# The NEW YORK CITY MARATHON® COOKBOOK

*Nutrition tips and recipes for high-energy eating and lifelong health*

## NANCY CLARK, M.S., R.D.

• • •

*Introduction by*
**FRED LEBOW**

*Marathon Information by*
**GLORIA AVERBUCH**

*Recipe Assistance by*
**JENNY HEGMANN, M.S., R.D.**

*RUTLEDGE HILL PRESS*

*Nashville, Tennessee*

Published in Nashville, Tennessee, by Rutledge Hill Press, 211 Seventh Avenue North, Nashville, Tennessee 37219. Distributed in Canada by H. B. Fenn & Company, Ltd., 1090 Lorimar Drive, Mississauga, Ontario L5S 1R7.

Photographs on pages 5, 57, 74, 106, 141, 164, 168, 185, 191, and 212 by Victah Sailer/Agence Shot

Photographs on pages 10, 98, 127, 192, and 201 courtesy of Duomo

Photograph on page 12 by Janeart, Inc.

Photograph on page 14 by Kathryn Dudek/Photo News

Photographs on pages 16, 45, 92, and 142 by Steve Sutton/Duomo

Photographs on pages 23, 51, and 162 by Nancy Coplon

Photographs on pages 35, 55, 80, 163, and 217 by Jack McManus/Agence Shot

Photograph on page 39 by Mark Shearman

Photographs on pages 40 and 195 by Elaine Seigel

Photographs on pages 52, 172, and 199 by Caroline Pallat

Photograph on page 60 by Norman Blake

Photographs on pages 67 and 216 by Michael Voudouris/Agence Shot

Photographs on Pages 71 and 207 by Jiro Mochozucki/Agence Shot

Photographs on pages 120, 142, and 214 by Paul Sutton/Duomo

Photographs on pages 105, 152, 153, and 175 by Lewis Bloom

Photograph on page 161 by Will Cofnuk

Photograph on page 178 by David Geltin Photography

Photograph on page 180 by H. Kluetmeyer

Photograph on page 198 by John Nugent

Photograph on page 213 by James Willis

Photo credits for color pictures given next to photographs themselves.

"The Race of a Lifetime" on page 194 is abridged and reprinted by permission of *Runner's World* magazine. Copyrighted 1993, Rodale Press, Inc., all rights reserved.

"A Splendid Human Race" on page 124 is excerpted from an editorial, October 31, 1980, with permission from the *Philadelphia Inquirer.*

Jacket and text design by Bruce Gore, Gore Studios, Inc.

Typography by D&T/Bailey Typesetting, Inc., Nashville, Tennessee

**Library of Congress Cataloging-in-Publication Data**

Clark, Nancy, 1951–
    The New York City Marathon cookbook : nutrition tips and recipes for high-energy eating and lifelong health / Nancy Clark.
       p.  cm.
    Includes index.
    ISBN 1-55853-306-0
    1. Runners (Sports)—Nutrition.  2. Athletes—Nutrition.  3. Cookery.  4. New York City Marathon, New York, N.Y.  I. Title.
TX361.R86C58   1994
613.2'024796—dc20              94-34915
                                CIP

*Printed in the United States of America*

1 2 3 4 5 6 7 8 9—99 98 97 96 95 94

This book is dedicated to
the true source of sugar and spice in my life—
My loving and patient husband, John McGrath
My fun-loving and fast-paced children,
John Michael and Mary

# Contents

# *Preface*
## *You Are Supposed to Eat. Enjoy It!*

 THE NEW YORK City Marathon Cookbook is designed to celebrate food for active people. After all, foods that are chosen wisely, prepared tastefully, and shared with friends can nourish our lives on many levels. This book provides the information you need to:

- eat healthfully and fuel your muscles optimally
- cook easily and enjoy eating pleasant meals

*The New York City Marathon Cookbook* also recognizes that food is a statement of cultural and ethnic heritage, traditions, lifestyles, and customs. To this extent, many people have contributed their food anecdotes and favorite family recipes—complete with stories about fond memories of cooking aromas and special meals enjoyed in their youth. The sidebar on the next page, *Comparing Dietary Guidelines*, delin-

---

### *TOM FLEMING*

*It used to be that I'd eat to run—and the more I ran, the more I needed to eat. But now I run to eat . . . I love to eat!*

---

eates some of the points that different government agencies deem important for healthy diets.

Due to either a lack of time or a lack of priority, pleasureable meals are rare among some active people and their families because they fail to plan their meals as a part of their lifestyle. They may perceive that sitting down to eat will take too much time away from work or training. Or they may fear meals as fattening. Taking time to enjoy a meal can seem to be

---

## *THREE TIPS TO BRING PLEASURE TO YOUR SPORTS DIET*

1. *Give yourself permission to eat relaxing meals.* If you have "no time" to stop and eat, remember that, without eating, you can't be effective from the time you get up until you collapse at night. Meal times should be used to relax, socialize, rejuvenate, and refuel so that you can maximize your effectiveness throughout the day. You do have time for meals if you make mealtime one of your priorities.

2. *During at least one meal a day, practice eating slowly.* If you gobble your meals, you miss out on

the best part of food: the taste. You can better enjoy the tastes, aromas, and textures of food if you eat slowly and savor the meal.

3. *Eat appropriate portions of your favorite foods.* Even chocolate chip cookies, holiday breads, and other treats included among these recipes can be balanced into an overall low-fat, high-carbohydrate sports diet. *Balance* and *moderation* are the keys to dietary health.

amoral. *The New York City Marathon Cookbook*, however, encourages you to bring aromas into your kitchen and nourishing meals into your life that will add strength and stamina to your sports program.

*The New York City Marathon Cookbook* is a valuable resource filled with quick and easy food suggestions. It addresses the tricks to eating a healthful, hassle-free sports diet, the kind of diet eaten by marathon champion Grete Waitz and many other athletes who prefer to spend their time training rather than cooking. The recipes are generally quick and easy, made from common foods, and will please the entire family. You can find tasty foods for Sunday brunches, carbo-loading parties, recovery feasts, and,

## JUDY MORRILL

*My friends and I like to do our own special "triathlon" on Sundays. We'll go for a long run, have a nice breakfast like French toast or pancakes, then go shopping or to the movies. That's what I call a nice day!*

of course, simple meals—all to help you win in the marathon called life.

Happy eating!

Nancy Clark

## *COMPARING DIETARY GUIDELINES*

The dietary guidelines in many societies include "take time to enjoy meals." Although a worthy goal, it's interesting to note that this guideline has been omitted in America.

### U.S. Dietary Guidelines

1. Eat a variety of foods.

2. Maintain a healthy weight.

3. Choose a diet low in fat, saturated fat, and cholesterol.

4. Choose a diet with plenty of vegetables, fruits, and grain products.

5. Use sugars only in moderation.

6. If you drink alcoholic beverages, do so in moderation.

### Commonsense Rules of Nutrition from the Norwegian Nutrition Council*

1. Take time to enjoy your meals.

2. Balanced meals of basic foods are vital.

3. Don't overeat. Eat only at fixed meal times.

4. Eat more bread, preferably whole grain.

5. Eat fish often, both for dinner and in sandwiches.

6. Eat more fruit, vegetables, and potatoes.

7. Use fats sparingly; eat lean.

8. Be careful with sugar, junk foods, and snacks.

9. If you are thirsty, drink water.

*Source: G. Waitz and G. Averbuch, *World Class* (New York: Warner Books, 1986).

# *INTRODUCTION*

FOOD AND THE New York City Marathon—what a perfect combination. Some runners eat to win, and others run to eat. But no matter why and how they do it, runners love their food! That's why *The New York City Marathon Cookbook* is such a great idea and filled with the best on food.

We at the New York Road Runners Club, the organizer of the Marathon, are excited by a series of celebrations for the race's twenty-fifth anniversary. As the event has evolved and grown over the past quarter century, we have refined its many aspects—from advanced computer systems to space blankets that warm every finisher. And along the way, our foodstuffs have also become state of the art.

The New York City Marathon has been called "an athletic world's fair," and I like to think of our food offerings as part of the total Marathon experience. The food comes from the sports bars and snacks consumed at the race-week Expo, to the International Breakfast Run, the Pasta Party, the breakfast fare at the start, and the post-race bag lunch. Believe me, no lack of thought or imagination has been spared on any of the extensive culinary details. It is this attention to detail that is also brought to this cookbook, with both recipes and food facts.

Once upon a time—twenty-five years ago to be exact—we were considered a handful of "fanatics," running a marathon in circles around New York City's Central Park. What

did we know about "carbohydrate loading" or "proper hydration" back then? We ran 26.2 miles, and maybe we had a soda afterward.

That's how it was in the first New York City Marathon in 1970. We were trendsetters in exercise then, and we are trendsetters in nutrition today. Now, the typical distance runner's diet—with its emphasis on complex carbohydrates—is recommended for everyone by experts who recognize our way of eating as the optimum nutrition for all.

New York is the largest marathon in the world. It brings together not only some of the world's best athletes in Olympic-level competition, but the tastes and cultures of runners from ninety-one countries. Over the years, they have shared their food stories and secrets—many of them now brought together in this book.

The favorite recipes of runners such as Grete Waitz, Alberto Salazar, and Bill Rodgers are included in these pages. And while crossing the finish line first may be their commonality—their different food favorites—from Norwegian to Cuban to all-American—are reflected in their recipe choices.

While these and other runners from around the world have lent their personal food styles to the event, they have also taken advantage of the great culinary diversity of New York City. When you come to New York, you can feast on the finest. That's because New York City is not only the financial, media, and business capital of the world, it is also the gastronomical capital as well. That's part of this book, too—from the history of the bagel to distributing apples to every Marathon finisher. In New York, we take being the "Big Apple" literally.

As a marathoner myself, I can tell you that despite appearances to the contrary (you rarely see a "heavy-weight" in our sport—another good reason to eat like we do), runners eat well and heartily. The true joy of cooking, and of eating, is combined here with the best health and nutrition advice.

With this book, we help celebrate twenty-five great years of the New York City Marathon. So for facts, fun, and good eating—read on. And, as it is said in one of the scores of languages represented in our race—bon appétit!

Fred Lebow

# *Acknowledgments*

SINCERE THANKS GOES to the following people who supported this effort:

Fred Lebow, father of the New York City Marathon, for inviting me to create this book.

Raleigh Mayer, Sue Ellen Silber, and Barbara Withers at the New York Road Runners Club, for their coaching along the way.

Mary-Giselle Rathgeber, R.D., for her nutrition advice from a New Yorker's perspective.

Christine Schlott, author of the "Eating Elite" food column in *New York Running News,* for sharing her collection of elite runners' recipes.

Larry Stone and Julie Pitkin, publisher and editor at Rutledge Hill Press, for compiling the ingredients of this book into a blue-ribbon product.

Jenny Hegmann, R.D., nutrition graduate student at Boston University's Sargent College of Allied Health Professions, for her marathon efforts to collect and test the recipes within a tight time line.

Fred Kirsch, Bob Fitzgerald, and Donni Richman for willingly devouring the tested recipes—including those that didn't make the final cut!

The runners and other athletes who have come to me for nutrition advice, little knowing they add to my knowledge as much as I try to add to theirs.

Dr. William Southmayd, medical director at SportsMedicine Brookline, for his continual support.

Jean Smith, my running partner, for patiently listening to miles of chatter about this book.

My family and friends, who nourish me with their love.

Nancy Clark

# The NEW YORK CITY MARATHON® COOKBOOK

# The NEW YORK CITY MARATHON® COOKBOOK

# 1 FOOD FOR RUNNERS
## Pleasure with a Purpose

 FROM A FAVORITE bowl of cereal to a special pasta dinner, active people welcome food that both tastes good and is good for them. But due to cramped and crazy schedules that dictate eating on the run, some runners find themselves struggling with roadblocks for good nutrition, particularly if they dislike cooking or have to contend with small apartment-style kitchens that cannot approach the pleasures of "home" cooking.

If this sounds familiar, you're probably frustrated and wondering, How can I work hard, train hard, and have enough energy left over to eat well? The answer is here in *The New York City Marathon Cookbook* in the form of some winning nutrition tips to help you enjoy a fast-paced life.

## ENERGY IN, ENERGY OUT

As an active person, you are constantly expending calories. To maintain a high level of energy, you need to deposit calories *regularly* into your calorie account throughout the day so you'll have energy when you need it. Think of your calorie needs as an accounting system. If you know how many calories you need, you can take the necessary steps to:

- maintain an even flow of energy all day long
- appropriately fuel-up and refuel from workouts
- lose weight, if desired, and maintain energy for running
- feel better, run better, and like your diet better

This balance sheet approach can be particularly helpful to marathoners who feel tired all the time. It can help you understand *why* you are tired. For example:

---

### GORDON BAKOULIS

*I could live on bagels. I have to make the effort to eat more than just bagels for breakfast, lunch, and dinner.*

---

- If you skip meals and deposit no calories into your daily bank account at breakfast and lunch, you can clearly see why you lack energy for your afternoon run.

- If you are a weight-conscious runner on a diet, calorie information allows you to determine how much food you should eat for fuel and still lose weight.

- If you are a food-loving runner who runs to eat, the calorie guidelines indicate how much you deserve to eat guilt-free, namely, hundreds of calories!

This budgeting system encourages you to eat and to eat *enough* at breakfast and lunch to support both an active life and a rigorous training program. Without a doubt, if you spend your calories evenly throughout the day by eating a variety of wholesome foods, you will invest in high energy, added stamina, strength, and smooth running, to say nothing of better health. Hungry runners need good food on a regular schedule. Why skimp on meals and feel tired all day just to spend your whole calorie budget in the evening?

## WHAT SHAPE IS YOUR DAILY DIET?

Most active people are very health conscious and care about what they eat. But due to the time constraints

# CALCULATING YOUR CALORIE NEEDS

How many calories do runners require? By using the following formula, you can estimate your personal calorie needs and gain a perspective on how to balance calories eaten versus calories expended.

1. To determine your *resting metabolic rate,* that is, the amount of calories you need to simply breathe, pump blood, and be alive:
   - *Multiply your weight in pounds by 10 calories per pound (22 cals/kg).* For example, if you weigh 120 pounds, you need approximately 1,200 calories (120 x 10) to simply do nothing all day except exist.

2. Add more calories for daily activity apart from your running and other purposeful exercise.
   - *If you are moderately active throughout the day, add about 50 percent of your resting metabolic rate.*

   - *If you are sedentary, add 10 to 30 percent less; if very active, 10 to 30 percent more.*

   For example, the moderately active 120-pound woman who requires 1,200 calories for her resting metabolic rate needs about another 600 calories for activities of daily living. This totals 1,800 calories per day—*without running.*

3. Add more calories for your purposeful exercise:

   The general rule of thumb is 100 calories per mile, but more precisely, this depends upon your weight. If you weigh more than 130 pounds, add a few more calories. If you weigh less, subtract a few, or go by these approximate guidelines:

Hence, if you are a 120-pound woman who runs five miles per day, you burn about 475 calories while running. This brings you to about 2,275 calories per day to maintain your weight. For simplicity sake, let's call that 2,300 calories.

4. If you want to lose weight, subtract 20 percent of your total calorie needs. That is,
   - .20 x 2,300 calories = 460 calories
   - 2,300 - 460 calories = 1,840 calories, or more simply 1,800 calories

   (Refer to chapter 4 for more weight reduction guidance.)

5. Take your calorie budget and divide it into three parts of the day. For the 120-pound woman on a diet, this comes to 600 calories per section of the day:

   | | |
   |---|---|
   | Breakfast/snack | 600 |
   | Lunch/snack | 600 |
   | Dinner/snack | 600 |

The next step is to read food labels to become familiar with the calorie content of the foods you commonly eat and then balance your calorie budget according to the rules for a well-balanced diet.

Here are approximate calorie needs for runners of different weights who are moderately active throughout the day:

| Weight, lbs (kg) | Approximate Calories per Mile |
|---|---|
| 120 (55) | 95 |
| 140 (64) | 110 |
| 160 (73) | 125 |

| Weight lbs (kg) | Calorie Needs for: | | |
|---|---|---|---|
| | Daily Living | With 5-mile Run | With 10-mile Run |
| 120 (55) | 1,800 | 2,300 | 2,700 |
| 140 (64) | 2,100 | 2,650 | 3,200 |
| 160 (73) | 2,400 | 3,000 | 3,650 |

*Two champions: Whereas Grete Waitz (#4) dislikes cooking, Joan Benoit Samuelson (#3) thoroughly enjoys making her own breads, soups, and meals. Both seem to be keeping pace with good nutrition, regardless of the source.*

that marathon training imposes upon already busy schedules, some runners fail to plan for meals. Rather, they simply grab whatever is convenient, which may be the same foods day after day, month after month. For example, one of my clients ate spaghetti for breakfast, lunch, and dinner. This repetitive eating kept life simple, minimized decisions, and simplified shopping, but it also created an unbalanced diet and chronic fatigue.

To be nutritionally sound, your diet should include a well-rounded variety of high quality sports foods, such as the cook-free, top sports foods listed in the sidebar on page 9. But if you eat a linear diet that lacks variety—for example, bagels, bagels, bagels or pasta, pasta, pasta—your body will have to chug along on a lackluster intake of vitamins, minerals, and other nutrients.

Take note: You don't have to be a good cook to eat well. Many active people, including New York City Marathon champion Grete Waitz, prefer to spend as little time as possible in the kitchen. Yet they still manage to eat well.

If your diet is linear, you might want to reshape it into a well-rounded diet or, better yet, a pyramid. The U.S. Department of Agriculture's newest model for healthy eating, the Food Pyramid, reflects the current thinking on nutrition in the 1990s (see the sidebar on page 6). The pyramid shape visually suggests that you should eat lots of grain foods for the foundation of your diet, include generous amounts of fruits and vegetables and lesser amounts of animal proteins and dairy foods. The tiny tip of the pyramid allows for just a sprinkling of sugars and fats.

Not everyone understands the Food Pyramid's messages of *balance, variety,* and *moderation.* Confusion abounds, in particular, regarding the recommended number of servings and how to fit them all into a day's menu:

    6–11 servings of grains
    2–4 servings of fruits
    3–5 servings of vegetables
    2–3 servings of milk and dairy foods
    2–3 servings of protein-rich foods such as meat
      and beans.

Although twenty-six servings may sound like several five-course meals and more recipes than you want to cook from this book, the calories range between 1,600 to 2,800. This is just the right amount of calories for a woman on a 1,600-calorie reducing diet or a businessman who trains for a half-hour per day and requires about 2,800 calories. Your calorie needs

## GRETE WAITZ

*I don't like to cook and I'm not good at it, so I never do it. But I am very good at heating food that has been already made. I'd rather not spend my time cooking when I can buy those services. There are lots of good grocery stores or delis with nice fresh ready-to-eat foods that simply need to be heated in the microwave.*

*I like basic foods that are quick and easy: cereal for breakfast with homemade bread (from my mother), bagels with goat cheese, lots of fruits, vegetables, and salads. Microwaved potatoes and "boil in the bag" rice help me to have a good diet.*

likely fall within this range. (Refer to the sidebar: *Calculating Your Calorie Needs.*)

### Carbs for Your Sports Diet

By eating according to the Food Pyramid, you'll consume about 60 to 70 percent of your calories from carbohydrates. This is exactly what you need for a high-energy sports diet. These carbohydrates are stored in your muscles in the form of glycogen, the energy you need to train hard day after day and to compete well on race day.

Grain foods are a popular source of carbohydrates for most active people. But even food-loving runners may balk at the recommendation of six to eleven servings of breads, cereals, and grains *every* day. Some believe that they would gain weight if they were to eat that much.

But this is not the case. The key to using the Food Pyramid is to understand the definition of "serving." Six to eleven grain servings is only two to four servings per meal (the equivalent of about 150–300 calories), not much for hungry runners who require at least 600–900 calories per meal.

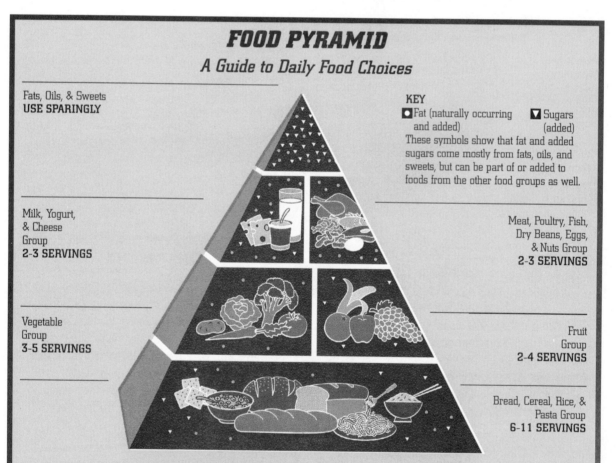

## FOOD PYRAMID
### A Guide to Daily Food Choices

Fats, Oils, & Sweets
**USE SPARINGLY**

KEY
◼ Fat (naturally occurring and added)   ▼ Sugars (added)
These symbols show that fat and added sugars come mostly from fats, oils, and sweets, but can be part of or added to foods from the other food groups as well.

Milk, Yogurt, & Cheese Group
**2-3 SERVINGS**

Meat, Poultry, Fish, Dry Beans, Eggs, & Nuts Group
**2-3 SERVINGS**

Vegetable Group
**3-5 SERVINGS**

Fruit Group
**2-4 SERVINGS**

Bread, Cereal, Rice, & Pasta Group
**6-11 SERVINGS**

Use the Food Guide Pyramid to help you eat better every day . . . the Dietary Guidelines way. Start with plenty of Breads, Cereals, Rice, and Pasta; Vegetables; and Fruits. Add two to three servings from the Milk group and two to three servings from the Meat group. Each of these food groups provides some, but not all, of the nutrients you need. No one food group is more important than another — for good health you need them all. Go easy on fats, oils, and sweets, the foods in the small tip of the Pyramid.

Source: U.S. Department of Agriculture/U.S. Department of Health and Human Services

| Food | Pyramid Serving Size | Runner's Portion | Number of Servings |
|------|---------------------|------------------|--------------------|
| *Carbohydrates: Recommended Intake—6 to 11 Servings per Day* | | | |
| cereal | 1 ounce | 2–4 ounces (1 big bowl) | 2–4 |
| bread | 1 average slice | 2 slices in sandwich | 2 |
| bagel | ½ small | 1 large | 3–4 |
| pasta | ½ cup cooked | 2–3 cups | 4–6 |
| rice | ½ cup | 1–2 cups | 2–4 |
| | | | |
| *Fruits: Recommended Intake—2 to 4 Servings per Day* | | | |
| Orange Juice | 6 ounces | 12 ounces | 2 |
| Apple | 1 medium | 1 large | 2 |
| Banana | 1 small | 1 large | 2 |
| Fruit Cocktail | ½ cup | 1 cup | 2 |
| | | | |
| *Vegetables: Recommended Intake—3 to 5 Servings per Day* | | | |
| Broccoli | 1 small stalk | 2 large stalks | 3–4 |
| Spinach | ½ cup | 10 ounces (1 box frozen) | 3 |
| Salad Bar | 1 small bowl | 1 large bowl | 3–4 |
| Spaghetti Sauce | ½ cup | 1 cup | 2 |

Fruits and vegetables are also great sources of carbohydrates. But eating the recommended two to four servings of fruits and three to five servings of vegetables per day is another story. As one marathoner sheepishly remarked, "I'm lucky if I eat that much in a week." The trick is to eat *large* portions.

Fruits and vegetables are truly nature's vitamin pills, chock full of vitamin C (to help with healing), beta-carotene (to protect against cancer), fiber (to aid with regular bowel movements), and numerous other vitamins and minerals. The sidebar, *Eat More Veggies* (page 8), offers more suggestions for ways to boost your veggie intake simply.

### Protein for Your Sports Diet

Like carbohydrates, protein-rich foods are also an important part of your sports diet. You should eat two to three servings per day. Athletes tend to either *over-* or *under*consume protein, depending on their health consciousness and lifestyle. Whereas some fill up on the saturated fats in animal proteins, others bypass these foods in their efforts to eat a low-fat or meat-free diet, but neglect to replace beef with beans. The protein section in chapter 2 contains additional information and guidelines.

Dairy foods such as milk, yogurt, and cheese are also quick and easy sources of protein. Plus, they are also rich in calcium (particularly important for

### ROD DIXON

*In the old days (the 1970s) when I was doing high-mileage training, no one understood the importance of carbohydrates. We used to train at two o'clock in the afternoon after stuffing ourselves on steak and eggs for breakfast. Then, we'd have dinners based on lots of lamb or meat. When I started traveling to Europe and Scandinavia, I noticed those runners were eating more breads and carbohydrates, and when living in Italy, my diet changed to include more pasta. It didn't take me long to figure out that these complex carbs are much better for my sports diet and my health.*

# EAT MORE VEGGIES!

People who live alone, work long hours, don't cook and/or eat primarily fast foods commonly have vegetable-poor diets. Case in point, Paula, a very busy graduate student, marathoner, and part-time receptionist, confessed, "I know I should eat more vegetables, but I just don't do it. The problem is finding time to buy them and then staying home long enough to cook and eat them before they go bad. I waste too much money throwing away smelly cauliflower and wilted lettuce."

If you, like Paula, struggle to consume the recommended three to five servings of vegetables per day, the following tips may help you to enhance your nutritional status.

- *Eat more of the best, less of the rest.* In general, *dark green, deep yellow, orange, and red* vegetables have far more nutrients than pale ones. Hence, if you dislike pale zucchini, summer squash, and green beans, don't work hard to acquire a taste for them. Instead, put your efforts into having more broccoli, spinach, and winter squash—the richly colored, more nutrient-dense choices.

- *Eat colorful salads* filled with tomatoes, green peppers, carrots, and dark lettuces and topped with low- or nonfat dressings. Pale salads with white lettuce, cucumbers, onions, celery, and other colorless veggies offer little more than crunch. When topped with oily dressing, this crunch simply becomes *greasy* crunch— a far cry from good nutrition. You'd be better off choosing tomato juice, vegetable soups (even canned soups are better than nothing), or a raw carrot for a pre-dinner snack.

- *Fortify spaghetti sauce with a box of frozen chopped broccoli or green peppers.* Cook it alongside the spaghetti (in a steamer over the pasta water) or in a covered saucepan with one-half inch of water before you add the tomato sauce.

- *Choose fast foods with the most veggies:*

  —pizza with peppers, mushrooms, and extra tomato sauce

  —Chinese entrées stir-fried with vegetables

  —lunchtime V-8 juice instead of diet soda

- *Even overcooked vegetables are better than no vegetables.* If your only option is overcooked veggies from the cafeteria, eat them. Cooking does destroy some of the vegetable's nutrients, but not all of them.

- *Keep frozen vegetables stocked in your freezer, ready and waiting.* They are quick and easy to prepare, won't spoil quickly, and have more nutrients than "fresh" vegetables that have sat in the store and your refrigerator for a few days. Because cooking (more than freezing) reduces a vegetable's nutritional content:

  —quickly cook vegetables only until *tender crisp* and use the cooking water as a broth

  —microwave them in a covered dish

  —stir-fry them with very little oil

  Refer to the recipe section on vegetables for additional cooking ideas and information.

- *When all else fails, eat fruit to help compensate for lack of vegetables.* The best alternatives include bananas, oranges, grapefruit, melon, strawberries, and kiwi. These choices are rich in many of the same nutrients found in vegetables.

| Protein-rich Foods | Pyramid Serving Size | Runner's Portion | Number of Servings |
|---|---|---|---|
| Tuna | ⅓ of 6 oz. can | 1 can | 3 |
| Chicken | 2 ounce drumstick | 6 ounce breast | 3 |
| Peanut Butter | 2 tbsp. | 2–4 tbsp. | 1–2 |
| Lentil Soup | 1 cup | 1 bowl | 2 |
| Kidney Beans | ½ cup | 1 cup | 1–2 |

growing teens and women who want to optimize bone density) and the B-vitamin riboflavin (for converting food into energy). For only 300 calories, even weight-conscious runners can easily enjoy the recommended three servings of low-fat dairy foods per day, such as:

- 8 oz. of low-fat milk on breakfast cereal
- a half-pint (8 oz.) container of milk with lunch
- an 8 oz. cup of yogurt for a snack

Although *nonfat* and *low-fat* dairy foods are preferable for heart-health and calorie control, you need not suffer with skim milk if you really don't like it. You can always cut back on fat in other parts of your diet. For example, a novice marathoner opted for cereal with 2 percent milk (five grams of fat), but saved on fat elsewhere in her diet by using fat-free salad dressing and low-fat granola. (For information on fat and calcium, see chapters 3 and 4.)

Runners who prefer a dairy-free diet or are lactose intolerant should take special care to eat adequate amounts of nondairy calcium sources. See the sidebar, *Calcium Equivalents* (page 11), for food suggestions.

### Sweets and Treats

Although nutritionists recommend eating a wholesome diet based on grains, fruits, and vegetables from the base of the Food Pyramid, some people eat too many fats, oils, and sweets from the tip. If you have a junk-food diet that topples the tip, you can correct this imbalance by eating more wholesome foods from the base and body of the pyramid *before you get too hungry*. Runners who get too hungry tend to choose foods low in nutrients and high in fats and sugar. The simple solution to the junk-food diet is to *prevent* hunger by eating wholesome meals.

The inclusion of fats and sweets in the tip of the pyramid suggests that you need not eat a "perfect diet" (*no* fats, *no* sugar) to have a good diet. Nothing is nutritionally wrong with having a cookie for dessert after having eaten a sandwich, milk, and fruit for lunch. But lots is wrong with eating cookies for lunch and skipping the sandwich. That's when nutrition and performance problems arise.

## SOME TOP SPORTS FOODS

The following top sports foods offer mainly cook-free and convenient best bets for people who eat and run.

**The best fruits for vitamins A and/or C:**
oranges, grapefruit, tangerines, bananas, cantaloupe, strawberries, kiwi

**The best vegetables for vitamins A and/or C:**
broccoli, spinach, green and red peppers, tomatoes, carrots, sweet potatoes

**The easiest sources of calcium for strong bones:**
Low-fat milk, yogurt, cheeses, calcium-fortified orange juice

**Convenient cook-free proteins for building and protecting muscles:**
Tuna, deli roast beef, ham and turkey, canned salmon, hummus, peanut butter

**Cook-free grains for carbohydrates and fiber:**
High-fiber breakfast cereals (preferably iron-enriched), wholesome breads and bagels, whole-grain crackers

*Priscilla Welch (#2) values good nutrition but knows that a good diet need not be a "perfect" diet. She enjoys occasional treats that are balanced into her overall winning food plan.*

The key to balancing fats and sugars appropriately into your diet is to observe the following guidelines:

- *10 percent of your calories can appropriately come from refined sugar* (about 200–300 calories from sugar daily for most runners)
- *25 percent of your calories can appropriately come from fat* (about 50–85 grams of fat per day)

Hence, moderate amounts of chips, salad dressing, jam, and cookies can nourish you with a liveable and tasty food plan. That's why I've included recipes for nonfat, low-fat, and full-fat foods. Even the Decadent Brownies (page 214) are not a "bad food" as long as you eat them as a part of a good *diet*.

If you want personalized dietary advice, I recommend that you have a nutrition checkup with a registered dietitian who is also interested in sports nutrition. To find one in your area, call the American Dietetic Association's referral network at (800) 366–1655.

## AM I SICK? AM I TIRED? IS SOMETHING WRONG WITH MY DIET?

Exercise energizes many people, enhancing their productivity as well as relieving their stress. But some runners complain of chronic fatigue. They feel run down, dragged out, and overwhelmingly exhausted. If this sounds familiar, you may wonder if you are

## *BALANCING YOUR DIET*

The trick to balancing the recommended servings of foods during your day is to plan to have at least three out of five food groups per meal, and one or two food groups per snack, such as:

|  | Grain | Fruit | Vegetable | Dairy | Protein |
|---|---|---|---|---|---|
| Breakfast | cereal | banana |  | milk |  |
| Lunch | bread | orange | vegetable soup |  | peanut butter |
| Snack | pretzels |  |  | yogurt |  |
| Dinner | spaghetti |  | tomato sauce | cheese | ground turkey |
| Snack | popcorn | juice |  |  |  |

sick, overtired, or if something is wrong with your diet.

Perhaps you can relate to Peter, a thirty-nine-year-old marathon runner, lawyer, and solo chef who bemoaned, "I just don't take the time to eat right. My diet is awful. I rarely eat fruits or vegetables, to say nothing of a real meal. I think that poor nutrition is catching up with me."

Peter lived alone, hated to cook in his cramped apartment, and tended to survive on fast (and fatty) foods. He rarely ate breakfast, barely ate lunch, but always collapsed after a long day with a generous feast of a large deli sandwich, Chinese take-out, or pizza. He struggled to wake up in the morning, to stay awake during afternoon meetings, and to grind through his daily ten-mile run.

Peter hoped that dietary improvements would restore his energy. I evaluated his diet, calculated that he had 3,000 calories in his daily energy budget (1,000 calories per section of the day—that is, morning, afternoon, and evening), and suggested a few simple food changes that could result in higher energy, greater stamina, and better running.

While trying to find some solutions to Peter's fatigue, I explored the following questions. Perhaps the answers will offer solutions for your energy problems.

■ *Are you tired due to low blood sugar?* Peter skipped not only breakfast but also often missed lunch because he "didn't have time." He would doze off in the afternoon because he had low blood sugar. With zero calories to feed his brain, he ended up feeling sleepy.

The solution was to *choose* to make time to eat. Just as he chose to sleep later in the morning, he

## CALCIUM REQUIREMENTS

The recommended calcium intake is

| | | |
|---|---|---|
| *Women:* | 11–24 years | 1,200 mg |
| | 24–50 | 800 |
| | Female athletes who have ceased menstruating | 1,200–1,500 |
| | Postmenopausal | 1,200–1,500 |
| *Men:* | 11–18 | 1,200 |
| | 18–50+ | 800 |

The following foods all provide about 300 milligrams of calcium. Two to three choices per day will contribute to meeting your calcium needs.

| *Calcium-rich Food* | *Amount* |
|---|---|
| milk, whole or skim | 1 cup |
| yogurt | 1 cup |
| cheese | 1½ ounces |
| cottage cheese | 2 cups |
| frozen yogurt | 2 cups |
| tofu | 8 oz. (½ cake) |
| broccoli | 2 cups |
| collard, turnip greens | 1 cup |
| kale, mustard greens | 1½ cups |
| canned salmon (with bones) | 4 ounces |
| canned sardines (with bones) | 2½ ounces |

## NATALIE UPDEGROVE PARTRIDGE

*I keep boxes of frozen chopped broccoli and spinach in my freezer. They quickly thaw in the microwave oven and add nutrients and flavor to pizza, quesadillas, and pasta dishes.*

could choose to get up five minutes earlier for breakfast; he could also choose to stop working for five or ten minutes to eat lunch.

■ *Is your diet too low in carbohydrates?* Peter's fast-but-fatty food choices filled his stomach but left his muscles poorly fueled without sufficient glycogen to support his training program. Higher carbohydrate snacks and meals would not only fuel his muscles but also help maintain a higher blood-sugar level, thereby providing energy for mental work as well as physical exercise. (See the upcoming sections on fast-food lunches and the four o'clock munchies for appropriate food ideas.)

*Thousands of runners: How many will win with good nutrition?*

- *Are you iron-deficient and anemic?* Peter ate little red meat and consequently consumed little iron, an important mineral in red blood cells that helps carry oxygen to exercising muscles. Iron-deficiency anemia can result in needless fatigue during exercise. I taught Peter how to boost his dietary iron intake with or without meat. (See chapter 3.) I also recommended blood tests (hemoglobin, hematocrit, ferritin, serum iron, and total iron-binding capacity) to rule out the question of anemia.

- *Are you getting enough sleep?* Peter's complaint of being chronically tired was justified because he *was* tired both mentally (from his intense job) and physically (from his strenuous training). He worked from 8:00 A.M. to 8:00 P.M. By the time he got home, ran, ate dinner, and "unwound," midnight had rolled around. The wake-up bell at 6:30 A.M. came all too soon—especially since Peter often had trouble falling asleep due to his having eaten such a large dinner.

I recommended that Peter try to get more sleep by eating lighter dinners (soup and sandwich, or even cereal), having bigger breakfasts, and scheduling his main meal at lunch (low-fat Chinese, pizza, or pasta). By trading in 1,200 of his evening calories for 600 more calories at breakfast and 600 more calories at lunch, he could determine if less food in his stomach before bed would result in better sleep.

- *Are you overtraining?* Although Peter took pride in the fact that he hadn't missed a day of running in seven years, he felt discouraged that he wasn't improving despite harder training. I questioned whether he was a "compulsive runner" who punished his body or a "serious athlete" who trained

---

### NINA KUSCSIK

*I find that as I get older—and I've been alive for a while now—I tend to eat more and more foods in their natural state. I like having fresh fruits, vegetables, and wholesome grains, and pack them every day into my lunch. This has become a daily habit that's now a part of my lifestyle.*

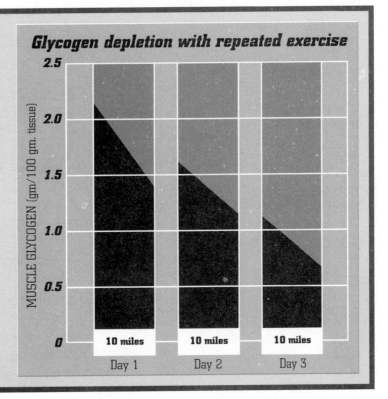

Exercise physiologist David Costill studied the rate of muscle glycogen depletion in five subjects who ran for 10 miles (6–8 minute mile pace) on three consecutive days. The runners ate their normal diet, which provided 40% to 60% of the calories from carbohydrates. They continually depleted, but did not replenish, the muscle glycogen.

Based on this information, you can understand why:

■ Carbohydrates are important for athletes who train every day; and why
■ Carbohydrates are an important part of an athlete's reducing diet.

Costill, D. et al. "Muscle Glycogen Utilization During Prolonged Exercise on Successive Days." *J. Appl. Physiol.* 31:834, 1971.

wisely and took rest days. One or two rest days or easy days per week are an essential part of a training program; they allow the body to replenish its depleted muscle glycogen.

■ *Are you stressed or depressed?* Peter not only had a stressful job, he was also dealing with the stress and depression associated with family problems. Since he was feeling a bit helpless with this situation, I encouraged him to take control in at least one aspect of his life—his diet. Simple dietary improvements could not only help him feel physically better, but also mentally better *about himself.* This would be very energizing in itself.

If you answered "yes" to many of the questions I asked Peter, you may be able to resolve your fatigue with better eating, sleeping, and training habits. Experiment with the simple suggestions in this book. Before long you may transform your current low-energy patterns into a food plan for success! Eating well is not as hard as you may think.

## BREAKFAST: THE MEAL OF CHAMPIONS

Good nutrition for runners starts at breakfast. This is *the* most important meal of the day because it sets the stage for eating healthfully. Breakfast eaters tend to eat a more nutritious diet, choose foods lower in fat, have lower blood cholesterol levels, enjoy more success with weight control. They are mentally alert, and

### PRISCILLA WELCH

*I'm watchful of my diet six out of seven days. And then I enjoy my "sin day." For example, when training in New Zealand, I would always eat fish and chips with salt and vinegar. I grew up on fish and chips and love them, but they are so greasy . . . so just one day out of the week, I enjoyed this treat.*

they have more energy to exercise. If you have at least 600 calories in your breakfast budget, you might as well deposit them so you'll have the energy to spend.

If breakfast is so great for us, then why do so many runners skip it? They have lots of excuses. But for every excuse to skip breakfast there is an even better reason not to.

*I don't have time:* If you have no time for breakfast, keep in mind that you can always make time to do what you want to do. Lack of *priority* is the real problem, not lack of time.

*The International Breakfast Run on the Saturday before the Marathon unifies the many cultures represented—and also starts the final day of carbohydrate-loading before the 26.2-mile event. The runners devour thousands of bagels afterward.*

## NORBERT SANDER

*For eighteen years now on every Tuesday and Thursday, I've eaten the same breakfast at Jimmy's Diner. When I walk in, the waitress shouts to the cook, "Give the Doc 'The Usual.'" I get my favorite: a bagel and coffee.*

Breakfast need not be an elaborate occasion. You can quickly prepare a simple breakfast to eat on the run:

- a baggie filled with raisins and dry cereal
- a pita pocket with a slice or two of low-fat cheese
- a frozen waffle popped into the toaster, then eaten plain, with honey or jam
- a glass of milk, then a banana while walking to the train.
- a travel mug filled with low-fat milk or juice (there will always be coffee at the office), a bagel or bran muffin and a banana during the morning commute.

The key to breakfast on the run is to *plan ahead.* Prepare your breakfast the night before so you can simply grab it and go during your morning rush hour. For example, on the weekends, you might want to make some muffins from the recipe section, freeze them, then take one or two out at night so breakfast will be ready and waiting in the morning. Or buy bagels by the dozen and keep them stocked in your freezer.

*Breakfast interferes with my training schedule:* If you are an early morning runner (5:00–7:00 A.M.), you will likely run better and avoid an end-of-the-run energy crash if you put just a little gas in your tank before leaving (assuming your stomach can tolerate food, of course). Coffee with extra milk, a swig of juice, a chunk of bagel, or a piece of bread are popular choices that can put your blood sugar on the upswing, contribute to greater stamina, and help you feel more awake. If you prefer to abstain, at least have a bedtime snack the night before. (The section on pre-exercise food in chapter 3 explains in greater detail the importance of morning food.)

Breakfast is equally important if you exercise at mid-day or in the afternoon. You need to fuel up in order to do a quality workout that afternoon. Breakfast is essential if you are doing double workouts. Because your muscles are hungriest for carbohydrates within the first two hours after hard exercise, a quick and easy recovery breakfast will set the stage for a strong second workout.

I sometimes hear athletes express the concern that breakfast interferes with their upcoming workout; that the food will sit heavily in their stomach or "talk back." This is unlikely. A low-fat meal at 7:00 to 8:00 A.M. (such as cereal and low-fat milk) should be well digested by noontime. Try it; you'll probably see a positive difference in your energy level.

*I'm not hungry in the morning:* If you have no morning appetite, the chances are you ate your breakfast calories the night before. Huge dinner? Ice cream? Too many cookies before bedtime? The solution to having no morning appetite is, obviously, to eat less at night so that you can start the day off hungry.

If running first thing in the morning "kills your appetite" (due to the rise in body temperature), keep in mind that you *will* be hungry within a few hours when you have cooled down. Plan ahead, so that when the hungry horrors hit, you will have healthful brunch options ready and waiting. Otherwise, you'll be likely to grab whatever's easy, which may include donuts, pastries, cookies, and other high-fat foods.

*I'm on a diet:* Too many weight-conscious people start their diet at breakfast. Bad idea. Breakfast skippers

tend to gain weight and to be heavier than breakfast eaters. A satisfying breakfast *prevents you from getting too hungry* and overeating.

Your best bet for successful dieting is to eat *during the day,* burn off the calories, and then eat reasonably at night. Chapter 4 has more details about how to lose weight and have energy to train.

*Breakfast makes me hungrier:* Many runners complain that if they eat breakfast, they seem to get hungry and eat more all day. This may result from thinking they have already "blown their diets" by eating breakfast, so they might as well keep overeating, then start dieting again the next day. Wrong.

Successful diets *start* at breakfast. If you feel hungry after breakfast you probably ate *too little* breakfast. For example, 100 calories of toast with jam is enough to whet your appetite but not to satisfy your calorie needs. Try budgeting about one-third of your calories for breakfast and/or a mid-morning snack—500–600 calories for most 120–150 pound runners. This translates into two slices of toast with jam, a banana, low-fat yogurt, *and* juice. Or yogurt and a bagel with peanut butter.

Note: If you *over*eat at breakfast, you can easily resolve the problem by eating less at lunch or dinner. You won't be as physically hungry for those meals and will be able to easily eat smaller portions.

## THE BREAKFAST OF CHAMPIONS

By now, I hope I've convinced you that breakfast is indeed the most important meal of the day for active

*Marathon champ Bill Rodgers may not eat breakfast, but he has developed a nutrition plan of wholesome lunches, dinners, and evening snacks that keeps him well nourished enough to be competing years after his first New York City Marathon victory.*

people. *What* should you eat, you wonder? If you feel like cooking, enjoy one of the recipes for French toast, pancakes, muffins, and other breakfast foods in the recipe section.

But if you are looking for a cook-free choice, I highly recommend cereal. Cereal is quick, convenient, and filled with the calcium, iron, carbohydrates, fiber, and other nutrients active runners need. A bowl of bran cereal with fruit and low-fat milk provides a well-balanced meal that includes three of the five food groups (grain, dairy, and fruit) and sets the stage for an overall low-fat diet.

Cereal is versatile. You can eat it dry if you're on the run, or preferably with low-fat milk and/or yogurt for a calcium booster. You can mix brands and vary the flavor with different toppings:

- sliced banana
- blueberries (a handful of frozen ones taste great—especially if microwaved)
- raisins
- canned fruit
- cinnamon
- maple syrup
- vanilla yogurt

Refer to the Breakfast and Brunches section for some more tasty cereal ideas.

## NONTRADITIONAL BREAKFASTS

Not everyone likes cereal for breakfast, nor do they want to cook pancakes. If you are stumped by what to eat for breakfast, choose a food that you *enjoy*. After all, you'll be more likely to eat breakfast if it tastes good. Remember that *any* food—even frozen yogurt—is better than nothing.
How about:
    leftover pizza
    leftover Chinese food
    mug of tomato soup
    potato zapped in the microwave while
        you shower
    tuna sandwich
    peanut butter and crackers

# HOW TO CHOOSE THE BEST BREAKFAST CEREAL

Needless to say, all cereals are not created equal. Some offer more nutritional value than others. Here are four tips to help you make the best choices.

1. *Choose iron-enriched cereals with at least 25 percent of the Required Daily Allowance for iron to help prevent anemia.*

   Note, however, the iron in breakfast cereals is poorly absorbed compared to the iron in lean red meats. But you can enhance iron absorption by drinking a glass of orange juice or enjoying another source of vitamin C (such as grapefruit, cantaloupe, strawberries, or kiwi) along with the cereal. *Any* iron is better than no iron.

   If you tend to eat "all-natural" types of cereals, such as granola and shredded wheat, be aware that these types have no additives, hence, no iron. You might want to mix and match all-natural brands with iron-enriched brands (or make the effort to eat iron-rich foods at other meals).

2. *Choose fiber-rich bran cereals with more than five grams of fiber per serving.*

   Fiber not only helps prevent constipation but also is a protective nutrient that may reduce the risk of colon cancer and heart disease. Bran cereals are the best sources of fiber, more so than even fruits and vegetables. Choose from All-Bran, 40% Bran Flakes, Raisin Bran, Fruit & Fibre, Corn Bran, Oat Bran, and any of the numerous cereals with "bran" in the name. You can also sprinkle raw bran on low-fiber corn flakes, shredded wheat, and muesli to boost their fiber value.

   Note: If you have very loose bowels, you may want to forgo bran cereals. The extra fiber may aggravate the situation.

3. *Choose cereals with whole grains listed among the first ingredients.*

   Whole wheat, brown rice, corn, and oats are among the grains popularly eaten in breakfast cereals. These should be listed first in the ingredients.

   Some runners overlook a cereal's grains and notice only the sugar or salt content. Remember:

   ■ Salt (sodium) in cereal is a concern if you have high blood pressure. Most athletes have low blood pressure and will suffer no health consequences from choosing cereals with a little added salt.

   ■ Sugar is simply carbohydrate that fuels your muscles. Yes, sugar calories are nutritionally empty calories. But given they are combined with lots of nutrition from the milk, banana, juice, and cereal itself, the twenty empty calories in five grams of added sugar are insignificant. Obviously, sugar-filled frosted flakes and kids' cereals with ten grams of sugar or more are somewhat more like dessert than breakfast. Hence, try to limit your breakfast choices to cereals with fewer than five grams of added sugar. Eat the sugar ones for snacks or dessert, if desired.

4. *Choose primarily low-fat cereals with less than two grams of fat per serving.*

   High-fat cereals such as some brands of granola and crunchy cookie-type cereals can add unexpected fat and calories to your sports diet. Select low-fat brands for the foundation of your breakfast, then use only a sprinkling of the higher-fat treats, if desired, for a topping.

## APPETITE CONTROL

The more you exercise, the hungrier you will get. Whereas most runners simply resolve their hunger with tasty foods, others feel confused by it and sometimes even feel guilty they are always eager to eat. One novice marathoner perceived that hunger was bad and wrong. Hunger is normal; it is simply your body's way of talking to you, requesting fuel. Plan to eat at least every four hours.

You should not spend your day feeling hungry—even if you are on a reducing diet (see chapter 4). If your 8:00 A.M. breakfast finds you hungry earlier than noon, your breakfast contained too few calories. You simply need a supplemental midmorning snack.

Come noontime, instead of feeling that something is wrong with you because you are hungry again, enjoy lunch as being the second-most-important meal of the day. Morning runners, in particular, need a hearty lunch to refuel their muscles; afternoon runners need a respectable lunch and afternoon snack to fuel-up for their after-work training. Ideally, lunch and snacks should provide about one-third of your day's calories.

### UTA PIPPIG

*I'm a big breakfast eater!!! That's typical German. My standard breakfast includes two cups of flavored coffee and a big bagel. I put honey-baked turkey on half the bagel, part-skim mozzarella cheese on one quarter, and blueberry marmalade on the other quarter.*

Whereas some runners like to satisfy their appetites with big meals, others prefer to divide their calories into mini-meals every two hours. That's fine if that is your preference and better suits your training schedule.

## LUNCH IDEAS

Brown-bagging it is a good way to save money, time, and sometimes calories if you are organized enough to pack your own lunch. Because of busy schedules,

# BROWN-BAG LUNCHES

The following suggestions may help you pack a super sports lunch.

- To reduce chaos in your morning rush hour, make your lunch the night before.

- To prevent sandwich bread from getting stale, keep it in the freezer and take out the slices as needed. Bread thaws in minutes at room temperature, or in seconds in the microwave oven.

- Make several sandwiches at one time, then store them in the freezer. The frozen sandwich will be thawed—and fresh—by lunch time. Sliced turkey, lean roast beef, peanut butter, and leftover pizza freeze nicely. Don't freeze eggs, mayonnaise, jelly, lettuce, tomatoes, or raw veggies.

- Instead of eating a dry sandwich with no mayonnaise, add moistness using:
  low-fat or nonfat mayonnaise

  plain yogurt or yogurt/mayo mixtures
  low-fat or nonfat bottled salad dressings, such as
    ranch or creamy Italian
  mustard and ketchup
  salsa
  lettuce and tomato

- Experiment:
  Peanut butter with sliced banana, raisins, dates, sunflower seeds, apple slices, and/or celery slices
  Cheese (preferably low-fat or a mixture of nonfat/full fat) with oregano, Italian seasonings, green peppers, and/or tomatoes

- Pack leftover soups, chili, and pasta dinners for the next day's lunch. You can either eat the leftovers cold or heat them in the office microwave oven.

few people make the effort to organize their lunch plans in advance of noontime (see the sidebar: *Brown-Bag Lunches*). Hence, fast foods can save the day . . . or do they spoil your sports diet?

### Fast-food Lunches

The good news is that most quick-service restaurants now offer more low-fat foods than ever before. But you'll likely be confronted by the many temptations that jump out at you while the healthier choices fade into the background. Before succumbing to grease, remind yourself that you will feel better *and feel better about yourself* if you eat well. Then, make the lower-fat choices:

| | |
|---|---|
| *Dunkin' Donuts:* | Low-fat muffins, bagels, juice, broth-based soups, hot cocoa |
| *Deli:* | Sandwiches or subs with lots of bread and half the filling, little or no mayo. (Or ask for two extra slices of bread or a second roll to make a sandwich for tomorrow's lunch with the excessive meat.) |
| *McDonald's:* | McLean burger or low-fat chicken sandwiches with high-carb fluids such as milkshakes, soft drinks, and juices |
| *Taco Bell:* | Bean burrito |
| *Pizza:* | Thick crust with extra veggies rather than extra cheese or pepperoni |
| *Pasta:* | Spaghetti or ziti with tomato sauce; a glass of low-fat milk for protein. Be cautious of lasagna, tortellini, or manicotti that are cheese filled (i.e., high fat). |
| *Chinese:* | Hot and sour or wonton soup; plain rice with stir-fried entrées such as beef and broccoli or chicken with pea pods. Request the food be cooked with minimal oil. Limit fried appetizers and fried entrées. |

Remember: You are better off having a substantial lunch than a huge dinner. Save the popular light salad-type lunch for the evening meal.

---

### NORBERT SANDER

*My favorite lunch that I've eaten on Tuesdays and Thursdays for eighteen years at Jimmy's Diner is a cheese sandwich and soup. The soup is not only delicious, but it's also a good source of fluid. I add a dash of Tabasco to warm me up on cold winter days.*

---

## THE FOUR O'CLOCK MUNCHIES

In many countries such as England or Germany, the natives enjoy an afternoon cup of coffee or tea along with a sweet. This scheduled meal in their day provides a pleasant break as well as an energy booster. In comparison, many American runners think eating in the afternoon is sinful. They self-inflict "Thou shalt not snack" as an Eleventh Commandment. Then they succumb and feel guilty.

As I mentioned before, hunger is not bad or wrong. It is a normal physiological function. You can *expect* to get hungry every four hours. For example, if you eat lunch at noon, you can appropriately be hungry by 4:00. Eat something! If you are craving sweets, you have gotten *too* hungry and should have eaten more food earlier.

Snacking is particularly important for dieters. As I will discuss in chapter 4, a *planned* afternoon snack of 100 to 200 calories (or whatever fits into your calorie budget) will prevent extreme hunger and reduce the risk of blowing your diet.

---

### JUDY MORRILL

*I like to eat cookies for my afternoon snack. I guess I could eat something healthier, but I like cookies. I also like frozen yogurt—chocolate raspberry swirl is my latest craze. I figure that because I eat an overall healthy, low-fat diet, I can include a few treats without feeling guilty.*

*Outrageous snacks:* If it's an ice cream sundae or insanity, I recommend that you satisfy your hankerings for even belt-busting snacks *by indulging at lunchtime.* By spending your lunchtime calories on the treat, you can still balance your day's calorie budget and you'll certainly have an incentive to run harder that afternoon. You also won't destroy your health with this occasional treat, as long as your overall diet tends to be wholesome. Some of the dessert recipes in this book fall into the "outrageous" category—enjoy them wisely!

*Vending machine snacks:* Vending-machine cuisine offers tough choices. Tucked between the lackluster choices, you may be able to find pretzels, peanuts, juice, yogurt, or even an apple. The good part about vending-machine snacks is that they are limited in size (e.g., only three cookies instead of the whole bag) and generally provide only 200 to 400 calories, not 2,000.

If trying to decide between fatty or sugary choices (i.e., chips v. jelly beans), remember that the sugar in jelly beans will appropriately fuel your muscles, whereas the fat in the chips will clog your arteries. After eating a sugary snack, brush or rinse your teeth.

## SOME SUPER SPORTS SNACKS

The best sports snacks include *wholesome* carbohydrates. If you *carry snacks with you,* you can avoid the temptations that lurk in every corner store, vending machine, or bakery. Or keep a supply of "emergency food" in your desk drawer to be ready and waiting for the four o'clock munchies.

Perishable snacks:
    bagels
    English muffins
    low-fat muffins
    microwaved potato
    yogurt
    thick-crust pizza
    fresh fruit
    leftovers

Nonperishable snacks to keep stocked:
    cold cereal (by the handful right out of the box
       or in a bowl with milk)
    hot cereal (packs of instant oatmeal are easy)
    pretzels
    lite popcorn
    low-fat crackers
    zwieback
    animal crackers
    low-fat granola bars
    sports bars
    noodle soups
    juice boxes
    dried fruit

## DINNER AND RUNNERS

Dinner generally marks the end of the workday. It's time to go home, relax, and enjoy a pleasant meal, that is, if you have the energy to prepare it. The trick to dining on a balanced dinner—the protein-starch-vegetable kind that mom used to make with at least three kinds of foods—is to arrive home with enough *energy* to cook. This means fueling your body and brain with adequate calories prior to the dinner hour.

The recipe section of this cookbook is filled with quick-and-easy pasta and potato ideas (see pages 133–46 and 179–86) that can be prepared by even the most basic of cooks. If you hesitate to cook even the simplest recipes, you might want to take a cooking class at your local center for adult education. But no number of cooking classes will help if you arrive home too hungry to cook or make wise food choices.

### Quick Fixes: Dinner Tips for Hungry Runners

Because good nutrition starts in the supermarket, you have a far better chance of achieving a super sports diet if your kitchen is well stocked with appropriate foods. You might want to muster up your energy to marathon shop at the discount food store once every two or three weeks and *really shop,* so that you have enough food to last for a while. To help accomplish this goal, post a copy of the sidebar: *Runner's Menu Ideas with Basic Foods to Stock* on your refrigerator and check off the foods you need.

If possible, you can use your morning shower/shave time to cook a potful of rice while getting ready for work. Come dinner time, you can simply brown hamburger or ground turkey in a large skillet, dump in the cooked rice, then add whatever is handy. The ratio of 1½ cups of raw rice per pound of lean meat results in two generous sports meals with 60 percent of the calories from carbohydrates. Some popular creations with rice and ground meat include:

- Mexican (canned beans + chili powder + grated low-fat Cheddar cheese + diced tomatoes)
- Chinese (broccoli zapped in a microwave oven while the meat cooks + soy sauce)
- Italian (green beans + Italian seasonings such as basil, oregano, and garlic powder)
- American (grated low-fat Cheddar cheese + onion browned with the meat + diced tomato)

Mary-Giselle Rathgeber, nutritionist, runner, and nutrition writer for *New York Running News,* offers these suggestions for quick-and-easy meals:

- pasta with clam sauce, tomato sauce and/or frozen vegetables, and/or low-fat cheese
- canned beans, rinsed then spooned over rice, pasta, or salads
- frozen dinners, supplemented with whole-grain bread and fresh fruit
- Pierogies, tortellini, and burritos from the frozen food section
- baked potato topped with cottage cheese
- whole-grain cereal (hot or cold) with fruit and low-fat milk
- thick crust pizza, fresh or frozen, then reheated in the toaster oven
- bean soups, homemade, canned, or from the deli
- quick-cooking brown rice—made double for the next day's rice-and-bean salad
- stir-fry, using precut vegetables from the market, salad bar, or freezer

For more dinner suggestions for your day-to-day training diet, as well as for carbo-loading parties and special feasts, refer to the recipe section.

## PASTA: A SUPERFOOD?

Every runner regardless of language understands the word *pasta.* Pasta parties are universally enjoyed around the world. Pasta is popular not only pre-

### RUNNER'S MENU IDEAS WITH BASIC FOODS TO STOCK

If you keep these foods stocked in your kitchen, you will have the makings for at least a week of simple meals:

- Spaghetti and tomato sauce, hamburger, ground turkey, tofu, beans, cottage cheese, grated cheese, and/or vegetables
- English-muffin or pita pizzas
- tuna noodle casserole
- soup and sandwiches (tuna, toasted cheese, peanut butter with banana)
- microwaved potato topped with cottage cheese, baked beans, or yogurt
- peanut butter crackers and V-8 juice

Cupboard: cereal, spaghetti, spaghetti sauce, rice, ramen noodles, crackers, kidney beans, baked beans, tuna, peanut butter, soups (mushroom for making casseroles, lentil, minestrone), baking potatoes, V-8 or other vegetable juices.

Refrigerator: low-fat Cheddar, mozzarella, and cottage cheese; low-fat milk and yogurt; Parmesan cheese; eggs; tofu; carrots; oranges; bananas (when refrigerated, the banana peel turns black but the fruit itself is fine and takes longer to ripen).

Freezer: bagels, pita, English muffins, multigrain bread, orange juice concentrate, broccoli, spinach, winter squash, ground turkey, extra-lean hamburger, chicken (pieces frozen individually in baggies).

## GORDON BAKOULIS

*Like most New York runners who work long hours and live alone, my diet is pretty simple. My kitchen is too small to enjoy cooking, so I eat lots of cooking-free foods: bagels, cereal with milk and banana, yogurt, cottage cheese, and peanut butter. Since I discovered frozen vegetables, my veggie intake has greatly improved.*

marathon, but also as a standard part of the training diet. Even runners who claim they can't cook can manage to boil pasta in one shape or another. Some choose to eat pasta at least five nights a week thinking it is a kind of superfood.

Granted, pasta is carbohydrate-rich, quick and easy to cook, heart-healthy, economical, fun to eat, and enjoyed by just about every member of the family. But in terms of vitamins, minerals, and protein, plain pasta is a lackluster food. Here's some information to help you to place pasta in perspective.

*Nutritional Value:* Pasta is an excellent source of carbohydrates for muscle fuel and is the equivalent of "gas" for your engine. But plain pasta is a marginal source of vitamins and minerals, the "spark plugs" you need for top performance. Pasta is made from refined white flour—the same stuff you get in "wonder breads"—with a few vitamins added to replace those lost during processing.

Note that whole-wheat pastas offer little nutritional superiority, because wheat (and other grains in general) are better respected for their carbohydrate-value than their vitamins and minerals. Even spinach and tomato pastas are often overrated since they contain relatively little spinach or tomato in comparison to having a serving of that vegetable along with the meal.

*Pasta and protein:* Pasta is popular not only for carbohydrates but also for being a vegetarian alternative to meat-based meals. However, many athletes live on *too much* pasta and neglect their protein needs. For example, Joe, an aspiring Olympian, thought his high-carbohydrate, low-fat diet of pasta and tomato sauce seven nights a week was top notch. He came to me wondering why he felt chronically tired and was not improving despite hard training.

The answer was simple. His linear diet was deficient in not only protein but also iron and zinc. Once he started to supplement the pasta with a variety of proteins, he started to feel better, run better, and recover better. He varied his choices between:

# PASTA V. POTATO V. RICE

If you have the choice between plain pasta or a potato for dinner, consider the potato. It offers far more vitamin C, potassium, fiber, and overall health value. A potato is even better than rice, and a sweet potato the best of all. Here's the lineup for these popular dinner starches:

| | Amount | Calories | Vit. C | Potassium | Thiamin | Fiber |
|---|---|---|---|---|---|---|
| Spaghetti, plain | 2 cups cooked; ¼ lb. dry | 420 | 0 | 230 | .5 | .2 |
| Spaghetti, 100% whole wheat | " | 420 | 0 | 440 | .7 | 3 |
| Brown rice, cooked | 2 cups cooked; ½ cup dry | 420 | 2 | 240 | .3 | 1 |
| Potato, plain baked | 2 large; 15 oz. total wt. | 420 | 90 | 2,270 | .5 | 3 |
| Sweet potato, baked | 2 large; 15 oz. total wt. | 420 | 100 | 1,400 | .3 | 6 |

*Carbohydrates galore: The pre-marathon pasta party celebrates the pleasure of eating. Thousands of excited runners come to this huge* *tent outside The Tavern on the Green in Central Park to share both the food and the camaraderie.*

- 2–3 ounces of extra-lean ground beef or turkey in tomato sauce
- ¼ cup of grated low-fat Mozzarella cheese
- ½ cake tofu
- ⅔ cup kidney beans
- ½ can of tuna
- 1 cup of low-fat cottage cheese

Or, instead of adding protein to the sauce, he drank two glasses of low-fat milk with the meal.

Pasta becomes more of a nutritional powerhouse when you top it with:

- tomato sauce rich in vitamins A and C and potassium
- pesto-type sauces rich in vitamins A and C and potassium

- clam sauce rich in protein, zinc, and iron

Pasta can be an artery-clogging nutritional nightmare if you eat it smothered with butter, cream, or greasy meat sauces. The recipe section includes several

### JUDY MORRILL

*Like many runners, I'm hungry all the time. I like to eat every two or three hours. I have cereal at home, then a bagel at the office, sandwich for lunch, then pre-run cookies, dinner and frozen yogurt. My nonrunning friends marvel at my appetite and wonder why I'm not fat.*

# SPUDS FOR RUNNERS

Not everyone is a pasta fan. Potatoes are pre-wrapped, convenient, nutritious, and a great source of carbohydrates, potassium, and vitamin C. A large baking potato offers 65 percent of the Required Daily Allowance for vitamin C and all the potassium you'd lose in three hours of sweaty exercise. A sweet potato offers the additional health benefits of beta-carotene.

Baked potatoes are a good sports food not only for meals but also snacks. Some runners carry them in a pocket, as they might a piece of fruit, and munch on them after workouts when they need an energy booster.

Potatoes can easily become an nutritious addition to your training diet:

- Pop a few bakers into a 400° oven just as you leave for your run. They will be ready and waiting to greet you when you return home. Or . . .
- Post-run, zap a potato in the microwave oven for about six to ten minutes while you shower.
- Top the potato with any of the numerous ideas listed in recipe section (pages 179 **to** 186).

low-fat pasta meals and suggestions that can contribute to a high-carbohydrate sports diet.

## SUMMARY

If you are like many active people who know what they "should" eat, but just don't do it, you need to remember the following keys to a successful sports diet:

1. Eat appropriately sized meals on a regular schedule so that you won't get too hungry. Notice how your diet deteriorates when you get too hungry.

2. Spend your calories on a *variety* of wholesome foods at each meal.

3. Pay attention to how much better you feel, run, and feel about yourself when you eat a well-balanced sports diet.

It's my opinion that getting *too* hungry is the biggest problem with most runners' diets. Carbohydrate-rich breakfasts and lunches set the stage for a top-notch sports diet.

# 2 NOT BY CARBS ALONE
## Protein, Fats, Fluids, and Vitamins

 RUNNERS AND CARBOHYDRATES are synonymous. But a runner cannot live by carbohydrates alone. An optimal sports diet includes a variety of nutrients. This chapter answers some of the questions active people commonly ask about protein, fats, fluids, vitamins, and minerals and offers handy tips to help you balance them into your daily food plan.

## PROTEIN FOR RUNNERS

Historically, protein was the fundamental part of a fitness diet because many thought it gave power and strength. That's why 1970 New York City Marathon winner Gary Muhrcke used to eat steak and eggs for his pre-marathon breakfasts when he first started running. Today we know that these types of animal proteins do a poor job of fueling muscles but a good job of increasing the intake of saturated fats and the risk of heart disease.

Although too much protein offers no benefits to a sports diet, adequate protein is essential. About 10 to 15 percent of your calories should come from protein to:

- build and repair muscles
- generate red blood cells
- make enzymes and hormones
- grow hair and fingernails

Most active people, being health conscious, have heard the public-health messages to eat less protein and have appropriately reduced their protein intake. Some have taken that advice to the extreme. They have eliminated meats from their diet but have failed to add any plant proteins. The result is a protein-deficient diet.

> ### GORDON BAKOULIS
> *I have to make the effort to eat enough protein because I could more easily live on just bagels. Cottage cheese, yogurt, and peanut butter are my staples.*

If you aspire to a vegetarian diet and have stopped eating meat, make sure you are addressing your overall protein needs. Also recognize that being a vegetarian may require lifestyle changes. Pay attention to the flip side of your higher-carbohydrate diet by eating a small amount of protein-containing food at each meal. Otherwise, you'll suffer the consequences of a dietary imbalance: chronic fatigue, anemia, lack of improvement, muscle wasting, and an overall rundown feeling. Note that a protein-deficient diet can also lack iron (which prevents anemia) and zinc (which helps with healing). These minerals will be discussed later.

### How Much Protein Is Enough?

The current recommended daily allowance (RDA) for protein is 0.4 grams per pound of body weight (0.8 gm/kg). This RDA was based on *sedentary* college students. Because runners have a slightly higher protein need, an adequate and safe protein intake is 0.5 to 0.75 grams of protein per pound of body weight (1.0–1.5 gms protein/kg). Growing teenagers, athletes building new muscles, marathoners doing lots of long runs, or dieters who restrict calories (which results in protein being used for fueling rather than maintaining muscles) should target the higher protein intake. Note that endurance runners burn some protein for energy during workouts.

### Combining Beans and Grains

The key to eating a high quality vegetarian diet is to eat a variety of foods that contain an assortment of the eight essential amino acids needed for building protein. Historically, vegetarians have been instructed to combine the amino acids from beans, grains, legumes, and/or seeds *in the same meal* in order to enhance the quality of their diet. Today we know this time frame can be expanded. You can receive the same results by simply eating a variety of these foods daily. Some effective protein-rich foods to combine throughout the day include:

| | |
|---|---|
| *Grains + milk products:* | bran muffin + yogurt |
| | cereal + milk |
| | pasta + cheese |
| *Grains + beans and legumes (such as peanuts, lentils, kidney, pinto, lima, and navy beans):* | bran muffin + peanut butter |
| | pasta + tomato sauce with canned kidney beans |
| | brown bread + baked beans |
| *Legumes + seeds:* | hummus (chickpeas + sesame paste) |
| | tofu + sunflower seeds (stir-fried with vegetables) |
| *Milk products + any food:* | milk, yogurt, or cheese added to any meal or snack |

### Red Meat: Eat or Avoid?

Red meats such as beef and lamb are indisputably excellent sources of high-quality protein. They are also rich in iron and zinc, two minerals important for optimal health and athletic performance. Some meat-eating athletes sound a bit unsure or even apologetic when asked if they eat red meat. Somehow eating beef seems out of vogue, and confusion abounds regarding the pros and cons of eating meat.

If you have pondered whether or not you should

---

**BARBARA ANDERSON**

*Being a vegetarian is a lifestyle that requires setting aside time for cooking. I'm pretty busy between work and running, but I still have time to cook because I've organized cooking into my daily schedule. Plus, I cook extra for leftovers, so that simplifies life.*

*I use the pressure cooker for brown rice. It cooks in only 20 to 30 minutes and tastes fabulous! I also have two Crock-Pots that do all the cooking while I work, run, and sleep. Slow-cooking beans, soups, and vegetarian stews make for wonderful flavors. I even travel with a Crock-Pot to out-of-town races, so that I can eat the foods I like to eat.*

---

eat or avoid red meat, know that the answer is not a simple yes or no but rather a weighing of nutrition facts, ethical concerns, personal values, and dedication to making appropriate food choices. Yes, you *can* get the nutrients needed to support your sports program from plant food sources, *but will you make the effort to do so?* The following facts can help you decide if adding two to four small (3–4 ounce) portions of red meat per week into your meals might enhance the quality of your diet.

*Meat for protein:* Animal foods are excellent sources of high-quality protein. But so are plant proteins if you eat *enough* of them. Active people with big appetites can do this more easily than calorie-conscious dieters. If you eat only a little peanut butter on a lunchtime sandwich and a sprinkling of garbanzo beans on a dinner salad, you likely fall short of meeting the approximate 50–70 grams of protein needed by active women and 70–90 grams of protein needed by men.

*Meat and cholesterol:* Meat, like chicken, fish, and other animal products, contains cholesterol because

---

**ALBERTO SALAZAR**

*Eat well-balanced meals but let your body advise you as to what you need. If you feel like you really want a steak, have it!*

---

cholesterol is a part of animal cells; plant cells contain no cholesterol. Most animal proteins have similar cholesterol values: 70–80 milligrams of cholesterol per four ounce serving of red meat, poultry, and fish.

Given that the American Heart Association recommends that healthy people with normal blood cholesterol levels take in less than 300 milligrams of cholesterol per day, small portions of red meat can certainly fit those requirements. People who know their blood cholesterol number can best make personalized dietary decisions about how much dietary cholesterol is appropriate for their bodies.

But note that the cholesterol content of meat is of less concern than the fat content. *Fatty* meats, such as greasy hamburgers, pepperoni, juicy steaks, and sausage, are the real dietary no-noes. Lean meats—

London broil, extra-lean hamburgers, top round roast beef—can fit into a hearty-healthy sports diet in appropriate amounts. The recipe section on meats lists the leanest cuts to buy (see page 167).

*Meat and iron:* Adequate iron in your sports diet is important to prevent anemia. Without question, the iron in red meat is more easily absorbed than that in popular vegetarian sources of iron (e.g., beans, raisins, spinach). In a study of eighteen women runners who consumed the recommended daily allowance for iron, eight of the nine women who ate no red meat (but did eat chicken and fish) suffered depleted iron stores as compared to only two of the nine red-meat eaters.

If you have an iron-poor diet and are tempted to

## QUICK AND EASY MEATLESS MEALS

Chapters 10, 14, and 15 (pasta, vegetarian main dishes, and potatoes and rice) offer numerous meat-free meal suggestions. Here are a few more ideas to help you with a meat-free diet that has adequate protein.

*Breakfast Suggestions:*

- Cold cereal (preferably iron-enriched, as noted on the label): eat with milk, yogurt, or soymilk; sprinkle with nuts
- Oatmeal, oat bran, and other hot cereals: add peanut butter, almonds or other nuts, and/or powdered milk
- Toast, bagels: top with low-fat cheese, cottage cheese, or a thin spreading of peanut butter

*Lunch and Dinner:*

- Salads: Add tofu, chickpeas, three-bean salad, marinated kidney beans, cottage cheese, sunflower seeds, chopped nuts.
- Protein-rich salad dressing: Add salad seasonings to plain yogurt, blenderized tofu, or cottage cheese (diluted with milk or yogurt).
- Spaghetti sauce: add diced tofu and/or canned kidney beans

- Pasta: Choose protein-enriched pastas that offer 13 grams of protein per cup, as compared to 8 ounces in regular pasta. Top with grated part-skim Mozzarella.
- Potato: Baked or microwaved, then topped with canned beans, baked beans, or low-fat cottage cheese.
- Hearty soups: Lentil, split pea, bean, and minestrone.
- Hummus with pita.
- Cheese pizza: A protein-rich fast food, half of a 12-inch pizza has about 40 grams of protein.

*Snacks:*

- Assorted nuts
- Peanut butter on rice cakes or crackers
- Yogurt (Note: frozen yogurt has only 4 grams of protein per 8 ounces. as compared to 8 grams of protein in regular yogurt.)

# HOW TO BALANCE YOUR PROTEIN INTAKE

If you wonder if you are eating too little (or too much) protein, you can estimate your daily protein needs by multiplying your weight by 0.5 to 0.75 grams of protein per pound.

| Weight (lbs) | Protein (grams per day) |
|---|---|
| 100 | 50–80 |
| 120 | 60–90 |
| 150 | 75–100 |
| 170 | 85–115 |

Use food labels and the following chart to calculate your protein intake. Pay close attention to portion sizes!

### Protein Content of Some Commonly Eaten Foods

#### Animal Proteins

| | |
|---|---|
| Beef, 4 ounces cooked* | 25 grams |
| Chicken breast, half, cooked | 30 |
| Tuna, canned, 7 ounces | 40 |
| Meat, fish, poulty, 1 ounce cooked | 7 |
| Egg, 1 | 7 |

#### Plant Proteins

| | |
|---|---|
| Lentils, beans, ½ cup | 7 |
| Baked beans, ½ cup | 8 |
| Peanut butter, 2 tablespoons | 8 |
| Tofu, ¼ cake (4 ounces) | 7 |

*4 ounces = size of a deck of cards
4 ounces raw = 3 ounces cooked

#### Dairy Products

| | |
|---|---|
| Milk, yogurt, 1 cup | 8 |
| Cheese, 1 ounce | 8 |
| Cheese, 1 slice American (⅔ ounce) | 6 |
| Cottage cheese, ⅓ cup | 8 |
| Milk, powder, ¼ cup | 8 |

#### Breads, Cereals, Grains

| | |
|---|---|
| Bread, 1 slice | 2 |
| Cold cereals, 1 ounce | 2 |
| Oatmeal, ⅓ cup, dry | 5 |
| Rice, ⅓ cup, dry, 1 cup cooked | 4 |
| Pasta, 2 oz. dry; 1 cup cooked | 8 |

#### Starchy Vegetables

| | |
|---|---|
| Peas, carrots, ½ cup | 2 |
| Corn, ½ cup | 2 |
| Beets, ½ cup | 2 |
| Winter squash, ½ cup | 2 |
| Potato, 1 small | 2 |

#### Fruits, Watery Vegetables

Negligible amounts of protein.
Most fruits and vegetables have only small amounts of protein. They may contribute a total of 5–10 grams of protein per day, depending on how much you eat.

take an iron supplement, note that animal iron is absorbed better than the iron in a pill. But any iron is better than no iron. (See the sidebar on page 30.)

*Meat and zinc:* Zinc is important for healing both the minor damage that occurs through daily training as well as major injuries and ailments. It is best found in iron-rich foods (e.g., red meat). Diets deficient in iron may then also be deficient in zinc. Like iron, the zinc in animal products is absorbed better than that in vegetable foods or supplements. (See the sidebar on page 31.)

*Meat and amenorrhea:* Female runners who are amenorrheic and have stopped having menstrual periods commonly eat no red meat. In one study, *none* of the amenorrheic runners ate red meat as compared to 44 percent of the runners with regular menses.

The question remains unanswered: Are these amenorrheic athletes simply protein deficient or is there a meat factor that affects the hormones involved with menstruation? Given that amenorrhea is a sign of poor internal health, athletes who do not menstruate should carefully evaluate the adequacy of their diets and acknowledge that red meat may reduce the higher risk of stress fractures that coincides with the loss of menses. Refer to chapter 5 for more information.

*Hormones in meats:* Fears abound regarding hormones given to cattle to enhance their growth. The U.S. Department of Agriculture claims the amount of hormones used is far less than one might get in a birth control pill or even in a cup of cole slaw, for that matter. If this is one of your concerns, you can shop for "all natural" meat to be on the safe side.

*Conclusion:* Active people who carefully select a vegetarian diet can certainly eat a high-quality sports diet that meets their nutritional needs. However, those who simply abstain from eating red meat and make no effort to include alternate sources of protein, iron, and zinc should rethink their diet and reorganize their food choices. Or they might want to reconsider including small portions of lean meat two to four times per week as a convenient, nutrient-dense sports food. Some sample meals might be:

- a roast beef sandwich with hearty bread
- 4 ounces of flank steak stir-fried with broccoli and eaten with rice
- a little extra-lean hamburger added to spaghetti sauce

Remember that the *fat* in greasy meats, not the red meat itself, is the primary health culprit. The recipe section includes several iron- and zinc-rich recipes with lean meat incorporated into the overall carbohydrate-rich, low-fat entrée. The recipe section also includes many vegetarian options.

## FATS AND YOUR SPORTS DIET

Many active people restrict their meat intake because of their desire to limit their intake of saturated fats.

This is a wise health practice until taken to the extreme. In this anti-fat era, some athletes think all they need to know about fat is that they are supposed to avoid it like the plague. Rumors abound:

- Fat instantly clogs the arteries or causes cancer.
- Fat slows you down; it's the worst food you could put in your body.
- If you eat fat, you'll get fat.

While there may be an element of truth to some of these statements, there is also room for more education. Let's look at the whole picture.

First of all, remember that fat is an essential nutrient needed for overall good health. Whereas a little fat is an appropriate part of your sports diet, too much leaves your muscles unfueled. Without question, a diet saturated with animal fats, fast-food grease, and obscene desserts may also contribute to heart disease and cancer and shorten your life. But if you are lean, fit, and healthy and have:

# HOW TO BOOST YOUR IRON INTAKE

- The RDA for iron is 10 milligrams for men and 15 milligrams for women. (Women have higher iron needs to replace the iron lost from menstrual bleeding.)
- Iron from animal products is absorbed better than that from plant products.
- A source of vitamin C at each meal may enhance iron absorption.

| Animal sources (best absorbed) | Iron (mg) | | Iron (mg) |
|---|---|---|---|
| Beef, 4 ounces cooked | 2 | **Beans** | |
| Pork, 4 ounces | 1 | Kidney, ½ cup | 2½ |
| Chicken breast, 4 ounces | 1 | Tofu, ¼ cake | 2 |
| Chicken leg, 4 ounces | 1½ | | |
| Salmon, 4 ounces | 1 | **Grains** | |
| | | Cereal, 100% fortified | 15 |
| **Fruits** | | Spaghetti, 1 cup, cooked | 2 |
| Prunes, 5 | 1 | Bread, 1 slice, enriched | 1 |
| Raisins, ⅓ cup | 1 | | |
| | | **Other** | |
| **Vegetables** | | Molasses, blackstrap, 1 tablespoon | 3½ |
| Spinach, ½ cup, cooked | 3 | Wheat germ | 2 |
| Broccoli, ½ cup, cooked | 1 | | |

- low blood cholesterol (or high levels of the good HDL cholesterol)
- a family history of longevity
- no family history of heart disease

you can appropriately include a reasonable amount of fat in your diet. The people who most likely need to severely restrict their fat intake to 10 to 20 percent of calories are overfat, under-fit folks with heart disease—not most healthy runners.

### Twenty-five Percent Fat: What's That?

I recommend that healthy runners target a sports diet with about 25 percent of the calories from fat. This:

- is in keeping with the 20 to 30 percent fat diet that is considered to be health-protective.
- allows for adequate carbohydrates (60–65 percent of all calories) and proteins (10–15 percent of all calories).
- provides fat-soluable vitamins such as vitamin E (an anti-oxidant that has a health-protective effect).
- allows for easier participation in life (i.e., eating at a party, enjoying a cookie guilt-free).

How does 25 percent fat translate into food? Let's say you have 1,800 calories a day in your calorie budget:

.25 x 1,800 total calories = 450 calories a day of fat

Because there are 9 calories per gram of fat, divide 450 calories by 9. Thus you have an allowance of 50 grams of fat for your daily fat budget. A 25-percent-fat diet includes a reasonable amount of fat and lets you enjoy a little fat at each meal. Preferably, you'll

### ROD DIXON

*I'm careful about my diet, and I still eat red meats. The meat is lean, 100 percent natural, and New Zealand farm-raised, of course!*

# HOW TO BOOST YOUR ZINC INTAKE

- The RDA for zinc is 15 milligrams.
- Animal foods, including seafood, are the best sources of zinc.

| Animal Sources | Zinc (mg) | Plant Sources | Zinc (mg) |
|---|---|---|---|
| Beef, tenderloin, 4 ounces | 7 | Wheat germ, ¼ cup | 3½ |
| Chicken leg, 4 ounces | 3½ | Lentils, 1 cup | 2½ |
| Pork loin, 4 ounces | 3 | Almonds, 1 ounce | 1 |
| Chicken breast, 4 ounces | 1 | Garbanzo beans, ½ cup | 1 |
| Cheese, 1 ounces | 1 | Spinach, 1 cup, cooked | ¾ |
| Milk, 1 cup | 1 | Peanut butter, 1 tablespoon | ½ |
| Oysters, 6 medium | 75 (!) | Bread, 1 slice, whole wheat | ½ |
| Tuna, 1 can (6½ ounces) | 2 | | |
| Clams, 9 small | 1 | | |

choose fats that have a positive health value such as olive oil, salmon and other oily fish, all-natural peanut butter, low-fat cheese, and tuna with light mayonnaise. But if you have the occasional hankering for a big burger with 25 grams of fat and 500 calories, simply fit it into your day's fat and calorie budget *and balance the rest of the day's meals.* (Refer to the sidebar, *Calculating Your Calorie Needs* on page 4.)

### Fat: Friend or Foe?

Without question, fat imparts a tempting taste, texture, and aroma and helps make food taste great. That's why fatty foods are hard to resist and are enjoyed to excess. Although *excess* fat-calories can easily turn into body fat, note that the "eat fat, get fat" theory is false. Many active people take in appropriate amounts of fat and stay thin. They simply don't overeat *calories.*

If you are weight-conscious and are obsessed about every gram of fat to the extent that you have a fat phobia, your fear of fat may be exaggerated! A little fat can actually aid in weight reduction because it adds *satiety,* the nice feeling of being satisfied after a meal. Satiety may actually *reduce* your desire to continue munching even after you've eaten your bulky but unfilling fat-free meal.

Believe it or not, many of my clients have lost

body fat after they reintroduced an appropriate amount of dietary fat back into their fat-free regimen. Refer to the weight reduction information in chapter 4 for additional help with resolving your "eat fat, get fat" fears.

Although all fats are equally caloric, some fats provide more health benefits than others. Olive oil, for one, is thought to be health protective. It is the foundation of the acclaimed heart-healthy Mediterranean diet. For centuries, the folks in Italy

### EINO

*The night before one New York City Marathon, one of the top runners asked me where he could find some raisins. He was worried about his iron intake and thought that some last-minute raisins would do the trick. He should have taken care of his iron intake as a part of his training diet—and also should have planned in a better source of iron than raisins!*

# FAT GUIDELINES

The following guidelines can help you appropriately budget fat into your food plan. If you need 1,600 calories per day, the number of grams of fat in a low-fat diet with 25 percent of calories from fat would be 45. If you need 1,800 calories per day, your grams of fat would be 50; 2,000 calories per day would be 55 grams, 2,200 calories per day would be 60 grams; and 2,400 calories per day would be 65 grams.

## Fat Content of Some Common Foods

| | Serving size | Grams fat | Total calories |
|---|---|---|---|
| **Dairy products** | | | |
| Milk, whole (3½% fat) | 8 oz. | 8 | 150 |
| 2% fat | 8 oz. | 5 | 120 |
| 1% fat | 8 oz. | 2 | 100 |
| skim (0% fat) | 8 oz. | – | 80 |
| Cheese, Cheddar | 1 oz. | 9 | 110 |
| Cheddar-lite | 1 oz. | 5 | 90 |
| Mozzarella, part-skim | 1 oz. | 5 | 80 |
| Cheese, cottage (4% fat) | ½ cup | 5 | 120 |
| low-fat (2% fat) | ½ cup | 2 | 90 |
| Cream cheese | 1 oz. (2 tbsp.) | 10 | 100 |
| light | 1 oz. (2 tbsp.) | 5 | 60 |
| Ice cream, gourmet | ½ cup | 15 | 250 |
| standard | ½ cup | 8 | 150 |
| light | ½ cup | 3 | 110 |
| Frozen yogurt, low-fat | ½ cup | 2 | 120 |
| nonfat | ½ cup | – | 100 |
| **Animal proteins** | | | |
| Beef, regular hamburger | 4 oz. cooked | 24 | 330 |
| flank steak | 4 oz. cooked | 12 | 235 |
| eye of round | 4 oz. cooked | 6 | 200 |
| Chicken, breast, no skin | 4 oz. cooked | 5 | 200 |
| thigh, no skin | 4 oz. cooked | 11 | 235 |
| Fish, haddock | 4 oz. cooked | 1 | 125 |
| swordfish | 4 oz. cooked | 6 | 175 |
| **Vegetable proteins** | | | |
| Beans, kidney | ½ cup cooked | – | 110 |
| Lentils | ½ cup cooked | – | 110 |
| Tofu | 4 oz. | 5 | 90 |
| Peanut butter | 1 tbsp. | 8 | 95 |
| **Vegetables** | | | |
| Vegetables, most varieties | negligible | | |

| | Serving size | Grams fat | Total calories |
|---|---|---|---|
| **Fats** | | | |
| Butter | 1 tbsp. | 12 | 108 |
| Margarine | 1 tbsp. | 11 | 100 |
| Oil, olive | 1 tbsp. | 13 | 120 |
| Mayonnaise | 1 tbsp. | 11 | 100 |
| **Grains** | | | |
| Bread, whole wheat | 1 large slice | 1 | 90 |
| Crackers, Saltines | 5 | 2 | 60 |
| Ritz | 4 | 4 | 70 |
| Rice cakes | 1 | – | 35 |
| Cereal, shredded wheat | 1 oz./⅔ cup | – | 90 |
| granola | 1 oz./¼ cup | 6 | 130 |
| oatmeal | 1oz; ⅓ cup dry | 2 | 100 |
| Spaghetti, plain | 2 oz. dry; 1 cup cooked | 1 | 210 |
| Rice | 2 oz. dry; 1 cup cooked | – | 200 |
| **Fast foods** | | | |
| Big Mac | 1 | 26 | 500 |
| Egg McMuffin | 1 | 11 | 280 |
| French fries | regular | 12 | 220 |
| Kentucky fried chicken | breast | 17 | 275 |
| Pizza, cheese | 1 slice large | 10–13 | 250 |
| **Snacks, Treats** | | | |
| Cookie, Chips Ahoy | 1 (½ oz.) | 2 | 50 |
| Fig Newton | 1 (½ oz.) | 1 | 60 |
| Brownie, from mix | 1 small | 5 | 140 |
| Graham crackers | 2 squares | 1 | 60 |
| Potato chips | 18 (1 oz.) | 9 | 150 |
| Pretzels | 1 oz. | 1 | 110 |
| Milky Way | 1¾ oz. bar | 8 | 220 |
| Peanut M&Ms | 1¾ oz. bag | 13 | 250 |
| Reese's Peanut Butter Cups | 1⁹⁄₁₀ oz. (2) | 15 | 280 |
| **Fruits** | | | |
| Fruit, most varieties | negligible | | |

*At one time, I tried to limit my fat intake to less than 10 grams a day so that I could lose weight. I was always hungry, ate lots of pretzels and bagels, and never lost weight. Then I went to a sports nutritionist who recommended that I include 50 grams of fat in my diet. With fear and hesitation, I took her advice and started eating more peanut butter, low-fat cheese, and olive oil (for cooking). I expected to blimp up, but much to my surprise I lost weight. I felt less hungry and simply ate fewer calories.*

and Greece have enjoyed good health and a 40 percent fat diet. Their diet is rich in monounsaturated fat from olive oil, not saturated fat from greasy meats and lard. Olive oil in combination with the Mediterranean diet's bounty of beans, fresh seafood, fruits, and vegetables are all positive factors that may combine with physically active lifestyles to enhance longevity. Many recipes in this book contain some olive oil; enjoy them in good health.

## WATER AND SPORTS DRINKS

Water is an essential nutrient equally important to carbohydrates, proteins, and fats. Active people need adequate water for:

- *blood* to help carry oxygen and fuel to working muscles
- *urine* to help carry away waste products
- *sweat* to dissipate heat
- *body fluids* to lubricate joints
- *gastric juices* to digest food

Today's runners know that water is an important part of their training and racing diet, but that wasn't always the case. For example, in 1953, running regulations stated that marathoners could take water *only* after 9.3 miles. This contrasts to the twenty-three water stations provided along today's New York City Marathon course!

All runners in all climates in all seasons should make the effort to replace sweat losses. This includes those who:

- race in the summer heat
- overdress for a winter training run
- sweat hard when working out on the health club's treadmill

The American College of Sports Medicine recommends that you drink 4 to 8 ounces of fluid every 15 to 20 minutes of hard running. You should never allow yourself to become thirsty. That's a clear sign of dehydration. Dehydration slows you down, and in extreme cases can contribute to medical problems.

Active people who replace fluid losses poorly during training and are chronically dehydrated tend to experience needless fatigue and lethargy. Don't let that happen to you! You can tell if you are well hydrated by monitoring your urine:

- You should urinate frequently throughout the day.
- The urine should be clear and of significant quantity.
- Your morning urine should *not* be dark and concentrated.
- To determine how much you should drink during your exercise time, weigh yourself before and after an hour of training. If you have lost one pound (16 oz.) in one hour, you've lost one pint (16 oz.) of sweat and should plan to drink accordingly during

*Don't let cold weather trick you into thinking you need less water. I once trained in cold weather, and because I didn't sweat much and feel thirsty I didn't drink enough replacement fluids. Race day turned out to be warm. I suffered in the race because of the low-grade dehydration from days and weeks of inadequate fluids. Recovery also took a long time.*

the next exercise session—at least 8 ounces every half-hour.

- Strive to lose no more than 2 percent of your body weight per exercise session. That is, if you weigh 150 pounds, try not to lose more than 3 pounds of sweat during a workout.

- Practice drinking fluids during training, so on marathon day you'll be familiar with the skills involved in drinking on the run as well as your body's capacity for fluids. If you plan to drink anything other than water (e.g., a sports drink), be sure that you have tried it during training as well.

### Sports Drinks

Although water always has been and always will be a popular thirst quencher and fluid replacer, sports drinks are rising in popularity, particularly among endurance runners. During a long run (60–90+ minutes), you'll perform better if you drink more than just plain water. That's where sports drinks come into the picture. They provide small amounts of carbohydrates to:

- enhance water absorption (sodium also helps with this transfer)

- supplement the limited amount of carbohydrate available to your muscles and brain

---

## NEW YORK CITY MARATHON FLUIDS

Here's how the fluid needs were met for 27,000 thirsty runners in 1993

- 23 water stations on the course serving New York City's finest water

- 1.6 million cups for water

- 150,000 12-ounce bottles of spring water at the start and finish

- 15,000 gallons of sports drink

- 30,000 sponges

---

## GORDON BAKOULIS

*What I like best about training in Central Park is that I can easily keep well hydrated. I simply plant a bottle of sports drink behind a bush, then take a swig every loop. This makes a big difference on helping me feel good during the whole long run.*

---

Some sports drinks are sweetened with glucose polymers, others with glucose or a combination of glucose and fructose. With the multitude of sports drinks on the market, it's easy to feel confused about what's best to drink and wonder if some are better than others. The bottom line is that you should choose the drink that you prefer; there are no significant advantages to one over the other.

The beverage perfect for all athletes in all events has yet to be designed. But in the quest for developing the ideal sports beverage, scientists have observed enormous individual differences among people's stomach function during exercise. This helps explain why some runners choose plain water, others seek out a particular brand of sports drink, and some prefer to make their own concoction. The most important point is to *drink enough*. Any fluid, be it water or sports drink, is better than no fluid during extended exercise.

### Electrolyte Replacement

When you sweat, you lose electrolytes such as sodium and potassium, two of the minerals that help maintain proper water balance in your tissues. Commercial sports drinks generally include these electrolytes. Although many runners believe the sodium and potassium are added to replace what is lost in sweat, these electrolytes are added primarily to increase the absorption rate of the water into your body.

Most runners don't have to worry about replacing electrolytes during exercise because the losses are generally too small to cause a deficit that will hurt performance and/or health. But if you will be running for more than five hours, electrolyte losses can become problematic, particularly if you are drinking *only* water during the run. Your best bet during extended runs is to drink sports drinks and eat foods that contain sodium and potassium.

### How to Keep Your Cool

The following true-false quiz is designed to test your knowledge about fluid replacement and help you survive the heat in good health and with high energy while you are training for or running in the New York City Marathon.

*Drinking cold water while running will cool you off.*
**True** (but by a small margin). Although drinking cold water will cool you off slightly more than warmer water, the difference is small. The more important concern is quantity. *Any* fluid of any temperature is better than no fluid.

*Wetting yourself down during a run with a cold sponge or towel will cool you off.*
**False.** Surprising as it may seem, research suggests that sponging the face, arms, and trunk every twenty minutes with a cold towel does not reduce core body temperature. Psychologically, this cold towel may provide surprising relief. Hence, your best bet is to drink often and sponge as desired, as long as you have enough fluids for both the inside and outside of your body.

*Drinking water thirty minutes before exercising eliminates the need to drink fluids during a long training run.*
**False.** Research suggests that drinking a quart of water pre-exercise is less effective than drinking an equal volume during exercise. Researchers aren't sure why, but they recommend the optimal approach: tank up beforehand *plus* drink enough to match your sweat losses during a long, strenuous run.

### ANDRES RODRIGUEZ, M.D.

*When you see runners at the end of the race who look like hell, inevitably they will tell you, "I didn't drink enough water."*

Water, an essential nutrient for runners, is more valuable in the body than splashed over the head. Be sure to hydrate both your inside and your outside!

*Soda is a poor choice during exercise because the carbon dioxide in the bubbles will slow you down.*
**False.** Historically, athletes were always warned to "de-fizz" carbonated beverages taken during exercise, fearing that the carbonation would interfere with oxygen transport and would also hurt performance. New studies comparing carbonated and noncarbonated soft drinks show that bubbles will not hurt your performance nor result in stomach discomfort.

*Drinking diet cola is as effective as drinking water to replace sweat losses.*
**False.** Water is better. Research has shown that ath-

letes who drank a volume of liquid equal to sweat losses replaced:

- only 54 percent of their sweat losses with diet cola
- 64 percent with water
- 69 percent with a sports drink

This difference relates primarily to the caffeine in the cola. Caffeine has a diuretic effect that makes you urinate more. When the weather is very hot, you want to be able to use every drop of water, not flush it down the toilet. Noncaffeinated drinks would be a better choice.

*Don't bother to drink during a run that is shorter than an hour because the fluid has too little time to get into your system.*
**False.** According to Larry Armstrong, exercise physi-ologist at the University of Connecticut, water can travel from stomach to skin in only 9 to 18 minutes after drinking. This water is essential for dissipating the 15 to 20 times more heat you produce during exercise as compared to that produced while you are at rest. Your safest bet is to try to match sweat losses with an equal volume of fluid during exercise.

*Beer is an appropriate recovery fluid.*
**False.** Although beer is a popular postexercise recovery drink, its alcohol content has both a dehydrating and depressant effect. If you drink beer on an empty stomach (as commonly happens post-race) you can quickly negate the pleasurable "natural high" that you would otherwise enjoy.

## VITAMINS AND SUPPLEMENTS

Vitamins are essential substances that your body can't make. They perform important jobs in your body, including helping to convert food into energy. Because vitamin supplements seem to be growing in popularity (surveys suggest that 75–90 percent of athletes take some type of supplement), you may wonder if you should "take" vitamins.

Although a supplement is certainly quick and easy health insurance, I highly recommend that you first make the effort to "eat" your vitamins. As a hungry athlete who requires more calories than the average person, you can easily eat larger doses of all nutrients (except possibly vitamin E) and potentially

## COMPARING COMMON FLUID REPLACERS

| Beverage | Calories (per 8 oz.) | Potassium (mg) | Sodium (mg) |
|---|---|---|---|
| Gatorade | 50 | 30 | 110 |
| Cola | 100 | - | 5 |
| Beer | 100 | 60 | 12 |
| Orange juice | 110 | 475 | 2 |
| Cranapple juice | 175 | 70 | 5 |
| Fruit yogurt | 250 | 465 | 150 |
| *Possible losses in 2 hours* | *1,000* | *180* | *1,000* |

benefit from this bonus. Chapter 1 provides more information about the best food sources of vitamins.

Because food consumption surveys suggest that many people fail to eat a well-balanced variety of wholesome foods, some runners may indeed suffer from marginal nutritional deficiencies, particularly those who restrict calories, eat a repetitive diet of bagels and pasta, skimp on fruits, vegetables, and dairy foods, or overindulge in fats and sweets. Even athletes who think they eat well sometimes miss the mark. For example, one runner who took pride in her high-carbohydrate, low-fat diet ate too many carbohydrates at the exclusion of other foods and had a diet deficient in iron, zinc, and protein.

As a result of Americans' unbalanced food choices, should public health officials recommend that the general public take a supplement to compensate for these poor eating habits? Or should we put more value on eating healthfully despite a hectic eat-and-run lifestyle? The answer is unclear. Let's take a look at some of what is and is not known about nutritional supplements, and then you can decide if you should spend more money on broccoli and spinach than on pills and potions.

Vitamins were originally studied to determine the

---

### UTA PIPPIG

*I drink lots of different kinds of herb tea. I use sleepytime tea for relaxation before I go to bed; peppermint tea if I have an upset stomach—or to prevent one. I even drink peppermint tea during marathons!*

---

minimal amount of a nutrient required to prevent deficiency diseases such as beriberi and scurvy. The recommended dietary allowances (RDA) were developed to guide people toward an appropriate intake. The RDA includes a large safety margin. For example, the RDA for vitamin C is 60 milligrams, which is six times the minimal amount needed to prevent the deficiency disease scurvy. The question remains unanswered: What is the *optimal* level of vitamins for lifelong health?

No amount of any supplement will compensate for a high-fat, hit-or-miss diet and stress-filled lifestyle. Taking supplements can also downplay the value of *whole* foods that offer protein, carbohydrates, and fiber—far more than just vitamins and minerals.

---

## HOW MUCH SODIUM DO YOU LOSE IN SWEAT?

During an hour of running in the heat, you might lose 900 to 1,800 milligrams of sodium. The average male's body contains about 75,000 milligrams sodium (11 tablespoons of salt). The amount of sodium you lose in sweat depends upon:

- *How much salt you eat.* The more salt you eat, the more salt you lose in sweat.

- *How much you exercise in the heat.* If you are acclimatized to hot weather, you will conserve sodium to defend against sodium depletion. The sodium in one pound of sweat may be:
  - 1,600 milligrams sodium for an unfit, unacclimatized person
  - 1,200 milligrams for a fit but unacclimatized person
  - 800 milligrams for a fit and acclimatized athlete

You can easily replace the sodium losses by eating some of these popular recovery foods:

| Food | Sodium (mg) |
| --- | --- |
| Pizza, ½ medium | 1,400 |
| Spaghetti sauce, 1 cup | 1,200 |
| Soup, 8 ounces | 750 |
| Saltines, 10 | 400 |
| Muffin | 500 |
| Salt, 1 packet | 500 |

Although sports drinks are thought to be a sodium-rich recovery beverage, they are actually sodium poor, containing about 50 to 110 milligrams per 8 ounces.

# SALT: SHAKE IT OR LEAVE IT?

Despite popular belief, salt for athletes is not a four-letter word. The public health recommendations to reduce salt intake are directed to the estimated one-third of adult Americans who are overweight, underfit, and have high blood pressure—*not* lean, fit runners with low blood pressure.

*How much salt do runners actually need?*

Salt (or more correctly *sodium,* the part of salt that is the health culprit) requirements depend upon how much you sweat. A "safe and adequate" sodium intake for the average person is 2,400 mg/day. The typical American intake is 3,000–6,000+ mg sodium/day—this tends to cover the sodium needs of most runners.

- The rule of thumb is to add extra salt to your diet if you have lost more than four to six pounds of sweat (3–4 percent of your body weight pre- to postexercise).

- Too little salt can result in fatigue, muscle cramps, and lack of thirst.

- Active people who sweat profusely day after day and eat primarily low-salt foods may benefit from adding a little sodium to replace that lost in sweat.

*If I crave salt, should I eat it?*

Yes. Salt cravings signal that your body wants salt. If you hanker for some pretzels or salty foods, eat them!

But supplements are indeed appropriate for certain populations, including:

- runners on low-calorie reduction diets
- pregnant women
- women who *might* become pregnant (expectedly or unexpectedly)
- vegetarians

Whole foods such as fruits and vegetables also offer hundreds, perhaps thousands, of substances called *phytochemicals* that protect our health. These include:

- *protease inhibitors* in soybeans that may slow tumor growth
- *isoflavones* in dried beans that may reduce the risk of breast or ovarian cancer
- *isothiocyanates* in broccoli that may help block carcinogens from damaging a cell's DNA

These phytochemicals may explain why the cruciferous vegetables such as broccoli, cabbage, and cauliflower are thought to protect against cancer, and onions and garlic are thought to protect against heart disease.

As you decide your nutritional fate, know that a diet based on a variety of wholesome foods is your best source of nutrition. If you choose to take a supplement for its health-protective effects, be sure to do so *in addition to eating well.* The anti-oxidant vitamins (C, beta carotene, and E) show the most promise. Although you can get sufficiently large amounts of C and beta carotene (and phytochemicals) from fruits and vegetables, you likely need a supplement to get an effective dose of E (100–400 IU). Because researchers have yet to unravel the whole vitamin/health mystery, stay alert to new findings and take care of your whole health. Phytochemicals and per-

## BARBARA ANDERSON

*I make my own formula of water, orange juice, and miso (for sodium and potassium). As you can imagine, this is an acquired taste. When I train in Central Park, I stash a bottle of sports drink behind a bush that's on my running loop. Sometimes people take my bottle. I can't imagine what they think when they open it.*

*On hot days enjoy the shower, but also take care to drink enough fluids, too.*

haps other substances in whole foods, but not in pills, may emerge as the winner.

### Pills and Potions

If you feel tired all the time and lack energy during workouts, you might be tempted to go to a health-food store and buy an impressive pharmacy of vitamins, amino acids, muscle-building powders, carbo-drinks, and other bottles filled with promises of enhanced athletic performance. One such runner, Jim, asked, "Do you think these can help me be a better marathoner? I'm spending more than $70 a month on these pills, but to date I haven't noticed any differences."

Because no amount of supplementation can compensate for poor eating habits, I first quizzed Jim about his daily diet before delving into the role of supplements. Jim sheepishly admitted that he tended to skip breakfast, eat fast-food lunches, and more

often than not dialed 1–800–PIZZA or TAK–EOUT for dinner. Mind you, not all of these are inherently poor sports foods, but Jim certainly managed to make the highest fat choices!

---

### GARY MUHRCKE

*Remember, if you can, back to 1970 when soda cans had no flip tops. That was the year when Fred Lebow went to the "thrifty store" and bought soda for the post-race refreshments. You can imagine the scene with hundreds of tired and thirsty runners in 83-degree heat trying to find a way to get at the contents. No one could open the cans!*

---

*Will supplements help you live a long and active life? Probably not. But years of nutritious eating and regular exercise will certainly enhance your health.*

After evaluating his daily diet, I concluded that Jim's complaints of chronic fatigue related primarily to inadequate carbohydrates; his lack of vim and vigor stemmed from skipping breakfast and lunch. He needed to enforce the following two food rules that would help him win with good nutrition rather than lose money with questionable hokum.

### ANN LEBARRON

*For four to eight mile runs on hot summer days, I carry a small water bottle with me. It's a perfect size to keep my stride smooth and just enough water to prevent me from getting too thirsty.*

*Rule #1. For energy, eat wholesome meals on a regular schedule.* Carbohydrates are the gas that provides energy. Vitamins are just spark plugs; they help convert carbohydrates into energy. Expensive carbohydrate powders are needless.

*Rule #2. For bigger muscles, lift weights and eat adequate protein and extra carbohydrates.* Protein supplements tend to be excessive and expensive; arginine, ornithine, growth hormone stimulants, and chromium picolinate have yet to be proven to enhance performance.

Based on these two fundamental rules, I taught Jim to make the dietary improvements outlined in chapter 1 that would help him feel better, have more energy, be stronger, run better, and save money. Food *does* work and is far safer than hokum. No magic potions have been found to date that will replace hard training and good nutrition.

The following supplements are currently popular among athletes. Although researchers have yet to study them extensively, here is some of what is known:

*Chromium:* Supposedly enhances the action of insulin, which thereby enhances muscle growth. Chromium will *not* contribute to steroidlike increases. Active people need adequate dietary chromium because they may excrete more chromium than couch potatoes. Good food sources include *mushrooms* (on pizza), *apples, raisins, chicken, wine* (instead of beer), and foods that are not highly processed. A safe and adequate chromium intake is 50 to 200 micrograms per day. The safety of long-term supplementation with chromium picolinate is questionable.

*Gamma Oryzanol:* Supposedly increases testosterone, a hormone that builds muscle. But the compound (extracted from rice bran, corn, and barley oils) is poorly absorbed from the stomach and gets left unused. There is no scientific evidence suggesting gamma oryzanol has any ergogenic effects.

*Inosine:* Supposedly enhances energy production. Inosine is needed to make ATP, the immediate source of energy for the muscles. This is true inside the muscle cells. But does inosine taken in pill form get to the cells? One study showed that inosine actually hurt aerobic performance.

*Medium-chain triglycerides:* Supposedly MCT oil increases energy and endurance, but it gets burned immediately by the liver before it even has a chance to get to the muscles.

*Arginine, ornithine, lysine:* These amino acids can stimulate the release of growth hormones, which theoretically might result in muscular development. Training itself stimulates growth hormone release, with endurance training stimulating more growth hormones than weight training. This raises the question: If growth hormones "work," why don't marathoners have bulkier muscles? No reliable studies to date have shown that supplemental amino acids result in greater anabolic (muscle-building) effects than does training alone.

## SUMMARY

Your best bet for nourishing your body with the safest balance of nutrients is to choose to eat a variety of foods and fluids from the different food groups. If you are tempted to take supplements as a kind of health insurance, do so only in conjunction with a healthful lifestyle. No amount of supplement, pill, or potion will compensate for an overall inadequate diet. You will always win with good nutrition.

### UTA PIPPIG

*After eight to ten years of very hard exercise and many experiments with my own body, including regular blood tests, I'm convinced that without using vitamins and minerals I wouldn't stay healthy. My use of supplements parallels my training schedule and the level of stress in my life, including exams, weather, and so forth.*

# 3 FUEL FOR RUNNING
## Nutrition Tips for Success

WHETHER YOU EAT to run or run to eat, as an active person you undoubtedly *love* to eat. That's why we've written this cookbook: to celebrate food as a pre-exercise energizer, a post-exercise reward for hard work, and a daily pleasure.

But food can sometimes be a problem for people who fear food-related upset stomachs that interfere with exercise, lack time to fuel themselves optimally, or lack the knowledge of how to win with good nutrition.

This chapter will focus on using food to its maximum potential; how to fuel up and refuel your body whether you are eating for a training run, a 10k race, the New York City Marathon, or any other form of exercise.

### EATING, EXERCISE, AND ABDOMINAL ACHES

As Bill Rodgers once commented, "More marathons are won or lost in the portable toilets than they are on the roads." Running jostles your stomach and enhances your risk of abdominal problems. An estimated 25 to 30 percent of runners may experience abdominal cramps, diarrhea, and/or the need for pit stops during or immediately after running. Thus the traditional warning: *Don't eat before you run.* Whereas this advice may be appropriate for people with sensitive gastrointestinal (GI) tracks, it's inappropriate for those who can tolerate pre-run food.

Pre-exercise food promises advantages that can contribute to greater stamina and endurance. If you have always abstained from pre-run food based only on hearsay and habit, I encourage you to *try* a light snack. You might be pleasantly surprised by the benefits that come from fueling up rather than running on empty.

### HAL GABRIEL

*I've trained my body to thrive on pre-exercise food. From the beginning of my running career, I have always run with food in my stomach. I'd eat meals and snacks with my children so that I could enjoy family time with them, and then I'd run at night. I now have an iron stomach. I can eat and run—nothing brothers me.*

Because eating ability and food preferences vary in relation to the type and intensity of exercise and time of day, you need to *practice* your pre-exercise eating. During training, you can learn through trial and error:

- what foods work best for your body
- when you should eat them
- what amounts are appropriate

Any of the following recommendations regarding pre-exercise eating should be pondered and experimented with *during training*. As the venerable Dr. George Sheehan once said, "We are each an experiment of one."

I emphasize *experiment during training* because of what typically happens: Runners read advertisements about special sports drinks, sports bars, supplements, or liquid meals. They are curious about trying these special products, but because of their high price tag they don't quite get around to buying them. Instead, they end up trying the free products provided by the sponsors on race day. In some instances they discover (much to their dismay) that the unfamiliar food causes upset stomach, heartburn, diarrhea, or cramps. If they had sampled these new foods or fluids during training, they would be confident about using or saving the race-day samples.

What (and whether) you eat before exercise will vary according to:

- *The type of exercise.* Pre-run food may make you feel uncomfortable, but pre-bike food might not cause any problems.

- *How hard you will be working.* You may be able to eat within ten minutes of a training run, an hour before a marathon, but need to wait three hours before a track workout.

- *How nervous you are.* Nothing will settle well if your stomach is in knots.

The general rule of thumb is that the harder you run the less likely you are to want to eat and the more likely you need to allow ample time between eating and exercising. Fast runners may feel nauseated at even the thought of pre-exercise food, but slower runners will appreciate the added energy.

If you exercise at a pace that you can comfortably sustain for more than thirty minutes, you can likely both exercise and digest food at the same time. At a training pace, the blood flow to your stomach is 60 to 70 percent of normal—adequate to maintain normal digestion processes.

If you are doing intense sprint work, your stomach essentially shuts down and gets only about 20 percent of its normal blood flow. This slows the digestive process so that any pre-exercise food will simply jostle along for the ride. It may feel uncomfortable and cause indigestion or heartburn.

If you are in the experimental stage of developing your pre-exercise food plan for various intensity runs, as well as for a marathon, the following information

provides some helpful facts about the benefits of pre-exercise food. This information can help you on marathon day when the right combination of food and fluids will make or break your ability to complete the distance comfortably.

1. *Pre-exercise food helps prevent low blood sugar.* Why suffer with lightheadedness, needless fatigue, blurred vision, and an inability to concentrate when you can prevent these symptoms of hypoglycemia?

    The carbohydrates in your pre-run snack are important because they fuel not only your muscles but also your mind. Adequate carbohydrates help you think clearly because your brain fuels itself with carbohydrates, the sugar in your blood. Successful athletes fuel both their muscles and their minds. As Grete Waitz once commented, "Novice runners often fail to recognize how much mental energy and concentration is needed to run—especially to run a marathon."

    Your blood sugar is maintained at a normal level by the release of sugar (glycogen) stored in your liver. If you have low blood sugar or low liver glycogen, your brain will go unfed. You will feel tired and you won't be able to concentrate on the task at hand. You may feel like you've "hit the wall." Why suffer when you can fuel yourself appropriately before you run? (And also while you run, as I'll soon explain.)

    If you run in the morning, you are likely to have to drag yourself through your routine if you haven't eaten anything between your 7:00 P.M. dinner and your 7:00 A.M. run. Similarly, if you

## NINA KUSCSIK

*I learned that food I could eat before a normal training run could take much longer to digest or was simply intolerable when there was pre-race excitement. For example, I can train one half-hour after eating cereal with milk, but I can't race on that! The milk does not digest well for me pre-race.*

*Alberto Salazar (center, with "Athletics West" singlet), well fueled with a late-night meal, is on his way to victory.*

choose to eat nothing between the pre-marathon pasta party and the 10:45 A.M. start of the New York City Marathon, you'll start out depleted and may end up devastated. Your blood sugar levels will have dropped, particularly if you tossed and turned all night with pre-race anxiety.

Note: Although many morning runners do exercise with an empty stomach and report that they have plenty of energy, they have likely eaten a substantial dinner and/or done serious late-night snacking to bolster liver glycogen stores and to reduce the need for a morning energizer. This is not bad or wrong, as long as this pattern works well for them.

2. *Pre-exercise food helps settle the stomach, absorbs some of the gastric juices, and abates hunger pangs.* For many athletes, the stress associated with competition stimulates gastric secretions and contributes to an "acid stomach." Eating a small amount of food can help alleviate that problem.

The caloric density of a snack or meal affects the rate at which food leaves your stomach. This explains why you can exercise comfortably soon after snacking on a few crackers or a piece of fruit but are better off waiting three or four hours after a heartier meal.

The general pre-exercise "rule of thumb" is to allow:

- 3–4 hours for a large meal to digest
- 2–3 hours for a smaller meal
- 1–2 hours for a blended or liquid meal
- less than an hour for a small snack, as tolerated

If you want to eat a full pre-marathon breakfast, simply allow sufficient time for it to digest by eating at 6:00 A.M.

3. *Pre-exercise food fuels the muscles.* The food you eat even an hour before you run is digested into glucose and burned for energy. For example, one study showed that runners who ate 400 calories of sugar three hours before an easy four-hour run burned about 70 percent of the sugar. Without question, pre-run food that is well tolerated

## ALBERTO SALAZAR

*The night before my first New York City Marathon, my younger brother, Fernando, was sharing my room with me. He got hungry around midnight, so I brought him out to get some pizza. Because I won the next day, I figured that the late-night pizza snack might have helped, so it became my last pre-race meal before all my morning marathons.*

## JUDY MORRILL

*Before any run, race, or marathon, I stick with my tried-and-true foods: a banana and a plain bagel. These foods settle well, digest easily, and keep me from feeling hungry. Before the New York City Marathon, I get up about 6:30 to eat the banana and bagel. Then I take a sports bar to eat before the start of the race, because the start is not until 10:47. Otherwise, I'd get hungry.*

provides an energy boost that can enhance your stamina.

Historically, athletes were told to choose starchy complex carbohydrates—such as bagels—for the pre-race meal over sugary simple carbohydrates—such as soft drinks. The theory was that starches would contribute to a stable blood sugar level and sugary carbohydrates would contribute to a debilitating "sugar low" (a hypoglycemic reaction). Today, we know that athletes should experi-

ment with pre-run carbohydrates based on their *glycemic index;* that is, the food's ability to contribute glucose into the blood stream (see the sidebar, *Glycemic Index of Some Common Foods*).

- Low glycemic index foods (oatmeal, bran cereal) are desireable before a long run because they provide sustained energy. They may reduce the need for consuming carbohydrates during endurance exercise to maintain normal blood sugar levels.

- High glycemic index foods (potatoes, rice) quickly elevate blood sugar. They can initiate hypoglycemic reactions in people sensitive to swings in blood sugar. Foods with a high glycemic index are preferable for recovery foods, when your depleted muscles readily absorb all available glucose.

Based on the latest research, you might want to experiment during training with your pre-run snack choices to determine if low glycemic index foods bolster your performance. For example, if you have been eating a pre-exercise microwaved potato (a food with a high glycemic index), see if a bowl of lentil soup contributes to better performance (that is, unless the fiber causes a laxative effect).

# GLYCEMIC INDEX OF SOME COMMON FOODS

The following list ranks foods according to their ability to elevate blood sugar given a 200 calorie (50 gram) dose of carbohydrates. Many factors influence this glycemic effect of a food, such as meal size, fiber content, amount of fat in the meal, and food preparation. Foods ranked higher than 70 are considered to have a high glycemic index.

| | | | | | |
|---|---|---|---|---|---|
| Glucose | 100 | Banana | 61 | Whole wheat pasta | 42 |
| Potato, baked | 98 | Soft rolls | 58 | Rye bread | 42 |
| Carrots, cooked | 92 | Corn | 58 | Apples | 39 |
| Honey | 87 | Peas | 51 | Ice cream | 36 |
| Corn flakes | 83 | All-Bran | 51 | Whole milk | 34 |
| White rice | 72 | White pasta | 50 | Kidney beans | 33 |
| Whole wheat bread | 72 | Oatmeal | 49 | Lentils | 29 |
| White bread | 69 | Orange juice | 46 | Barley | 22 |
| Mars Bar | 68 | Oranges | 43 | Carrots, raw | 16 |
| Raisins | 64 | Grapes | 43 | Peanuts | 11 |

4. *Pre-exercise beverages can provide fluid to hydrate your body fully as well as additional carbohydrates.* By tanking up on diluted juice or sports drinks before you exercise, you can help prevent dehydration as well as boost your carbohydrate and energy intake. Whereas you are unlikely to starve during the marathon, you may become seriously injured due to dehydration. The best pre-exercise fluid choices include water, sports drinks, and diluted juices.

You should drink plenty of fluids not only before races but also every day during training, in both hot and cold weather. You can confirm that you've had enough to drink by frequent urination and clear-colored urine. If your urine is dark and concentrated with metabolic wastes, you need more fluids. Refer to the section on water and sports drinks in chapter 2 for more details.

5. *Pre-exercise food can pacify your mind with the knowledge that your body is well fueled.* Before a long training run, and particularly before the Marathon, you don't want to waste any energy

## PRE-RUN MEALS

To be sufficiently fueled for long training runs, hard track workouts, shorter races, or the marathon, eat according to this schedule. *Always* drink additional fluids with and between meals to ensure complete hydration. If you are overly nervous, stressed, or have a sensitive stomach prior to the event, you may have to abstain from food on the day of competition. You should make a special effort to eat extra food the day before.

*Morning events:*
- The day before:  Minimal exercise
- The night before:  Eat a hearty, high-carb lunch, dinner, and bedtime snack
- Race morning:  Eat a light snack/breakfast to abate hunger feelings, and replenish liver glycogen stores.

*Afternoon events:*
- Day before:  Minimal exercise
  Eat a hearty high-carb dinner
- Race day:  Hearty high-carb breakfast to be followed by a light lunch

*Evening events:*
- Day before:  Minimal exercise
  Carbohydrate-rich meals

- Day of:  Hearty carbohydrate-rich breakfast and lunch, followed by a light snack 1–3 hours prior to the event

# HOW MUCH SHOULD YOU EAT BEFORE YOU RUN?

How much should you eat before you run? If you will be eating within an hour of running, exercise physiologist Mike Sherman recommends 0.5 gram carbohydrate per pound of body weight (1 gm carbohydrate/kg).

| Body Weight lbs. (kg) | Carbohydrates one hour before-exercise gm carb. | calories carb. |
|---|---|---|
| 120 (55) | 60 | 240 |
| 140 (64) | 70 | 280 |
| 160 (73) | 80 | 320 |
| 180 (82) | 90 | 360 |

To translate this into food, choose from the following popular items:

| Food | gm carb. | calories |
|---|---|---|
| Bagel, large New York-style | 60 | 320 |
| Fruit yogurt, 1 cup | 50 | 260 |
| Fig Newtons, 4 | 44 | 240 |
| Spaghetti, 1 cup cooked | 40 | 200 |
| Orange juice, 8 ounces | 25 | 110 |
| Graham crackers, 4 | 22 | 120 |
| Oatmeal, ⅓ cup dry | 20 | 110 |
| Banana, 1 medium | 25 | 105 |

wondering if you've eaten enough. Appropriate eating can resolve that concern!

Pre-exercise food has great psychological value. If you firmly believe that a specific food or meal will enhance your performance, than it probably will. Your mind has a powerful effect on your body's ability to perform at its best. If you do have

a "magic food" that assures athletic excellence, you should take special care to be sure this food or meal is available to you prior to the race. This is particularly important if you are traveling to an event. The last section in this chapter has suggestions for the traveling athlete.

### Facts about Pre-exercise Foods

When experimenting with your pre-exercise foods, note the following information:

- *Liquid foods leave the stomach faster than solid foods.* If you have trouble with solid foods, such as a bagel, you might want to experiment with liquids, such as juice or a canned liquid meal. One study showed that a 450-calorie meal of steak, peas, and buttered bread took six hours to leave the stomach, whereas a blenderized variation of the same meal emptied from the stomach in four hours.

- *Carbohydrates are digested more easily than fatty foods.* Low-fat foods (such as those listed in the sidebar, *High Carbohydrate Meal Suggestions*) tend to digest easily and settle well. In comparison, high-fat bacon-and-fried-egg breakfasts, greasy hamburgers, tuna sandwiches loaded with mayon-

## BILL RODGERS

*In 1977, four-time Olympic gold medalist Lasse Viren entered the New York City Marathon, and I recall the media hullabaloo as to whether he'd challenge to win. My brother, Charlie, saw Lasse enjoying a large breakfast of eggs and bacon the morning of the race and reported this to me. I then knew he wasn't serious and went on to defend my title without a challenge from Lasse. (He had a car waiting for him on the far side of the Queensboro Bridge.)*

# HIGH-CARBOHYDRATE MEAL SUGGESTIONS

Some high-carb meal suggestions for both training and pre-marathon include tried-and-true foods such as:

**Breakfast:** cold cereals, oatmeal and other hot cereals, bagels, English muffins, pancakes, fruit, juice

**Lunch:** sandwiches (with the bread being the "meat" of the sandwich), fruit, hearty broth-based soups, thick-crust pizza

**Dinner:** pasta, potato, or rice entrées and veggies, breads, juice, fruit

**Snacks:** flavored yogurt, pretzels, crackers, fig bars, frozen yogurt, dry cereal, leftover pasta, zwieback, simple biscuit-type cookies, animal crackers, canned and fresh fruits, juices

naise, and peanut butter sandwiches have been known to settle heavily and feel uncomfortable.

Too much fat slows digestion, so the meal lingers longer in the stomach and may contribute to a weighed-down feeling.

A little fat, however, such as a slice of cheese on toast, a teaspoon of peanut butter on a bagel, or the fat in some brands of sports bars, can be appropriate. It provides both sustained energy and satiety during long runs. Note that some runners can break all the sports nutrition rules and do well with even very high-fat foods. After all, steak and eggs was the pre-marathon breakfast of champions for many years!

- *Pre-exercise sweets may cause a hypoglycemic reaction.* Although some runners can tolerate pre-exercise sweets without experiencing negative effects on their performance, other runners are very sensitive to the swings in blood sugar that can

### HAL GABRIEL

*I love to eat. My sports nutrition philosophy is the more I eat, the better I do. When I ran New York in 1977, I managed to wheedle my way into a press tent, where I enjoyed eight cups of coffee and ten pieces of lemon cake before the marathon. Then I ran a 2:43. I thrive on food!*

### MARSHA JONES

*I hate that feeling of being lightheaded and weak that I get after I eat sugary foods. I should know better than to eat sweets . . . my body just can't handle sugar unless it's after I've eaten a big meal.*

occur after eating sugary foods. (Large doses of sugar can stimulate large amounts of insulin to transport the excessive sugar out of the bloodstream. If too much sugar is removed, you'll feel lightheaded and shakey.) If you are "sugar sensitive" and believe that sugar hurts your performance, refer back to the glycemic index information and take note of the low glycemic index foods that are least likely to cause blood sugar problems.

The best advice regarding pre-exercise sugar is for you to *avoid the need for* a sugar fix by having appropriately timed meals prior to exercise. For example, if you crave sugar before an afternoon training run, know that you could have *prevented* the desire for quick-energy foods by having eaten a bigger breakfast and lunch. Skimping on those meals leaves you looking for a last-minute energizer that may hurt your performance.

Note that sugar taken *during* exercise does not contribute to a hypoglycemic reaction because

49

# *POPULAR RECOVERY FOODS*

Your muscles are most receptive to replacing depleted glycogen stores *immediately* after a run. For optimal recovery, target approximately 0.5 gram carbohydrate per pound of body weight (or 1 gm carbohydrate/kg) every two hours.

Carbohydrates for recovery:

| Body Weight lbs (kg) | Grams Carb | Calories |
|---|---|---|
| 120 (55) | 60 | 240 |
| 140 (64) | 70 | 280 |
| 160 (73) | 80 | 320 |
| 180 (82) | 90 | 360 |

Some popular choices include:

| Food: | Amount | Grams Carb | Total Calories |
|---|---|---|---|
| Apple juice | 1 cup | 30 | 120 |
| Cranapple juice | 1 cup | 45 | 180 |
| Cola | 12 oz. can | 38 | 150 |
| Banana | 1 large | 35 | 150 |
| Fruit yogurt | 1 cup | 40 | 240 |
| Baked potato | 1 large | 50 | 220 |

If you can't tolerate solid foods immediately following a hard run or marathon, simply drink carbohydrate-rich fluids and/or eat watery foods with mini-meals or snacks every two hours.

---

## GARY MUHRCKE

*When I ran my first marathon in 1959, my mom got up and cooked me steak and eggs.*

your muscles quickly use the sugar without the need of extra insulin.

## RECOVERING FROM LONG RUNS

You've just trained for hours and hours and hours, or so it seems. You are pleased but tired, sore, and hungry. You wonder if any special foods or fluids will hasten your recovery and help you feel better quickly. Here are the answers to questions athletes commonly ask about recovery foods during training.

*What's the best recovery food plan?*

Eating a proper recovery diet every day *during training* is very important if you are to endure repeated days of hard workouts. To optimize the recovery process, you should eat 200 to 400 calories of high-glycemic carbohydrates within two

hours of the exercise bout, then repeat this two hours later. Good choices include apple juice, sweetened yogurt, soft drinks, potatoes, and, if you like the Bill Rodger's approach, a swig of maple syrup straight up!

Because you may have burned 1,000 to 2,000 calories during a 10 to 20 mile run, sooner or later you'll be hungry and ready to eat. The replacement eating process can take twenty-four to forty-eight hours and even longer when your muscles are damaged. If exercise initially kills your appetite or if even the thought of post-exercise food makes you nauseated, you can still drink the carbohydrates while you quench your thirst.

Soft drinks, particularly colas, are extremely popular recovery fluids. Granted, soft drinks lack nutri-

## MICHAEL KEOHANE

*I like to use a high-carb sports drink right after I run. . . . It really helps with recovery. . . . I'm sure glad I work in a running store and can get a good deal!*

## NORBERT SANDER

*I love to eat peanuts before training runs. They taste good and do the trick for me even though they are a high-fat food.*

tional value and are filled with empty calories, but they do offer both carbohydrates and fluids. Note that most colas also offer caffeine. Because caffeine has a diuretic effect that hampers your efforts to replace fluids, juices are perhaps a better (and more nourishing) refresher.

*Note that juices and soft drinks offer more recovery carbohydrates than do commercial fluid replacers that are designed to be taken during exercise. In 16 ounces of cranapple juice you can get the same amount of carbohydrates as in 48 ounces of a commercial fluid replacer.*

*What and how much should I drink?*

After a long training run, you need to replace fluid losses as soon as possible to help your body restore normal water balance. Carry a water bottle (preferably filled with juice) with you so you'll easily be able to drink enough to quench your thirst, and then drink some more. You may not feel thirsty, but your body may still need more fluids. Your goal is to have pale-colored urine in large volumes, then you'll know that you are well hydrated. Refer back to chapter 2 for more information.

*Do I need extra salt to replace what I lose in sweat?*

Athletes lose some sodium (a part of salt) in sweat but are unlikely to deplete body stores even

## BILL RODGERS

*When I come back from a long hard training run, I'm generally exhausted and in need of some quick energy. I've been known to drink maple syrup right from the bottle. Tastes great!*

*Carbo-loading companions: Part of the fun of the marathon is enjoying eating beforehand. The pasta party serves more than five thousand pounds of pasta and twenty-five hundred gallons of sauce to the eager runners.*

## UTA PIPPIG

*After very hard training workouts, I crave fresh fruits, like melon and banana, and sweet things. I follow the cravings of my body. When I crave sweets, I eat sweets because my body probably needs carbs. When I crave chicken, I eat chicken because my body probably needs protein.*

*Water station madness: Be sure to drink your share and not be pushed away by the competition.*

during a marathon. As I mentioned in chapter 2, during a three-hour run, you might lose about 1,800 to 5,600 milligrams of sodium. Since the average 150-pound person's body contains about 97,000 milligrams of sodium, this 2 to 6 percent loss is relatively insignificant. In most cases, runners can replace more than enough salt through standard post-exercise foods.

Athletes who may need extra salt include those who train in cold weather yet run a marathon in warm weather. This sometimes happens, for example, with Boston Marathoners if they train throughout the winter but compete on what turns out to be an unusually warm spring day. New York City Marathon runners (excluding those from Australia, New Zealand, and other countries in the Southern Hemisphere) have the benefit of training during the summer heat, then competing on what is likely to be a cooler day (but may not be!).

If you crave salt, you should respond appropriately by eating salty, carbohydrate-rich foods such as salted pretzels, soups, crackers, and/or baked potatoes sprinkled with salt. Salt replacement is more commonly needed for novice marathoners, ultradistance runners, and triathletes who exercise continuously for more than four to six hours.

*Do I need extra potassium?*

Like sodium, you lose some potassium when you sweat, but you are unlikely to deplete your body stores. During three hours of exercise, you might lose 300 to 1,200 milligrams of potassium (.001–.007 percent of your body stores). The typical American diet

provides 4,000 to 7,000 milligrams of potassium and can easily replace that lost in sweat, particularly if you eat potassium-rich foods, such as fruits and vegetables. Chapter 2 provides more information about how to replace potassium losses.

## PREPARING FOR THE NEW YORK CITY MARATHON

Because 26.2 miles is a long way to run, you want to be sure to fuel yourself optimally for the New York City Marathon. Carbohydrate-loading, after all, means more than just eating a pile of pasta. Here's some food for thought.

## BILL RODGERS

*When I was racing in Japan, I noticed the runners eating rice out of containers before the race. I guess that was the Japanese equivalent to our sports bar.*

**GRETE WAITZ**

*Runners commonly ask me what I eat before the marathon. I don't like to change anything in my regimen. I normally eat a high-carbohydrate diet, so I stick with the same foods. I may eat two potatoes instead of my typical one, but I don't stuff myself.*

### Pre-marathon Training Diet

You can't simply eat a big dinner at the pasta party the night before the marathon and expect to run well. Your muscles have to be trained to store carbohydrates, and that naturally happens as a part of a daily running program.

To support the rigors of marathon training, you need to eat a carbohydrate-rich sports diet *every* day as the foundation for *every* meal. Runners who carbo-load every day (i.e., eat a diet with 60 to 70 percent of the calories from carbohydrates):

- can train better because their muscles are better fueled
- can continue eating the same foods pre-marathon

The last thing you want to do is change your diet before the marathon.

To avoid nutritional mistakes on Marathon Day, during training you should:

- Practice eating your planned pre-marathon breakfast. If you are a traveling athlete, be sure this tried-and-true food will be available on Marathon Day.
- Start your long training runs at 10:30 to 11:00 A.M. (the time you'll be running on Marathon Day).
- Learn how much food you can eat and then still run comfortably.
- Practicing drinking the sports drink that will be available as well as any mid-run foods you plan to eat.

These preparations will help reduce surprises!

### The Week Before the Marathon

The biggest change in your schedule during the week before the marathon should be in your *training*, not in your food. You'll want to taper off your running so that your muscles have an opportunity to become fully fueled. Don't bother with any last-minute hard training that will burn off carbohydrates rather than allow them to be stored. Instead, limit yourself to four miles on Tuesday, six on Wednesday, four on Thursday, none on Friday, and up to two on Saturday.

You need not eat hundreds more calories this week. As Grete Waitz says, "Carbo-loading does not mean stuffing yourself." You simply need to exercise less. This way, the 600 to 1,000 calories you generally expend during training can be used to fuel your muscles. All during this week, you should maintain your tried-and-true high-carbohydrate training diet. Drastic changes commonly lead to upset stomachs, diarrhea, or constipation. For example, carbo-loading on an unusually high amount of fruits and juices might cause diarrhea. Too many low-fiber bagels, breads, and pasta might clog your system.

Be sure that you are *carbo*-loading, not fat-loading. Some runners eat two pats of butter per dinner roll, big dollops of sour cream on a potato, and enough dressing to drown a salad. These fatty foods fill the stomach and the fat cells but leave the muscles less fueled. Your best bet is to trade the fats for extra carbohydrates. That is,

- instead of having one roll with butter for 200 calories, have two plain rolls for 200 calories
- have pasta with tomato or other low-fat sauces rather than oil-based or cheese-based toppings.

**THOMAS STEFFENS**

*Even though I'm German, I still prefer pasta to potatoes for my favorite pre-marathon meal. Even foreign runners who speak no English understand what a pasta party is.*

The recipe section has several high-carbohydrate, low-fat entrées to help guide your menu planning. Perhaps Uta Pippig's Pasta Dinner can help you be a winner, too!

Many runners totally avoid protein-rich foods in the days before a marathon. This is unnecessary because your body still needs protein on a daily basis. Also, endurance runners even burn a little protein for energy. Hence, you can and should eat a small serving of either low-fat proteins, such as poached eggs, yogurt, turkey, or chicken, as the *accompaniment* to the meal (not the main focus), or plant proteins such as beans and lentils (as your intestines can tolerate them).

### Saturday Before the Marathon

Fully fuel your muscles by resting your legs and putting your feet up; today is not the time to try to see all the sights in New York City! Relax with some juices and other tried-and-true carbohydrates by your side. Start visualizing yourself running smoothly, strongly, and successfully.

By now, you may have gained about three to four pounds, but don't panic. This weight gain reflects water weight. For every ounce of carbohydrate stored in your body, you store about three ounces of water. You can tell if your muscles are well saturated with carbohydrates if your weight has gone up a few pounds.

Instead of relying on a huge pasta dinner the night before the Marathon, you might want to enjoy a substantial carbo-feast at breakfast or lunch. This ear-

> ## PAM DUCKWORTH
>
> *New York was the first marathon I ran. The friend who talked me into it told me not to eat beforehand. Not knowing any better, I followed his advice. We got up at 5:30 and by the time we got to the start area, I was starved. The donuts and coffee were all gone, but I found half a donut on the ground. In desperation, I ate it. I was hungry all morning, and by the time I finished the marathon I was starved.*

> ## HAL GABRIEL
>
> *There's more to preparing for the marathon than just eating carbs. The marathon is a mind game. You have to program your mind in order to do it.*

lier meal allows sufficient time for the food to move through your system. Another option would be to eat at both times! After all, how often do you have the chance to enjoy the world's largest pasta party with marathoners from one hundred different countries?

You'll be better off eating a little bit too much than too little on the eve of the Marathon. But you don't want to *over*eat either. Learning the right balance takes practice. Let each preparatory race and long run be opportunities to learn.

Be sure to drink extra water, juices, and even carbohydrate-rich soft drinks if desired. But abstain from wine, beer, and alcoholic beverages because they have a dehydrating effect. You want to be well saturated with water, not flushing needed fluids down the toilet.

### Marathon Morning

With luck, you'll wake up to a clear, crisp day that makes you want to jump out of bed and run! Before embarking upon your day's task, be sure to eat breakfast. One of the biggest nutritional mistakes made by New York City Marathoners is eating too little beforehand, fearing that eating will result in an upset stomach.

As I've repeatedly mentioned, be sure to eat pre-marathon foods that are familiar. That is, don't feast on a pancake breakfast on the morning of the marathon only to discover that pancakes settle like a lead balloon. Some runners can eat a bagel, juice, or a light breakfast one to three hours before the marathon; many carry familiar foods with them to the start. Others want six hours for their stomach to empty; they've learned they run best if they wake up at 4:00 A.M., eat a bowl of oatmeal, then go back to bed.

Drink plenty of fluids on Marathon morning. Water and sports drinks are popular choices. Some runners drink coffee for stimulation; others prefer to abstain because they are already nervous and jittery and have no need for an added buzz. Do what's best for your body, keeping in mind that caffeine contributes to water loss. If the weather is warm, every drop of fluid lost can matter.

Because water takes about 45 to 90 minutes to move through your system, you can drink several glasses up to two hours before the marathon, have time to urinate the excess, then tank up again 5 to 15 minutes before the starting gun. With pre-race nerves,

*Dehydration is a major concern among marathon runners. Try to drink eight ounces of fluid every fifteen to twenty minutes.*

don't be surprised if you are urinating twenty times!

### Fluids and Foods During the Marathon

During the Marathon be sure to drink water and/or sports drinks every 15 to 20 minutes. Take advantage of the twenty-three water stations along the route. Your goal is to *prevent* dehydration. Don't let yourself get thirsty.

With *programmed drinking* (i.e., a target of 8 ounces of water or sports drink every fifteen minutes), you can minimize dehydration, maximize your performance, and reduce your recovery time. Be sure to drink according to a schedule, not by how thirsty you are. And don't miss the early water stops—once you are dehydrated, you won't catch up. Losing only 2 percent of your body weight (i.e., three pounds, if you weigh 150 pounds) from sweating hurts your performance and upsets your ability to regulate your body temperature. Refer to chapter 2 for more details.

You will feel better and run better if you can replace not only water but also carbohydrates while running. These carbohydrates help to maintain a normal blood sugar level as well as provide a source of energy for your muscles. Then when you come to the Willis Avenue Bridge, which is just before the 20-mile mark, you can better run up the slight incline, which many have found to be their "wall."

According to research, you might be able to increase your stamina by as much as 18 percent if you take in 0.5 grams of carbohydrates per pound of body weight (or 1 gm/kg) per hour of endurance exercise. For example, if you weigh 150 pounds, target about 75 grams of carbohydrates (300 calories) per hour. This could be:

- six 8-ounce glasses of a sports drink (50 calories per 8 ounces)
- four cups of sports drink and a banana

## POPULAR SNACKS DURING A LONG RUN

| Solids: | Liquids: |
|---|---|
| Banana | Cola + water |
| Sports bars | Sports drinks |
| Bagel | Iced tea with honey |
| Tootsie Rolls | Juice + water |
| Hard candies | Iced coffee with sugar |
| Chocolate bar | Water (+ solid foods) |
| Gummy Bears | |
| Chocolate chip cookies | |

- two cups of sports drink plus a sports bar (plus extra water)

This is more calories than many runners voluntarily consume during long runs. Hence, you should have already practiced *programmed* eating and drinking to replace energy and sweat losses. On Marathon Day, you should know:

- what and how much you can tolerate
- how you can comfortably carry the nourishment

You might want to tuck snacks into either a pocket of your running shorts or a waist pack (if you plan to be out on the course for four or five hours and have a big appetite). You must also be flexible. Who knows what happens when your body is pushed to the limit. Even tried-and-true favorites can become unpalatable.

### UTA PIPPIG

*Nobody can believe this, but it's true. During the marathon I drink sweetened peppermint tea. One year in New York, my coach unknowingly prepared the wrong tea—the one I use for relaxing—for my water bottles. During the race, I thought the taste was different than I'd expected, but I figured it was due to the heat or hard effort. I'm lucky I didn't fall asleep in Central Park!*

### SCOTT MCGUFFIN

*Before running in New York (my first marathon), I'd never eaten while running. In fact, I'd gotten the impression that eating was the sissy thing to do. Runners just don't do that. I was supposed to train my body to go the distance without food. My coach had never mentioned anything about eating during the marathon, nor had any of the numerous books I'd read, so I had assumed that food was forbidden. Now I know differently.*

*As I approached the halfway point in Queens, I was delighted to see people in the crowd giving out pretzels, orange sections, and banana halves. I was running on empty and extremely hungry. I took as much as I could carry (the banana oozed out of my fingers . . . this really looked quite comical). I could immediately feel an energy difference. At 20 miles, I ate again, and I attribute my success in the last 10K (50 minutes, which for me was good) to all the food.*

*For my next marathon I plan to eat more often instead of getting into a hole like I did in New York.*

Note that elite runner Willie Mtolo, from South Africa, ate something "magic" before he won in 1992. With two miles to the finish, he took something out of his wristband. He claimed this "secret thing" gave him the energy to move into first place and be fresh to the finish. Although race officials were at first concerned, they relaxed when they learned the "magic" was nothing but glucose pills. This little bit of sugar seems to have given the winning edge.

Most runners consume carbohydrates by drinking some type of sugary fluid such as a sports drink, defizzed cola, or diluted juice. But solid foods work

*Like these two Marathon champions—Douglas Wakiihuri and Juma Ikangaa (#1)—everyone wins with good nutrition.*

well, too, as long as you drink plenty of water. Whereas the fastest runners may be able to do well with just carbohydrate-containing fluids, slower runners will likely do better with solids that contain more calories (assuming they can tolerate the food). Given that the average finish time in the New York City Marathon is 4:10, the majority of runners can benefit from significantly supplementing their bodies' limited glycogen stores.

The carbohydrates you consume during the Marathon will also keep you in good spirits. Some runners become moody, irritable, and irrational toward the end of the Marathon. Running partners can become either the best of friends or the worst of enemies.

Many runners fear that fluids or foods taken during running will cause diarrhea. Diarrhea commonly occurs in runners who lose more than 4 percent of their body weight during the race (6 pounds for a 150-pound runner). Hence, the fluids you drink may actually help *prevent* diarrhea, not cause it.

I once talked to a runner who tried to abstain from drinking anything—even water—during a marathon in fear it would upset his stomach. He held off as long as he could without fluids. Then when he did succumb, he experienced diarrhea. Although he blamed the diarrhea on the drink, I tend to think the lack of prior fluid intake was the bigger problem.

### Recovering from the Marathon

Congratulations! After you complete the Marathon, you deserve a round of applause and lots of water,

carbohydrates, and tasty reward foods. Because you'll have plenty of time after the Marathon to replace depleted glycogen stores, you can be less strict with choosing recovery carbohydrates (as discussed at the beginning of this chapter) and go with what you crave. Allow yourself to rest, heal, and eat well. And if your legs and feet will allow, you might even enjoy the post-marathon dance party.

Yes, you do want to continue to eat:

# *INTERNATIONAL SPORTS FOODS*

New York offers a veritable cornucopia of foods from around the world. International runners can enjoy familiar meals at all hours of the day and night. If you want to venture into an unfamiliar menu, Mary-Giselle Rathgeber, R.D. recommends the following low(er) fat choices for your sports diet (adapted from Fred Lebow and Gloria Averbuch, *The New York Road Runner's Club Complete Book of Running* [New York: Random House, 1992]).

|  | *Good Choice* | *Poor Choice* |
| --- | --- | --- |
| Italian | Cioppino | Antipasto |
|  | Minestrone soup | Parmigiana dishes |
|  | Marinara and marsala dishes | Alfredo/cream sauces |
|  | Red or white clam sauce | Lasagna, cannelloni |
|  | Chicken cacciatore | Stuffed shells |
|  | Pasta |  |
|  | Fruit or fruit ice |  |
| Chinese | Won ton soup | Egg rolls |
|  | Moo goo gai pan | Egg dishes |
|  | Steamed dumplings | Fried dumplings |
|  | Brown rice | Fried noodles and rice |
|  | Vegetarian dishes | Sweet and sour |
|  | Stir-fry | Duck |
| Mexican | Fajitas | Nachos |
|  | Plain, "soft" tortillas (not fried) | Quesadillas |
|  | Vegetable, chicken, beef dishes | Cheese dishes |
|  | Burritos | Refried beans |
|  | Bean soup, rice, and beans | Tostados |
|  | Enchiladas | Taco salad |
|  | Seviche | Guacamole, sour cream |
| Indian | Tandoori | Malai (coconut sauce) |
|  | Vegetable curries | Samosas |
|  | Naam, roti (breads) | Poori |
|  | Dahl | Fried Appetizers |
|  | Shish kebab | Muglai |
| Japanese | Sushi, sashimi | Tempura |
|  | Miso soup | Tonkatsu |
|  | Teriyaki, yakatori |  |
|  | Tofu |  |
| Middle Eastern | Couscous, rice dishes |  |
|  | Kabobs |  |
|  | Tabouli |  |
| Greek | Greek salads | Gyros |
|  | Kabobs | Spanakopita |
|  | Plaki (fish) | Moussaka |
|  | Souvlaki |  |

## JEFF GALLOWAY

*The New York City Marathon is where I first learned the benefits of eating on the run. I had tried eating a sports bar during my training runs and found that it worked well. So during New York, I carried a sports bar with me and started eating it after the halfway point—one chew every two miles, along with plenty of water. I felt good the whole marathon. And afterward, I continued to feel good— the food shortened my recovery time.*

- plenty of post-marathon recovery carbohydrates to refuel your muscles
- adequate protein (to help with healing damaged muscles)
- potassium-rich fruits and juices and salty foods to replace electrolyte losses

But you need not be as meticulous as during training. Your most important job after the Marathon is to relax and enjoy yourself. Indulge in a special reward food, if desired, such as the Carrot Cake in the recipe section or some Big Apple Pie. A nice massage and a gentle swim or bike ride to loosen stiff muscles without pounding the joints are also good ideas. The standard practice is to allow an easy day for every mile run. That's almost a month of gentle exercise.

### CARBOHYDRATES "TO GO": TIPS FOR THE TRAVELING RUNNER

New Yorkers take pride in welcoming the thousands of runners from more than one hundred countries who travel to New York. These traveling runners who stay in hotels have an added nutritional challenge:

- finding their familiar sports foods pre-marathon
- avoiding the rich temptations that lurk in every restaurant, deli, and pushcart

All too often when traveling, you can get sidetracked by the convenience, cost, confusion, and excitement of being in a new city.

Even runners who are staying with New Yorkers can be a little surprised. As Mike Turmala, a member of the Greater Boston Track Club, explained, "I stayed with a friend when I came to New York City. We ate out all the time because the kitchen in the apartment was too small to cook in. I missed home cooking, especially the night before the race."

One key to selecting a topnotch sports diet when you are traveling is to bring some fundamental foods with you. This is not foolproof, however. For example, Gelindo Bordin of Italy (known as a food-lover extraordinaire) schlepped not only his own pasta and grateable hard cheese to New York, but also a small hot plate on which to cook in his hotel. The only problem was the water was different in New York City. To his dismay, this not only affected his cooking but also negated his beloved espresso.

The 1992 New York City Marathon winner Willie Mtolo also bought a hot plate to cook his traditional pre-marathon food: phutu, a cornmeal-based porridge. His cooking, however, promptly set off the hotel's fire detectors. Mtolo and his fiancée used

## JUDI FLEISCHNER ECOCHARD

*Rather than stuff myself beforehand, I've learned to rely upon food that I eat during the marathon. I figure my muscles can store about 1,800 calories of glycogen, and I burn about 100 calories per mile. So, starting at the eighteenth mile, First Avenue, I start munching on leftover Halloween candy. What a treat to enjoy sugar and candy in a positive way! (I'm thankful the New York City Marathon comes at a time that very conveniently helps me get rid of my leftover candy.)*

*I also have friends feed me defizzed cola at key locations. And in the Bronx, there's always some guy with cola every year! I make sure I get 800 calories worth of sugar to get me over the finish line.*

towels to fan the smoke out the windows, waited for the firefighters to leave, then finished their meal in peace. Such can be the price of eating your familiar foods in preparation for the Marathon!

To help you better accommodate a high-carbohydrate sports diet into your traveling routine, here are a few tips from New York nutritionist and runner Mary-Giselle Rathgeber, R.D.

**Breakfast:**

1. At a restaurant or deli, order pancakes, French toast, whole wheat toast, or English, bran, or corn muffins. Add jelly, jam, or maple syrup for extra carbohydrates, but hold the butter or request that it be served on the side so that you can better control the amount of fat in your meal.

2. Order a *large* orange or tomato juice. This can help compensate for a potential lack of fruits or veggies in the other meals.

3. For a hotel stay, you might want to save time and money by packing your own cereal, raisins, and spoon. Either bring powdered milk or buy a half-pint of low-fat milk at a local convenience store. A water glass or milk carton can double as a cereal bowl.

**Lunch:**

1. Find a deli or restaurant that offers wholesome breads. Request a sandwich that emphasizes the

*Dehydration can contribute to muscle cramping. Adequate fluids can keep you running smoothly.*

---

### TOM FLEMING

*In one New York City Marathon, for some unknown reason (my training and eating had not changed), I ran out of gas after 21 miles. I hit the wall, as they say. My body was screaming for sugar, so I ran into a store and bummed two bucks off a stranger and bought a cola and a package of Twinkies. I felt great for the next five miles until I ran out of gas again. . . . I crawled in the last mile and a half, humbled by the marathon.*

---

bread rather than the filling (preferably lean beef, turkey, ham, or chicken). Hold the mayonnaise and, instead, add moistness with mustard or ketchup, sliced tomatoes, and lettuce. Add more carbohydrates with juice, fruit, fig bars (brought from a corner store), or yogurt for dessert.

2. At fast-food restaurants, the burgers, fried fish, special sandwiches, and French fries have a very high fat content. You'll get more carbohydrates by sticking to the spaghetti, baked potatoes, chili, or thick-crust pizza selections.

3. Request *thick-crust* pizza (with veggie toppings)

rather than thin-crust pizza with pepperoni or sausage.

4. At a salad bar, generously pile on the chickpeas, three-bean salad, beets, and fat-free croutons. Take plenty of bread. But don't fat-load on butter, salad dressings, and mayonnaise-smothered pasta and potato salads.

5. Baked potatoes are a super choice if you request them plain rather than drenched with butter, sour cream, and cheese toppings. For moistness, try mashing the potato with milk (usually by special request) rather than butter.

6. Hearty soups (such as split pea, minestrone, lentil, vegetable, or noodle) accompanied by crackers, bread, a plain bagel, or English muffin provide a satisfying carbohydrate-rich, low-fat meal.

7. Both juices and soft drinks are rich in carbohydrates. Juices, however, are nutritionally preferable for vitamin C, potassium, and wholesome goodness.

Dinner:

1. If possible, check out the restaurant beforehand to make sure that it offers wholesome carbohydrates (pasta, baked potatoes, rice, steamed vegetables, salad bars, homemade breads, fruit, or juice), broiled foods, and low-fat options. To be on the

> ### BILL FRANKS
>
> *One of the reasons I run New York is because I love being in the city and enjoying the food. There's so much variety. Pre-marathon I stick with familiar foods and go to Little Italy, but after the race I venture into Greenwich Village to enjoy any number of exotic ethnic restaurants that I can't find in New Hampshire.*
>
> *On Marathon eve, the streets in Little Italy are crowded and somewhat like a zoo, but a wonderful zoo. For example, one year Halloween happened to be marathon eve. My running friends and I were attracted to this restaurant where the waiters were dressed up as ghosts and goblins. They brought us food and more food and more food. . . . What a great experience!*

safe side, save the exotic restaurants for *after* the Marathon! Don't be shy! Inquire how dishes are made. Request they be prepared with minimal fat.

2. Eat the breads and rolls either plain or with jelly. Replace the butter calories with another slice of bread, a second potato, soup and crackers, juice, sherbet, or frozen yogurt—all high-carbohydrate choices.

3. When ordering salads, always request the dressing be served on the side. Otherwise, you may get as many as 400 calories of oil or mayonnaise—fatty foods that fill your stomach but leave your muscles unfueled.

Snacks and Munchies:

1. Pack your own snacks. Some suggestions include: whole-grain bagels, muffins, rolls, crackers, pretzels, fig bars, oatmeal-raisin cookies, granola, oranges, raisins, dried or fresh fruit, and juice boxes.

> ### GLORIA AVERBUCH
>
> *The year Alberto Salazar set the world record, I was privileged to attend his family's victory celebration at a prominent Cuban restaurant in midtown Manhattan. Alberto's father, standing in front of a large Cuban flag that had been hung from the wall, raised a glass of red wine and made a touching speech filled with a father's pride. Then, after his sister sang, we all feasted on rice, black beans, and other Cuban delicacies. What a great memory!*

> ## SCOTT MCGUFFIN
>
> *After the marathon, I was hungry and very thirsty. Three of us went to a Chinese restaurant and ate enough food for six. What a feast! And then for days I craved bananas, rice, and bagels.*

2. Buy wholesome snacks at the convenience store: small packets of trail mix, bananas, dried fruit, yogurt, V-8 juice or fruit juice, bagel, hot pretzel, slice of thick-crust pizza, small sandwich, or cup of soup.

## SUMMARY

The carbohydrate-rich foods that you eat before, during, and after the Marathon should be an extension of your daily 60 to 70 percent carbohydrate training diet. During training, you should experiment to determine the foods and fluids that settle best and contribute to top competitive performance. Because each runner has individual tolerances and preferences, you have to learn through trial and error what foods and fluids work best for your body. Traveling runners should take special care to fuel themselves with familiar foods . . . perhaps an easier task in New York than other cities.

> ## JUDY MORRILL
>
> *After a marathon, I really crave red meat. It's like my body needs extra protein to repair the muscles.*

# 4 WEIGHT AND RUNNERS

EXERCISE BURNS CALORIES! And that's why many people exercise. Consistent training helps them manage their weight and allows more freedom with eating. For some active people, however, weight remains a significant issue. If you are discontent with the readings of your bathroom scale, the following information can help you find peace with your physique whether you want to trim down or bulk up.

## HOW TO LOSE WEIGHT AND HAVE ENERGY TO RUN

I spend hours helping runners who struggle to lose weight. Most feel frustrated that they just can't seem to shed those final few pounds. Inevitably, the first words they say to me are, "I know what I *should* do to lose weight. I just can't do it." They think they should follow a strict diet with rigid rules and regulations.

Wrong. Diets don't work. If diets worked, every runner would be as thin as desired. The key to losing weight is to:

- stop thinking about *going on a diet*
- start learning *how to eat healthfully*

Marsha, a 3:15 marathoner, thought that *not eating* was a good way to diet and felt frustrated by her lack of weight loss. She explained, "I don't eat breakfast. I run at lunchtime and then just eat a yogurt and a banana. Nighttime is my troubletime. I eat everything in sight. Cookies are my downfall. It seems the more I diet, the more weight I gain."

Clearly, *not* eating was Marsha's problem. Dieting and denial were getting her nowhere. I reminded Marsha that she is *supposed* to eat and encouraged her to trust that appropriate eating would contribute to an appropriate weight.

> ### KATHRINE SWITZER
>
> *I used to think it was important to keep my weight down, so I cut back on food, forgetting that food is fuel and I needed to eat enough good food to train hard. I was then tired and depressed in workouts and didn't run well.*
>
> *I found that when I ate more I could keep my energy up and really train hard. Then weight just fell off me. Best of all, I felt wonderful and my running really improved. It took me years to figure this out. I wish I had known this in my twenties.*

### How Much Is OK to Eat?

As I outlined in chapter 1, active people need more than a few morsels to fuel themselves. To determine just *how much* you can appropriately eat, refer back to page 4. Note that your body requires an amazing amount of calories to pump blood, breathe, produce urine, grow hair, and simply exist. Also note that you deserve to eat those maintenance calories even if you are injured and unable to run.

> ### BILL RODGERS
>
> *I think runners are crazy to diet. Their better bet is to eat sensibly and not diet.*

A sensible reducing diet knocks off *only 20 percent of your calorie needs.* Many weight-conscious runners try to eat as little as possible. That's a big mistake. Perhaps the following case study will help you understand why.

Ann, a 120-pound nurse, runs five miles most days. She requires about 2,200 to 2,300 calories to maintain her weight.

- 1,200 calories for her resting metabolic rate (10 cal/lb x 120 lbs)

- 600 calories for general daily activity (50% of 1,200 calories)

- 475 calories for purposeful running (95 cal/mile x 5 miles)

To appropriately lose weight, I recommended she cut her calorie intake by 20 percent (about 400 to 500 calories), leaving her with 1,800 calories for her diet plan.

To Ann, 1,800 sounded like too many calories. She exclaimed, "I could never eat that much without turning into a blimp. If I can't lose weight on my self-prescribed 1,000-calorie diet, how could I possibly do so on 1,800? *My* metabolism is *so slow.* I seem to gain weight just smelling cookies."

Although Ann challenged my calorie recommendations, I suggested she keep an open mind. The latest research on athletes' calorie needs theorizes that very few runners actually have slow metabolisms. Researchers have even studied runners like Ann who

claim to maintain weight despite eating next to nothing. When carefully monitored, these women burned the calories one would expect based on standard calculations. Their metabolism was fine, but they had problems acknowledging how much food they actually ate. Their nibbles on bagels, apples, rice cakes, and broken cookie pieces added up! (For more information, refer to the sidebar, *Slow Metabolism Woes* in chapter 5, Women and Running.)

Because Ann claimed she ate far less than her peers, I suggested she heighten her awareness of her food intake by keeping food records. Food records can be extremely useful to help you understand your eating habits. For example, by listing *everything* you eat, you might notice that you:

- eat when reading and don't even notice the portion

- eat too little at breakfast and lunch, only to overeat at night

- diet Monday through Thursday, then splurge on weekends

Accurate food records can help you lose weight because you'll likely end up eating about 20 percent less, which, after all, is an appropriate reducing diet!

### Five Keys to Successful Weight Reduction

Using your calorie guidelines, you can lose weight with the following five keys to successful weight reduction.

## *WEIGHT EXPECTATIONS*

Although only nature knows the best weight for your body, the following guidelines offer a *very general* method to estimate a healthy weight.

**Women:**   100 pounds for the first 5 feet of height; 5 pounds per inch thereafter

**Men:**   106 pounds for the first 5 feet of height; 6 pounds per inch thereafter

Although runners commonly want to be lighter than the "average" person, heed this message: If you are striving to weigh significantly less than the weight estimated by this general guideline, think again. Pay attention to the genetic design for your body and don't struggle to get too light. The best weight goal is to be *fit* and *healthy* rather than sleek and skinny.

## CANDACE STROBACH

*For a while I was trying to eat less so that I could weigh less, but I'd end up eating more and weighing more. I finally learned that if I eat sensibly–three meals per day–that my weight is fine. I feel better and run better.*

*Key #1. Eat enough. Don't get too hungry or you'll blow your diet.* For example, Lori, a receptionist and a runner, tried to self-impose the following bare-bones diet:

| Breakfast: | coffee | 0 calories |
| Lunch: | dry salad | 100 |
| Snack: | big apple | 150 |
| Dinner: | frozen diet meal | 300 |
| Total calories: | | 550 |

This totaled *less than a quarter* of the 2,400 calories she required. No wonder she lacked energy for running. She'd often skip workouts and then at night eat everything in sight, only to get up the next morning with a food hangover. She'd then vow to get back on her diet, skip breakfast, skimp on lunch, lack energy to enjoy running, and blow her diet again at night. Although Lori deserved a lot of credit for having the will power to survive the day on 550 calories, her method was mistaken. Her diet was too strict.

If you, like Lori, are trying to lose weight by eating as little as possible and exercising as hard as you can, remember that the less you eat, the more likely you are to blow your diet. Even if you can successfully restrict your intake, the less you eat, the more your body adjusts to having fewer calories. In short, you'll start to hibernate similar to what a bear does in winter when food is scarce. That is, your metabolic rate will drop to conserve on calories and you'll feel lethargic, cold, and lack energy to exercise.

Research comparing dieters who either crash dieted or followed a more reasonable reducing plan showed that both groups lost the same amount of fat. The strict diet caused the metabolic rate to drop. Why bother to eat next to nothing when you can lose weight with eating just 20 percent less than you need to maintain your weight?

Most of my clients follow 1,800 to 2,200 calorie *reduction* diets. This is far more than most 800 to 1,200 calorie diets that are designed for couch potatoes who can function with eating very little. *You* need a substantial amount of energy to fuel your muscles and have energy to enjoy your training.

*Key #2. Be sure that you eat during the day, so that you'll be able to diet at night.* For a sensible reducing program, I recommend that you divide your calories evenly throughout the day. Because runners tend to get hungry every four hours, an appropriate diet for a 120-pound female runner might be:

| Breakfast: | 8:00 A.M. | 500 calories |
| Lunch: | Noon | 500 |
| Snack: | 4:00 P.M. | 200–300 |
| Run: | 6:00 P.M. | |
| Dinner: | 8:00 P.M. | 500 |

Your goal is to eat on a schedule to *prevent* yourself from getting too hungry. I call this my "eat more, lose weight" food plan.

Your training program may require creative meal scheduling if you exercise during meal times. For example, if you run at 6:00 P.M.—potentially at the height of your hunger—you might better enjoy your run if you eat part of your dinner beforehand. For example, trade in your 200-calorie dinner potato for 200 calories of a bagel at 4:00 P.M. Similarly, if you run at 6:00 A.M., you might enjoy greater energy if you eat part of your breakfast beforehand, such as a slice of toast and a glass of juice, and then eat the rest afterward to recover from the workout and satisfy your hunger. (As I mentioned in chapter 3, you need to experiment with pre-exercise food to determine

## GEOFF SMITH

*When I had to retire from running because of injuries, I was a little concerned about gaining weight. I started eating just a little less; my weight went up only a few pounds to the natural weight for my body.*

## STOP BLOWING YOUR DIET!

If blown diets are your downfall, I recommend that you take the following steps:

- Experiment with bigger breakfasts and lunches.
- Plan a substantial afternoon snack, especially if you won't be eating dinner until after 7:00 P.M.
- "Diet" at night by eating smaller portions than usual.

the right amount of calories that boost your energy without making you feel heavy and sluggish.)

*Key #3. Eat a sufficient amount of fat.* If you are currently eating a high-fat diet filled with butter, mayonnaise, salad dressing, greasy meals, and rich desserts, you should cut back on these fattening foods. Excess dietary fat easily turns into excess body fat, if not clogged arteries.

But many of today's runners avoid fat. They believe that if they eat fat, they'll instantly get fat. Not always the case. Take a look around and notice the number of runners whose diets include some fat.

If you are trying to knock *all* the fat out of your diet, think again and reread the section on fat in chapter 2. Some fat in your food may actually help you lose weight. Runners who try to eat a no-fat diet:

- commonly feel hungry, denied, and deprived
- feel guilty when or if they "cheat" by eating fat
- eat an unbalanced diet that may be too low in protein and can hurt their performance

One study showed that dieters who ate 1,200 calories of a high-fat diet actually lost more body fat than the group who ate 1,200 calories of a very low-fat diet. Why? Because the high-fat dieters were better able to comply with their regimen. Fat is helpful for dieters because it takes longer to digest and provides a nice feeling of satisfaction that can prevent you from searching through the kitchen, scrounging for something to eat.

You'll enjoy better luck with weight loss if you give yourself a reasonable calorie and fat budget to spend on the foods that you want to eat. By choosing the 25 percent fat diet that I described in chapter 2, you can add a little fat to each meal, feel less hungry, and be better able to stick to your diet. For generations, people have lost body fat even though their diets included fat. You can too!

*Key #4. You don't have to diet every day.* Losing weight requires enough mental energy to tell yourself, "I'd rather be thinner than eat more calories." Some days you may lack that mental energy. For example, Paul, a lawyer and a runner who wanted to lose five pounds before the New York City Marathon, was stressed out by his demanding workload, training schedule, and family problems. Although he wanted to drop a few pounds, he lacked the mental energy he needed to cut calories. At the end of the day, he'd inevitably succumb to ice cream. It seemed like a nice reward for having survived the day, but it also contributed to weight gain.

I reminded Paul that he was only human, with a limited amount of mental and physical energy. Rather than punish himself for lacking energy to diet, he needed to accept the fact that he was stressed and in need of comfort. Like it or not, food provided that comfort.

I recommended that Paul let go of his current goal to lose fat and focus instead on fueling his muscles adequately. Well-fueled muscles might enhance his running more than would poorly fueled muscles, especially if they were depleted from improper dieting. I also reminded Paul that he had the rest of his life to lose fat. In this already stressful season in his life, he might be happier removing the additional self-imposed stress of trying to lose weight. He reluctantly agreed with that reality.

## BILL RODGERS

*Although I have been known to eat lots of fatty foods, I've never had a weight problem. I now try to eat mostly low-fat foods, and my weight is still the same.*

Stressful times are often poor times to try to reduce body fat. Rather, focus on exercising regularly to help cope with stress and on eating healthfully to prevent the weight gain that sometimes occurs during stressful times. Eat every four hours to keep your appetite under control. Note that runners who are both stressed and hungry can *easily* succumb to overeating. But no amount of food will solve any problem. In fact, it only adds to your feeling out of control.

*Key #5. Have realistic weight goals.* Weight is more than a matter of will power; genetics plays a large

*This mother-daughter duo certainly have similar physiques. Weight is under significant genetic control.*

> ### *NATALIE UPDEGROVE PARTRIDGE*
> *I used to suffer through nonfat foods that I didn't really enjoy, like nonfat cheeses. But now I let myself enjoy low-fat cheeses and welcome the addition of this little bit of fat into my overall low-fat diet.*

role. If you are eating during the day, exercising regularly, dieting at night, and waking up eager for breakfast but still have not lost weight, perhaps you have an unrealistic goal. It's possible that you have no excess fat to lose and are already very lean for your genetic blueprint. Like it or not, weight is somewhat controlled by genetics. Although you might wish for a sleeker physique, nature may want you to look more like a discus thrower!

Marsha, a 3:15 marathoner, was short and had thin hair and big thighs, "just like my mother and sisters." Although she wasn't concerned with trying to grow taller or thicken her hair, she obsessed about the fat on her thighs and spent lots of energy trying to reduce them.

I reminded Marsha that although she could remodel her body to a certain extent, she couldn't totally redesign it. Plain and simple, runners, like fruits, come in varying sizes and shapes. No one body type is right or wrong.

In order to determine a proper weight for your body, I recommend you stop looking at the scale and start looking at your family. Imagine yourself at a family reunion.

> ### *LINDA PERKINS*
> *I still find it hard to believe that when I started eating more at breakfast and lunch, I lost weight. I felt as though I was cheating all the time. My running times even improved because I was actually well fueled instead of half-starved.*

> ## *PRISCILLA WELCH*
>
> *I like to train at 115 to 116 pounds and race at 108 to 109. I naturally drop the weight as I train. Getting on the track really brings it down.*

- How do you compare to other members of your family?
- Are you currently leaner than they are? fatter? the same?
- If leaner, are you straining to stay that way?

If you are significantly leaner, you may already be underfat for your body.

I counsel many runners who put their lives on hold, struggling to lose a final few pounds. As Marsha said when she grabbed onto her thighs, "I hate being seen in running shorts. But no matter how much I exercise, I can't get rid of these fat thighs. I must be doing something wrong."

Marsha was simply trying to get to a weight that was abnormal for her genetics. She was already leaner than other members of her family. I helped her to understand the reason why women (as compared to men) have "fat thighs": the fat in the thigh area is sex-specific. It is a storehouse of energy for potential pregnancy and breast feeding and is *supposed to be there*. Just as women have breast tissue (which is generally deemed desireable), women also have thigh tissue (which is generally deemed *un*desireable). Women have fatter thighs than men because women are women. Marsha needed to accept the realities of being a woman and stop comparing herself to the magazine models who indeed have unusual physiques.

If you are wasting time complaining about your body, keep the following in perspective:

- Life is a gift.
- Life is too short to be spent obsessing about food and weight.

Yes, you do want to be fit and healthy, but you need not strive to be sleek and skinny. The cost attached to achieving the perfect weight and the perfect body is often yo-yo dieting, poor nutrition, lack of energy for exercise, guilt for eating, a sense of failure that can play havoc with your self-esteem, and, of course, poor athletic performance.

Food is fuel, healthful, and health giving. You are supposed to eat even if you are trying to lose weight. Be realistic about your expectations and remember:

## CASE STUDY: PAM, A JOGGER

*Question:* I jog four miles every day and eat only foods with no fat in them. I haven't lost any weight. What am I doing wrong?

*Answer:* Pam was eating 2,400 calories of fat-free foods, oblivious to their calories. She required only 2,200 calories per day.

Pam's overall diet was very limited, unbalanced, and rather boring. Every day she ate the following items:

| | |
|---|---|
| 6 big apples | 900 calories |
| 4 big bagels | 1,000 |
| 10 hard pretzels | 500 |
| Total intake | 2,400 calories of fat-free snacks. |

*Daily needs:*     2,200 calories

I suggested that Pam add some peanut butter, cheese, and tuna with low-fat mayonnaise to her diet so she could:

- boost her protein intake
- satisfy her appetite
- reduce her desire to eat yet another bagel (with yet more calories) and reduce her overall calorie intake

She did, and this helped her successfully meet her weight goal.

- The thinnest runner may not be the fastest runner.
- The best fueled runner will always win with good nutrition.

Also remember the following keys to successful weight control:

1. You are supposed to eat even if you want to lose fat. Deduct only 20 percent of your calorie budget, but don't starve yourself.

2. You need to eat during the day, then diet at night. Morning hunger is a sign you didn't overeat the night before.

3. Your diet should include a little fat to keep you from feeling hungry and also from feeling denied.

4. You don't have to lose weight every day; stress-filled days can be for maintaining weight.

5. You may have no weight to lose, according to your genetics. Weight is more than a matter of will power.

## HOW TO GAIN WEIGHT HEALTHFULLY

If you are among the athletes who struggle with being too thin, food may seem a medicine, meals a burden, and the expense of food budget-breaking. Through discipline and diet, you can change your physique to

---

### WHY ARE YOU EATING?

If you tend to overeat for reasons other than fuel, stop and ask yourself, Am I eating because I am hungry? angry? lonely? tired? If you are eating inappropriately, remember that no amount of food will solve any problem. Don't start eating if you know you'll have problems stopping.

Food has many roles. It:

- satisfies our hunger
- fuels our muscles
- rewards us at the end of a stressful day
- is a social pleasure and a part of celebrations
- has a calming affect

---

a certain extent, but first, have a clear picture of your genetic blueprint and a realistic goal:

- What do other people in your family look like?
- Was your mother or father very slim at your age?
- When did s/he gain weight?
- What does s/he look like now?

If at your age, a parent was equally thin, you probably are genetically predisposed to be thin and may have trouble adding pounds. Some people are simply "hard gainers." For example, in an overfeeding study on identical twins, some pairs of twins gained more weight than others, despite the fact that everyone overate by an equal amount—1,000 extra calories per day. In another study, some subjects who theoretically should have gained eleven pounds during a month-long overfeeding study gained an average of only six pounds. Why the difference? No one knows!

### Six Rules for Gaining Weight

If you are a hard gainer, you may require a significant amount of calories to add weight. There is no instant cure or magic solution. The bottom line is that you have to consume more calories than you expend.

---

### GRETE WAITZ

*Weight is a very individual matter. Each runner has a different body with a weight that is normal for that body. You have to look in your family tree to understand what weight is appropriate for your body. I hate to see so many runners struggling to be a few pounds lighter when the cost of the lightness is their health and strength. It's just not true that the lightest runner is the best runner.*

> ### *TOM FLEMING*
>
> *Weight was a big issue for me. When I was competing at 6' 1" and 155 pounds, I always felt at a disadvantage compared to Bill Rodgers [5' 8" and 122 pounds]. I had a lot more to lug up those hills. Twenty years later, I'm only 10 pounds heavier (but I could easily be at my natural weight of 175 if I weren't running off the calories!).*

Adding muscle-building exercise, such as weightlifting, helps convert the extra calories into muscle rather than fat. Although you may gain a little body fat through this process, the bulk of the weight will be muscle if you eat and exercise appropriately.

I encourage my clients to consume an additional 500 to 1,000 calories per day. If you are committed to the weight-gain process, you can expect to gain one-half to one pound per week, perhaps more depending on your age. For example, high school and collegiate athletes may bulk up more easily than the fully mature thirty-five-year-old who is genetically skinny.

The trick to successful weight gain is to pay careful attention to these six important rules.

1. *Eat consistently.* Have three hearty meals plus one or two additional snacks daily. Do *not* skip meals! You may not feel hungry for lunch if you've had a big breakfast, but you should have lunch regardless. Otherwise, you'll miss out on important calories that you need to accomplish your goal.

2. *Eat larger portions.* Some people think they need to buy expensive weight-gain powders. They don't need special powders; standard food works fine. The only reason commercial powders seem to "work" is because they provide additional calories. For example, one runner religiously drank the recommended three glasses per day of a 300-calorie weight-gain shake. This gave him an extra 900 calories and the desired results. Although he credited the weight-gain formula for his success, he could have less expensively consumed those calories with supermarket foods. I suggested that he invest his food budget in readily available foods:

   - a bigger bowl of cereal
   - a larger piece of fruit

## HOW TO BOOST YOUR CALORIES

| Choose more: | Calories | Amount | Instead of: | Calories | Amount |
|---|---|---|---|---|---|
| Cranberry juice | 170 | 8 ounces | Orange juice | 110 | 8 ounces |
| Grape juice | 160 | 8 ounces | Grapefruit juice | 100 | 8 ounces. |
| Banana | 170 | 1 large | Apple | 130 | 1 large |
| Granola | 780 | 1½ cups | Bran flakes | 200 | 1½ cups |
| Grape-Nuts | 660 | 1½ cups | Cheerios | 130 | 1½ cups |
| Corn | 140 | 1 cup | Green beans | 40 | 1 cup |
| Carrots | 45 | 1 cup | Zucchini | 30 | 1 cup |
| Split pea soup | 130 | 1 cup | Vegetable soup | 80 | 1 cup |
| Baked beans | 260 | 1 cup | Rice | 190 | 1 cup |

## PETER SMITH

*When I started to train for the marathon, I also started to lose weight. I felt self-conscious about my scrawny legs and hated to be seen in my running shorts. I questioned whether I should bother to train for the marathon because I was afraid I'd burn off too many calories and turn into a bag of bones. Although I was eating all the time, I just couldn't seem to eat enough. Drinking lots of juice solved the problem.*

*Even elite runners come in different sizes and shapes. No one shape or size is best.*

- an extra sandwich for lunch or a large submarine sandwich

- three potatoes at dinner instead of two

- a larger glass of milk

When he did this, he met his goal of 1,000 extra calories per day and continued to see the desired results.

3. *Select higher calorie foods but not higher fat foods.* Excess fat calories easily convert into body fat that fattens you up rather than bulks up your muscles. They also diminish your appetite. The better bet for extra calories is to choose carbohydrate-rich foods that have more calories than an equally enjoyable counterpart (see sidebar, *How to Boost Your Calories*). These extra carbohydrates will give you the energy you need to do muscle-building exercise. By reading food labels, you'll be able to make the best choices.

4. *Drink lots of juice and low-fat milk.* Beverages are a simple way to increase your calorie intake. Instead of drinking primarily water, quench your thirst with calorie-containing fluids. One high school runner gained thirteen pounds over the summer by simply adding six glasses of cranapple juice (about 1,000 calories) to his daily diet. Extra juices are not only a great source of calories but also of carbohydrates to keep your muscles well fueled. You might want to make some of the high-calorie drinks described in the recipe section for beverages and fluids.

## MICHAEL BUCKHEIM

*I'm 6' 4" and have always been thinner than desired. When I started to run, I gained six pounds, from 180 to 186. To my surprise, running stimulated my appetite and I got hungrier. Running encourages me to pay more attention to my diet. I feel better when I run, so I tend to eat better.*

5. *Do resistence exercises* (pushups, weightlifting) to stimulate muscular development, so that you *bulk up* instead of *fatten up*. Note that extra *exercise,* not extra protein, is the key to muscular development. If you are concerned the extra exercise will result in weight *loss* rather than weight gain, remember that exercise tends to stimulate the appetite. Yes, a hard run may *temporarily* "kill" your appetite right after the workout because your body temperature is elevated, but within a few hours when you have cooled down, you will be plenty hungry. The more you exercise, the more you'll want to eat—*assuming you make the time to do so.*

6. *Be patient.* If you are in high school or college and

> ### ROD DIXON
>
> *Weight has never been an issue for me. In 1972, when I was doing high mileage, I weighed 152 pounds. Today, on low mileage, I weigh 156. I think it's genetic and a good, balanced diet.*

don't easily bulk up this year, you may do so more easily as you get older. Focus on improving your athletic skills and know that you can be a strong runner by being well fueled and skilled. Your skinny legs may hurt your self-esteem more than your athletic ability.

# 5 WOMEN, RUNNING, AND SPECIAL FOOD CONCERNS

 ACTIVE WOMEN OF all ages and abilities appreciate the fitness, fun, and physical benefits that come with exercise. To support their exercise programs, women clearly benefit from good nutrition to help them:

- attain their athletic goals
- maintain energy to handle their fast-paced lifestyles
- ensure having regular menstrual periods
- reduce the risk of injuries

This chapter highlights some of the special nutritional concerns of active women.

## WOMEN AND WEIGHT

Due to the prevailing myths that thinness contributes to both better performance and happiness, some women consider food to be a fattening enemy rather than a friendly fuel. With the fear that eating meals will make them heavy and slow, they may deny themselves permission to eat adequately. Appropriate meals are placed on hold until those final few pounds get lost and the dieter begins to feel better about her weight.

Fueled by this "thinner is better" philosophy, the women runners who strive to be abnormally thin commonly pay a high price: poor nutrition, poorly fueled muscles, loss of menses, stress fractures and other injuries, to say nothing of reduced stamina, endurance, and performance. In their overconcern about their weight, they forget this formula for success:

*Appropriate eating + regular exercise =*
*appropriate weight*

Whereas chapter 4 offered guidance about how to lose weight and maintain energy for running, this

> ## GORDON BAKOULIS
> *I'm saddened by how many women runners have eating disorders. I know, because I struggled with food for a while, and I can pick out the runners who are currently struggling. They think they have a secret, but they don't.*
>
> *I can remember how tired I used to be. Then I started eating better and my running got better. I was surprised by how well food worked. It really helps runners to run better!*

chapter provides an additional perspective to help resolve the special food and weight concerns of women runners.

Clearly, in the running community, weight is a bigger issue for women than for men. As the saying goes, "Men eat and women weep!" Why is this? Let's look at the possible explanations.

1. *Women are supposed to have more body fat than men.* Plain and simple, nature prescribes to women a certain amount of body fat that is essential for two reasons:

- to protect their ability to create and nourish healthy babies
- to be a storehouse of calories for pregnancy and breast feeding

This essential body fat is stored not only in the breasts but also the hips and upper legs. That's why women tend to have heavier thighs than most men.

Whereas 11 to 13 percent of a woman's body weight is essential fat stores, only 3 to 5 percent of a man's body weight is essential body fat. Hence, women who try to achieve the "cut look" of male athletes create physiological turmoil and often have to pay the price by starving, bingeing, and obsessing about food in order to reach their desired image.

2. *Women commonly target an unnatural weight.* Women who try to get below their natural weight are the ones most likely to struggle with food and to fight the battle with the bulge. Given that even some of those very lean, front-of-the-pack women runners wish they could be lighter, I'm not surprised that eating disorders abound. The majority of male runners, in comparison, seem to be more at peace with their natural weight—and consequently at peace with food.

3. *Women hold distorted body images.* The Madison Avenue image that adorns every storefront and magazine ad leads us to believe that nature makes all women universally lean. Any aberration is thought to be a result of gluttony and lack of willpower. Wrong!

Nature makes us in different sizes and shapes, like it or not. If the runners who are discontent with their weight could only learn to accept and love their bodies, eating disorders would be rare. As one food-obsessed woman—5'7" and 115 pounds—lamented, "I don't have the gaunt look of my peers. I wish I could weigh 110." She was unable to see that she was already very lean. She was training harder and harder to burn calories and lose body fat. Her running contrasted with that of other runners, commonly men, who train primarily to enhance performance, not to reshape their bodies.

### The Slow Metabolism Woes

Some women runners comment that the fitter they are, the fewer calories they need. As Priscilla Welch once said, "I'm amazed at what nonrunners can tuck away." These comments raise questions about metabolic efficiency. Does nature slow a female runner's

metabolism to protect her from getting too thin and having inadequate fat stores to support pregnancy?

Frustration with a perceived inability to lose weight abounds among women who claim they have a slow metabolism and eat less than they "deserve," given their rigorous daily exercise regimen. Perhaps

*As a health-conscious medical student, Uta Pippig knows how to eat well and yet wisely to maintain her lean physique.*

> ## UTA PIPPIG
>
> *In running, the relationship between weight and strength is important. Yes, if you are a highly competitive runner, you want to be as light as possible. But the lightest runner may not be the fastest runner. I think every runner has an optimal weight.*

you've heard your buddies express complaints similar to the following:

- I eat less than my friends but I still don't lose weight. There must be something wrong with my metabolism.

- I maintain weight on only 1,000 calories per day. I want to lose a few pounds, but I can't imagine eating any less.

- I run at least eight miles every day and eat only one meal a day. I can't understand why I don't lose weight.

What's going on? Is it true that some athletes are "energy efficient?" Do they efficiently utilize every calorie that enters their body so they are able to maintain weight on fewer calories than their counterparts who more unproductively burn them off? According to Dr. Jack Wilmore, exercise physiologist at the University of Texas at Austin, the energy-efficient athlete does *not* exist. His research suggests that metabolic rates are closely tied to muscle mass. Because many women who restrict calories end up burning muscle tissue for energy, they tend to have less muscle mass. Consequently, they require fewer calories. Wilmore concluded, "Athletes who have well-developed muscles require more calories than those who have less muscle."

Other researchers support the energy-efficiency theory, believing that a slower metabolism may be nature's way of conserving calories. After all, the women who perceive themselves as being energy efficient commonly complain about being cold all the time, feeling lethargic, and lacking regular menstrual cycles. These symptoms suggest that their diet is too

meager to support normal body functions. While the debate continues, your solution comes in finding the right amount of calories and nutrients to support a healthy weight for your body.

## WOMEN, RUNNING, AND AMENORRHEA

If you are a runner who previously had regular menstrual periods but currently has stopped menstruating, you are experiencing *amenorrhea*. Although you may think the loss of menses is because you are *too* thin or are running *too* much, thinness and exercise may not be the causes of amenorrhea. After all, many very thin runners *do* have regular menses.

Studies have shown that both regularly menstruating and amenorrheic runners commonly have the same amount of body fat. Clearly, leanness and intense exercise are not the simple explanation to the complexities of amenorrhea. But the question remains unanswered: Why, given a group of women who have a similar running program and the same low percent of body fat, do some experience menstrual problems and others don't?

Amenorrheic runners often strive to maintain an unhealthy low weight. If you perceive yourself as struggling harder than your counterparts to maintain your desired leanness, note that the *cost of achieving that leaness* is likely inadequate nutrition and, consequently, loss of menses. Athletic amenorrhea is commonly a nutritional problem and sometimes a red flag for an eating disorder. If you stop having regular menstrual periods, be sure to consult with your gynecologist and nutritionist for professional guidance.

### Health Risks

Although you may deem amenorrhea a desireable side effect of running because you no longer have to deal with the hassles and possible discomfort of monthly menstrual periods, amenorrhea can lead to

> ## JOAN BENOIT SAMUELSON
>
> *I quickly returned to my prepregnancy weight. I can remember being too busy to eat!*

undesirable problems that can interfere with your health and ability to perform at your best. These problems include:

- almost a three times higher increase of stress fractures
- premature osteoporosis (weakening of the bones) that can affect your bone health in the not-too-distant future
- possible higher risk of heart disease
- inability to conceive should you want to have a baby

If the amenorrhea is caused by anorexia, it is a symptom of pain and unhappiness in your life. Note that the "absence of at least three consecutive menstrual cycles" is part of the American Psychiatric Association's definition for anorexia.

Amenorrheic women who resume menses do restore some of the bone density lost during their months of amenorrhea, particularly if they are younger than seventeen years. But they do not restore all of it. Your goal should be to minimize the damages of amenorrhea by eating appropriately and taking the proper steps to regain your menstrual period. Remember: Food is fuel, healthful and health giving, not the "fattening enemy."

### Resolving Amenorrhea

The possible changes required to resume menses include the following steps:

- running 5 to 15 percent less (50 minutes instead of an hour)

---

### JACQUELINE GARREAU

*When my son was eighteen months old, I was five pounds heavier than my prepregnancy weight. I felt good and chose to not diet because I needed the energy to be a mom as well as a runner. I figure the weight will come off naturally as I train more.*

---

## RISK FACTORS FOR AMENORRHEA

You are more likely to become amenorrheic if you have any of the following:

- a restrictive diet
- a rapid weight loss
- low body weight
- low percent body fat
- a rigorous exercise program
- irregular menstrual periods even before you started to train hard
- significant emotional stress

---

- eating 10 percent more calories each week until you consume an appropriate amount given your activity level (see chapter 1)
- choosing more protein-rich foods, particularly red meat
- gaining a few pounds

Some amenorrheic runners have resumed menses with just reduced exercise and no weight gain. Those who totally stop training, such as happens at the time of an injury, often resume menses within two months. Other runners resume menstruating after having gained less than five pounds. And despite what you may think, this small amount of weight gain does not result in your "getting fat" and can be enough to achieve better health.

If you have stopped menstruating and believe that poor eating may be part of the problem, you should consider getting a nutrition checkup with a registered dietitian who specializes in sports nutrition.

The following tips may help you resume menses, or at least rule out nutrition-related factors.

1. *Throw away the bathroom scale.* Rather than striving to achieve a certain number on the scale, let your body weigh what it weighs. Weight is more than a matter of willpower and a "numbers game." Remember that genetics plays an important role.

2. *If you have weight to lose, don't crash diet but rather moderately cut back on your food intake by about 20 percent.* Severe dieters commonly lose their menstrual periods, suggesting that amenorrhea may be an adaptation to the calorie deficit produced either by low calorie intake alone or by increased energy expenditure via exercise. In particular, *rapid* weight loss may predispose you to amenorrhea. By following a healthy reducing program, such as outlined in chapter 4, you'll not only have greater success with long-term weight loss, but also have enough energy to run.

3. *If you are at an appropriate weight, practice eating as you did as a child: eat when you are hungry, stop when you are content.* If you are always hungry and are constantly obsessing about food, you are undoubtedly trying to eat too few calories. Your body is complaining and requesting more food. Remember that you want to eat adequate calories to support your training program. Chapter 1 can help you determine an appropriate calorie intake and eating schedule that may differ from your current routine, particularly if you yo-yo between starving and binge eating.

4. *Eat adequate protein.* Research has suggested that amenorrheic runners tend to eat less protein than their regularly menstruating counterparts. In one study, 82 percent of the amenorrheic women ate less than the recommended dietary allowance for protein. Even if you are a vegetarian, remember that you still need adequate protein (see chapter 2).

5. *Eat at least 20 percent of your calories from fat.* Amenorrheic runners commonly avoid meat and other protein-rich foods because they are afraid of eating fat. They think that if they eat fat, they'll get fat. Although *excess* calories from fat are fattening, some fat (20 to 30 percent of total calories) is an appropriate part of a healthy sports diet. For most runners, this translates into about 40 to 60+ grams of fat per day. Clearly, this differs from a no-fat diet and allows lean beef, peanut butter, cheese, nuts, and other wholesome foods that balance a sports diet (see chapter 2).

6. *Include small portions of red meat two or three times per week.* Surveys of runners show that those with amenorrhea tend to eat less red meat and are more likely to follow a vegetarian diet than their regularly menstruating counterparts. They are also likely to have a diet deficient in iron (see chapter 2).

Even among nonrunners, vegetarian women are five times more likely to have menstrual problems than meat eaters. It's unclear why meat seems to have a protective effect upon menses. Some researchers believe that women who eat meat take

## MARSHA JONES

*I loved being very light, lean, and unburdened by menstrual periods. That is, until I got a stress fracture, then another one, and then a third one. They took forever to heal. I think my poor diet was the problem.*

*I made an effort to eat more protein, like tuna, cottage cheese, and even lean roast beef. I started to feel stronger, run better, and eventually got my period in three months and three pounds. I now feel better knowing that my body is healthier inside and functioning the way it should.*

in fewer calories from fiber-rich foods. A high-fiber vegetarian diet can alter hormones—vegetarians tend to excrete twice as much estrogen as meat eaters. The high fiber intake common to vegetarian diets may also affect calcium absorption, another concern for the amenorrheic woman who needs to optimize calcium intake.

7. *Maintain a calcium-rich diet.* You should choose a high-calcium diet to help maintain bone density. Because you build peak bone density in your teens and early adult years, your goal is to protect against future problems with osteoporosis by eating calcium-rich foods today. As I mentioned in chapter 1, a safe target is at least 800 milligrams of calcium per day if you are between twenty-four and fifty years old, and between 1,200 and 1,500 milligrams of calcium per day if you are a teenager, amenorrheic, or postmenopausal. This is the equivalent of three to four servings of (low-fat)

---

### MARSHA JONES

*As a runner who has gone from a size 5 to a size 8, I've had to come to peace with my heavier body. I certainly am a much happier human being at a bigger size, and I'm less invested in running to make my life. Now that I'm over forty, my shape is even harder to maintain. I'm just glad the races have age categories, so I can compete with all the other women who are experiencing the same physical changes!*

---

milk, yogurt, and other dairy or calcium-rich foods.

Chapter 1 provides guidelines for getting an optimal amount of calcium. Although you may

---

## STEPS TO RESOLVE EATING DISORDERS

*If you think that you are struggling too much with food and have an eating disorder,* seek help by contacting:

- America Anorexia and Bulimia Association, 418 East 58, New York, NY 10021 (212) 734-1114
- National Association of Anorexia Nervosa and Related Disorders, P.O. Box 7, Highland Park, IL 60035 (708) 831-3438
- American Dietetic Association, 216 W. Jackson Blvd #800, Chicago, IL 60606-6995 (800) 877-1600
- Overeaters Anonymous. Look in the phone book for your local chapter.

*If you think that a runner/friend is struggling with food issues,* speak up! Anorexia and bulimia are self-destructive eating behaviors that may signal underlying depression and can be life threatening.

- Approach the runner gently but be persistent. Say that you are worried about her health. She, too, may

be concerned about her loss of concentration, light-headedness, or chronic fatigue. These health changes are more likely to be a steppingstone to accepting help, since the athlete clings to foods and exercise for feelings of control and stability.

- Don't discuss weight or eating habits. Address the fundamental problems of life.
- Focus on unhappiness as the reason for seeking help. Point out how anxious, tired, and/or irritable the athlete has been lately. Emphasize that she/he doesn't have to be that way.
- Post a list of local resources (with a tear-off phone number at the bottom) where the runner will see it (see resources listed above).
- Remember that you are not responsible and can only try to help. Your power comes from using community resources and health professionals, such as a counselor, nutritionist, or eating disorders clinic.

cringe at the thought of spending so many calories on dairy foods, remember that milk is not an "optional fluid" but rather a wholesome food that contains many important nutrients.

If you are eating a very high-fiber diet (e.g., lots of bran cereal, fruits, and vegetables), you may have a higher need for calcium because the fiber may interfere with calcium absorption. For you, adequate calcium intake will be particularly important.

Calcium is only one factor that affects bone density. Other variables include your genetic predisposition to osteoporosis, how much you weigh (heavier women have denser bones than lighter women), and adequate exercise and estrogen to help prevent osteoporosis. Being athletic, your bones benefit from the protective effect of exercise, but this does not compensate for lack of calcium or lack of estrogen (as occurs with amenorrhea). So bone health is closely related to regular menstrual periods.

## WOMEN, RUNNING, AND MOTHERHOOD

Some women runners dream about the day they'll become a mom but also may have nightmares about the effect that pregnancy will have on their bodies. Competitive runners, in particular, worry about gaining too much weight and being left with excess fat in addition to a child that may disrupt their exercise program and active lifestyle.

If you are contemplating parenthood, the following information addresses some of the concerns common to runners and may offer a helpful perspective on how to build a blue-ribbon baby.

### JOAN BENOIT SAMUELSON

*If you feel like eating, eat. Let your body tell you what it wants. Cravings are a good indication of what your body needs, be it water to quench your thirst, sugar for quick energy, meat for protein, or fat for calories. I always eat when I'm hungry—even if it's before a race.*

### FOODS RICH IN FOLIC ACID

Folic acid is found primarily in dried beans, vegetables, and a few fruits. The RDA is 400 micrograms per day.

| Food | Amount | Folic acid (micrograms) |
|---|---|---|
| Asparagus | 5 spears | 100 |
| Avocado | ½ medium | 110 |
| Broccoli | 1 cup cooked | 160 |
| Spinach | 1 cup cooked | 260 |
| Orange | 1 large | 60 |
| Chickpeas | ½ cup canned | 80 |
| Kidney beans | ½ cup, canned | 65 |
| Lentils | ½ cup | 180 |

1. If you're anticipating getting pregnant, start eating wholesome foods *today* so that you can stockpile lots of vitamins and minerals. Who knows what you'll be eating during pregnancy? Your tastes may change to chips and ice cream!

   One nutrient of particular concern to women contemplating motherhood is folic acid, a B vitamin involved in fetal brain development. An optimal intake of folic acid (found in oranges, spinach, kale, and other green vegetables) *at the time of conception* can help reduce certain types of birth defects. Start eating foods rich in folic acid today as well as taking a multivitamin with 400 micrograms of folacin.

2. During pregnancy, listen to your body's cravings, especially if you are feeling nauseous and know that certain foods will help make you feel better. Any food is better than no food.

   Assuming that you *are* able to tolerate a nice variety of wholesome foods, the primary focus should be on the nutrition basics:

   - calcium-rich food such as low-fat yogurt, milk, and cheese four times a day.
   - lots of dark green or colorful vegetables and citrus fruits like oranges
   - whole-grain breads and cereals

- protein-rich foods like chicken, tuna, beans, and fish.

Women who have not eaten meat for years may find themselves hankering for a hamburger. Others crave potato chips, as if their body wants some salt.

Try to moderate sweet cravings with the most healthful choices, such as frozen yogurt instead of ice cream, raisins and dried fruits instead of candy. The reality of the situation may be that there's only one food that will do the trick—the food you crave, no substitutions allowed! Strange cravings and morning sickness are two reasons why you want to eat healthfully *prepregnancy*, to be sure you start off well nourished.

3. When exercising during pregnancy, be sure to eat adequate calories. You should be gaining the appropriate amount of weight, as recommended by your care provider. If you are exercising because you're worried about "getting fat," switch your thought pattern and remind yourself that you are *pregnant*, not *fat*, and that you are *supposed* to gain weight.

4. Be sure to drink extra fluids. Drink enough for you and the baby. You should be urinating frequently, and the urine should be in significant amounts.

5. After pregnancy, trust that normal eating and regular exercise will contribute to a return to your normal weight. Let Mother Nature do her thing, as opposed to forcing yourself to go on a diet. Yes,

you can moderate your calorie intake and eat wisely, but don't be overly restrictive. Your body needs adequate calories and plenty of fluids to recover, maintain your energy, and to produce milk for breast-feeding. Good nutrition will also help you to better cope with all the new stresses of having a baby.

6. Yes, many moms lead a lean life after pregnancy! Now is *not* the time to brood about your postpregnancy flab. Life has seasons, and the first year

*Lisa Ondieki is but one of many women who has given birth to a child and regained fitness and a slim figure.*

---

### NANCY CLARK

*When I was pregnant, all of my favorite foods made me nauseated. I didn't eat broccoli or cereal for nine months! I was exhausted all the time and felt too tired to run. I can't comprehend how some women, like Joan Samuelson, could run up to the day they delivered!*

## WEIGHT GAIN DURING PREGNANCY

The twenty-four pounds that women commonly gain during pregnancy can be accounted for by the weight of the:

| | |
|---|---|
| baby | 7 pounds |
| placenta | 2 |
| amniotic fluid | 3 |
| uterus | 3 |
| breast tissue | 2–3 |
| water, fat, and blood volume | 6–7 |

Athletic women who are initially underweight commonly gain more than twenty-four pounds; overweight women may gain less. Your care provider can offer guidelines personalized to you.

postpregnancy may not be your season to be as lean or as athletic as you'd like. Remember: You were pregnant for nine months, and you may need nine months to a year to return to your prepregnant physique. Surveys of women runners do suggest that many returned to running five weeks after delivery, and some were at their prepregnancy weight in five months.

### UTA PIPPIG

*How do I stay so thin? I eat as much as I can—sometimes more than seems possible. But I train very hard . . . you don't know my training!*

*Participants in the 1971 New York City Marathon included Erich Segal (#91), author of Love Story, and Fred Lebow (#24).*

*Olympic runner Frank Shorter and New York Road Runners Club president Fred Lebow before the 1976 New York City Marathon*

*The starting line of the 1975 New York City Marathon, which at that time was run entirely in Central Park*

RIGHT: *New York City Marathon race director Fred Lebow*

FAR RIGHT: *Mom Edith Farias (center, age 66) and all her daughters ran the 1990 Marathon.*

LOWER LEFT: *Runners love those carbohydrates!*

LOWER RIGHT: *Runners from some of the ninety-one countries represented in the Marathon celebrate in the International Breakfast Run.*

FAR LEFT:  *If lined up, the buses that transport the runners to the starting line on Staten Island would stretch one mile.*

ABOVE:  *Timing is everything. Runners hit their watches at the Marathon start.  They will also hear their times called out at every mile of the race.*

LEFT:  *A boat showers red, white, and blue water at the Marathon start.*

ABOVE: *The women's field in the New York City Marathon—more than six thousand— is the largest in the world.*

RIGHT: *Volunteers pass out water and encouragement along the entire route.*

LEFT: *The runners take off from three separate starts on the Verrazano Narrows Bridge and head for Brooklyn.*

BELOW: *The one-mile carpet, the world's longest, stretching across the Queensboro Bridge, protects the runners' feet from grating on the bridge's surface.*

ABOVE: *There is live music—rock, reggae, salsa, and more—by volunteer bands along all 26.2 miles of the Marathon.*

BELOW: *Supporters and runners wait at the finish of the race.*

# INTRODUCTION TO RECIPES

THE FOLLOWING RECIPES reflect a mixture of tried-and-true family favorites that were submitted by runners, friends, and sports nutritionists. Some are simply quick-and-easy ideas that you can create in minutes; others involve more preparation. Most are low fat and healthful; a few are decadent reward foods to be enjoyed in moderation. We have sometimes modified the ingredients to simplify the recipe and/or stay within the guidelines for a low-fat, heart-healthy diet appropriate for runners and nonrunners alike. We did not restrict salt usage because most active people have low blood pressure; you can add more or less salt as desired, based upon your taste preferences and health needs.

The nutrition analysis reflects approximate values for the basic recipe, without optional ingredients. If two amounts of ingredients are listed (i.e., 2 to 4 tablespoons oil), the nutrition analysis is based on the lower amount. Remember that your total daily caloric intake should be approximately 60 percent carbohydrate, 25 percent fat, and 15 percent protein. How this translates into calories and grams is shown in the chart below. Because some of the recipes are high in protein or fat, you'll need to balance them into your overall day's calorie and fat budget.

## HOW TO COOK EFFICIENTLY

Once you've decided to make a recipe, you certainly want the process to go smoothly. Here are a few tips:
1. Read the recipe completely before you start making it. Make sure that you have a clear understanding of the entire process before you begin.
2. Make sure you have all the ingredients on hand and in adequate amounts. Consider doubling the ingredients to either freeze or enjoy for planned-overs the rest of the week.
3. Post a grocery list in a convenient place in your kitchen, so you can easily add to the list before you run out of any items.
4. Use frozen or pre-cut vegetables from the grocery store.
5. Use pre-chopped garlic (in a jar in the produce section of the market) and use dried onions instead of chopping fresh.

## HOW TO SPICE UP YOUR DIET

If you are like many runners, you may eat the same ten to fifteen foods repeatedly. To add variety to this limited repertoire, take advantage of the flavor changes that come with adding herbs, spices, and other seasonings.

| Calorie needs | 60% Carbohydrate | | 25% Fat | | 15% Protein | |
| | cal | gm | cal | gm | cal | gm |
|---|---|---|---|---|---|---|
| 1,500 | 900 | 225 | 375 | 40 | 225 | 55 |
| 2,000 | 1,200 | 400 | 500 | 55 | 300 | 75 |
| 2,500 | 1,500 | 375 | 625 | 70 | 375 | 95 |
| 3,000 | 1,800 | 450 | 750 | 80 | 450 | 110 |

### Basic Herbs and Spices

- Use about ¼ teaspoon dry herbs (or ¾ teaspoon fresh) for a dish that serves four people. You are better off underseasoning and adding more than overseasoning and having to double the recipe!

- To enhance their flavor, crumble the herb between your fingers.

- Heat the herbs in oil to heighten and extend their flavor.

- With soups and stews, add the herbs during the last hour of cooking.

- Store herbs in a cool place to retain their flavor—*not* near the stove.

Some harmonious combinations include:

| | |
|---|---|
| Basil | Tomato dishes, salads, fish |
| Marjoram | Fish, meat, poultry, stuffing |
| Oregano | Tomato dishes, fish, salads |
| Parsley | Soups, salads, vegetables, garnish |
| Poppy seeds | Cottage cheese, noodles, cole slaw, baked goods |
| Rosemary | Fish, meat, poultry, stuffing vegetables |
| Sage | Soups, stews, stuffing |
| Thyme | Tomato dishes, stews, salads, vegetables |
| Cinnamon | Cooked fruits, winter squash, baked goods |
| Cloves | Hot cider or tea, cooked fruits tomatoes, winter squash |
| Ginger | Cooked fruits, curry, chicken, stir-fry |
| Nutmeg | Apple desserts, puddings, winter squash |

The classic combinations in international dishes are:

| | |
|---|---|
| Italian: | Basil, oregano, parsley, garlic |
| Mexican: | Cumin, chili, cayenne pepper |
| Indian: | Curry, turmeric, coriander cumin |
| Chinese: | Soy sauce, ginger, hot chili oil, garlic |
| French: | Dill, fennel, rosemary, tarragon |

Some additional flavor boosters that are worth stocking include:

| Flavor booster | Combines nicely with |
|---|---|
| Balsamic vinegar | Salads, vegetables |
| Sun-dried tomatoes | Pasta and tomato sauces |
| Dijon mustard | Chicken, fish |
| Sesame oil | Chicken, fish, vegetables, soups |
| Hot chili oil | Stir-fry, soups, vegetables, pasta |
| Tabasco (hot pepper sauce) | Stir-fry, soups, vegetables pasta |
| Salsa | Fish, chicken |
| Chicken broth | Rice, vegetables |
| Canned green chilies | Eggs, tomato, cheese |

## STANDARD MEASURES

| | |
|---|---|
| 3 teaspoons | = 1 tablespoon |
| 2 tablespoons | = 1 liquid ounce or ⅛ cup |
| 4 tablespoons | = ¼ cup |
| 8 tablespoons | = ½ cup |
| 16 tablespoons | = 1 cup |
| 1 cup | = ½ pint (8 ounces) |
| 2 cups | = 1 pint (16 ounces) |
| 4 tablespoons flour | = 1 ounce |
| 4 cups flour | = 1 pound |
| 2 cups white sugar | = 1 pound |
| 2⅔ cups brown sugar | = 1 pound |

Basic metric conversions

| | |
|---|---|
| 1 teaspoon | = approximately 5 ml |
| 1 tablespoon | = approximately 15 ml |
| 1 cup (8 oz.) | = approximately 250 ml |
| 1 quart (4 cups) | = approximately 1 liter |
| 1 pound (16 oz.) | = approximately 450 grams |
| 2.2 pounds | = approximately 1 kilo |
| 350° | = 180 degrees C |

NOTE: Initials following some recipe introductions denote the speaker: NC—Nancy Clark; JLH—Jenny Hegmann; AS—Alberto Salazar; KS—Kathrine Switzer.

# 6 BREAKFASTS AND BRUNCHES

Breakfast or brunch is a wonderful meal that is meant to be enjoyed on days when you don't have to rush out of the house in the morning. Even dieters can enjoy a satisfying breakfast, because they'll have the chance to burn off the calories the rest of the day.

The following breakfast and brunch ideas are perfect for refueling after long runs or fueling up for a busy day.

## Jeff Galloway's Oat Bran

Jeff recommends that you make this the night before, or else before your morning run. The oat bran puffs up and tastes like it is cooked. He also has eaten this without waiting—a bit "gritty," he claims, but it does the job of providing a hearty, healthy, high-fiber breakfast!

½  cup oat bran, uncooked
1   cup yogurt
1   medium banana, sliced

1. In a serving bowl mix together the oat bran, yogurt, and banana.
2. Let it sit for an hour or overnight, then eat with gusto.

YIELD: 1 serving

| Total calories: | | 320 |
|---|---|---|

| | Grams | % of recipe |
|---|---|---|
| CARB | 58 | 75 |
| PRO | 15 | 20 |
| FAT | 3 | 5 |

## Grete Waitz's High-Fiber Breakfast

Grete likes to let high-fiber cereals soften in yogurt while she showers and stretches after her morning run. The following is her basic breakfast, eaten along with home-made bread, or a bagel if she is in the States. (Bagels are the closest match she can find to Norwegian breads.)

1   cup All-Bran
1   cup plain nonfat yogurt
1   medium banana
¼  cup raisins

1. In a serving bowl combine the All-Bran and yogurt. Refrigerate the mixture while you shower and stretch.
2. Top with sliced banana and a handful of raisins.

YIELD: 1 serving

| Total calories: | | 450 |
|---|---|---|

| | Grams | % of recipe |
|---|---|---|
| CARB | 95 | 80 |
| PRO | 17 | 15 |
| FAT | 2 | 5 |

## Cold Cereal with Warm Blueberries

This tastes more like a dessert than a breakfast. The combination of warm blueberries and cold milk reminds me of blueberry cobbler with ice cream. You may vary the types of cereals—this combination just happens to be my favorite.
—NC

1   cup Life cereal
½  cup All-Bran
¼  cup low-fat granola
½  cup (or a generous handful) of blueberries, either fresh or frozen
1   cup low-fat milk

1. In a microwaveable bowl combine the cereals.
2. Sprinkle with fresh or frozen blueberries
3. Heat in the microwave oven for 30 to 60 seconds, until the blueberries are warm.
4. Pour the cold milk over the warm blueberries, so the flavors blend. On your mark, get set, go!

YIELD: 1 serving

| Total calories: | | 500 |
|---|---|---|

| | Grams | % of recipe |
|---|---|---|
| CARB | 85 | 70 |
| PRO | 22 | 20 |
| FAT | 7 | 10 |

# MARATHON HISTORY

### THE ORIGIN OF THE MARATHON

In the year 490 B.C., Persia invaded Greece. The two armies battled on the Plain of Marathon in northeast Attica. Although the Athenians were the less powerful army, they emerged victorious. A historically inaccurate legend has it that the news of the great victory was brought to Athens by Pheidippides, who ran some 20 miles with his message. From this story, the concept of the marathon was born.

It was not until the first modern Olympic Games in 1896, however, that the marathon road race came into being. The current marathon distance was established in the 1908 Olympics, with a 26-mile race that started at Windsor Castle. At Queen Alexandra's insistence, the event ended in front of her box at the Olympic stadium, a distance of 26 miles, 385 yards. This has remained the marathon distance ever since.

### NEW YORK CITY MARATHON HISTORY

In 1959 the newly formed New York Road Runners Club (NYRRC), under the guidance of Olympic marathoner Ted Corbitt and race director Joe Kleinerman, sponsored a 26.2-mile run that began in the Bronx, near Yankee Stadium. Because a cherry tree stood at a turn on the course and because the event was usually scheduled on Washington's Birthday, it was dubbed the Cherry Tree Marathon. The Cherry Tree race was held each year until 1970, when Central Park was opened to runners by Mayor John Lindsay's weekend traffic ban.

### 1970

The first New York City Marathon consisted of four loops around Central Park. There were more runners (127) than spectators. Winner Gary Muhrcke remembers his running outfit was "something close to underwear." The awards ceremony took place at the finish line, among the hot dog vendors, dogs, and horses. The race was conceived, conducted, directed, and spon-

sored by one of the 55 finishers, Fred Lebow, and co-directed by Vince Chiappetta.

Awards for the winners were a problem; there was not enough money to buy trophies. So old baseball and bowling trophies were gathered and redistributed as running awards. There were still not enough, so Fred Lebow handed them out onstage and secretly retrieved them from local winners to give to those from out of town. The top ten finishers were also awarded wristwatches.

### 1971

Fuller Brush salesman Norm Higgins from New London, Connecticut, won the men's race. Five women started, and nineteen-year-old Beth Bonner won the women's division in 2:55:22. She and Nina Kuscsik (2:56:04), finishing thirty-fourth and thirty-fifth overall, became the first women in the world to break the three-hour mark.

A finish banner was added to the race, but it was printed on only the runner's side, thus photographers' pictures featured a blank banner.

### 1972

The six women were the focus of this race. Led by Nina Kuscsik and Jane Muhrcke, they staged a sit-down strike protesting a rule by the Amateur Athletic Union (AAU), then the governing body of the sport, that required their race begin ten minutes after the men's. The women got up and ran with the men, and the AAU added ten minutes to their times. The winners were Sheldon Karlin, a student at the University of Maryland, and Nina Kuscsik (3:08:41 minus ten minutes).

### 1973

Race winner Tom Fleming set a course record (2:21:54) and was awarded an all-expense paid trip to the Marathon-to-Athens Marathon in Greece by the first cash-sponsor of the race, Olympic Airways.

*Continued on page 89*

## Breakfast Cookie

If you lack the time to sit down for a bowl of cereal, this breakfast cookie can be a wholesome alternative. Because of its reduced fat content, the cookie is soft, not crisp. If desired, you can make these cookies into sandwiches with either low-fat cream cheese or peanut butter for the filling. Put each sandwich into a small plastic bag, then freeze. Take one out at night, and your breakfast will be ready and waiting for the rush hour!

⅓ cup margarine
½ cup firmly packed brown sugar
¾ cup unsweetened applesauce
½ cup oatmeal
½ cup oat bran
¼ cup milk powder
1 egg (or substitute)
½ teaspoon baking soda
½ teaspoon baking powder
½ teaspoon salt
½ teaspoon cinnamon
¾ cup flour, preferably half white, half whole-wheat
½ cup raisins

**Optional:**

¼ teaspoon cloves
½ cup chopped walnuts

1. In a mixing bowl cream together the margarine and brown sugar.
2. Add the remaining ingredients, stirring the raisins in last.
3. Drop by tablespoonful onto a greased or nonstick cookie sheet. Bake at 375° for 10 to 12 minutes.

YIELD: 12 big cookies

| Total calories: | 2,500 |
|---|---|
| Calories per cookie: | 210 |

|  | Grams | % of recipe |
|---|---|---|
| CARB | 35 | 65 |
| PRO | 4 | 10 |
| FAT | 6 | 25 |

*John Kelly (the younger) wins the 1956 Yonkers Marathon, the second oldest marathon in the United States. (Only Boston is older.) The New York Road Runners Club was established two years later, in 1958, and it began the Cherry Tree Marathon, which was first run in February 1959 in the Bronx. In 1970 the race, by then known as the New York City Marathon, moved to Central Park, and in 1976 it was run throughout the entire five boroughs, as it is today.*

## Norb Sander's French Toast

When he's not eating at his local diner, one of Norb's favorite breakfasts is French toast. He says the trick is to use really good bread.

1 thick slice bakery bread
1 egg (or substitute)
½ cup milk
1 to 2 dashes cinnamon, or to taste
*Salt and pepper to taste*

1. Cut the bread into 1-inch thick slices.
2. In a flat bowl that will hold the bread, mix together the egg, milk, and seasonings.
3. Soak the bread in the milk mixture for 10 minutes, then place it on a preheated griddle that has been treated with cooking spray or a little margarine.
4. Cook over medium heat until golden, then turn with a spatula and cook the other side.
5. Serve with maple syrup, and get ready to relax and refuel after your hard run!

YIELD: 1 serving

| Total calories without syrup: | 350 |
|---|---|

|  | Grams | % of recipe |
|---|---|---|
| CARB | 52 | 60 |
| PRO | 16 | 20 |
| FAT | 9 | 20 |

With 2 tablespoons syrup and 1 teaspoon butter or margarine:

| Total calories: | 500 |
|---|---|

|  | Grams | % of recipe |
|---|---|---|
| CARB | 78 | 65 |
| PRO | 16 | 10 |
| FAT | 13 | 25 |

## Hearty Wheat Germ and Cottage Cheese Pancakes

These pancakes are a tasty way to add protein and whole-grain goodness to your sports diet. The wheat germ adds vitamin E, B vitamins, and fiber. Although cottage cheese may sound like an unusual addition, you won't even notice it.

½ cup cottage cheese, preferably low-fat
½ cup wheat germ
2 to 4 tablespoons firmly packed brown sugar or honey
1 egg (or substitute)
1 to 2 tablespoons oil
1 cup milk, preferably low-fat
1 teaspoon vanilla extract
1 teaspoon baking powder
½ teaspoon baking soda
1 cup flour, preferably half white, half whole-wheat

**Optional:**
½ teaspoon cinnamon or ¼ teaspoon nutmeg

1. In a medium bowl beat together the cottage cheese, wheat germ, brown sugar, egg, and oil.
2. Beat in the milk and vanilla, then the baking powder and soda. Gently stir in the flour.
3. Pour onto a hot griddle. Cook until the edges are done and bubbles form on top. Turn and cook until golden.
4. Tasty plain or served with maple syrup, applesauce with cinnamon, or yogurt.

YIELD: 3 servings

| Total calories: | 1,200 |
|---|---|
| Calories per serving: | 400 |

| | Grams | % of recipe |
|---|---|---|
| CARB | 54 | 55 |
| PRO | 19 | 20 |
| FAT | 12 | 25 |

## Kathrine Switzer's Toast with Manuka Honey

Kathrine submitted what she calls her New Zealand recipes, just to be sure we would all be left drooling—and eager to come visit and train during the American winter. This recipe is one you could enjoy for breakfast or snack.

Manuka raw honey is a special honey from the manuka bush and is famous for its supposed antibacterial qualities. It has a strong taste and a grainy texture with bits of pollen, but runners in New Zealand swear by it, including the famous Arthur Lydiard. If it's good enough for Arthur, Kathrine says it's also good enough for her!

2 slices (4 ounces) bread, made with whole grains
2 spoonfuls Manuka raw honey

**Optional:**
A little bit of butter

1. Make or buy some good bread, then cut your own (read thick) slices and toast them.
2. Add a little butter if you want or dare.
3. Slather on Manuka raw honey.

YIELD: 1 serving

| Total calories: | 400 |
|---|---|

| | Grams | % of recipe |
|---|---|---|
| CARB | 84 | 80 |
| PRO | 10 | 10 |
| FAT | 4 | 10 |

## The Baked "Big Apple" French Toast

This is a beautiful dish with wonderful aroma, perfect for company. The dish may be prepared the night before and baked the next morning.—JLH

1 loaf French or Italian bread (about 1 pound), cut into 1-inch slices
4 eggs (or substitute)
1½ cups milk
½ cup sugar, divided
1 tablespoon vanilla extract
3 Granny Smith apples, peeled and cored
2 teaspoons cinnamon

1. Spray a 9x13-inch baking dish with cooking spray. Arrange the bread slices in a layer in the pan.
2. In a medium bowl combine the eggs, milk, ¼ cup of sugar, and vanilla. Blend well. Pour half of the liquid mixture over the bread.
3. Slice the peeled and cored apples into rings and arrange them over the bread.
4. Pour the remaining liquid mixture over the apples. Combine ¼ cup of sugar and the cinnamon, and sprinkle the mixture over the apples. The dish may be refrigerated overnight at this point, if desired.
5. Bake at 400° for 35 to 40 minutes. Let the meal cool for 5 to 10 minutes before serving. Serve with maple syrup.

YIELD: 5 servings

| Total calories: | 2,250 |
|---|---|
| Calories per serving: | 450 |

| | Grams | % of recipe |
|---|---|---|
| CARB | 77 | 70 |
| PRO | 17 | 15 |
| FAT | 8 | 15 |

Twelve women were in the field. The ages of the participants ranged from twelve to eighty. Medical help was provided for the first time, as were T-shirts, and a start banner.

It was also the first year traditional laurel wreaths were worn by the winners. They were made by Jane Muhrcke (wife of the first NYC Marathon winner, Gary Muhrcke), and she has made them ever since.

### 1974

The race is the Metropolitan AAU Women's Championship, and Kathrine Switzer, in fifty-ninth place overall, takes the title. Men's winner was New York doctor Norbert Sander. Rising star Bill Rodgers took an early lead, but faded to fifth and was briefly hospitalized due to the effects of the heat and humidity.

This was the first year electronic timing equipment was used and the first year the race was covered on local television.

### 1975

Two course records were set by Tom Fleming and twenty-year-old Wisconsin college student Kim Merritt. Aristotle Onassis's death leaves the Marathon without its lone sponsor, Olympic Airways, but 160 people send in donations.

### 1976

The race celebrated the bicentennial by going out into the streets—all five boroughs of New York.

Fifty percent of the field was made up of first-time marathoners. The expansion of the race is made possible by the first major sponsors. The field included fifty-eight women, the most ever for a marathon. Bill Rodgers's 2:10:10 was a new course record and was the fastest time in the world in 1976. Miki Gorman, aged forty-one, won the women's race in 2:39:11.

### 1977

The race included 36 world-class entrants with marathon times under 2:20. The women's field of 250 nearly tripled from the year before.

After receiving hearty greetings in the various neighborhoods the year before, the race moved farther

*In the first NYC Marathon in 1970, Jane Muhrcke, wife of winner Gary Muhrcke, made the winners' laurel wreaths (pictured here on Lisa Ondieki). She has made them every year since.*

into the communities, crossing five bridges and passing 360 intersections. This was the first year runner's blankets were used and the first time carpeti was used to cover the grating on the Queensboro Bridge.

### 1978

For the first time in any road race, bar codes on numbers and multiple start and finish lines were used.

Designated the race "rabbit" by Fred Lebow, unknown Norwegian Grete Waitz ran the entire course, setting a new women's world record by more than two minutes.

In 1976, the Hasidic Jews in Williamsburg ignored the Marathon completely. In 1977, they stopped and watched for a while. This year, when temperatures rose to 80 degrees, Fred Lebow implored them in Yiddish to bring water. They brought the runners seltzer.

*Continued on page 90*

### 1979

Grete Waitz smashed the 2:30 barrier with 2:27:33 and was the subject of a *New York Times* editorial for her achievement. Bill Rodgers won his fourth consecutive title. The first live television coverage of the race signed off at 2:27 P.M., without mentioning Waitz's record. But astute viewers realized her accomplishment, as she could be seen crossing the line in the closing credits.

### 1980

Alberto Salazar ran the fastest debut marathon in history, 2:09:41. There were also women's world and American records by Grete Waitz and Patti Catalano, respectively. Runners from China participated for the first time.

An examination of the case of fraudulent Boston Marathon winner Rosie Ruiz resulted in the discovery of her falsely recorded NYC Marathon time the year before. It turned out that Ruiz had taken the subway for a good portion of the route. Subsequently, this year NYC Marathon organizers installed a system of checking runners at the start, along the course and at the finish with videotape machines. They have used this system ever since.

### 1981

This was the first year ABC Sports telecast the race. Network officials said that it was their biggest undertaking outside of the World Series and the Olympic Games. Alberto Salazar broke a twelve-year-old world record, throwing in a 4:33 seventeenth mile, and Allison Roe set a women's world record at 2:25:29.

### 1982

The live ABC telecast was viewed by 22 million people, making it the highest-rated sports show of the day. This was the first year for the waiting list system, which guaranteed those who did not run and who turned in their numbers would have a spot in next year's race. Two thousand took advantage of the system, opening places for that many more marathon hopefuls. The Soviet Union sent a delegation of runners for the first time.

### 1983

Geoff Smith of Great Britain came in second by mere seconds but ran the fastest debut marathon ever, 2:09:08. Eleven men ran under 2:12. Postcards giving the runners' results were mailed the day after the race and featured a special Marathon postmark. This was the first year every woman finisher was given a rose, a tradition Fred Lebow adopted from the Berlin Marathon.

### 1984

Due to the heat (the temperature was 74 degrees with 96 percent humidity), the race was the slowest since expansion in 1976 into the five boroughs. Despite the more than 10,000 runners on one of the starting lines, it took only one minute, 41.3 seconds for all of them to cross the line. This was the first year open prize money was awarded, along with a Mercedes-Benz to both the male and female winners.

### 1985

New York became the largest marathon in the world with 15,881 finishers, surpassing the London Marathon. The 100,000th finisher crossed the line.

### 1986

Italian men finished 1, 4, 7, and 9, and three Italian women were in the top ten (3, 7, 8). Grete Waitz won her eighth Marathon, making her the only athlete with that many wins in a major marathon.

After several years of unseasonably hot weather, beginning this year the race is scheduled a week later, the first Sunday in November.

### 1987

Kenyan Ibrahim Hussein became the first African to win the race. Pete Pfitzinger, who came in third, became the first to win $10,000 in a prize money bonus structure designed to develop American marathoners. The Marathon message was flashed from a record number of electronic billboards, buses, posters, and storefronts.

*Continued on page 93*

## French-Toasted Cheese Sandwiches

This is a quick and easy brunch as well as supper. For variety, add sliced ham to the sandwich filling. Serve with maple syrup.

1    egg (or substitute), beaten
¼    cup milk
Salt, as desired
2    slices wholesome bread
1½ ounces low-fat cheese, sliced
**Optional:**
Margarine for cooking
Sliced ham
Sliced tomato
Sautéed mushrooms
Mustard

1. In a medium bowl combine the egg, milk, and salt.
2. Heat a nonstick skillet.
3. Dip the slices of bread in the egg mixture until all soaked and place in the skillet.
4. Cook the French toast on one side, flip one slice over, add the cheese slices, then flip the cooked side of the second piece onto the cheese, making a sandwich.
5. Cover the pan and continue cooking. Slowly brown on both sides over low heat until golden.

YIELD: 1 sandwich

| Total calories: | | 375 |
| --- | --- | --- |
| | *Grams* | *% of recipe* |
| CARB | 43 | 50 |
| PRO | 26 | 25 |
| FAT | 11 | 25 |

With 2 tablespoons of maple syrup:

| Total calories: | | 450 |
| --- | --- | --- |
| CARB | 75 | 60 |
| PRO | 26 | 20 |
| FAT | 11 | 20 |

## Honey Nut Granola

New Zealand runner Anne Audain likes this granola because it is a delicious and healthful way to start the morning. It is also wonderful with fresh fruit and yogurt after a run or workout. The milk powder and nuts add a protein boost.

4    cups rolled oats
2    cups wheat or oat bran
1    cup chopped almonds
1    cup powdered milk
2    teaspoons cinnamon
1    teaspoon salt
¼    cup firmly packed brown sugar
1    cup honey
⅓    cup oil (preferably canola)
**Optional:**
1    cup wheat germ
1    cup whole-wheat or soy flour
1    cup sesame seeds
1    cup shelled raw sunflower seeds, unsalted
1    cup chopped dates, dried fruit, raisins, etc.

1. In a large bowl combine the oats, bran, almonds, powdered milk, cinnamon, salt, and brown sugar.
2. In a saucepan or microwaveable container combine the honey and oil. Heat until almost boiling. Pour the honey mixture over the oat mixture, and stir well.
3. Spread the mixture into 2 large pans.
4. Bake at 225° for 1 hour, stirring every 15 minutes.
5. After the granola has cooled, add the optional ingredients. Store in an airtight container.

YIELD: 16 ½-cup servings

| Total calories: | | 4,700 |
| --- | --- | --- |
| Calories per ½ cup: | | 300 |
| | *Grams* | *% of recipe* |
| CARB | 44 | 55 |
| PRO | 10 | 15 |
| FAT | 9 | 30 |

## Blue-Ribbon Breakfast Cereal

According to Gloria Averbuch, this makes a great breakfast. If you're heading for a race out of town, this mixture is also portable; simply omit the fresh apple, add dried fruit and/or nuts, and powdered milk. Carry it in a plastic container. Just add water and shake.

½    cup raw rolled oats
¼    cup Grape-Nuts cereal (or ½ cup of your favorite)
½    cup diced apple (or other fruit)
¼    to ⅓ cup raisins
1    cup low-fat milk

1. In a serving bowl combine the oats, Grape-Nuts, apple, and raisins.
2. Pour milk over all.

YIELD: 1 serving

| Total calories: | | 520 |
| --- | --- | --- |
| | *Grams* | *% of recipe* |
| CARB | 102 | 80 |
| PRO | 17 | 15 |
| FAT | 5 | 5 |

Fred Lebow, center, in a vintage Central Park Track Club team picture. He remembers, "What turned out to be an eventful day didn't seem like much at the time. I was sitting in front of the Plaza Hotel in the spring of 1970. Vince Chiappetta, then NYRRC president, wandered up and sat down, showing me his hand-typed entry blank for the New York City Marathon. I was surprised to see my name listed as co-race director. When I questioned Vince why, he lightheartedly answered, 'It was your idea.' Well, okay. Little did I realize how that one day would signal a permanent change in my lifestyle and career."

## Soufflé à la Stale Bagels

This is a hearty, delicious dish, perfect for brunch or even dinner. Use a variety of bagels such as rye, pumpernickel, and plain to give it color and interesting flavor.

3   large day-old bagels
4   ounces low-fat Cheddar cheese, grated
4   eggs (or substitute), beaten
2¼ cups milk
2   to 3 teaspoons Dijon mustard
Salt and pepper to taste
**Optional:**
2   green onions, chopped
1   cup chopped fresh spinach (or ½ cup frozen, drained)
Parmesan cheese

1. Cut the bagels into 1-inch cubes.
2. In a medium bowl combine the remaining ingredients except the Parmesan cheese. Add the bagels and mix well.
3. Refrigerate for 20 to 30 minutes.
4. Spray an 8-inch square baking pan with cooking spray. Pour the bagel mixture into the prepared pan. Sprinkle with Parmesan cheese, if desired. Bake at 325° for 50 to 60 minutes.

YIELD: 4 servings

| Total calories: | | 1,700 |
| Calories per serving: | | 425 |

|  | Grams | % of recipe |
| --- | --- | --- |
| CARB | 52 | 50 |
| PRO | 23 | 20 |
| FAT | 14 | 30 |

## Peanut Butter Granola

This delicious cereal comes out in clumps, and is yummy with milk for breakfast or plain as a nutritious snack. It is handy for breakfast-in-a-bag, if you are eating on the run. The peanut butter adds protein and also some fat that will "stick to your ribs" and keep you from feeling hungry for a while.

¼   to ⅓ cup peanut butter
½   cup firmly packed brown sugar
½   cup apple juice
1   teaspoon salt
2½ cups old-fashioned rolled oats
**Optional:**
1   teaspoon vanilla extract
½   cup raisins
½   cup chopped dried apricots, dates, and/or dried apple
½   cup sunflower seeds or coconut
½   cup wheat germ

1. In a medium bowl combine the peanut butter, sugar, apple juice, and salt. Mix well.
2. Add the oats and mix well. Add more apple juice if the mixture seems too dry or isn't clumping together. Stir in the vanilla if desired.
3. Spray a baking sheet with cooking spray. Spread the granola on the prepared baking sheet.
4. Bake at 300° for 20 to 25 minutes, stirring occasionally, until golden brown.
5. After the granola has cooled, add the optional ingredients. Store in an airtight container.

YIELD: about 3½ cups, 7 servings

| Total calories: | | 2,000 |
| Calories per ½ cup: | | 285 |

|  | Grams | % of recipe |
| --- | --- | --- |
| CARB | 50 | 70 |
| PRO | 7 | 10 |
| FAT | 6 | 20 |

## 1988

The men's field was the strongest it had been for this race in five years. In their first match-up since American Joan Samuelson's victory in the 1984 Olympics, Grete Waitz emerged victorious, recording her ninth NYC Marathon win. Steve Jones of Great Britain notched his first NYC Marathon win, recording the second fastest time for the race, barely missing the course record by seven seconds.

## 1989

For the first time in the same race the field included the Olympic Marathon gold medalist, the defending champion, and the world record holder. More personal best times were set than ever before. Juma Ikangaa left all challengers by 15 miles and ran 12 seconds faster than the 1981 course record (set by Alberto Salazar.) He finished literally jumping up and down for joy.

Ingrid Kristiansen finished one second off the women's course record and won her thirteenth of twenty-one career marathons.

There were so many runners this year that they surrounded the starting cannon. It was decided not to use it for safety reasons.

## 1990

Kenyan native Douglas Wakiihuri won the race. Sometime before the race, his meticulous Japanese coach spent an entire day being driven over every mile of the route, asking scores of questions. John Campbell of New Zealand placed fifth overall, and clocked a new NYC masters (over age forty) record of 2:14:34.

American Kim Jones stalked Polish-born Wanda Panfil through Central Park, only to come up five seconds short. Adopted New Yorker Grete Waitz finished a creditable fourth after a two-year battle with injuries. Broadcasts, both live and taped, reached approximately twenty-six countries. The race was dedicated to Fred Lebow. Runners rallied behind the fund-raising theme, "Fred, This Run's for You" to raise $1.2 million for cancer research.

## 1991

This was the year of the Mexicans, three of whom placed in the top five. Winner Salvador Garcia ran his best time, followed by Andres Espinoza, with Isidrio Rico fifth. Scottish native Liz McColgan ran the fastest marathon debut for a woman, winning in 2:27:32. Fred Lebow's campaign for cancer research continued and was titled "Put Cancer on the Run."

## 1992

Fred Lebow celebrated his sixtieth birthday and his remission from brain cancer by running in the race he helped create. His partner and coach was nine-time NYC Marathon winner Grete Waitz, who finished together with Lebow in 5:32:34. Lisa Ondieki of Australia set a women's course record of 2:24:40. Willie Mtolo, competing soon after the lifting of international sanctions that had previously banned South African athletes from competing outside their own country, outsprinted Andres Espinosa for the win.

## 1993

After placing second twice, Andres Espinosa of Mexico had his victory day. German medical student Uta Pippig took the women's race. The cancer fundraising continued for the fourth year with the theme, "This One's for the Children." This year's race boasted more than one hundred male and female runners over the age of seventy.

## Swiss Bircher Muesli

Olympian marathoner Gabriele Andersen says that in Switzerland this is often eaten at lunch or as a light dinner with some bread and cheese. It is also great for breakfast.

½ cup oats (regular or quick-cooking)
4 ounces plain low-fat yogurt
1 tablespoon lemon juice
1 small apple, grated
1 small banana, sliced
3 tablespoons raisins
Honey or sugar to taste
**Optional:**
½ cup hazelnuts or walnuts, grated or chopped
1 cup strawberries, raspberries, blackberries, or blueberries
1 cup peaches, apricots, or pears, sliced
1 cup pitted cherries

1. In a large bowl combine the oats and yogurt. Add the lemon juice and grated apples. Mix immediately to avoid discoloration of the apples.
2. Add the banana and raisins. Add any of the optional ingredients desired.
3. Sweeten to taste with honey or sugar.

YIELD: 1 serving

| Total calories: | | 450 |
|---|---|---|
| | Grams | % of recipe |
| CARB | 95 | 85 |
| PRO | 12 | 10 |
| FAT | 3 | 5 |

## Fruit and Rice Cereal

When you cook rice, plan to cook extra to have on hand for an excellent high-carbohydrate breakfast food. The following rice-based cereal is nourishing, delicious, crunchy, and anything but boring. When made with brown rice it has a nice nutty flavor.

To simplify preparation, cut the fruit and nuts with a paring knife right over the saucepan into the heating rice, oat, and milk mixture.

½ cup cooked rice
⅓ cup uncooked rolled oats
¾ cup milk, more or less as needed for consistency
1 tablespoon brown sugar
3 dashes cinnamon
Salt to taste
**Optional:**
3 dried apricots, cut into small pieces
8 raw almonds, chopped
¼ tart apple, cut up
¼ cup blueberries, fresh or frozen

1. In a saucepan combine all of the ingredients except the blueberries. Cook over medium-high heat, stirring often, for about 3 to 5 minutes or until thick and hot.
2. Add the blueberries and continue cooking just until the blueberries are heated, less than 1 minute.
3. Pour the cereal into a serving bowl and serve immediately with more brown sugar and milk.

YIELD: 1 serving

| Total calories (without fruit): | | 300 |
|---|---|---|
| | Grams | % of recipe |
| CARB | 58 | 80 |
| PRO | 12 | 15 |
| FAT | 2 | 5 |

## Pumpkin Oatmeal

Vegetable for breakfast?! Why not? Pumpkin oatmeal is a delicious way to start the day and you'll be getting a jump on your daily requirement for vitamin A before lunchtime.

½ cup rolled oats
1 cup water
¼ cup cooked (canned) pumpkin
Dash cinnamon
Salt to taste
1 tablespoon brown sugar or molasses
**Optional:**
Chopped pecans or sunflower seeds

1. In a saucepan cook the oats in the water according to the package directions.
2. When the oatmeal is done, add the pumpkin, cinnamon, salt, and brown sugar. Continue cooking over high heat, stirring constantly, for about 1 minute or until hot.
3. Pour the cereal into a serving bowl and serve immediately with more brown sugar and milk.
4. For a special touch, sprinkle with chopped pecans or sunflower seeds.

YIELD: 1 serving

| Total calories: | | 225 |
|---|---|---|
| | Grams | % of recipe |
| CARB | 45 | 80 |
| PRO | 5 | 10 |
| FAT | 3 | 10 |

## Breakfast Bars

These are packed with iron and carbohydrates, a perfect breakfast-on-the-run or quick snack.

½   cup chopped dried apricots
½   cup chopped dates
½   cup yogurt or buttermilk
1   egg (or substitute)
1   tablespoon vegetable oil
⅓   cup firmly packed brown sugar
¼   teaspoon salt
1   cup bran flakes
1   teaspoon baking soda
½   cup whole-wheat flour

**Optional:**
1   teaspoon grated orange rind
¼   cup chopped almonds or walnuts
1   teaspoon vanilla extract

1. Soak the apricots and dates in hot water for about 10 minutes while you prepare the other ingredients, then drain.
2. In a mixing bowl beat together the yogurt, egg, oil, sugar, and salt. Add the bran flakes. Add the baking soda and flour, then stir in the drained apricots and dates.
3. Spray an 8-inch baking dish with cooking spray. Pour the batter into the prepared dish.
4. Bake at 375° for 25 minutes. Cook before cutting into bars.

Yield: 12 bars

| Total calories: | | 1,300 |
|---|---|---|
| Calories per serving: | | 110 |

| | Grams | % of recipe |
|---|---|---|
| CARB | 21 | 75 |
| PRO | 2 | 10 |
| FAT | 2 | 15 |

## Oatmeal Pancakes

These pancakes are light and fluffy prizewinners, perfect for carbo-loading or recovering from a long run.

½   cup rolled oats
½   cup yogurt or buttermilk
½   to ¾ cup milk
1   egg (or substitute)
1   tablespoon oil, preferably canola
2   tablespoons firmly packed brown sugar
½   teaspoon salt, or to taste
1   teaspoon baking powder
½   teaspoon baking soda
1   cup flour, half white, half whole-wheat

**Optional:**
Dash cinnamon
1   cup blueberries or raspberries
¼   cup raw, shelled, unsalted sunflower seeds

1. In a medium bowl combine the first three ingredients. Set the bowl aside for about 15 to 20 minutes. This allows the oatmeal to soften.
2. When the oatmeal is through soaking, beat in the egg and oil, and mix well. Add the sugar, salt, and cinnamon, then the baking powder, baking soda, and flour.
3. Heat a large nonstick or lightly oiled skillet over medium heat.
4. For each pancake, pour about ⅓ cup of the batter onto the skillet. Cook pancakes until the edges are dry, and bubbles and holes form on top, about 2 minutes, being careful not to overcook the bottom. Flip each cake and continue cooking until lightly browned.
5. Serve with maple syrup.

Yield: 3 servings

| Total calories: | | 1,000 |
|---|---|---|
| Calories per serving (2 6" pancakes): | | 330 |

| | Grams | % of recipe |
|---|---|---|
| CARB | 52 | 65 |
| PRO | 13 | 15 |
| FAT | 8 | 20 |

With 2 tablespoons maple syrup:

| Calories per serving: | | 460 |
|---|---|---|

| | Grams | % of recipe |
|---|---|---|
| CARB | 84 | 75 |
| PRO | 13 | 10 |
| FAT | 8 | 15 |

## Blueberry Pancakes

Any pancake can be made fancy with blueberries. Keep frozen berries on hand so you can enjoy wonderful blueberry pancakes anytime. A half-cup of blueberries contains 40 calories and 10 grams of carbohydrates.

*Fresh or frozen blueberries*
1   recipe pancake batter (see Oatmeal Pancakes or Whole-Wheat Pancakes)

1. Prepare the pancake batter according to the recipe.
2. Preheat a nonstick or lightly greased skillet over medium heat. Pour about ⅓ cup of batter onto the skillet for each pancake.
3. Dot the top of each pancake with blueberries. Cook until the edges of the pancakes are done and bubbles form on top.
4. Turn and cook until golden. Watch the bottoms carefully as the blueberries tend to darken easily.

## THE INTERNATIONAL BREAKFAST RUN

1994 marks the sixteenth year of this celebration, a virtual "United Nations on the Roads." The event is always held the Saturday before the Marathon, when runners from ninety-one countries assemble at the United Nations headquarters in Manhattan. Carrying their national flags, they jog several miles to the finish line in Central Park for breakfast outside the Tavern on the Green restaurant. More than ten thousand international runners participate—ranking this as one of the largest races in the United States. Two runner's standards are part of the morning: food, in the form of a continental breakfast, and special T-shirts.

## Whole-Wheat Pancakes

These basic pancakes provide loads of carbohydrates to keep you going all morning long. Serve with maple syrup, honey, preserves, or fresh fruit and yogurt.

1   egg (or substitute)
1   cup milk
1   tablespoon oil, preferably canola
2   tablespoons firmly packed brown sugar
¼   teaspoon salt, or to taste
2   teaspoons baking powder
½   cup whole-wheat flour
½   cup white flour

**Optional:**
*Diced fruit or chopped nuts*

1. In a medium bowl beat together the egg, milk, oil, sugar, and salt. Add the baking powder and flour.

2. Heat a large nonstick or lightly oiled skillet over medium heat. For each pancake pour about ⅓ cup of batter onto the skillet.

3. Cook until the edges are dry and bubbles and holes appear on top of the pancake. Flip over and continue cooking until the bottom is lightly browned, being careful not to burn them.

YIELD: 2 servings

| Total calories: | 700 |
| --- | --- |
| Calories per serving (2 6" pancakes): | 350 |

|  | Grams | % of recipe |
| --- | --- | --- |
| CARB | 57 | 60 |
| PRO | 13 | 15 |
| FAT | 9 | 25 |

With 2 tablespoons syrup:

| Total calories: |  | 480 |
| --- | --- | --- |
| CARB | 99 | 80 |
| PRO | 13 | 10 |
| FAT | 9 | 10 |

# 7 BREADS AND MUFFINS

Although man cannot live by bread alone, many runners thrive on this fundamental carbohydrate-rich food. Here are some baking tips adapted from Nancy Clark's Sports Nutrition Guidebook (Leisure Press, 1990) to help you bake the yummiest of breads.

1. The secret to light and fluffy quick breads, muffins, biscuits, and scones is to stir the flour lightly and for only 20 seconds. Ignore the lumps! If you beat the batter too much, the gluten (protein) in the flour will toughen the dough. This tip is particularly important when making low-fat quick breads because the reduced fat content results in a tougher dough even if not over-stirred.

2. Breads made entirely with whole-wheat flour tend to be heavy and less popular. In general, half whole-wheat and half white flour is an appropriate combination, and these recipes have been developed using this ratio. But you can alter this ratio as you desire. In general, when substituting whole-wheat for all-purpose flour in other recipes, use ¾ cup whole-wheat for 1 cup white flour.

3. Most of these recipes have reduced sugar content (or a range from which you can choose). To reduce the sugar content of your own recipes, use one-third to one-half less sugar than indicated; the finished product will be just fine. If you want to replace white sugar with honey, brown sugar, or molasses, use only ½ teaspoon baking powder per 2 cups of flour and add ½ teaspoon baking soda. This prevents an "off" taste.

4. To reduce the cholesterol content, substitute ¼ cup cholesterol-free egg product or 2 egg whites for 1 egg.

5. Most quick bread recipes instruct you to sift together the baking powder and flour. This method produces the lightest breads and the best results. In some of these recipes, I instruct you to mix the baking powder in with the wet ingredients and gently add the flour last. My method is easier, produces an acceptable product, and saves time and energy.

"To believe this story you must believe that the human race can be one joyous family, working together, laughing together, achieving the impossible. I believe it because I saw it happen. Last Sunday, 12,000 men, women, and children from 40 countries of the world, assisted by 2.5 million black, white, and yellow people, Protestants and Catholics, Jews and Muslims, Buddhists and Confucians, laughed, cheered, and suffered during the greatest folk festival the world has seen."

—CHRIS BRASHER, now Director of the London Marathon after his first NYC Marathon in 1979

"We are here to be heroes. The marathon is one way we prove it to ourselves. . . . The marathon is a theater for heroism, the common man and an uncommon challenge. [It shows] the extraordinary powers of ordinary people."

—the late GEORGE SHEEHAN, M.D., author and runner.

*Miki Gorman, New York City Marathon champion in 1976 and 1977, was the first woman to run the race under 2:40.*

6. *To prevent breads from sticking, use nonstick baking pans, treat the pan with cooking spray, or place a piece of waxed paper in the baking pan before pouring the batter. When using waxed paper, let the bread cool for five minutes after baking, tip it out of the pan, then peel off the paper.*

7. *To hasten cooking time, bake quick breads in an 8-inch square pan instead of a loaf pan. They*

*will bake in half the time. You can also bake muffins in a loaf or square pan, eliminating the hard-to-wash muffin tins!*

## Nina Kuscsik's Holiday Pulla Bread

Nina always looks forward to enjoying this holiday bread that is a family tradition for Easter and Christmas. The nutmeg (or cardamon) adds a distinctive and special taste. Cardamon is an expensive spice, so you may replace it with nutmeg and will barely notice the difference.

This bread is so good it's worth making all seasons of the year, especially if you want to fuel yourself with tasty carbohydrates. To shorten the process, eliminate the first rising and let the dough rise once you have made it into braids. The bread will come out almost as well textured, and just as tasty.

| | |
|---|---|
| 1 | *package active dry yeast* |
| ¼ | *cup lukewarm water (110°)* |
| ½ | *teaspoon sugar* |
| 1 | *cup milk* |
| 1 | *egg (or substitute)* |
| 2 | *teaspoons salt* |
| ½ | *cup sugar* |
| 1 | *to 2 teaspoons nutmeg or cardamon* |
| ⅓ | *cup butter or margarine* |
| 5 | *to 6 cups flour* |
| 1 | *tablespoon sugar for sprinkling on top* |

**Optional:**
*Slivered almonds*

1. In a small bowl sprinkle the yeast and ½ teaspoon of sugar over the lukewarm water.

2. In a separate bowl beat the egg slightly. Set aside 1 tablespoon for brushing on top.

3. In a large bowl combine the sugar, salt, nutmeg or cardamon, butter, and the rest of the beaten egg.

4. Scald 1 cup of milk, then pour it on top of the sugar mixture. Mix well. Cool until lukewarm.

5. Add the yeast mixture, then 4 to 5 cups of flour.

6. Turn the dough onto a slightly floured board, cover, and let it rest for 10 minutes (if you are patient). Knead until smooth and elastic, working in the rest of the flour as needed.

7. Place the dough in a lightly oiled bowl, turning the dough over so it is all covered with oil. Cover and set aside to rise in a warm place until double in bulk.

8. Punch down and divide into 6 equal portions. Cover the portions and let them rise for 10 minutes (if you are patient). Roll each portion into lengthwise strips and use 3 strips for each braid.

9. Braid the dough. Place the braids on the prepared baking sheet. Lightly oil a baking sheet or spray it with cooking spray.

10. Dilute the beaten egg with 1 teaspoon of water. Brush the braids with the mixture. Dust very lightly with sugar and sprinkle with slivered almonds (as desired). Let the braids rise until almost double.

11. Bake at 350° for 25 to 30 minutes.

YIELD: 2 braids, 32 slices

| Total calories: | 3,800 |
|---|---|
| Calories per slice: | 120 |

| | Grams | % of recipe |
|---|---|---|
| CARB | 21 | 70 |
| PRO | 3 | 10 |
| FAT | 3 | 20 |

## Breadsticks

In Amy Pohlman's family, these delicious breadsticks are as much a part of the Thanksgiving dinner as the turkey and cranberry sauce. They are also a great addition to a pasta party. You can vary them by adding Italian seasonings to the dough, or by sprinkling garlic powder or sesame seeds on top. Because these breadsticks are addictive, Amy suggests that you might want to double the recipe!

1   package active dry yeast
¼   cup lukewarm water (110°)
1   teaspoon sugar
1   cup milk, scalded
2   to 4 tablespoons butter or margarine
1½   tablespoons sugar
1   teaspoon salt
2   egg whites
3½   to 4 cups flour, or half white, half whole-wheat

1. In a small bowl sprinkle the yeast and 1 teaspoon of sugar over the lukewarm water.
2. Scald the milk, then cool it in a large mixing bowl. Mix in the margarine, 1½ tablespoons of sugar, salt, and yeast mixture.
3. In a small bowl, beat 1 egg white until stiff. Add it alternately with the flour to the milk-yeast mixture.
4. Turn the dough onto a lightly floured board and knead for 10 minutes, until smooth and elastic. Place the dough in a lightly oiled bowl, turning the dough over so it is thoroughly covered with oil. Cover and set aside to rise in a warm place until double in bulk.

5. Punch the dough down and divide it into 12 "golf balls." Roll each ball into a 12-inch breadstick.
6. Spray a baking sheet with non-stick cooking spray, and then dust with flour or cornmeal. Place the sticks 1 inch apart on the prepared baking sheet.
7. In a small bowl beat the remaining egg white with 2 tablespoons of cool water and brush the mixture onto the breadsticks. Sprinkle with cornmeal.
8. Bake at 400° for 10 minutes or until golden brown. Serve warm.

YIELD: 12 breadsticks

| Total calories: | | 2,150 |
| --- | --- | --- |
| Calories per serving: | | 180 |

| | Grams | % of recipe |
| --- | --- | --- |
| CARB | 33 | 75 |
| PRO | 6 | 15 |
| FAT | 3 | 10 |

## Single-Rise Yeast Bread

Jean Smith, member of the Greater Boston Track Club, routinely uses this recipe because it is very simple. The use of powdered milk eliminates the need to scald milk and the single rise (in the bread pan) cuts preparation time to a minimum.

The bread has a slightly sweet taste and a substantial texture. The sesame seeds add a very nice taste and crunch, if you choose to add them. Jean says that if you make this bread into a peanut-butter-and-banana sandwich, you'll have a meal that will stay with you for the long run!

1½   tablespoons yeast (1½ packages)
½   cup lukewarm water (110°)
1   teaspoon sugar
¾   cup oatmeal
2   tablespoons powdered milk
1   tablespoon salt, as desired
2¼   cup boiling water
3   cups whole-wheat flour
¼   cup oil, preferably olive or canola
¼   cup honey
3   to 4 cups white flour
**Optional:**
2   tablespoons sesame seeds

1. In a small bowl sprinkle the yeast over the water. Stir in the sugar and set aside.
2. In a large bowl combine the oatmeal, sesame seeds, powdered milk, and salt. Pour in the boiling water and mix well.
3. Add the whole-wheat flour, and by now the dough should be cool enough to add the yeast without deactivating it.
4. Add the yeast mixture, oil, and honey. Beat well.
5. Mix in the white flour. Turn the dough onto a floured board and knead until smooth and elastic, about 10 minutes.
6. Shape into 2 loaves. Place the loaves in 2 greased bread pans. Cover and set the dough aside to rise until almost double in bulk, about 30 to 45 minutes.
7. Bake at 350° for about 50 minutes while you go for a run. Come back and enjoy the aroma—and the bread.

YIELD: 2 loaves, 32 slices

| Total calories: | | 4,000 |
| --- | --- | --- |
| Calories per slice: | | 125 |

| | Grams | % of recipe |
| --- | --- | --- |
| CARB | 24 | 75 |
| PRO | 3 | 10 |
| FAT | 2 | 15 |

## Oatmeal Yeast Bread

This recipe is submitted by Joan Benoit Samuelson. To shorten this preparation time, let the dough rise only once (in the pan). This makes for a slightly courser texture, but otherwise is fine.

Homemade bread is a wonderful gift not only for yourself, but also for hungry friends. If you want to be the most popular person around, try making this recipe. Who knows, perhaps all the carbs will help us ordinary mortals run as fast as Joan!

1   cup rolled oats
1   teaspoon oil, preferably canola
3   tablespoons molasses
¼   cup sugar
1   tablespoon salt
2   cups boiling water
1   package active dry yeast
½   cup lukewarm water (110°)
2   teaspoons sugar
5   cups flour, preferably half
    white, half whole-wheat

1. In a large bowl combine the oats, oil, molasses, sugar, and salt. Pour the boiling water on top and mix together. Set the bowl aside to let the oats soften and the mixture cool.
2. In a small bowl sprinkle the yeast over the water. Stir in the sugar.
3. When the oat mixture has cooled to lukewarm, add the yeast mixture, then the flour.
4. Pour the dough onto a floured board, knead for 10 minutes until smooth and elastic. Place the dough in a lightly oiled bowl, turning the dough over so it is thoroughly covered with oil. Cover and let rise until double in bulk.

5. Punch down the dough, knead again for a few minutes, and then divide into two loaves.
6. Place in bread pans treated with cooking spray. Cover and let rise for 15 to 20 minutes.
7. Bake at 350° for 45 minutes.

YIELD: 2 loaves, 32 slices

| Total calories: | | 3,000 |
| --- | --- | --- |
| Calories per slice: | | 90 |

| | Grams | % of recipe |
| --- | --- | --- |
| CARB | 19 | 85 |
| PRO | 2 | 10 |
| FAT | .5 | 5 |

## Homemade Bagels

This recipe is shared by marathoners Terry and Susan Martell, owners of two bagel shops. Some Bagels in Richmond, Washington, and Some Bagels Too in Kennewick, Washington. They invite you to try this recipe, then come visit their store to see how the products compare! Homemade bagels are more effort, for sure, but a fun project—especially for entertaining kids on a rainy day. Terry and Susan suggest this topping: add chopped green olives into cream cheese, first adding a little milk to get the desired consistency. Spread on a hot bagel. Yes!

2   packages active dry yeast
2   cups lukewarm water (110°)
3   tablespoons sugar
1   tablespoon salt
5   to 6 cups flour, preferably high-
    gluten bread flour
Cornmeal
1   egg (or substitute), beaten with
    1 tablespoon water
**Optional:**
Sesame, poppy, and/or caraway
    seeds to sprinkle on top

1. In a large bowl sprinkle the yeast over the lukewarm water. Stir in the sugar and salt.
2. Slowly add 4 cups of flour, mixing well. Blend in the remaining flour until the dough is firm enough to handle.
3. Turn the dough onto a floured surface and knead for about 10 to 20 minutes, until it is smooth and no longer sticky, using more flour as needed. Bagel dough will be stiffer than bread dough.
4. Place the dough in an oiled bowl, turning it over so the top of the dough is slightly oiled. Cover and set aside to rise in a warm place for about 40 minutes.
5. Punch the dough down and form to resemble French bread. Divide into 18 pieces. Try not to handle the dough too much.
6. Form the bagel using one of two methods: The easiest is to roll the bagel piece into a ball, hold the ball with two hands and push a thumb through to create the hole. The second method is more traditional. Roll each piece into a rope about 8-inches long and tapered at the ends. Shape the ropes into rings, rolling the ends together firmly.
7. Place the bagels on a surface lightly covered with cornmeal. Cover and let rise in a warm place for about 20 minutes.
8. Bring a large pan of water to a boil. Place the bagels a few at a

time into the boiling water. Boil for 1 to 2 minutes on each side. Remove from the boiling water with a slotted spoon and place on a baking sheet that has been sprinkled with corn-meal.

9. Brush* each bagel with the beaten egg (or just egg white), then sprinkle with sesame, poppy, or caraway seeds, as desired. Plain bagels do not need an egg wash. (*If you

have no brush, simply use your fingertips.)

10. Bake at 410° for about 20 to 25 minutes or until golden.

YIELD: 18 bagels

| Total calories: | | 2,700 |
| Calories per bagel: | | 150 |

| | Grams | % of recipe |
| --- | --- | --- |
| CARB | 32 | 85 |
| PRO | 5 | 12 |
| FAT | .5 | 3 |

### Pesto Bagel

This bagel is a popular flavor at Terry and Susan Martell's bagel shop. They say that it is great with sandwiches and hamburgers. To the above bagel recipe, make this variation: When adding the sugar and salt, add 2 tablespoons of garlic powder and ¼ cup of chopped fresh basil leaves. After boiling, brush the bagel with the egg wash then top with Parmesan cheese.

# THE NEW YORK ROAD RUNNERS CLUB

Every year, scores of spectators are inspired by the New York City Marathon. They decide to start running—or walking. That's when many call the New York Road Runners Club (NYRRC).

The NYRRC, best known as the organizer of the New York City Marathon, is the largest and most active running organization in the world. Now serving more than thirty thousand members, the club was founded in 1958 and is dedicated to developing the sport of running for fun, fitness, and competition.

Members primarily come from the New York metropolitan area, but many also come from the fifty states and more than fifty foreign countries. Runners of all ages and occupations belong.

Working in partnership with corporate sponsors, the NYRRC conducts some of the best-known sponsored events in the country. In addition to the Marathon, these include the Chemical Corporate Challenge, the Advil Mini Marathon, the Race for the Cure, the Trevira Twosome, and the Reebok New York Games.

The club conducts more than one hundred events each year for runners and walkers, from age two and

up and including physically challenged athletes. In addition to road races, the NYRRC conducts classes, clinics, safety programs, and fundraising to improve city services, specifically in recreational areas such as parks.

The club's headquarters features a comprehensive international library and the Running Gallery that sells New York City Marathon and NYRRC merchandise. Throughout the year, prominent athletes, medical specialists, and other fitness experts are part of the club's programs. A core staff of about forty-five is supplemented by hundreds of volunteers.

The NYRRC provides technical services to races and sporting events around the world, including other international marathons and races and the Olympic Games. The club is a founding member of AIMS (Association of International Marathons), the professional marathon association.

For further information, including a free calendar of events and the many benefits of club membership—which include regular mailings and a subscription to *New York Running News* magazine—send a self-addressed stamped envelope to the NYRRC at 9 East 89th Street, New York, NY 10128, or call (212) 860–4455.

## Pumpkin Cranberry Bread

Although cranberries and the winter holidays are synonymous, this recipe uses canned cranberry sauce so you don't need to worry about trying to find fresh ones. Whatever the season, bake a loaf and enjoy!

Because the recipe calls for using half-cans of pumpkin and cranberry sauce, you might want to double the recipe and freeze one loaf or give it to a friend.

1   cup pumpkin (½ of a 16-ounce can)
1   cup whole berry cranberry sauce (½ of a 16-ounce can)
¼   cup oil, preferably canola
1   to 2 eggs (or substitute), slightly beaten
½   to ¾ cup sugar
½   to 1 teaspoon salt
1   teaspoon cinnamon
2   cups flour, half white, half whole-wheat as desired
1   teaspoon baking soda
½   teaspoon baking powder

**Optional:**
¼   teaspoon ginger
¼   teaspoon nutmeg
¼   teaspoon cloves
1   teaspoon vanilla extract
½   cup chopped walnuts or pecans

1. Grease a 9x5-inch loaf pan.
2. In a large bowl stir together the cranberry sauce, pumpkin, oil, eggs, and sugar until well mixed.
3. Add the cinnamon, salt, baking soda, and baking powder.
4. Gently stir in the flour until all ingredients are just moistened. Add nuts, if desired.
4. Pour the batter into the prepared pan. Bake at 350° for 45 to 60 minutes or until a toothpick inserted near the center comes out clean.
5. Cool the loaf in the pan for 10 minutes then remove to a cooling rack.

YIELD: 1 loaf, 16 slices

| Total calories: | | 2,300 |
|---|---|---|
| Calories per slice: | | 145 |

|  | Grams | % of recipe |
|---|---|---|
| CARB | 25 | 70 |
| PRO | 2 | 10 |
| FAT | 4 | 20 |

# THE BEST BAGEL

Without a doubt, carbohydrate-rich bagels are the mainstay of many runners' diets—not just the runners who live in New York. But runners disagree about what makes the best bagel. What's your vote?

- The best bagel is crispy and crusty, not doughy on the inside and *covered* with sesame seeds.—*L. Lynder*

- The best bagel is fresh, warm, chewy, and big enough to be a meal.—*G. Bakoulis*

- The best bagel is not too big, not too thick, not doughy. I like them petite, with a golden sheen, lots of sesame seeds, and a little bit of butter and cream cheese.—*N. Sander*

- Big and doughy. Because I like a variety of kinds of bagels, I keep an assortment in the freezer, then defrost one quickly in the microwave oven, and top it with peanut butter.—*M. Keohane*

- I like lighter bagels, like egg bagels, that aren't too dense, topped with cream cheese, lox, and onion, what else! It has to have a nice round hole, and it should fight back a little when I bite into it.—*F. Kirsch*

- When I'm in the mood for something sweet, I go for a cinnamon raisin bagel—big, warm, fresh from the oven. But it has to be a New York bagel. New York bagels are the best because they are made with New York water (or so I overheard from some women talking in the bakery).—*J. Morrill*

- When I'm in the States, a pumpernickle bagel is the closest I can find to resemble the Norwegian bread that I miss. I toast the bagel, then top it with thin slices of Norwegian Goat Cheese. The cheese has a different but sweet, nutlike flavor that I enjoy.—*G. Waitz*

- Big and soft—not hard, toasted with preserves or jam for a snack, or with lettuce, sun-dried tomato, and onion for lunch.—*P. Welch*

- Poppyseed, sesame seed—anything but plain.—*B. Franks*

## Cheese Danish

Fred Lebow's sister, Sarah, shares this recipe that was enjoyed not only at Fred's bar mitzvah, but also as a part of family living. As children growing up in Romania, Fred and Sarah's family was among the few that had a telephone, so neighbors would commonly come to their house to do business. Mrs. Lebowitz would always have coffee and often these cheese danishes. No wonder the house was a popular gathering place!

1    package active dry yeast
1    teaspoon sugar
¼    cup lukewarm water (110°)
½    cup butter or margarine
4    to 5 cups white flour
⅓    cup sugar
1    tablespoon salt
1    egg
½    cup club soda or water or scalded milk

**Filling:**
2    tablespoons cream of wheat cooked in ½ cup milk
1    cup part-skim Ricotta or farmer cheese
1    egg yolk (save the white for later use)
⅓    cup sugar
1    teaspoon vanilla extract
1    tablespoon lemon juice
Grated rind of half a lemon
1    egg white beaten with 1 teaspoon water

**Optional:**
Grated rind of half a lemon
Confectioners' sugar for sprinkling on the top

1. In a small bowl dissolve yeast and 1 teaspoon of sugar in the lukewarm water. Set aside.

2. In a large bowl blend the butter or margarine into 2 cups of flour until crumbly. Make a well, and add the yeast-water mixture, sugar, salt, egg, club soda, and grated lemon rind. Mix well, then blend in the remaining flour. Turn the dough onto a floured surface and knead until smooth and elastic.

3. Make the filling. In a mixing bowl combine the cooked cream of wheat, Ricotta cheese, egg yolk, sugar, vanilla, lemon juice, and grated lemon rind. Set aside.

4. Roll out the dough on a floured surface to ¼-inch thickness. Cut into 4-inch squares. Place a spoonful of the cheese filling in the center, then fold in the side corners, pinching the sides together as best you can to prevent the filling from oozing out. (Practice helps!)

5. Place the pastries on a baking sheet. With your finger tips or a brush, coat the dough with the beaten egg white. Let the pastries rise for 10 to 20 minutes. Bake at 350° for about 25 to 30 minutes or until golden.

6. Sprinkle with confectioners' sugar if desired.

YIELD: 20 danish

| Total calories: | | 4,000 |
|---|---|---|
| Calories per danish: | | 200 |

| | Grams | % of recipe |
|---|---|---|
| CARB | 30 | 60 |
| PRO | 5 | 10 |
| FAT | 7 | 30 |

## Priscilla Welch's Favorite Banana Bread

When Priscilla has too many bananas that are getting too ripe, she makes a loaf of banana bread—perfect for breakfast and snacks. Her favorite recipe is taken from Nancy Clark's first book, *The Athlete's Kitchen*.

3    large bananas, the riper the better
1    egg (or substitute)
2    tablespoons oil, preferably canola
⅓    to ½ cup sugar
¼    cup milk
1    teaspoon salt, as desired
1    teaspoon baking soda
½    teaspoon baking powder
1½   cups flour, preferably half white, half whole-wheat

1. Spray a 9x5-inch loaf pan with cooking spray.

2. In a large bowl mash the bananas with a fork.

3. Add the egg, oil, sugar, milk, and salt. Beat well, then add the baking soda and baking powder.

4. Gently blend the flour into the banana mixture. Stir for 20 seconds or until just moistened.

5. Pour the batter into the prepared pan.

6. Bake at 350° for 45 minutes or until a toothpick inserted near the middle comes out clean.

YIELD: 1 loaf, 12 slices

| Total calories: | | 1,600 |
|---|---|---|
| Calories per slice: | | 140 |

| | Grams | % of recipe |
|---|---|---|
| CARB | 24 | 70 |
| PRO | 3 | 10 |
| FAT | 3 | 20 |

## Irish Soda Bread

This bread tastes best when laced with caraway seeds, but if you have none on hand, make it anyway and you'll still have a good-tasting product. Or, if you buy some especially for making this bread and wonder what to do with the leftovers, try making Rice with Celery and Caraway (page 183), or sprinkle on the tops of Homemade Bagels (page 100).

2   cups flour, half white, half
    whole-wheat as desired
2   teaspoons baking powder
½   teaspoon baking soda
½   teaspoon salt
2   teaspoons caraway seeds
1   cup raisins
1   egg (or substitute)
⅓   cup oil
1   cup milk, preferably low-fat

1. Spray a 9-inch round baking pan with cooking spray.
2. In a mixing bowl, combine the flour, baking powder, baking soda, salt, caraway seeds, and raisins.
3. In a separate bowl beat together the egg, oil, and milk. Add the liquid ingredients to the flour mixture. Gently stir until just blended.
4. Put the dough in the prepared baking pan, forming it into a round loaf. Make an 'X' in the top of the dough with a knife.
5. Bake at 375° for 35 to 40 minutes or until nicely browned. Slice into wedges.

YIELDS: 1 loaf, 16 wedges

| Total calories: | | 2,000 |
| --- | --- | --- |
| Calories per wedge: | | 125 |

| | Grams | % of recipe |
| --- | --- | --- |
| CARB | 18 | 60 |
| PRO | 2 | 5 |
| FAT | 5 | 35 |

## Whole-Wheat Raisin Quick Bread

This is delicious toasted for breakfast, with peanut butter for lunch, with soup and salad for supper, and plain for snacks.

1½  cups plain yogurt, or 1½ cups
    milk with 2 tablespoons of
    vinegar, or 1½ cups buttermilk
¼   cup oil, preferably canola
½   cup molasses
½   cup sugar
½   cup raisins
1   teaspoon salt
1½  teaspoons baking soda
1½  teaspoons baking powder
½   cup white flour
2½  cups whole-wheat flour

1. Spray a 9x5-inch loaf pan with cooking spray.
2. In a large bowl mix together the yogurt, oil, molasses, sugar, raisins, and salt. Beat well.
3. Add the baking powder and baking soda, then gently add the flour, stirring just until blended.
4. Pour the batter into the prepared pan.
5. Bake at 350° for 1 hour, or until a toothpick inserted near the center comes out clean.

YIELD: 1 loaf, 16 slices

| Total calories: | | 2,850 |
| --- | --- | --- |
| Calories per serving: | | 180 |

| | Grams | % of recipe |
| --- | --- | --- |
| CARB | 33 | 75 |
| PRO | 3 | 10 |
| FAT | 3 | 15 |

## Whole-Wheat Yogurt Biscuits

Margaret Groos, winner of the 1988 Olympic Marathon Trials, likes this recipe. The biscuits are extra good when served with honey or preserves—all in the name of carbo-loading!

1   cup whole-wheat flour
1   cup white flour
2   teaspoons baking powder
½   teaspoon baking soda
½   teaspoon salt
⅓   cup butter or margarine
1   cup plain nonfat yogurt
2   to 4 tablespoons honey

1. Spray a baking sheet with cooking spray.
2. In a large bowl stir together the dry ingredients.
3. With the back of a large spoon, blend the butter into the dry ingredients until the mixture resembles cornmeal.
4. Add the yogurt and honey, stirring just until moistened. The dough will be very sticky.
5. On a floured surface with floured hands pat or roll the dough out to ¾-inch thickness. Cut with a glass or biscuit cutter. Arrange the biscuits on the prepared baking sheet.
6. Bake at 425° for about 10 minutes. Watch very carefully, they burn easily.

YIELD: 12 biscuits

| Total calories: | | 1,650 |
| --- | --- | --- |
| Calories per biscuit: | | 140 |

| | Grams | % of recipe |
| --- | --- | --- |
| CARB | 19 | 55 |
| PRO | 3 | 10 |
| FAT | 6 | 35 |

# FRED LEBOW

**FRED LEBOW** is widely acknowledged as the genius behind orchestrating marathons in major cities. He is also one of the major influences on the running boom in this country and abroad and renowned for contributing innovative ideas and programs to the sport. He has been the director of the New York City Marathon since its inception in 1970, the president of the New York Road Runners Club (NYRRC) from 1972–93, and is currently the club chairman.

Lebow was instrumental in turning the New York City Marathon from a small event in Central Park to its present five-borough version. He also created the Club's many other original events, such as the Advil Mini Marathon, the original and most prestigious women's long-distance running event in the world, the Fifth Avenue Mile, and the Empire State Building Run-Up.

Lebow established the New York Games, an international Grand Prix track and field meet, reintroduced the Six Day Run in New York, and successfully bid for and conducted the IAAF XII World Cross Country Championships in 1984 (the first time the event had been held in North America), and conducted America's Ekiden Relay in 1987–88.

Lebow built the NYRRC from a kitchen-table operation with several hundred members to the largest organization of its kind in the world. The organization is housed in the International Running Center, a headquarters for running worldwide.

Lebow was born in 1932 in Transylvania, Romania. He spent extensive time in Ireland, Czechoslovakia, and several other European countries before coming to the United States. After moving to New York City, he was able to make a successful career in the textile and garment industry. He first started running to improve his stamina for tennis. One thing led to another, however, and what Lebow took up as a hobby became his entire life. In 1979, he gave up the garment industry and became affiliated with the NYRRC full time.

He has completed a total of sixty-nine marathons in more than thirty countries. He first ran his own marathon in its first edition in 1970. In 1992, two years after being diagnosed with brain cancer, while in remission, he ran his first five-borough New York City Marathon.

Lebow is the co-author of *The New York Road Runners Club Complete Book of Running* (Random House, 1992).

## Corn Bread

Homemade corn bread is a delightful accompaniment to bean soups. What a wonderful way to eat complementary proteins! This version is low in fat and full of flavor, using molasses and whole corn. Because overcooked corn bread tends to be very dry, be careful to remove this from the oven when it is just lightly golden. Cooking tip: Measure the molasses in the same cup as the oil and the molasses will slide right out without sticking.

1    cup milk
¼    cup oil, preferably canola
2    tablespoons molasses
¼    cup sugar
1    egg (or substitute), slightly beaten
1    teaspoon baking powder
½    teaspoon baking soda
½    teaspoon salt
1¼   cups flour, half white, half whole-wheat, as desired
¾    cup cornmeal
½    to 1 cup corn, fresh, frozen, or canned

**Optional:**
¼    cup sesame seeds

1. Grease a 9-inch square baking dish.
2. In a mixing bowl combine the milk, oil, molasses, sugar, and egg.
3. Add the baking powder, baking soda, and salt. Blend in the flour, cornmeal, and corn kernels. Stir until just moistened, being careful not to overmix.
4. Pour the batter into the prepared baking dish. Bake at 400° for 15 to 20 minutes.
5. Cut into 12 squares and serve warm, plain, or with jam or honey.

YIELD: 12 squares

| Total calories: | | 1,900 |
|---|---|---|
| Calories per serving: | | 158 |

| | Grams | % of recipe |
|---|---|---|
| CARB | 20 | 65 |
| PRO | 3 | 10 |
| FAT | 3 | 25 |

# ALLAN STEINFELD

**ALLAN STEINFELD** is the Technical Director of the New York City Marathon. If Fred Lebow has dreams, Allan Steinfeld makes them reality. Steinfeld has a reputation as the nation's leading authority on the technical aspects of road running. For nearly two decades, he has developed methods that have become the standard for marathons and other races. His New York City Marathon magic is also a family affair. His wife, Alice Schneider, helped create and develop the innovative computer scoring system for the race that has also served as a model worldwide.

At the 1984 Los Angeles Olympics, Steinfeld was chief referee of the men's and women's marathons. Additionally, he has been a technical adviser for the network television broadcasts of the Olympic Games since 1984.

Steinfeld, who has worked at the NYRRC since 1978, is currently the president of the club and the race director of other prestigious events. Besides his involvement with the NYRRC, he is also a member of an executive committee of USA Track & Field, the governing body of the sport.

Steinfeld earned a master's degree from Cornell University in electrical engineering and radio astronomy. His most memorable New York City Marathon food experience is from 1993. After working feverishly at the finish line every year, he had finally delegated enough responsibilities to his capable staff that he was able to sit down and have lunch for the first time in sixteen years of Marathon monitoring.

## Red Pepper Biscuits

These biscuits have a lot of flavor and are easy to make. They have a beautiful yellow color with red flecks, a festive addition to a brunch or dinner, or reheat in the toaster oven for a quick snack.

1½ cups flour, half white, half whole-wheat, as desired
1 tablespoon baking powder
½ teaspoon salt
1 to 2 dashes cayenne pepper
1 to 2 dashes black pepper
1 teaspoon sugar
¼ cup butter or margarine, at room temperature
⅔ cup finely chopped, drained, bottled roasted red peppers (patted dry before chopping)
⅓ cup milk

**Optional:**
½ cup shredded Monterey Jack cheese, preferably low-fat

1. In a mixing bowl stir together the flour, baking powder, salt, cayenne, sugar, and pepper.
2. Blend the butter into the dry ingredients until the mixture resembles coarse crumbs.
3. Add the roasted peppers, milk, and cheese and stir just until the mixture forms a dough. (Overmixing will make a tough dough.)
4. Spoon the dough into 12 mounds on a nonstick baking sheet.
5. Bake at 425° for 15 to 18 minutes, or until they are golden brown.

YIELD: 12 medium biscuits

| Total calories: | | 1,200 |
|---|---|---|
| Calories per biscuit: | | 100 |

| | Grams | % of recipe |
|---|---|---|
| CARB | 14 | 55 |
| PRO | 2 | 10 |
| FAT | 4 | 35 |

## Joan Benoit Samuelson's Blueberry Muffins

Joan claims that these muffins are best when made with freshly picked Maine blueberries (of course!). They are indeed delicious and can double as a sweet snack. Each muffin has about 9 grams of fat. This is similar to the amount in a standard bakery muffin. If desired, you can cut the oil by half, and still have a tasty product, but it will be less tender and less moist.

1 egg (or substitute)
½ to 1 cup sugar
½ cup oil, preferably canola
¾ cup milk
1 teaspoon salt
1 teaspoon vanilla extract
2 teaspoons cinnamon
2 teaspoons baking powder
2 cups flour, preferably half white, half whole-wheat
2 cups blueberries, fresh or frozen, preferably from Maine

1. Spray 12 muffin cups with cooking spray.
2. In a mixing bowl beat together the egg, sugar, and oil. Add the milk, salt, vanilla, and cinnamon.
3. Stir in the baking powder and flour, then gently fold in the blueberries.
4. Divide the batter into muffin cups. Bake at 400° for 20 minutes or until golden.

YIELD: 12 large muffins

| Total calories: | | 2,500 |
|---|---|---|
| Calories per muffin: | | 210 |

| | Grams | % of recipe |
|---|---|---|
| CARB | 28 | 55 |
| PRO | 3 | 5 |
| FAT | 9 | 40 |

## Wheat-Germ Muffins

These muffins filled with vitamin E-rich wheat germ can boost your daily intake of this hard-to-find vitamin that may protect against heart disease, cancer, and even muscle injuries.

This recipe makes only 10 nice-sized muffins; fill the empty muffin cups with water before putting the pan into the oven.

1 egg (or substitute)
⅓ cup firmly packed brown sugar
¼ to ⅓ cup oil
1¼ cup low-fat milk
1 teaspoon salt
½ teaspoon baking soda
2 teaspoons baking powder
1 cup wheat germ
1 cup flour, preferably half white, half whole-wheat

**Optional:**
1 teaspoon cinnamon
½ cup raisins or chopped fruit

1. Spray 10 muffin cups with cooking spray.
2. In a medium bowl beat together the egg, sugar, oil, and milk.
3. Stir in the salt, baking powder, baking soda, and wheat germ. Gently add the flour. The mixture will be soupy, but the wheat germ will absorb the excess moisture. Add optional ingredients as desired.
4. Fill the prepared muffin cups ⅔ full. Bake at 425° about 15 to 20 minutes.

YIELD: 10 muffins

| Total calories: | | 1,800 |
|---|---|---|
| Calories per muffin: | | 180 |

| | Grams | % of recipe |
|---|---|---|
| CARB | 23 | 50 |
| PRO | 6 | 15 |
| FAT | 7 | 35 |

## Oat Bran Muffins

If you have high cholesterol, oat bran eaten in combination with an overall low-fat diet can help lower your cholesterol level. These muffins are one way to boost your oat-bran intake. You can add chopped fruits (fresh, canned, or dried) of your choice for variety.

1½ cups oat bran, uncooked
¼ cup firmly packed brown sugar
1 teaspoon cinnamon
1 teaspoon salt or to taste
2 teaspoons baking powder
1 egg (or substitute)
2 tablespoons oil, preferably canola
1¾ cups low-fat milk
1 cup flour, preferably half white, half whole-wheat

**Optional:**
1 cup chopped apples, peaches, pears, fruit cocktail, etc.
½ cup chopped nuts
½ cup raisins or chopped dried fruits

1. Spray 12 muffin cups with cooking spray. (Do not use paper liners because these muffins tend to stick to them.)
2. In a medium bowl combine the oat bran, brown sugar, cinnamon, salt, and baking powder. Mix well.
3. In a separate bowl, beat the egg with the oil. Add the milk. Blend the liquid mixture into the oat bran mixture. Gently blend in the flour, mixing until just moistened. Add the fruits, as desired.
4. Fill the muffin cups ⅔ full. Bake at 400° for about 20 minutes or until light golden.

YIELD: 12 muffins

| | | |
|---|---|---|
| Total calories: | | 1,550 |
| Calories per muffin: | | 130 |

| | Grams | % of recipe |
|---|---|---|
| CARB | 20 | 60 |
| PRO | 5 | 15 |
| FAT | 4 | 25 |

## The Complete Breakfast Muffin

If you are a muffin lover, this complete breakfast muffin contains a variety of wholesome foods for you to eat on the run, take to the office, or enjoy for an afternoon snack. If the orange juice adds too strong of an orange taste for your liking, simply replace part or all of the juice with milk or water. These taste good spread with a little peanut butter to boost protein and add satiety.

1 cup oatmeal
1 cup All-Bran cereal
2 big bananas, mashed
1 cup orange juice
½ cup nonfat dry milk
½ cup brown sugar
1 egg (or substitute)
¼ cup oil, preferably canola
1 teaspoon salt
1 teaspoon cinnamon
2 teaspoons baking powder
1 cup flour, preferably half white, half whole-wheat

**Optional:**
½ cup raisins or chopped dried fruits
½ cup chopped nuts

1. Spray 12 large muffin cups with cooking spray.
2. In a medium bowl mix together the oatmeal, bran cereal, mashed bananas, orange juice, dry milk, and brown sugar. Mix well.

3. Beat in the egg, oil, salt, and cinnamon. Add the baking powder, flour, raisins, and nuts.
4. Fill the prepared muffin cups ⅔ full.
5. Bake at 400° for 15 to 20 minutes.

YIELD: 12 hefty muffins

| | | |
|---|---|---|
| Calories per muffin: | | 200 |

| | Grams | % of recipe |
|---|---|---|
| CARB | 33 | 65 |
| PRO | 5 | 10 |
| FAT | 5 | 25 |

## Basic Bran Muffins

These are basic bran cereal muffins, tasty and a good source of fiber (5 grams per muffin). Add lots of extras such as raisins, nuts, dried apricots, and spices for extra flavor and variety.

2 cups All-Bran cereal
1¼ cups milk
½ cup firmly packed brown sugar
1 to 2 eggs (or substitute)
¼ cup oil, preferably canola
½ teaspoon salt
1 teaspoon baking powder
½ teaspoon baking soda
1¼ cups flour, half white, half whole-wheat, as desired

**Optional:**
1 teaspoon vanilla extract
½ teaspoon cinnamon
¼ teaspoon nutmeg or allspice
¼ teaspoon cloves
½ cup raisins or walnuts, dried apricots, or dates

1. Spray 12 muffin cups with cooking spray.
2. In a mixing bowl combine the bran cereal and milk. Let the mixture stand until soft, about 3 minutes.

3. Add the brown sugar, eggs, oil, salt, vanilla, cinnamon, nutmeg, cloves, and raisins.
4. Add the baking powder and baking soda. Gently stir in the flour, mixing only until combined.
5. Fill the prepared muffin cups ⅔ full. Bake at 400° for 20 minutes.

YIELD: 12 muffins

| Total calories: | 2,000 |
|---|---|
| Calories per muffin: | 170 |

| | Grams | % of recipe |
|---|---|---|
| CARB | 27 | 60 |
| PRO | 3 | 10 |
| FAT | 5 | 30 |

## Bran Muffins with Molasses and Dates

These muffins are sweet and moist, despite having no added fat. Nice for breakfast or a late-night snack. The acid in the yogurt and molasses, when combined with the baking soda, makes the muffin batter puff up, and contributes to a light texture in the finished product.

½  cup chopped dates
1  cup boiling water
1  egg (or substitute)
⅓  cup molasses
1  cup yogurt or buttermilk
¾  cup unprocessed bran
½  teaspoon salt
1  teaspoon baking soda
1  cup whole-wheat flour
**Optional:**
½  teaspoon cinnamon
1  teaspoon orange rind
1  teaspoon vanilla extract
Cinnamon and sugar

# THE BEST OF NEW YORK

Bagels may be served around the world, but for the real thing, come to New York. Since 1976, every finisher of the New York City Marathon has received a bagel—the quintessential symbol of New York City. Where did this doughnut-shaped bread originate? There are many theories. Here are a few compiled by the Court of Historical Review in San Francisco.

One theory, although disputed, is that the bagel was invented in Vienna by a Polish baker in 1638. It was first fashioned to look like the Polish king's stirrup, which represented military prowess against the Turks. It acquired the name "beugel," a Germanism for "stirrup." Some centuries later, bagels made their way to New Jersey, then across the Hudson to New York. Eventually, Jewish bakers, mostly from Eastern Europe, made them a staple. Bagels, which today come with a variety of toppings and in various flavors, are made by first boiling the dough ring, then baking.

According to Leo Rosten's *The Joys of Yiddish*, bagels were first mentioned in print in the "community regulations of Krakow, Poland, for the year 1610, which stated that bagels would be given as a gift to any woman in childbirth."

1. Soak the chopped dates in boiling water while you prepare the other ingredients.
2. In a large bowl mix together the egg, molasses, yogurt, bran, and salt.
3. Drain the dates and add them to the batter.
4. Gently stir in baking soda, flour, cinnamon, orange rind, and vanilla. Stir just to blend.
5. Spray 9 muffin cups with cooking spray, then fill ⅔ full. Sprinkle the top of each muffin with cinnamon and sugar, if desired.
6. Bake at 350° for 18 to 20 minutes.

YIELD: 9 muffins

| Total calories: | 1,330 |
|---|---|
| Calories per muffin: | 150 |

| | Grams | % of recipe |
|---|---|---|
| CARB | 30 | 85 |
| PRO | 4 | 10 |
| FAT | 1 | 5 |

## Basic Fruit Muffins

These sweet, light muffins are slightly different because the fruit is tucked in the middle, making a nice surprise when you bite into it. Pennsylvania sports nutritionist Marci Leeds invites you to experiment with hiding a variety of fresh, frozen, or canned fruits inside the muffin—peaches, blueberries, raspberries, canned pineapple, banana chunks—whatever suits your fancy.

To reduce the fat content to 25 percent, simply use only ¼ cup of oil, instead of ⅓ cup. For a less sweet muffin, you may also reduce the sugar to ⅓ cup.

1    egg (or substitute)
⅓    to ¼ cup oil, preferably canola
½    to ⅓ cup sugar, as desired
1    cup low-fat milk
½    teaspoon salt
½    tablespoon baking powder
2    cups flour, half white, half whole-wheat, as desired
1½   cups fruit, diced

**Optional:**
1    teaspoon cinnamon
¼    teaspoon cardamon
¼    teaspoon nutmeg
1    teaspoon vanilla extract
2    tablespoons sugar mixed with ½ teaspoon cinnamon

1. Spray 12 muffin cups with cooking spray.
2. In a medium bowl beat together the egg, oil, sugar, milk, and salt. Add either cinnamon, cardamom, or nutmeg if desired, and vanilla extract.
3. Gently blend in the baking powder and the flour.
4. Fill the prepared muffin cups ½ full. Spoon 1 heaping teaspoon of diced fruit into each cup. Fill the rest of each cup with batter.
5. Sprinkle the muffin batter with the cinnamon sugar mixture, if desired.
6. Bake at 400° for 18 to 20 minutes.

YIELD: 12 muffins

| Total calories: | | 2,100 |
| --- | --- | --- |
| Calories per muffin: | | 175 |

|  | Grams | % of recipe |
| --- | --- | --- |
| CARB | 27 | 65 |
| PRO | 3 | 5 |
| FAT | 6 | 30 |

## Jelly Belly Muffins

You can make these with any of your favorite muffin recipes, (either homemade or from a mix). I enjoy mixing and matching flavors, such as orange marmalade with corn muffins, raspberry jam with plain muffins, and grape jelly with bran.

1    recipe muffin mix, prepared according to directions
½    cup jelly or jam of your choice

1. Spray muffin cups with cooking spray.
2. Make the muffin mix according to the directions.
3. Put the batter into the prepared muffin cups, filling each ⅔ full.
4. Gently press 1 teaspoon of jelly into the middle of each cup of batter.
5. Bake at 400° for 20 to 25 minutes.
6. Warning: Watch out for the hot jelly—it can burn you!

# 8 SOUPS, STEWS, AND CHILIS

One of the nicest things about making homemade soups and stews is having their aroma fill the house. What a wonderful greeting upon returning from a long winter run! I like to keep soup or stew on hand for quick evening meals that simply need to be heated. A bowl of warm soup is a relatively effortless dinner, thanks to the microwave oven.

If you frequently make soups or stews, you might want to:

- Save the cooking water from vegetables in a jar in the refrigerator to use as a soup base.

- Limit the seasonings and add the seasoning-of-the-day into the individual portion you will be eating. That way, you can have Chinese-style soup one day, curried soups another, and Mexican a third. See the herb chart in the recipe introduction for ideas.

There's nothing wrong with using canned soups or broth for the foundation of a quick and easy meal. Because the canned products tend to have more sodium than do some homemade soups and stews, runners with high blood pressure should choose the low-sodium canned soups.

Here are some ways to convert plain ol' canned soup into a more exotic meal, light supper, or snack:

- Combine soups such as onion and chicken noodle; tomato and vegetable.

- Add ingredients such as diced celery, broccoli, tomatoes, or whatever fresh or frozen vegetable is handy; leftover rice, noodles, pasta; leftover vegetables, salads, casseroles; whatever in the fridge needs to be eaten.

- Add seasonings such as curry powder to chicken soup; cloves to tomato soup; wine, sherry, or vermouth to mushroom soup.

- Add toppings such as Parmesan cheese, grated low-fat cheeses, cottage cheese, sesame seeds, or croutons.

## Vegetable Soup with Beef or Turkey

This recipe can be made in a Crock-Pot. Combine the ingredients and let them simmer all day. Serve with some bread and a glass of milk, and you have a balanced meal. Add extra potatoes or beans for more carbs.

½ to 1 pound lean ground beef or ground turkey
1 cup chopped onion
4 cups water
1 cup cut-up carrots
1 cup diced celery
1 cup cubed pared potatoes
2 teaspoons salt
1 teaspoon bottled bouquet sauce
¼ teaspoon pepper
1 bay leaf
⅛ teaspoon basil
6 tomatoes, peeled and chopped or 1 28-ounce can of tomatoes

1. In a large saucepan cook the meat until browned. Drain the fat.
2. Add the onions and cook until the onions are tender, about 5 minutes.
3. Stir in the remaining ingredients except the tomatoes and bring the soup to a boil. Reduce the heat, cover, and simmer for 20 minutes.
4. Add the tomatoes, cover, and simmer 10 minutes longer or until the vegetables are tender. Remove the bay leaf before serving.

YIELD: 4 servings

| Total calories: | 800 |
|---|---|
| Calories per serving: | 200 |

| | Grams | % of recipe |
|---|---|---|
| CARB | 17 | 35 |
| PRO | 16 | 30 |
| FAT | 8 | 35 |

## Chicken Black Bean Soup

Peter Hermann submitted this recipe because it is simple, delicious, and nutritious. You can make it into a heartier meal by adding cooked pasta (or cooking the pasta along with the soup).

4   chicken breast halves, skinned and boned
5   cups water or broth
2   carrots, peeled and sliced
2   tomatoes, chopped
½   onion, chopped
3   to 5 cloves garlic, crushed
2   16-ounce cans black beans, rinsed and drained
1   tablespoon fresh oregano leaves or 1 teaspoon dried
Salt and pepper to taste
**Optional:**
2   to 4 cups cooked pasta, shells or bow-ties
2   ounces grated Cheddar cheese
Hot red pepper flakes
½   cup marsala wine

1. In a large stock pot cover the chicken breasts, vegetables, garlic, beans, and seasonings in water. Bring the water to a boil, reduce the heat, and simmer for about 20 minutes or until done.
2. Remove the chicken pieces from the broth and set them aside to cool. Keep the broth warm over low heat. (Optional: Add the cooked pasta.)
3. Dice the chicken into small pieces. Return it to the soup and heat through.
4. Garnish with grated cheese and red pepper flakes if desired.

YIELD: 4 servings

| Total calories: | 1,200 |
| --- | --- |
| Calories per serving: | 300 |

|  | Grams | % of recipe |
| --- | --- | --- |
| CARB | 33 | 45 |
| PRO | 34 | 45 |
| FAT | 3 | 10 |

## Macrobiotic Soup

Barbara Anderson has followed a macrobiotic lifestyle for 5 years. She uses a Crock-Pot to simplify cooking. The following is her favorite soup recipe that she enjoys for breakfast as well as other meals. It's a good source of beta carotene.

3   quarts water
1   acorn squash, cut in half and seeded
1½   cups red lentils
1½   cups barley or millet
6   dried shiitake mushrooms
4"   seaweed strip
1   to 2 teaspoons miso per bowl, to taste

1. In a 3½-quart Crock-Pot combine the water, acorn squash, lentils, barley, mushrooms, and seaweed. Cook for several hours or overnight. Or cook for two hours over low heat in a large soup pot.
2. Carefully remove the squash with a slotted spoon, scoop the flesh into the soup, and discard the peel.
3. Stir well, then serve for breakfast, lunch, or dinner.
4. Add the miso to the individual bowls to taste.

YIELD: 10 servings

| Total calories: | 2,300 |
| --- | --- |
| Calories per serving: | 230 |

|  | Grams | % of recipe |
| --- | --- | --- |
| CARB | 47 | 80 |
| PRO | 10 | 20 |
| FAT | 0 | 0 |

## Egg Drop Soup

This soup is so easy and low calorie. It makes a nice lunch, or an appetizer to a light dinner. By adding spinach leaves, broccoli, bean sprouts, or other vegetables, you can increase the nutritional value. Add rice for carbs.

1   cup chicken broth, homemade, canned, or from bouillon
2   teaspoons cornstarch mixed with a little cold water
1   egg (or substitute)
Dash soy sauce
**Optional:**
Spinach leaves
Chopped broccoli
Green bell pepper, chopped
Bean sprouts
Chinese cabbage, shredded
Scallions, chopped
Cooked rice

1. In a stock pot bring the broth to a boil.
2. Stir in the cornstarch to slightly thicken the broth.
3. In a small bowl lightly beat the egg with the soy sauce. Stir the soup quickly. While it swirls, slowly add the beaten egg. Remove the pan from the heat. Do not stir.
4. Add the vegetables. They will cook from the heat of the soup, crunchy but warm.
5. Serve immediately.

YIELD: 1 serving

| Total calories: | 120 |
| --- | --- |

|  | Grams | % of recipe |
| --- | --- | --- |
| CARB | 12 | 40 |
| PRO | 6 | 20 |
| FAT | 5 | 40 |

## Lentil Soup I

Make this soup in quantities and freeze it in individual portions. When heating it up, add fresh vegetables such as chopped celery or broccoli, to add a crunchy texture.

Lentils are a good source of protein as well as carbohydrates. To get the most protein value serve this soup with bread and low-fat cheese or milk. Or complement the protein in the lentils by cooking them with 1 cup of raw rice and 2 additional cups of water.

2   cups dried lentils (1 pound)
12  cups water
2   large onions, chopped
2   large carrots, chopped
1   clove garlic, crushed
1   tablespoon salt or 5 beef bouillon cubes or 1 package dried onion soup mix
Black pepper to taste
**Your choice of:**
1   tablespoon curry or 1 teaspoon cloves
2   tablespoons Worcestershire sauce
1   tablespoon molasses
1   6-ounce can tomato paste
Soup bones

1. In a large soup pot combine all of the ingredients, including one of the optional seasonings or flavorings. Bring the soup to a boil.
2. Reduce the heat, cover, and simmer for 1 hour.

YIELD: 10 servings

| Total calories: | | 1,800 |
| Calories per serving: | | 180 |

| | Grams | % of recipe |
| --- | --- | --- |
| CARB | 37 | 80 |
| PRO | 8 | 20 |
| FAT | 0 | 0 |

## Lentil Soup II

If you want to spend a little more effort, this is a wonderful lentil soup recipe. If desired, add rice or barley to it for variety and additional flavor. Or, make it with less water and use it for a pasta sauce.

2   tablespoons olive oil
2   to 3 cloves garlic, minced
1   medium onion, chopped (about 1 cup)
1   large celery stalk, chopped (about 1 cup)
1   large carrot, chopped (about 1 cup)
½   large green bell pepper, chopped (about ½ cup)
1½  cups lentils, rinsed
1   16-ounce can Italian-style peeled whole tomatoes
8   cups chicken or vegetable broth
1   teaspoon dried oregano
1   teaspoon dried basil
Salt and pepper to taste
**Optional:**
1   teaspoon cumin
1½  teaspoons dried marjoram
1   bay leaf
½   cup rice or barley (increase broth by 1 cup)

1. In a large heavy pot heat the oil and sauté the garlic, onion, celery, carrot, and bell pepper over medium-low heat for 5 to 10 minutes.
2. Add the remaining ingredients and bring the soup to a boil. Reduce the heat and simmer for about 1 hour, adding more water or broth as needed for consistency.

YIELD: 6 servings

| Total calories: | | 1,500 |
| Calories per serving: | | 250 |

| | Grams | % of recipe |
| --- | --- | --- |
| CARB | 42 | 65 |
| PRO | 12 | 20 |
| FAT | 4 | 15 |

## Homemade Chicken Rice Soup

This will cure all of your ailments.

1   large chicken, cut up
4   carrots, cut up
3   stalks celery, cut up
2   large onions, chopped
1   tablespoon salt
⅛   teaspoon pepper
1   cup rice, uncooked
**Optional:**
1   bay leaf
⅛   teaspoon thyme
1   teaspoon parsley

1. In a large pot cover the chicken with cold water. Add the vegetables and spices. Bring the mixture to a boil, reduce the heat, and simmer for 2 hours. Skim the fat as necessary.
2. Remove the chicken pieces and set them aside to cool.
3. Cook the rice or noodles in the skimmed broth.
4. Remove the meat from the bone and dice it. Return the chicken meat to the soup and heat through.

YIELD: 8 servings

| Total calories: | | 1,600 |
| Calories per serving: | | 200 |

| | Grams | % of recipe |
| --- | --- | --- |
| CARB | 20 | 40 |
| PRO | 17 | 35 |
| FAT | 6 | 25 |

The start of the 1973 New York City Marathon, which at that time was run entirely in Central Park

## Joan Benoit Samuelson's Minestrone Soup

Mmmm good! Top with cheese if desired.

2   to 4 tablespoons olive oil
2   cloves garlic, minced
1   cup diced yellow onion
1   cup diced carrot
1   cup diced celery
2   cups diced, peeled potatoes
2   cups diced zucchini
1   cup fresh or frozen green beans
3   cups shredded green cabbage
1   28-ounce can whole or crushed tomatoes with liquid
6   cups broth or water
Salt and pepper to taste
1   16-ounce can cannellini beans (white kidney beans)

1. In a large pot heat the oil and sauté the onion and garlic until the onion is softened.

2. Add the remaining ingredients except the cannellini beans. Bring the soup to a boil, reduce the heat, and simmer for 30 to 45 minutes.
3. Add the cannellini beans and heat through. Adjust the seasonings.

YIELD: 6 large servings

| Total calories: | 1,300 |
| --- | --- |
| Calories per serving: | 220 |

|  | Grams | % of recipe |
| --- | --- | --- |
| CARB | 36 | 65 |
| PRO | 10 | 20 |
| FAT | 4 | 15 |

## Orlando Pizzolato's Pasta e Fagioli (Pasta with Beans)

New York City Marathon winner Orlando Pizzolato of Italy knows how to cook up a super soup! This recipe makes a large amount and can be frozen in individual servings for quick meals. This soup is rich in carbohydrates, potassium, B vitamins, and very low in fat. The original recipe included two large potatoes, but it works well without them and saves on effort.—JLH

1   cup chopped onion
3   to 4 cloves garlic, minced
1   28-ounce can tomatoes with juice
2   stalks celery, chopped
¼   cup minced fresh parsley
8   cups broth or water
1½  cups short tubular pasta, uncooked
2   teaspoons sage
½   teaspoon cinnamon
2   16-ounce cans cannellini beans (white kidney beans), drained and rinsed
Salt and pepper to taste
Grated Parmesan cheese

1. In a large pot combine the onion, garlic, tomatoes, celery, parsley, and broth. Bring the soup to a boil, reduce the heat, and simmer for 1 hour, until the vegetables are tender.
2. Add the pasta and cook until it is al dente.
3. Add the beans and correct the seasonings. Heat through.
4. Garnish each serving with freshly grated Parmesan cheese.

YIELD: 8 servings

| Total calories: | 1,600 |
| --- | --- |
| Calories per serving: | 200 |

|  | Grams | % of recipe |
| --- | --- | --- |
| CARB | 39 | 80 |
| PRO | 9 | 18 |
| FAT | 1 | 2 |

## Pasta and White Bean Soup with Sun-Dried Tomatoes

This soup is delicious—worth the trip to the store to get sun-dried tomatoes if you don't have them on hand. Terri Smith, Director of the Dietetic Internship at Boston's Beth Israel Hospital, says this is among the most popular soups served in the cafeteria. Try it and you'll know why.

If desired, add more beans and pasta to the soup and you'll have a hearty high-carb dinner.

1   tablespoon oil, preferably olive or canola
1   large onion, diced
1   medium carrot, diced
¼   to ½ teaspoon red pepper flakes
12  ounces cannellini beans, drained
5   cups chicken or vegetable broth
3   ounces bowtie or shell pasta (about ⅔ cup)
⅓   cup sun-dried tomatoes, diced
Salt and pepper to taste
**Optional:**
1   clove garlic, minced or 1 teaspoon garlic powder
1   bay leaf
3   tablespoons fresh parsley
Parmesan cheese

1. In a large pot heat the oil and sauté the onion, carrot, garlic, and red pepper flakes. Cover and cook for about 10 minutes, stirring occasionally.
2. Add the drained beans, broth, and bay leaf. Bring the soup to a boil.
3. Add the pasta and sun-dried tomatoes. Reduce the heat and simmer until the pasta is tender, about 10 minutes.
4. Season to taste with salt and pepper. Add the parsley. Serve with grated Parmesan cheese.

YIELD: 4 12-ounce servings

| | | |
|---|---|---|
| Total calories: | | 900 |
| Calories per serving: | | 225 |

| | Grams | % of recipe |
|---|---|---|
| CARB | 38 | 70 |
| PRO | 9 | 15 |
| FAT | 4 | 15 |

## Simple Winter Squash Soup for One

When you are hankering for something sweet for lunch or supper, this will do the job with wholesome carbohydrates rich in beta-carotene. To make this soup into a more substantial meal, simply add some cooked ground turkey and/or leftover rice.

1   10-ounce package frozen winter squash
1   cup milk
2   to 3 teaspoons brown sugar
1   teaspoon salt, or to taste
**Optional:**
A few dashes ginger or nutmeg
Cooked ground turkey
Leftover rice

1. In a saucepan or a microwave-able dish heat the squash with the milk.
2. Add the brown sugar, salt, seasonings, and other add-ins as desired. Stir until blended.
3. Pour into a bowl or mug, and enjoy.

YIELD: 1 serving

| | | |
|---|---|---|
| Total calories: | | 220 |

| | Grams | % of recipe |
|---|---|---|
| CARB | 40 | 75 |
| PRO | 11 | 20 |
| FAT | 2 | 5 |

## Pumpkin Soup

Pumpkin, like all dark yellow and orange vegetables, is an excellent source of beta carotene and vitamin A. Chef Peter Hermann of Boston gets rave reviews when he serves this soup.

1   to 2 tablespoons margarine, butter, or oil
3   green onions, sliced
2   cups puréed pumpkin (canned is fine)
2   tablespoons all-purpose flour
½   teaspoon ginger
Salt and pepper to taste
2   cups low-fat milk
3   cups chicken broth, homemade, canned, or from bouillon
Chives or parsley for garnish
**Optional:**
¼   teaspoon turmeric

1. In a large stock pot melt the margarine (or butter or oil) and sauté the onions until translucent. Stir in the pumpkin.
2. Blend the flour with the ginger, salt, pepper, and ⅓ cup of milk, stirring until smooth. Add the mixture to the soup.
3. Add the remaining milk and cook, stirring constantly, for 5 to 10 minutes, until thickened. Do not allow the soup to boil.
4. Add the broth and heat almost to boiling.
5. Garnish each serving with chives or parsley.

YIELD: 5 large servings

| | | |
|---|---|---|
| Total calories: | | 500 |
| Calories per serving: | | 100 |

| | Grams | % of recipe |
|---|---|---|
| CARB | 16 | 60 |
| PRO | 3 | 10 |
| FAT | 3 | 30 |

## Vegetable Cheese Chowder

Joan Benoit Samuelson enjoys this nice warm chowder in the cold Maine winters. Because the vegetables are only cooked briefly, they are still tender-crisp and offer a nice crunch. The low-fat cheese and milk are calcium and protein boosters for runners who tend to skimp on these nutrients.

By eating this chowder with some of Joan's Oatmeal Yeast Bread (see page 100) or serving it over rice, you'll be better able to fuel your muscles with adequate carbohydrates.

2   medium carrots, diced
2   to 4 tablespoons margarine
2   cups chopped cabbage
1   medium onion, diced
3   stalks celery, diced
1   cup green peas, fresh or frozen
1   16-ounce can creamed corn
2½  cups milk
1   teaspoon salt
Dash pepper
¼   teaspoon thyme
4   to 8 ounces (1 to 2 cups) low fat
    Cheddar cheese, grated

1.  In the bottom of a large pot sauté the carrots in margarine for 5 minutes. Add the cabbage, onion, celery, and peas, and sauté for 8 to 10 minutes.
2.  Add the creamed corn, milk, and seasonings. Heat at low temperature, stirring often.
3.  Add the grated cheese, stirring until melted.

YIELD: 6 big bowls

| Total calories: | | 1,450 |
| --- | --- | --- |
| Calories per serving: | | 240 |

| | Grams | % of recipe |
| --- | --- | --- |
| CARB | 30 | 50 |
| PRO | 12 | 20 |
| FAT | 8 | 30 |

# THE ACHILLES TRACK CLUB

The Achilles Track Club is an international running organization with more than 110 chapters that encourages people with disabilities to participate in long-distance running. It has organizations in 30 countries and 40 chapters in the United States. In 1982, Dick Traum, the president of Achilles and a member of the board of directors of the New York Road Runners Club, suggested that a program be established to encourage disabled people to participate in long-distance running. Fred Lebow merely said, "Do it." Lebow felt that if only three people came out the program would be successful. When two people showed up, Lebow, feeling a little embarrassed, said, "Well, it *will* be successful." In 1983, five Achilles members participated in the New York City Marathon. By 1993, more than 170 Achilles members from a total membership of more than 3,500 competed in the Marathon, with 153 completing the distance.

- After he ran the 1990 Marathon, the New York Eye and Ear Infirmary provided a complimentary corneal transplant for Tuul, the president of the Achilles Track Club of Mongolia. Following the transplant, Tuul went on to compete in the marathon in the 1992 Barcelona Olympics as a sighted runner.

- The Achilles Track Club of South Africa had four chapters represented in the 1993 Marathon. After the event, three members of the Soweto chapter received artificial legs. It is anticipated that two of them will be running the '94 Marathon on their new prostheses.

- In 1994, Achilles members from Vietnam will run the Marathon. Amputees and Vietnam War veterans from the Hanoi chapter will be running with volunteer escorts—Vietnam War veterans from the United States. Following the race, both Hanoi runners will be fitted with artificial legs.

- After a world-class running career in which he twice placed third in the New York City Marathon (1976, 1977), Chris Stewart of Great Britain went on to establish an Achilles Track Club program in Bosnia in 1994. In 1994, he will run with a blind member from the Bosnian chapter.

- Ketil Moe, president of the Achilles Track Club of Norway, will run his eleventh New York City Marathon. Moe, who was born with cystic fibrosis, is chasing the record number of NYC Marathons of his coach, Grete Waitz—which is eleven. Helping him do it will be his 1994 escort: triple Olympic gold medalist, the Norwegian speed skater Johann Koss.

## Cauliflower Soup

It seems that sometimes the most delicious things are also the most simple. This is true of the following recipe. The soup is low calorie, has a light taste, and is equally delicious served warm in winter or cold in summer.

To simplify cooking, you can cook the onions with the cauliflower, rather than sautéing them first.

1   to 2 tablespoons margarine, butter, or oil
1   head cauliflower, cut in florets, or 1 20-ounce bag frozen
4   cups chicken or vegetable broth (homemade, canned, or bouillon)
*Salt and pepper to taste*
**Options:**
1   large onion, diced
1   clove garlic, minced, or ⅛ teaspoon garlic powder
*Dash cayenne powder*
½   to 1 cup milk, fresh or evaporated
*Chopped fresh parsley*
*Toasted bread, cut into cubes*

1. In a large heavy pot melt the margarine (or butter or oil) and sauté the onion and garlic until translucent.
2. Add the cauliflower and stock, and bring the soup to a boil. Reduce the heat and simmer for about 30 minutes, until the cauliflower is soft.
3. Purée the soup in a blender or food processor until smooth, and return it to the pot. Season with salt, pepper, and cayenne to taste.
4. If desired, add the milk and reheat to the simmering point.
5. Optional: Garnish each serving with toast cubes and fresh parsley.

Yield: 3 servings

| Total calories: | | 300 |
|---|---|---|
| Calories per serving: | | 100 |

|  | Grams | % of recipe |
|---|---|---|
| CARB | 13 | 50 |
| PRO | 3 | 15 |
| FAT | 4 | 35 |

## Fish and Broccoli Soup

This soup is easy, delicious, slightly different, and low calorie. For a heartier soup add cooked rice. Serve with homemade bread.

4   cups chicken broth (homemade, canned, or bouillon)
¼   cup cornstarch
¼   cup cold water
½   pound white fish
2   stalks broccoli, chopped
**Optional:**
*Cooked rice*
*Sesame oil*
*Chopped scallions*

1. In a stock pot bring the chicken broth to a boil.
2. In a small bowl blend the cornstarch with the cold water. Add the mixture to the broth, stirring to blend.
3. Cut the fish into 1-inch chunks. Add the fish and the broccoli to the broth. Reduce the heat and simmer for 6 minutes. Add the rice and sesame oil if desired.
4. Optional: Garnish each serving with scallions and sesame oil.

Yield: 2 servings

| Total calories: | | 300 |
|---|---|---|
| Calories per serving: | | 150 |

|  | Grams | % of recipe |
|---|---|---|
| CARB | 3 | 10 |
| PRO | 28 | 75 |
| FAT | 3 | 15 |

## Manhattan Clam Chowder

Try making this chowder when you want to get into the spirit of training for the New York City Marathon! It is a flavorful, rich soup, best if prepared a day or two ahead to let the flavors mature.

1   tablespoon butter or margarine
1   onion, chopped
2   tablespoons all-purpose flour
1   carrot, chopped
1   stalk celery, chopped
4   potatoes, cubed
16  ounces clam juice
14  ounces canned whole tomatoes
2   6½-ounce cans minced or chopped clams, drained and liquid reserved
*Salt and pepper to taste*
**Optional:**
2   tablespoons fresh, minced parsley
¼   teaspoon dried thyme leaves
1   bay leaf

1. In a stock pot melt the butter and sauté the onions until softened. Blend in the flour and cook for 1 to 2 minutes, or until the flour begins to brown slightly.
2. Add the carrot, celery, potatoes, clam juice, tomatoes, reserved clam juice, parsley, thyme, and bay leaf. Cook over medium-low heat for about 45 minutes, until the vegetables are tender.
3. Add the clams, salt, and pepper. Cook until heated through. Remove the bay leaf before serving. Serve with oyster crackers.

## Gazpacho

This wonderful recipe was adapted from Jane Brody's *Good Food Book*, which contains many excellent and healthy recipes. Gazpacho is a delicious summertime recipe that uses garden vegetables at their peak. It is nutritionally rich in vitamins A and C, beta carotene, potassium, and carbohydrate, and very, very low in fat. This goes nicely with tabouli or hummus and pita bread.

1   large cucumber, peeled, halved lengthwise and seeded, divided
2   large tomatoes, peeled, cored, and seeded, divided
1   green bell pepper, halved and seeded, divided
1   medium onion, peeled and halved, divided
3   cups tomato juice or vegetable juice cocktail
⅓   cup red wine vinegar
1   tablespoon olive oil
¼   teaspoon hot pepper sauce
¼   teaspoon salt, if desired
¼   teaspoon pepper
3   to 4 cloves garlic, minced

1. In a blender or food processor combine half of the cucumber, 1 tomato, half of the pepper, half of the onion, and 1 cup of the juice. Purée the mixture until smooth.
2. Chop the remaining cucumber, tomato, pepper, and onion. Place the chopped vegetables in a bowl, cover, and refrigerate until serving time.
3. In a large serving bowl combine the purée, remaining 2 cups of juice, vinegar, oil, hot sauce, salt, pepper, and garlic. Cover and refrigerate for at least 2 hours.

4. Just before serving add the chopped vegetables and stir well. Check the seasonings and adjust to taste.

YIELD: 3 servings

| Total calories: | 360 |
| Calories per serving: | 120 |

|  | Grams | % of recipe |
| --- | --- | --- |
| CARB | 18 | 60 |
| PRO | 3 | 10 |
| FAT | 4 | 30 |

## Brew Stew

The Irish stout used in this recipe lends a special flavor to this stew. Other types of beer will also work, but they might be less flavorful.

To simplify preparation and slightly boost the nutritional value, simply leave the peels on the vegetables. Then serve with homemade bread or biscuits, and you have a wholesome, high carbohydrate meal!

The best stews are made by first browning the meat. This adds to the flavor. You can save time by deleting that step, and simply toss all the ingredients (except the flour) into the pot, and thicken the gravy afterward with the flour mixed into cold water and added to the hot broth.

⅓   cup flour
¾   teaspoon thyme
1   pound extra-lean stew beef, cut into cubes
2   to 3 tablespoons oil
2   onions, chopped
5   medium carrots, sliced
5   potatoes, diced
1   16-ounce bottle Irish stout
2   to 3 cups beef broth
1   to 2 tablespoons firmly packed brown sugar
Salt and pepper to taste
**Optional:**
1   bay leaf

1. On a plate, blend together the flour, pepper, and thyme. Dip the beef cubes in the flour mixture to fully coat.
2. In a large stew pot heat the oil and add the beef and cook until the cubes are browned on all sides. Add extra oil as needed. Remove the beef from the pan and reserve.
3. Place the onion in the pot and sauté over gentle heat until soft. Add the beef, carrots, potato, stout, broth, sugar, and bay leaf. Cover the pot and simmer over medium-low heat or bake at 350° for 1 hour, stirring occasionally.
4. Add salt, more pepper, any extra flour mixture, and more brown sugar if desired. Continue cooking for another 15 to 30 minutes or until the vegetables and meat are tender.

YIELD: 5 large servings

| Total calories: | 2,200 |
| Calories per serving: | 440 |

|  | Grams | % of recipe |
| --- | --- | --- |
| CARB | 40 | 40 |
| PRO | 29 | 25 |
| FAT | 17 | 35 |

## Irish Stew

This recipe is from the kitchen of John Treacy, 1984 Olympic Marathon Silver Medalist, a native of Ireland. By cooking the potatoes separately, they offer a sharper flavor that contrasts well with the beef.

1 tablespoon olive oil
1½ pounds round steak, cubed
3 medium onions, cut in eighths
1 pound carrots, sliced
3 cloves garlic, minced
3 tablespoons Worcestershire sauce
3 cups beef broth or water
1 pound mushrooms
Salt and pepper to taste
3 tablespoons cornstarch
3 tablespoons cold water
Rice or hot boiled potatoes

1. In a heavy skillet heat the oil and brown the meat on all sides. Add the garlic and onion, and sauté until tender.
2. Add the sliced carrots, salt, pepper, and Worcestershire sauce. Add the broth and bring the soup to a boil. Simmer for 30 minutes to 2 hours or until the meat is tender. The longer, the better.
3. Add the mushrooms.
4. In a small bowl blend together the cornstarch and water. Add the mixture to the soup and cook until the gravy thickens, about 10 minutes.
5. Serve with rice or hot boiled potatoes. Nutritional analysis includes 1 large potato per serving.

YIELD: 8 servings

| Total calories (without potatoes): | 2,200 |
|---|---|
| Calories per serving (with potatoes): | 470 |

|  | Grams | % of recipe |
|---|---|---|
| CARB | 64 | 55 |
| PRO | 27 | 25 |
| FAT | 12 | 20 |

## Quick and Easy Chili

Dennis Monahan of Hawaii claims this is a family favorite. Using the packaged chili seasonings simplifies the cooking process—why not? Adding a second can of beans and halving the meat makes this into a higher carbohydrate meal.

1 pound extra-lean beef or ground turkey
1 16-ounce can stewed tomatoes, preferably Cajun-style
1 16-ounce can beans, kidney, or pinto
1 package chili seasonings, hot or mild
1⅔ cups rice, uncooked

1. In a saucepan brown the ground turkey or beef. Drain fat if any.
2. Add the stewed tomatoes, beans, and chili seasonings. Bring the mixture to a boil, then reduce the heat.
3. Simmer for 5 to 50 minutes, depending on your patience.
4. While the chili is simmering, cook the rice.
5. Serve the chili over rice.

YIELD: 6 servings

| Total calories without rice: | 1,650 |
|---|---|
| Calories per serving without rice: | 275 |

|  | Grams | % of recipe |
|---|---|---|
| CARB | 20 | 30 |
| PRO | 23 | 35 |
| FAT | 11 | 35 |

| Calories per serving with 1 cup rice: | 500 |
|---|---|

|  | Grams | % of recipe |
|---|---|---|
| CARB | 64 | 55 |
| PRO | 27 | 20 |
| FAT | 13 | 25 |

## Chili
### (Vegetarian, Turkey, or Beef)

This easy recipe is a standby for sports nutritionist and marathoner Natalie Updegrove Partridge. Serve plain or with corn bread, or over pasta or rice.

1 tablespoon oil
2 cloves garlic, minced
1 onion, chopped
1 green bell pepper, chopped
1 10-ounce box frozen whole-kernel corn
1 20-ounce can of kidney beans, drained and rinsed
1 16-ounce can tomatoes, chopped, reserving liquid
1 8-ounce can tomato sauce
1½ tablespoons chili powder (more or less depending on how hot you like it)
Salt and pepper to taste
**Optional:**
¼ teaspoon cayenne pepper
1 teaspoon oregano
1 teaspoon basil
1 pound cooked ground beef or turkey, drained of fat
Grated cheese

1. In a large pot heat the oil and sauté the garlic, onion, and bell pepper for about 5 minutes over medium-high heat.
2. Add the remaining ingredients except the grated cheese. Bring the chili to a slow boil, reduce the heat, and simmer for 30 minutes.
3. Garnish with grated cheese if desired.

YIELD: 4 servings

| Total calories: | 1,000 |
|---|---|
| Calories per serving: | 250 |

|  | Grams | % of recipe |
|---|---|---|
| CARB | 48 | 80 |
| PRO | 8 | 10 |
| FAT | 3 | 10 |

## NYPD V. NYFD
## A Friendly Competition

Since 1979, the New York City Police and Fire departments have held a Marathon competition. Each department has between two hundred and three hundred runners in the race. The Fire Department holds the large trophy kept by the winning team at the Union Hall Fire Station near City Hall.

The squads rent adjacent suites in the Mayflower Hotel, near the Marathon finish, to celebrate after the race with family and friends. Medals are awarded to the top ten finishers in each department at the annual Police-Fire race held in April.

Kevin Malley of the Fire Department says that the FDNY Running Club was started to promote fitness within the department.

*Norway's Grete Waitz on her way to winning her first New York City Marathon in 1978*

### Savory Scallop and Cauliflower Stew

This pretty red and white soup can also be served over rice or pasta. Serve with a green salad and French bread for a delicious supper.

1   to 2 tablespoons olive oil
1   onion, chopped
¼   to ½ teaspoon crushed red pepper flakes
½   teaspoon thyme
¼   teaspoon dried oregano
1   28-ounce can tomatoes, cut in chunks
1   8-ounce bottle clam juice
2   teaspoons sugar
⅓   cup white wine
½   medium head cauliflower, cut into small florets, or 10 ounces of frozen cauliflower
¾   pound scallops
Salt and pepper to taste
**Optional:**
1   large carrot, peeled and sliced
2   cloves garlic, minced
¼   teaspoon cumin
2   tablespoons chopped fresh parsley

1. In a stock pot heat the oil over medium heat and sauté the onion until translucent, about 5 to 7 minutes.
2. Add the carrot, garlic, cumin, red pepper, thyme, and oregano, and cook for 1 minute.
3. Add the tomatoes (with juice), clam juice, sugar, wine, parsley, and cauliflower, and cook until tender, about 12 to 15 minutes.
4. Add the scallops and cook just until opaque, about 1 to 2 minutes. Season with salt and pepper. Let the soup stand for a few minutes to let the flavors blend.

YIELD: 2 servings

| Total calories: | | 660 |
| --- | --- | --- |
| Calories per serving: | | 330 |

| | Grams | % of recipe |
| --- | --- | --- |
| CARB | 35 | 40 |
| PRO | 31 | 40 |
| FAT | 7 | 20 |

# 9 SALADS AND DRESSINGS

Salads, whether served as a main dish or an accompaniment, are a simple way to boost your intake of fresh vegetables. The keys to making a healthy salad are:

- Use fresh vegetables.
- Choose a variety of colorful vegetables—dark green lettuces, red tomatoes, yellow peppers, orange carrots—for a variety of vitamins and minerals.
- Monitor the dressing. Some runners drown 50 calories of healthful salad ingredients with 400 calories of fatty dressing!

The trick to making a substantial sports salad is to add extra carbohydrates:

- dense vegetables such as corn, peas, beets, carrots
- beans and legumes such as chick-peas, kidney beans, and three-bean salad
- cooked rice or pasta

- oranges, apples, raisins, grapes
- toasted croutons
- whole-grain bread on the side

If you choose to use regular dressings, try to select ones made with olive oil for the flavor and the health-protective monounsaturated fats. If you want to reduce your fat intake, simply dilute regular dressings with water, more vinegar, or even milk (in ranch and other mayonnaise-based dressings). Or choose from the plethora of low-fat and nonfat salad dressings available in stores and even salad bars. The commercial low-fat and nonfat dressings are good not only for salads, but also sandwiches, baked potatoes, and dips.

If you know the salad vegetables you buy will soon be wilting in your refrigerator, consider salad bars at the grocery store and deli as an easy and economical alternative to preparing your own.

## Tomato-Pepper Salad

This colorful salad will supply 100 percent of the RDA for vitamins A and C. It attractively complements colorless pasta and fish dishes.

| | |
|---|---|
| 3 | large tomatoes, diced in ½-inch cubes |
| 1 | large green pepper, diced |
| ¼ | cup wine vinegar |
| 2 | to 3 tablespoons oil |

**Optional:**
Garlic powder
Pepper
Salt
Basil
Chopped onion
A pinch of sugar

1. In a salad bowl combine the tomatoes and peppers.
2. In a separate bowl combine the vinegar, oil, and remaining ingredients, as desired.
3. Pour the dressing over the salad and chill until ready to serve.

YIELD: 4 servings

| Total calories: | 340 |
|---|---|
| Calories per serving: | 85 |

| | Grams | % of recipe |
|---|---|---|
| CARB | 6 | 30 |
| PRO | 1 | 5 |
| FAT | 6 | 65 |

### Comparing Salad Ingredients

Here are how some popular salad ingredients compare. Note that the vegetables with the most color have the most nutritional value.

| SALAD INGREDIENT RDA | VITAMIN C (MG) 60 MG | VITAMIN A (IU) 5,000 IU | MAGNESIUM (MG) 400 MG |
|---|---|---|---|
| Broccoli, 5" stalk | 110 | 2,500 | 24 |
| Green pepper, ½ | 65 | 210 | 20 |
| Spinach, 2 cups | 50 | 8,100 | 90 |
| Tomato, medium | 35 | 1,400 | 20 |
| Romaine, 2 cups | 20 | 1,900 | 20 |
| Iceburg, 2 cups | 5 | 330 | 10 |
| Cucumber, ½ med | 5 | 125 | 5 |
| Celery, 1 stalk | 5 | 120 | 10 |

## Bill Rodgers's Spinach Salad with Sweet and Spicy Dressing

The secret to this recipe is the dressing. As Bill's wife, Gail, reports, "We have never served this salad without people fighting over the last scraps!"

1   10-ounce package or large bunch fresh spinach
1   cup sliced mushrooms
2   fresh tomatoes, cut into wedges

**Dressing:**
¼   cup olive oil
2   tablespoons red wine vinegar
1   tablespoon sugar
1   teaspoon salt as desired
1   tablespoon ketchup

**Optional:**
2   hard-boiled eggs, sliced
½   cup broken walnuts
3   to 5 slices bacon, crisply cooked and crumbled

1. In a salad bowl combine the spinach, mushrooms, and tomatoes.
2. In a jar combine the olive oil, vinegar, sugar, salt, and ketchup. Cover and shake until well blended.
3. Portion the salad onto 4 plates. Over each serving spoon 2 tablespoons of dressing. Garnish with egg slices, walnuts, and bacon.

YIELD: 4 servings

| Total calories: | | 400 |
|---|---|---|
| Calories per serving: | | 100 |

| | Grams | % of recipe |
|---|---|---|
| CARB | 10 | 40 |
| PRO | 1 | 5 |
| FAT | 6 | 55 |

## Oriental Spinach Salad with Soy Sauce and Sesame Dressing

This recipe from Angella Hearn, masters runner from New York, New York, is a good source of iron, calcium, and fiber. Angella suggests serving this salad with a sourdough baguette and chilled white wine.

1   pound spinach, rinsed well and cut up
4   ounces water chestnuts, sliced
½   pound mushrooms, sliced
½   pound bean sprouts

**Dressing:**
⅓   cup light soy sauce
1½  teaspoons fresh lemon juice
¼   cup rice vinegar
½   teaspoon sugar
½   teaspoon grated ginger
2   to 4 tablespoons sesame oil

**Optional:**
½   teaspoon finely chopped shallot
½   teaspoon toasted sesame seeds

1. In a blender combine the soy sauce, lemon juice, vinegar, sugar, shallot, and ginger. Mix until well blended. Slowly dribble the oil into the mixture to thicken the dressing.
2. In a salad bowl combine the spinach, water chestnuts, mushrooms, and bean sprouts. Pour the dressing over the salad.
3. Sprinkle the sesame seeds over the salad.

YIELD: 4 servings

| Total calories: | | 550 |
|---|---|---|
| Calories per serving: | | 140 |

| | Grams | % of recipe |
|---|---|---|
| CARB | 13 | 40 |
| PRO | 6 | 25 |
| FAT | 7 | 35 |

## Snow Peas and Cucumber Salad

A colorful, crunchy salad that is especially good with barbecued fish or meat. You can alter the salad ingredients, depending on what you have available.

6   ounces snow peas, cut diagonally in half
1   8-ounce can water chestnuts
3   cucumbers, peeled, seeded, cut into crescent-shaped slices
1   yellow or red bell pepper, seeded, cut into thin strips

**Dressing:**
2   tablespoons chopped onion
1   tablespoon grated fresh ginger
¼   cup vinegar, preferably rice vinegar

Salt to taste
2   to 3 tablespoons oil

1. Toss the snow peas into boiling water for a minute or less, just until they lose their raw crunch. Drain and drop into ice water. When cooled, pat dry.
2. In a salad bowl combine the peas, water chestnuts, sliced cucumber, and bell pepper.
3. In a separate bowl whisk together the onion, ginger, vinegar, and salt to taste. Add oil.
4. Pour the dressing over the salad and toss to coat. Chill. Refrigerate for no longer than 7 hours, because the cucumbers will give off too much liquid and the snow peas will discolor.

YIELD: 5 servings

| Total calories: | | 500 |
|---|---|---|
| Calories per serving: | | 100 |

| | Grams | % of recipe |
|---|---|---|
| CARB | 13 | 55 |
| PRO | 1 | 5 |
| FAT | 5 | 40 |

## Carrot-Raisin Salad

Carrots are an excellent source of vitamin A. This vitamin helps your eyes adjust to the dark, as they do when you come indoors after running outside on a sunny day.

4   medium carrots, grated
½   cup raisins
3   tablespoons orange juice
**Optional:**
½   cup walnuts, chopped
½   cup low-fat yogurt or low-fat mayonnaise
1   tablespoon honey

1. In a salad bowl combine the carrots, raisins, and orange juice.
2. Add the walnuts, mayonnaise, and honey if desired.

YIELD: 4 servings

| Total calories: | | 440 |
|---|---|---|
| Calories per serving: | | 110 |

| | Grams | % of recipe |
|---|---|---|
| CARB | 26 | 95 |
| PRO | 1 | 5 |
| FAT | 0 | 0 |

## Cabbage and Carrot Salad

Red cabbage is popular because of its pretty color and sweet crunch. This slaw is rich in vitamins, especially beta-carotene, and goes nicely with baked fish.

2   cups shredded carrot
2   cups shredded red cabbage
**Dressing:**
¼   cup rice or cider vinegar
2   teaspoons sugar or to taste
1   tablespoon oil
Salt to taste

1. In a salad bowl toss together the carrot and the cabbage.

2. In a small bowl whisk together the remaining ingredients.
3. Just before serving, add the dressing to the vegetables and toss the slaw well.

YIELD: 4 servings

| Total calories: | | 320 |
|---|---|---|
| Calories per serving: | | 80 |

| | Grams | % of recipe |
|---|---|---|
| CARB | 4 | 40 |
| PRO | trace | trace |
| FAT | 3 | 60 |

## Three-Bean Salad

This salad is best made the night before to allow the flavors to blend. You can use frozen or fresh green and wax beans, if desired. Canned are easier, and have somewhat similar nutritional value, except for added sodium.

1   16-ounce can wax beans, drained
1   16-ounce can green beans, drained
1   16-ounce can kidney beans, drained
**Dressing:**
¼   cup sugar
½   cup cider vinegar
2   to 4 tablespoons oil
¼   cup finely chopped onion

1. In a salad bowl combine the wax beans, green beans, and kidney beans.
2. Add the remaining ingredients and toss.
3. Chill until ready to serve.

YIELD: 6 servings

| Total calories: | | 1050 |
|---|---|---|
| Calories per serving: | | 175 |

| | Grams | % of recipe |
|---|---|---|
| CARB | 30 | 65 |
| PRO | 5 | 15 |
| FAT | 4 | 20 |

## Cabbage and Carrot Salad with Fruit

Jaqueline Marcus, a sports nutritionist in the Chicago area, submitted this recipe that has lots of crunch, and is high in fiber and low in fat. The red cabbage adds wonderful color and a sweet flavor, and is a good source of vitamins A and C. Any extra dressing makes a delicious calcium-rich topping for fruit.

2   cups shredded red cabbage
2   medium carrots, grated
1   stalk celery, diced
⅓   cup raisins, preferably golden
1   small apple, diced
**Dressing:**
½   ripe banana
⅓   cup plain yogurt
½   cup part-skim Ricotta or cottage cheese
1   tablespoon honey or sugar or apple juice concentrate
**Optional:**
2   tablespoons sunflower seeds or chopped walnuts

1. In a mixing bowl combine the cabbage, carrots, celery, raisins, and apple. Add the sunflower seeds if desired.
2. In a blender or food processor combine the remaining ingredients. Process until smooth. Pour the dressing over the salad.

YIELD: 4 servings

| Total calories: | | 600 |
|---|---|---|
| Calories per serving: | | 150 |

| | Grams | % of recipe |
|---|---|---|
| CARB | 25 | 70 |
| PRO | 6 | 15 |
| FAT | 2 | 15 |

# A SPLENDID HUMAN RACE
# 12,260 WINNERS, AND MORE

It has neither the enduring charm, rooted deep in history, nor the warm civility of Philadelphia, but New York City is, so to speak, a nice place to visit. It does have a way with things on the grand scale. And so it was with the 11th New York City Marathon Sunday. We dropped in at Central Park shortly after noon to watch for two treasured friends, a man who had run the race before and his wife, the mother of a not-quite 2-year-old, who had not.

The closest we could get to the end-point was the 26-mile marker, 385 yards short of the finish line. Even there, the crush was so great as to make it difficult to see every runner as he or she swept or plodded, soared or agonized, sprinted or staggered, up the last, long, grueling hill to the finish. We missed seeing either of our special marathoners.

Missing our friends did not detract from being part of an almost magical sense of unity with the runners and the crowd: a feeling of common identity, an experience that was rare in its personal, individual intensity and yet even more rare in its sense of universal sharing. All of it spoke one thing: "It's in you," the crowd seemed to tell every runner, "you *can* finish. It's important. You are." And the runners responded. As the roar rose to them, their bodies and their faces showed belief, and then relief, from pain and fatigue, and they surged forward with new strength.

After the race was done we heard wonderful stories of support and encouragement. Near the finish line there was an almost unbroken stream of urging that flowed from the bystanders to the runners as they came in sight. Three men completed the course as they had begun, in wheelchairs. Spectators sent forth particular warmth, and visible tears, for three blind runners who finished. Small children and women and men in their sixties and even their seventies got special attention and affection.

But no one was begrudged; there were no villains in the drama, nor even bit-players. The outpouring surged from strangers to strangers, and yet it truly seemed to be that most beautiful and most dignified, that singularly most accepting and uncritical of all human experiences: love.

We learned later that our friend, the veteran, had finished in 3 hours, 59 minutes and 10 seconds. But wait, we said later, two years ago our friend had run the same course 21 minutes more quickly. Surely, that was a sort of defeat? No, our friend said, not at all. Two years ago, he had been able to train almost perfectly; this year for five of the seven weeks before the race, he had been traveling and unable to run. To break four hours was a fine victory.

Over whom, we asked. Over those who came in behind?

Oh, no, he said. His wife had finished 4 hours, 44 minutes and 16 seconds, and that was a great and wonderful victory too.

But victory is beating someone, isn't it?

Or some *thing*, he insisted. Personal challenge. A sense of one's own limits. The finiteness of self.

The following day, we went over the published list of the 12,260 names, tabulated in order of their finishing times. It came upon us very strongly what had caused an enormous crowd of legendarily uninvolved, impersonal New Yorkers to behave so they had on Sunday—what had led them to weep and shout and urge with as much caring, with the same spontaneous passion, for people finishing a race behind 10 and more thousands of others as they did for those who finished in the lead.

What did it, for the runners and the spectators alike, was the sure knowledge that in each of them was the capacity for victory, true personal victory, and the equal certainty that for a person of strength and perseverance and character to win does not mean that another human being has to lose.

*The Philadelphia Inquirer*, October 31, 1980

## Cauliflower and Broccoli Salad

This is a wonderfully simple salad and so healthy. Broccoli and cauliflower are cruciferous vegetables that may help in the fight against cancer. They are also high in vitamins and fiber. Sometimes I add a little blue cheese to the dressing for an elegant touch.—JLH

3   cups cauliflower, cut into small florets
2   cups broccoli, cut into small florets
½   cup red onion slices or 3 or 4 green onions with tops, chopped
**Dressing:**
¾   cup fat-free or reduced fat mayonnaise
½   cup plain yogurt
3   drops Tabasco sauce
1   teaspoon Worcestershire sauce
1   tablespoon sugar
1   tablespoon vinegar
Salt and pepper to taste
**Optional:**
Blue cheese, crumbled
Paprika

1. In a serving bowl combine the cauliflower, broccoli, and onion.
2. In a separate bowl combine the remaining ingredients and blend well.
3. Pour the dressing over the vegetables and toss to coat.
4. Refrigerate overnight to allow the flavors to blend.

YIELD: 6 servings

| Total calories: | | 480 |
|---|---|---|
| Calories per serving: | | 80 |

| | Grams | % of recipe |
|---|---|---|
| CARB | 16 | 80 |
| PRO | 4 | 20 |
| FAT | 0 | 0 |

## Tom and Barbara Fleming's South African Platter with Yogurt-Honey Dressing

This recipe from Tom's wife has a wonderful and unusual combination of flavors. It makes an excellent summertime salad to serve with homemade rolls or French bread.

1   head lettuce, shredded
1   tablespoon lemon juice
1   large red apple, cored and chopped
1   large banana, peeled and sliced
1   large orange, peeled and segmented
½   cantaloupe, peeled and cubed
¼   pound Roquefort cheese, cubed
**Dressing:**
2   tablespoons lemon juice
1   teaspoon honey, heated
¾   cup plain yogurt
1   clove garlic, crushed
Salt and pepper to taste
1   tablespoon mint, finely chopped
Optional:
1   to 2 ounces chopped pecans

1. In a small bowl combine the lemon juice, melted honey, and yogurt, blending well. Add the garlic, salt, pepper, and mint, and stir to blend. Refrigerate the dressing for 1 hour to allow the flavors to blend.
2. In a salad bowl arrange the lettuce.
3. In a mixing bowl toss the apples in the lemon juice. Add the banana, orange, and cantaloupe. Spoon the fruit mixture onto the lettuce.
4. Add the Roquefort cheese and mix lightly.
5. Pour the dressing over the salad and sprinkle with the nuts.

YIELD: 4 servings

| Total calories: | | 1,200 |
|---|---|---|
| Calories per serving: | | 300 |

| | Grams | % of recipe |
|---|---|---|
| CARB | 48 | 65 |
| PRO | 9 | 15 |
| FAT | 8 | 25 |

## Sunset French Dressing

This is a tempting French dressing that is yummy on mixed salads. It's a lovely bright orange color, and tangy-sweet. Due to its high sugar content, it's even a reasonable source of carbohydrates! Feel free to use half the sugar and oil, depending upon your taste preferences.—JLH

½   cup oil
⅓   cup sugar
2   teaspoons salt
¼   cup vinegar
⅓   cup firmly packed brown sugar
2   teaspoons paprika
⅓   cup ketchup
1   clove garlic, minced
Juice of 1 lemon (¼ cup)
**Optional:**
2   tablespoons grated onion

1. In a shaker, blender, or food processor combine all of the ingredients. Blend until smooth.
2. Refrigerate the dressing for several hours to allow the flavors to blend.

YIELD: 10 servings

| Total calories: | | 1,550 |
|---|---|---|
| Calories per serving (2 tablespoons): | | 155 |

| | Grams | % of recipe |
|---|---|---|
| CARB | 17 | 45 |
| PRO | 0 | 0 |
| FAT | 10 | 55 |

## Italian Bread Salad

Mary Abbott Hess of Chicago says this is a tasty, high-carb salad.

1   1-pound loaf firm Italian bread
1   cup cold water
4   small red onions, thinly sliced
1   cucumber, pared and sliced
4   ripe tomatoes, cut into wedges
1   small head romaine lettuce,
    torn into bite-sized pieces
10  fresh basil leaves or ¾ teaspoon
    dried basil
¼   cup olive oil
2   tablespoons red wine vinegar
1   teaspoon salt
½   teaspoon fresh ground pepper

1. Remove the bread crust and cut or tear the bread into cubes. Let the bread stand uncovered until it dries out, about 3 hours.
2. Sprinkle the bread with about 1 cup of cold water. The bread should be wet but not soggy. Refrigerate for several hours.
3. In a large salad bowl combine the bread cubes, onions, cucumber, tomato, lettuce, and basil.
4. In a small bowl combine the olive oil, vinegar, salt, and pepper.
5. Drizzle the dressing over the salad and serve immediately.

YIELD: 8 servings

| Total calories: | | 1,840 |
| Calories per serving: | | 230 |

| | Grams | % of recipe |
| --- | --- | --- |
| CARB | 25 | 65 |
| PRO | 5 | 10 |
| FAT | 7 | 25 |

## Tunisian Pita Salad

This is an interesting blend of common and unusual tastes. Sports nutritionist Jacqueline Marcus suggests you serve it with pita bread or on a bed of romaine.

2   medium green bell peppers,
    diced
1   cup minced onions
2   medium tomatoes, peeled,
    seeded, and diced
2   large tart apples (such as
    McIntosh), unpeeled, cored and
    diced
2   teaspoons hot salsa (or more if
    your salsa is mild) or hot relish
1   cup garbanzo beans, preferably
    halved
1   tablespoon crushed dried mint
    leaves, or minced fresh
3   to 4 tablespoons each oil and
    vinegar
Romaine lettuce
3   whole-wheat pita loaves, halved
    or quartered

1. In a mixing bowl combine all of the ingredients except the lettuce and pita bread. Refrigerate until chilled.
2. Spoon the salad into the pita pockets. Add lettuce.

YIELD: 6 servings

| Total calories: | | 1,440 |
| Calories per serving: | | 240 |

| | Grams | % of recipe |
| --- | --- | --- |
| CARB | 37 | 65 |
| PRO | 7 | 10 |
| FAT | 7 | 25 |

## South-of-the-Border Bean Salad

This healthy, tangy salad is a great way to enjoy legumes. Serve in a pita pocket or on a bed of greens.

8   ounces chickpeas (half of a 16-
    ounce can), drained
8   ounces black beans (half of a
    16-ounce can), drained
1   16-ounce can kidney beans,
    drained
1   cup corn, fresh, frozen, or
    canned
3   tomatoes (or 6 Italian plum
    tomatoes), chopped
1   large red onion, thinly sliced
1   to 2 cloves garlic, minced
**Dressing:**
3   tablespoons olive oil
¼   cup balsamic vinegar
1   teaspoon Tabasco or other hot
    sauce
Salt and pepper to taste
**Optional:**
2   tablespoons chopped fresh
    cilantro

1. In a serving bowl combine the chickpeas, black beans, kidney beans, corn, tomatoes, onion, and garlic.
2. In a small bowl combine the remaining ingredients. Pour the dressing over the salad.
3. Refrigerate the salad overnight to allow the flavors to blend.

YIELD: 7 servings

| Total calories: | | 1,275 |
| Calories per serving: | | 180 |

| | Grams | % of recipe |
| --- | --- | --- |
| CARB | 24 | 55 |
| PRO | 7 | 20 |
| FAT | 5 | 25 |

## Mango-Chicken-Rice Salad

This recipe was submitted by Barbara Barran of Brooklyn, New York.

2 cups cooked plain or saffron rice (see note)
1½ cups diced cooked chicken
1 cup seedless white grapes
1 cup peeled, cubed peaches
1 cucumber, seeded and chopped
Lettuce leaves
2 tablespoons raisins or currants
**Dressing:**
1 medium mango, very ripe
1 cup low-fat yogurt
¼ teaspoon ginger

1. Peel the mango and remove the meat from the core. Reserve the juice.
2. In a blender combine the mango, juice, yogurt, and ginger. Purée the mixture until smooth.
3. In a mixing bowl combine the rice, chicken, grapes, peaches, and cucumber.
4. Pour the mango purée over the salad mixture. Toss until well blended.
5. Arrange lettuce leaves on a platter. Spoon the salad onto the lettuce. Sprinkle with raisins.

**Note:** Saffron rice is regular white rice prepared with 1 to 2 threads of saffron added before cooking.

YIELD: 4 servings

| | Grams | % of recipe |
|---|---|---|
| Total calories: | | 1,300 |
| Calories per serving: | | 325 |
| CARB | 48 | 60 |
| PRO | 25 | 30 |
| FAT | 3 | 10 |

## 26.2-MILE PAINT JOB

Painting the blue line is one of the coveted rituals of Marathon preparation. In the silence of the early morning hours, the enormous machines of the New York Traffic Department ride through the streets of the city, accompanied by Fred Lebow and other course staff. The blue line, modeled on the one used in the 1976 Olympic Games and painted in patented Marathon Blue, takes two nights to paint. In 1978, three culprits were arrested for attempting to paint a fake Marathon blue line in order to misdirect the runners.

Assistant Course Coordinator Adam Kaufman paints the finish line and the NYRRC apple logo using a special paint that, according to its instructions, is "ideal for machinery, like tanks, and in extreme weather conditions."

*In 1976, the Marathon went from a course run within Central Park to a course through all five boroughs of New York City.*

# THE START

New York City Fire Department Lt. Vic Navarra was preparing to run the Marathon in 1980 when he broke his ribs while fighting a fire. Because he couldn't run, he decided to work. Since then, he has become the Start Coordinator, recruiting fifteen hundred volunteers from community groups in Staten Island, where the race begins. Among the recruits are his fellow firefighters and his wife, Joanne, and two daughters, April and Christy, who coordinate various work teams.

Work begins in early August, with an inventory of equipment. Orders are made for items like barrels, tables, and cups. The start banners are sent to the cleaners. The week prior, telephone lines and electric lines are installed and the Verrazano Bridge expansion joints are covered with rubber matting. The day before the event, tents are assembled as well as the world's longest urinal and portable toilets.

The two most overwhelming aspects of the start, according to Navarra, are crowd control and cleanup. "It's scary—the masses. It's difficult enough directing in one language. But one-third of the field is international. And they are really cranked. After all that travel and waiting to run the biggest and the best—they seem afraid they are not going to get to do it."

The rising energy of the international runners builds as they begin to chant. In an effort to keep them calm, members of the psyching team stand at each exit gate with small bullhorns and talk to them. Since 1993 the Fire Department has provided Navarra with a ninety-five foot (ten stories high) tower ladder to enable him to see and thus better coordinate the entire start.

Thousands of runners form a picturesque scene when they simultaneously bend, stretch, and reach during the Marathon warm-up exercises, which are conducted in three different sessions at the staging area at Fort Wadsworth.

Every year, staffers have a betting pool to see who can guess what time the first runner will arrive. About twenty-five people toss a dollar in the hat along with their name and the predicted time written on it. Navarra recalls the first runner one year, an international entrant, dressed only in T-shirt and shorts, who wandered up to him at the chilly morning hour of 3:30 A.M.

The schedule for the pre-Marathon activities includes the following:

1:00 A.M.  Removal of the concrete divider on the bridge (to be replaced immediately after runners depart)

2:30  "Chef" Colin Cuskley arrives to cook breakfast for the workers.

3:00  Fire Department searchlight arrives to light up the starting area field.

3:30–4:00  The first runners arrive.

3:30  The Red Cross sets up its coffee and donuts for the runners.

4:00  Portable toilets unlocked.

4:30  Videotaped check-in is set up.

5:00  The entrance is opened.

5:15  First bus with runners arrives.

5:30  Water stations are opened; coffee is served.

6:30–8:30  Three groups of the Achilles Track Club (disabled) start their Marathon run.

8:30  Call to worship for various religious services.

9:20  Psyching team heads to the exits.

9:40  Clean-up crew lines up in toll booths.

9:45  Army band and cannon arrive and set up on bridge.

10:00  "Human chain" of firefighter and police entrants assembles to hold back runners.

10:05–10:24  Release of three separate starts.

10:34  Elite runners take their place at the start.

10:44  Playing of the National Anthem.

10:48  Race start.

Noon  Pizza arrives for clean-up crew.

6:30 P.M.  Start Coordinator Vic Navarra goes to bed

## Dreamy Tuna, Chicken, Turkey, or Salmon Salad

This recipe was submitted by Barbara Day, sports nutritionist in Louisville, Kentucky. Serve on a bed of lettuce or stuff it into pitas, buns, or hollowed tomatoes.

1½  cups cooked, diced or crumbled tuna, chicken, turkey, or salmon
¼  cup frozen peas
¼  cup shredded carrot
2  tablespoons raisins
⅛  teaspoon celery seed
¼  cup chopped shallots or green onions

**Dressing:**
1  tablespoon Dijon mustard
3  tablespoons lemon juice
1  cup plain yogurt, low- or nonfat
1  tablespoon mayonnaise, preferably low-fat

**Optional:**
1  dash Tabasco sauce or
   ½ teaspoon curry powder or
   ½ teaspoon dill weed
1  to 2 tablespoons minced shallots or green onions

1. In a salad bowl combine the first 6 ingredients.
2. In a small bowl combine the mustard, lemon juice, yogurt, and mayonnaise. Add Tabasco, herbs, and shallots as desired.
3. Toss the dressing with the salad.

YIELD: 3 servings

| Total calories: | | 700 |
|---|---|---|
| Calories per serving: | | 235 |

| | Grams | % of recipe |
|---|---|---|
| CARB | 16 | 30 |
| PRO | 32 | 55 |
| FAT | 4 | 15 |

## Chicken Salad with Fruit

4  small chicken breasts, skinless and boneless, about 1 pound
2  stalks celery, diced
1  large red delicious apple, skin on, diced
1  cup seedless grape halves

**Dressing:**
½  cup low-fat mayonnaise
2  tablespoons orange juice
2  tablespoons vinegar
Salt and pepper to taste

**Optional:**
1  head lettuce, shredded
½  cup coarsely chopped walnuts
1  tablespoon minced fresh parsley

1. Steam the chicken in 1 inch of water for about 15 to 20 minutes, until cooked.
2. When cooled, cube into ½-inch pieces.
3. In a bowl combine the chicken, celery, apple, grapes, and walnuts.
4. In a separate bowl combine the mayonnaise, juice, vinegar, salt, pepper, and parsley. Blend well. Pour over the chicken mixture and combine.
5. Serve over a bed of shredded lettuce or in a pita pocket.

YIELD: 4 servings

| Total calories: | | 1,200 |
|---|---|---|
| Calories per serving: | | 300 |

| | Grams | % of recipe |
|---|---|---|
| CARB | 24 | 35 |
| PRO | 30 | 40 |
| FAT | 9 | 25 |

## Spiced Turkey Salad

Runner and sports nutritionist Lisa Dorfman of South Miami, Florida, submitted this recipe for a different and tasty turkey salad. Serve the salad with pita bread. The dressing also goes nicely with chicken, leftover fish, canned tuna, or even beans.

¾  pound turkey (unsliced deli, leftover, or fresh cooked), cut into bite-sized cubes
1  large golden Delicious apple, diced
½  cup raisins
½  cup mayonnaise, preferably low-fat
½  to 1 teaspoon cumin
½  to 1 teaspoon ginger
½  to 1 teaspoon curry
½  to 1 teaspoon cinnamon
Salt and pepper to taste

**Optional:**
4  ounces (1 cup) smoked Cheddar cheese, grated

1. In a salad bowl combine the turkey, apple, raisins, and Cheddar cheese, if desired.
2. In a separate bowl combine the mayonnaise, cumin, ginger, curry, cinnamon, salt, and pepper to taste.
3. Add the mayonnaise mixture to the turkey mixture, tossing to coat.

YIELD: 4 servings

| Total calories: | | 1,400 |
|---|---|---|
| Calories per serving: | | 350 |

| | Grams | % of recipe |
|---|---|---|
| CARB | 26 | 30 |
| PRO | 26 | 30 |
| FAT | 16 | 40 |

## Central Park Salad with Chicken

This is a fast, flavorful, fix-ahead meal in one bowl, submitted by sports nutritionist Merle Best of Westfield, New Jersey.

1   head romaine lettuce, shredded
3   carrots, shredded
1   10-ounce package frozen green peas, thawed and drained
½   red onion, sliced
3   to 4 small skinned, boned chicken breasts, cooked and diced

**Dressing:**
1   cup plain nonfat yogurt
1   cup cottage cheese, nonfat or low-fat, whipped in the blender
1   cup fat-free or low-fat mayonnaise
Sugar to taste
Salt and pepper to taste
Dashes onion powder
**Optional:**
Cherry tomatoes

1. In a salad bowl layer half of the lettuce, half of the carrots, half of the peas, half of the onion, and half of the chicken.
2. In a small bowl combine the remaining ingredients except the tomatoes. Pour half of the dressing over the layers.
3. Repeat the layers of vegetables and chicken. Pour the remaining dressing over the salad.
4. Refrigerate the salad for 2 to 4 hours or overnight.
5. Top with the tomatoes.

YIELD: 4 servings

| Total calories: | | 1,100 |
| Calories per serving: | | 275 |

| | Grams | % of recipe |
| --- | --- | --- |
| CARB | 28 | 40 |
| PRO | 33 | 50 |
| FAT | 4 | 10 |

## Fresh Fruit Salad with Yogurt Dressing

This recipe is a favorite of Melissa Kalman's because of its healthy nature. She can remember her mother buying large amounts of fruit and displaying them in beautiful bowls. Her father would return from a long run with all of his running friends and they would enjoy this light meal and have a great time socializing and relaxing with each other. This is a very simple and enjoyable recipe.

Vanilla Yogurt
A variety of fresh fruits cut up into bite-sized pieces (try cherries, strawberries, melon, bananas)

In a serving bowl combine the fruit and yogurt, in whatever quantity you may desire, and enjoy!

## Wild Rice Chicken Salad

New Yorker Christine Schlott submitted this recipe for success. It is a good source of complex carbohydrates, protein, and B vitamins. For simplicity, cook the chicken and rice together in the same pot.

1   6-ounce package seasoned long-grain and wild rice mix
½   pound boneless, skinless chicken breast
1   cup water
2   to 4 tablespoons olive oil
¼   cup lemon juice
**Optional:**
¼   cup thinly sliced scallions

1. Prepare the rice according to the package directions.
2. While the rice is cooking, in a covered saucepan, steam the

chicken in the water for 15 to 20 minutes.
3. Chop the chicken into bite-sized pieces when cool enough to handle.
4. In a mixing bowl combine the rice, chicken, and remaining ingredients. The salad may be stored in the refrigerator for 2 to 3 days, but is best served at room temperature.

YIELD: 3 servings

| Total calories: | | 1,200 |
| Calories per serving: | | 400 |

| | Grams | % of recipe |
| --- | --- | --- |
| CARB | 49 | 50 |
| PRO | 28 | 25 |
| FAT | 10 | 25 |

## Avocado-Black Bean Pasta Salad

Barbara Barran of Brooklyn, New York, submitted this low-fat salad entrée. She says it is especially good the next day after the flavors have had a chance to marry. The dressing itself makes a great dip or salad dressing.

1   pound pasta (rotelli, ziti, shells, etc.), cooked and rinsed
½   avocado, cubed
1   10-ounce can black beans, drained and rinsed

**Dressing:**
½   cup plain low-fat yogurt
½   cup low-fat cottage cheese
1½   avocados
4   to 5 dashes cayenne pepper
¼   teaspoon dried dill
1   to 2 cloves garlic
Salt and pepper to taste

**Optional:**
1   cup sliced mushrooms
1   cucumber, seeded and chopped
½   red onion, chopped

1. In a blender combine the yogurt, cottage cheese, 1½ avocados, cayenne, dill, garlic, salt, and pepper. Purée the mixture until smooth.
2. In a mixing bowl combine the pasta, cubed avocado, beans, mushrooms, cucumbers, and onion if desired.
3. Add the dressing and toss to coat.
4. Line a serving bowl with lettuce. Spoon the salad onto the lettuce. Refrigerate until chilled.

YIELD: 5 main-dish servings

| Total calories: | | 2,600 |
|---|---|---|
| Calories per serving: | | 520 |

| | Grams | % of recipe |
|---|---|---|
| CARB | 81 | 60 |
| PRO | 17 | 15 |
| FAT | 14 | 25 |

*The throngs at the start can barely maintain their adrenaline. The first signs of discarded warm-up clothes decorate the roof of the tent.*

## Sea Legs Salad with Sun-Dried Tomatoes

If you want a new dish that reduces the amount of meat and fat in your diet, try this. Barbara Barran has found that a base of yogurt and cottage cheese works quite well in summer salads.

1   pound pasta (rotelli, ziti, shells, etc.), cooked and rinsed
¾   pound Sea Legs crab substitute, cut in bite-sized pieces
4   to 5 sun-dried tomatoes, thinly sliced

**Dressing:**
¾   cup low-fat yogurt
¾   cup low-fat cottage cheese
¼   cup low-fat mayonnaise
¼   teaspoon dried dill
Salt and pepper to taste

**Optional:**
Lettuce leaves
1   cup sliced fresh mushrooms
1   cucumber, seeded and chopped
½   Haas avocado, cubed

1. In a blender combine the yogurt, cottage cheese, mayonnaise, dill, salt, and pepper. Purée the mixture until smooth.
2. In a mixing bowl combine the pasta, crab substitute, sun-dried tomatoes, mushrooms, cucumber, and avocado. Toss until well mixed.
3. Add the dressing mixture and toss to coat.
4. Arrange the lettuce leaves on a platter. Spoon the salad onto the lettuce.

YIELD: 5 servings

| Total calories: | | 2,250 |
|---|---|---|
| Calories per serving: | | 450 |

| | Grams | % of recipe |
|---|---|---|
| CARB | 80 | 70 |
| PRO | 26 | 25 |
| FAT | 3 | 5 |

131

## Colorful Vegetable Pasta Salad with Honey-Mustard Dressing

Joy Cunningham of Chicago submitted this recipe because it is colorful and tasty—pretty to look at and pretty to eat.

8   ounces thin spaghetti
1   cup cherry tomato halves
1   cup zucchini slices
1   cup yellow pepper strips
1   cup broccoli florets
1   cup carrot slices
½   cup onion slices

**Dressing:**
2   tablespoons olive or canola oil
¼   cup cider vinegar
¼   cup honey
1   tablespoon Dijon mustard
1   teaspoon ginger
Salt and pepper to taste

1. Cook the pasta according to the package directions. Drain and rinse with cold water.
2. In a large bowl toss together the spaghetti, tomatoes, zucchini, yellow pepper, broccoli, carrots, and onion.

3. In a small bowl whisk together the oil, vinegar, honey, mustard, ginger, salt, and pepper.
4. Pour the dressing over the pasta mixture. Stir gently, cover, and refrigerate until ready to serve.

YIELD: 4 servings

| Total calories: | 1,500 |
|---|---|
| Calories per serving: | 375 |

|  | Grams | % of recipe |
|---|---|---|
| CARB | 70 | 75 |
| PRO | 8 | 10 |
| FAT | 7 | 15 |

## Tropical Pasta Salad with Chickpeas

Sports nutritionist and runner Lisa Dorfman of South Miami, Florida, likes this recipe because it is colorful, easy, tastes good, and is a crowd pleaser.

1   pound pasta (preferably tri-colored rotelli), cooked, drained, and cooled
1   cup chickpeas, drained
1   cup frozen green peas, thawed

1   cup corn (frozen or canned)
1   cup mandarin oranges, drained
¼   cup raisins

**Dressing:**
3   tablespoons oil
3   tablespoons orange juice
1   teaspoon cinnamon
¼   teaspoon ginger
¼   teaspoon nutmeg

**Optional:**
¼   teaspoon orange peel

1. In a large bowl combine the pasta, chick peas, green peas, corn, mandarin oranges, and raisins.
2. In a small bowl combine the remaining ingredients. Pour the dressing over the salad and toss to coat.

YIELD: 6 servings

| Total calories: | 2,700 |
|---|---|
| Calories per serving: | 450 |

|  | Grams | % of recipe |
|---|---|---|
| CARB | 78 | 70 |
| PRO | 16 | 15 |
| FAT | 8 | 15 |

# 10 PASTA

## HOW TO COOK PASTA

The perfect boiled pasta is tender, yet firm to the teeth; "al dente" as the Italians say. To cook pasta perfectly, follow these rules:

1. Use a big pot filled with water, so the individual pieces of pasta can float freely. Allow 10 minutes for the water to reach a rolling boil.

2. Allow 4 quarts (4 liters) water per pound (½ kilo) dry pasta. Plan to cook no more than 2 pounds of pasta at a time: otherwise, you may end up with a gummy mess.

3. To keep the water from boiling over, add 1 tablespoon of oil to the cooking water. You may also add 1 to 2 tablespoons salt if desired to heighten the flavor of the pasta.

4. Bring the water to a vigorous, rolling boil before you add the pasta. Then add the pasta in small amounts that will not cool the water too much and cause the pieces to clump. When cooking spaghetti or lasagna, push down the stiff strands as they soften, using a long handled spoon.

5. If the water stops boiling, cover the pan, turn up the heat, and bring the water to a boil again as soon as possible.

6. Cooking time will depend on the shape of the pasta. Pasta is done when it starts to look opaque. To tell if it is done, lift a piece of pasta (with a fork) from the boiling water, let it cool briefly, then carefully pinch or bite it (being sure not to burn yourself!). The pasta should feel flexible but still firm inside.

7. When done, drain the pasta into a colander set in the sink, using potholders to protect your hands from the steam. Shake briefly to remove excess water, then return it to the cooking pot or to a warmed serving bowl.

8. To prevent the pasta from sticking together as it cools, toss the pasta with a little oil or sauce.

## PASTA PRIMER

Pasta comes in at least 26 shapes, ranging from plain spaghetti strands to bowties. All the shapes are made from the same wheat-and-water dough, some times tinted with vegetable juice (spinach, tomato). The best pasta is made from durum wheat that has been ground into fine granules called semolina or into durum flour. Durum wheat has a high gluten (protein) content, that gives the pasta a firm texture. Whole-wheat pasta, in comparison, tends to have more fiber and be softer; soy pastas are softer.

When trying to decide which shape of pasta to use for a meal, the rule of thumb is to use twisted and curved shapes (such as twists and shells) with meaty, beany, and chunky sauces. The shape will trap more sauce than would the straight strands of spaghetti or linguine.

Although pasta is an international favorite food of runners, you may struggle with understanding which shape is named what. Here is the translation into English for runners who are not fluent in pasta:

| | |
|---|---|
| Capelli d'angelo | Angel's hair |
| Conchiglie | Shells |
| Conchigliette | Little Shells |
| Farfalle | Butterflies (or bow ties) |

> "The biggest thrill came from passing other Jewish runners and calling to them 'chazak veematz.' It is an ancient Jewish salute dating back to Joshua. It means 'be strong and have courage.'"
>
> **—ZEV STERN,**
> Ph.D., AOJT, November 1990.

> "The New York City Marathon—a fantastic event."
>
> **—POPE JOHN PAUL II**
> to Fred Lebow, 1982.

| | | | |
|---|---|---|---|
| Fusilli | Twisted spaghetti strands | | |
| Fettuccine | Flat, wide spaghetti | | |
| Linguine | Thinner than fettuccine; wider than spaghetti | | |
| Manicotti | Big tubes | | |
| Orzo | Rice-shaped pieces | | |
| Penne | Skinny tubes with pointed ends | | |
| Rigatoni | Tubes | | |
| Rotelle | Twists | | |
| Route | Cart wheels | | |
| Stelline | Little stars | | |
| Vermicelli | Thin, flat spaghetti | | |
| Ziti | Small tubes | | |

Some international pasta names include:

| | |
|---|---|
| Fen ssu | Oriental bean-thread noodles / cellophane noodles |
| Somen | Oriental thin wheat flour noodles |
| Udon | Oriental thick wheat-flour noodles |
| Mi fen | Oriental rice stick noodles |
| Lug-lug | Thick rice-stick noodles |
| Soba | Buckwheat noodles |
| Tan mien | Oriental egg noodles |

| | |
|---|---|
| Couscous | North African rice-shaped pellets |
| Egg noodles | German egg noodle |
| Wonton | Oriental egg noodle |

The quickest cooking pastas include angel hair, alphabets, and the tiny stars, stelline. The time consuming part of cooking pasta is bringing the water to a boil. If desired, you can cook the pasta in half the amount of water, and it will cook okay in less time.

## PASTA FOR CARBO-LOADING

A favorite carbo-loading dinner among runners is pasta with oil and/or cheese. Be aware that if you nonchalantly add oil to pasta, you might end up fat-loading more than carbo-loading. The following chart shows how one innocent tablespoon of oil with 120 calories and 13 grams of fat can alter the calorie profile of a plate of pasta.

| Pasta | Oil | Total calories | % Carb | % Fat (gms) |
|---|---|---|---|---|
| 2 ounces dry; 1 cup cooked | 0 | 210 | 80 | 5 (1) |
| 2 ounces dry; 1 cup cooked | 1 tablespoon | 330 | 50 | 40 (14) |
| 3 ounces dry; 1½ cups cooked | 1 tablespoon | 435 | 60 | 30 (14) |
| 4 ounces dry; 2 cups cooked | 1 tablespoon | 540 | 62 | 25 (14) |
| 5 ounces dry; 2½ cups cooked | 1 tablespoon | 645 | 65 | 22 (14) |

For runners who want to carbohydrate load, the best ratio that provides a 60 to 70 percent carbohydrate sports meal is 1 tablespoon of oil per 4 to 5 ounces of dry pasta (about 2 to 2½ cups cooked pasta). Using a measuring spoon, measure out 1 tablespoon of oil so that you can see what it looks like. Similarly, if you nonchalantly sprinkle Parmesan cheese on pasta, you might add more fat and calories than anticipated.

| Pasta | Parmesan Cheese | Total calories | % Carb | % Fat (gms) |
|---|---|---|---|---|
| 4 ounces dry | 2 tablespoons | 465 | 73 | 10 (5) |
| 4 ounces dry | 4 tablespoons (¼ cup) | 500 | 63 | 15 (8) |

The fat and calories from oil and Parmesan combined really adds up quickly:

| Pasta | Oil (tablespoon) | Parm (tablespoon) | Total calories | % CARB | % FAT (gm) |
|---|---|---|---|---|---|
| 4 ounces dry | 1 | 2 | 580 | 58 | 28 (18) |
| 4 ounces dry | 1 | 4 | 620 | 54 | 30 (21) |

## Runner's Basic One-Pot Pasta

The following is Michael Keohane's standard dinner. Like many runners, Michael cooks foods that are easy to fix and result in minimal dishes to wash. Otherwise, he claims he can't be bothered.

Michael simplifies the cooking process by boiling the broccoli in with the pasta. Because this results in greater nutrient losses, you might want to buy a spaghetti pot with a vegetable steam basket that fits on top. (Or simply cook the veggies in another pot or the microwave oven.) To hasten the cooking process, use angel hair pasta or the little alphabet letters that cook in only 2 to 3 minutes.

¼ to ½ pound pasta (depending on how hungry you are)
1 to 2 big stalks broccoli (or 1½ to 3 cups of other veggies)
2 to 4 tablespoons Parmesan cheese

1. Cook the pasta according to the package directions.
2. Cook the broccoli in with the pasta or in a steamer on top of the boiling water.
3. Drain. Serve on large plate sprinkled with Parmesan cheese (or low-fat cheese of your choice).

YIELD: 1 serving

| Total calories: | | 500 |
|---|---|---|
| | *Grams* | *% of recipe* |
| CARB | 92 | 75 |
| PRO | 22 | 15 |
| FAT | 5 | 10 |

## Runner's Basic Pasta with Vegetables

Judy Morrill, veteran of three New York City Marathons, submitted this recipe for her standard pasta dinner. As an investment portfolio manager she works hard, trains hard, and arrives home eager to eat. This suits her needs for a meal that is quick, easy, healthy, and satisfying. She claims it is best when followed by chocolate raspberry swirl frozen yogurt!

New York City Marathon winner Kathrine Switzer also makes a similar dinner. Her favorite combinations are tomatoes, mushrooms, celery, zucchini, broccoli, eggplant, and green beans. She loves it not only because it tastes good, but because it cleans out the refrigerator!

¼ to ½ pound pasta of your choice
1 tablespoon olive oil
1 to 2 cloves garlic, crushed
2 to 3 cups fresh vegetables (zucchini, summer squash, red, yellow, or green bell peppers), chopped

**Optional:**
1 to 2 tablespoons fresh basil
2 tablespoons grated Parmesan cheese
2 tablespoons pine nuts

1. Cook the pasta according to the package directions. Drain.
2. In a large skillet heat the oil and sauté the garlic, chopped vegetables, and basil over medium-low heat until the vegetables are cooked to taste.
3. Mix the vegetables into the drained pasta. Add more olive oil to taste. Sprinkle with Parmesan and pine nuts, as desired.

YIELD: 1 big serving

| Total calories: | | 650 |
|---|---|---|
| | *Grams* | *% of recipe* |
| CARB | 113 | 70 |
| PRO | 16 | 10 |
| FAT | 15 | 20 |

## Uta Pippig's Pasta Dinner

This is Uta's standard pasta fare. She eats it with a plate of freshly steamed vegetables, such as her favorites, red peppers and bean sprouts.

¼ pound pasta
⅔ cup spaghetti sauce
1 large tomato, diced into small pieces
1 to 2 tablespoons fresh basil and parsley
2 ounces part-skim mozzarella cheese

1. Cook the pasta according to package directions.
2. In a saucepan combine the spaghetti sauce and fresh tomatoes.
3. Add the fresh basil and parsley. Simmer for 5 minutes.
4. Serve the sauce on top of a pile of pasta. Sprinkle with mozzarella cheese.

YIELD: 1 large serving

| Total calories: | | 750 |
|---|---|---|
| | *Grams* | *% of recipe* |
| CARB | 116 | 60 |
| PRO | 33 | 20 |
| FAT | 17 | 20 |

## Spinach Lasagna

This recipe makes a good luck lasagna that Joan Benoit Samuelson claims is welcomed before endurance events. She particularly likes this recipe because it eliminates the step of cooking the lasagna noodles before assembly. (Note: This can be done with any lasagna recipe.)

When eating lasagna pre-event, be aware that about half the calories come from protein and fat. Be sure to boost your carb intake with breads and juices.

1  pound (2 cups) part-skim Ricotta or cottage cheese or mixture
1  egg (or substitute)
1  10-ounce package frozen chopped spinach, thawed
1  teaspoon salt, as desired
1  teaspoon dried oregano
Dash pepper

1  30-ounce jar spaghetti sauce
1  pound lasagna noodles
4  to 6 ounces (1 to 1½ cups) mozzarella cheese, shredded
4  cups water
**Optional:**
4  cups diced vegetable (onions, mushrooms, carrots, zucchini, summer squash, etc.), steamed or sautéed in a little oil

1. In a bowl mix the Ricotta cheese with the egg, spinach, salt, pepper, oregano, and vegetables.
2. In a 9x13-inch pan alternate layers of dry (uncooked) lasagna noodles, cheese/vegetable mixture, and tomato sauce, starting and ending with noodles and tomato sauce, making 3 layers of ricotta filling and 5 layers of noodles (3 noodles per layer).
3. Sprinkle shredded mozzarella over the tomato sauce on the top layer.
4. Pour water around the edges of

---

## QUICK AND EASY PASTA TOPPINGS

The following quick and easy pasta toppings are a change of pace from the standard tomato sauce straight from the jar:

- Steamed, chopped broccoli
- Salsa
- Salsa heated in the microwave, then mixed with cottage cheese
- Red pepper flakes
- Low-fat Italian salad dressing mixed with a little Dijon mustard
- Low/no-fat salad dressings of your choice
- Low/no-fat Italian salad dressing with tamari, chopped garlic, steamed vegetables
- Nonfat sour cream and Italian seasonings
- Parmesan cheese and a sprinkling of herbs (basil, oregano, Italian seasonings)
- Chicken breast sautéed with oil, garlic, onion, and basil
- Chili with kidney beans (and cheese)
- Lentil soup (thick)
- Spaghetti sauce with a spoonful of grape jelly (adds a "sweet 'n' sour" taste)
- Spaghetti sauce with added protein: canned chicken or tuna, tofu cubes, canned beans, cottage cheese, ground beef or turkey

---

the uncooked noodles after the layers are finished.
5. Cover with foil. Bake at 350° for 1 hour and 15 minutes. The noodles will expand to fit the size of the pan. (Try to prevent the foil from sticking to the top cheese by covering it carefully.)
6. Serve with additional sauce if desired.

YIELD: 8 servings

| Total calories: | | 3,700 |
|---|---|---|
| Calories per serving: | | 460 |

| | Grams | % of recipe |
|---|---|---|
| CARB | 59 | 50 |
| PRO | 22 | 20 |
| FAT | 14 | 30 |

## Pasta Omelet

Fran Richman created this as a part of the "refrigerator bingo" game that she plays from night to night. It's a tasty way to vary leftover spaghetti with tomato sauce, and it adds ever-so-important protein.

2  cups leftover pasta with tomato sauce
2  eggs (or substitute), beaten

1. In a bowl mix together the eggs and leftover pasta with tomato sauce.
2. Pour the mixture into a preheated nonstick frying pan that has been treated with cooking spray or a little oil.
3. Cook the omelet on one side, then flip it or put it under the broiler to cook the top.

YIELD: 1 big serving

| Total calories: | | 600 |
|---|---|---|

| | Grams | % of recipe |
|---|---|---|
| CARB | 90 | 60 |
| PRO | 24 | 15 |
| FAT | 17 | 25 |

## Gourmet Vegetarian Lasagna

This lasagna, submitted by Linda Press Wolfe, has a wonderful flavor that is indeed a nice variation from standard lasagnas. The sun-dried tomatoes and pine nuts make the difference! The original recipe called for 2 pounds of Ricotta, which would make the lasagna much richer. I make it with one pound, and it comes out fine and offers less fat and more carbs per serving for fueling your muscles. As is, only 50 percent of the calories come from carbohydrates. The target sports diet is 60 to 70 percent carbohydrates.

If you should have any lasagna left over, Linda suggests that you cut it into individual servings, wrap, and freeze. It defrosts/heats successfully in the microwave oven.

| | |
|---|---|
| 1 | 16-ounce box lasagna noodles |
| 8 | to 9 sun-dried tomatoes |
| ½ | cup pine nuts (pignoli nuts) |
| 1 | to 3 cloves garlic, peeled and finely chopped |
| 1 | teaspoon oil, preferably olive or canola |
| 1 | to 2 pounds Ricotta cheese, part-skim or nonfat |
| 4 | to 8 ounces (1 to 2 cups) shredded mozzarella cheese |
| 1 | to 2 dashes nutmeg |
| ¼ | teaspoon oregano |
| 1 | 10-ounce package frozen chopped spinach, cooked and drained |
| 1 | 30-ounce jar spaghetti sauce |

**Optional:**
| | |
|---|---|
| 1 | tablespoon grated Parmesan cheese |

1. Cook the lasagna noodles according to the package directions.
2. Put the sun-dried tomatoes in a small bowl. Cover with boiling water and set aside for 5 minutes if oil-packed, 10 to 15 minutes if dried. Drain, cool, and chop finely. Set aside.
3. Toast the pine nuts in the oven at 350° for 5 minutes or on the stovetop in a nonstick skillet over medium-high heat for 2 to 3 minutes.
4. In a separate skillet sauté the garlic in oil for 2 minutes. Do not brown. Set the pan aside.
5. In a large mixing bowl combine the Ricotta cheese, Mozzarella, nutmeg, oregano, chopped spinach, chopped sun-dried tomatoes, pine nuts, and garlic. Blend well.
6. In a 9x13-inch lasagna pan pour enough tomato sauce to coat the bottom. Layer the noodles, cheese mixture, and tomato sauce, totaling 5 layers of noodles with three noodles per layer.
7. Cover the top layer of lasagna noodles with tomato sauce. Sprinkle with Parmesan cheese if desired.
8. Cover the pan tightly with foil. Bake at 350° for 30 to 40 minutes, or until hot.

YIELD: 10 servings

| Total calories: | | 4,000 |
|---|---|---|
| Calories per serving: | | 400 |

| | Grams | % of recipe |
|---|---|---|
| CARB | 50 | 50 |
| PRO | 19 | 20 |
| FAT | 14 | 30 |

## Orzo

Fred Lebow's sister, Sarah Katz, submitted this recipe for an extremely colorful dish that is appealing to the eye as well as the stomach. This makes enough for several hungry runners or leftovers for the week for solo cooks.

| | |
|---|---|
| 1 | pound orzo |
| 1 | green bell pepper |
| 1 | red bell pepper |
| 1 | yellow bell pepper |
| 2 | to 4 tablespoons butter or margarine |
| 1 | package onion soup mix |

1. Cook the orzo according to the package directions, adding no salt to the cooking water.
2. While the orzo is cooking, finely dice the peppers. In a skillet melt the butter and sauté the peppers until tender. Or skip this step and bake the peppers in the oven with the orzo.
3. Drain the orzo and transfer it to a large baking dish. Stir in the peppers and onion soup mix. Cover and bake at 325° for 20 to 30 minutes. Or if you lack patience, simply mix well, cover, and let the orzo stand for 10 to 15 minutes over low heat to allow the dried onions in the soup mix to soften and the flavors to blend.

YIELD: 10 side-dish servings

| Total calories: | | 2,400 |
|---|---|---|
| Calories per serving: | | 240 |

| | Grams | % of recipe |
|---|---|---|
| CARB | 43 | 75 |
| PRO | 8 | 10 |
| FAT | 4 | 15 |

## Macaroni and Cheese I

This recipe is a no-brainer that uses American cheese because it melts so nicely. The only challenge is to balance the amount of cheese, so that you end up carbo-loading and not fat-loading. This recipe with 8 slices of American cheese (6 ounces) results in an entrée with 30 percent of the calories from fat, the upper limit for athletes who need to eat enough carbohydrates for fuel. Six slices (4 ounces) would be 25 percent fat, a slightly better way to carbo-load.

½   box (8 ounces) elbow macaroni, or any shape pasta you desire
6   ounces (8 slices) American cheese or any grated cheese of your choice
1   cup milk
**Optional:**
1   tablespoon flour
¼   cup milk

1. Cook the pasta according to the package directions. Drain.
2. In a large saucepan heat the milk and melt in the cheese.
3. Add the pasta and blend well. Add more milk, as needed.
4. Serve in a bowl, because the cheese sauce will be a little bit soupy. Or dissolve the flour in ¼ cup of milk and stir the mixture into the cheese sauce before adding the pasta.
5. Add more milk as desired if the pasta absorbs too much liquid.

YIELD: 4 side-dish servings

| Total calories: | 1,500 |
|---|---|
| Calories per serving: | 375 |

|  | Grams | % of recipe |
|---|---|---|
| CARB | 50 | 50 |
| PRO | 20 | 20 |
| FAT | 12 | 30 |

## Macaroni and Cheese II (Low-Fat)

This recipe requires slightly more preparation than Macaroni and Cheese I, but it's worth the effort.

16   ounces macaroni
2   cups fat-free cottage cheese
2   cups skim milk
2   tablespoons flour
4   ounces grated low-fat Cheddar
Salt and pepper to taste
**Optional:**
2   tablespoons grated Parmesan
2   tablespoons bread crumbs
¼   teaspoon paprika

1. Cook the macaroni until al dente, 8 to 10 minutes. Drain in a colander and rinse with cold water; set aside.
2. Purée cottage cheese in a blender or food processor until smooth; set aside.
3. In a saucepan, heat 1½ cups of the milk over medium heat until steaming.
4. In a small bowl stir together the flour and the remaining ½ cup of milk until smooth.
5. Stir this into the hot milk and cook, stirring constantly, until the sauce is smooth and thick, about 2 minutes.
6. Remove from heat and stir in the Cheddar cheese, puréed cottage cheese, salt, and pepper.
7. Add the cooked macaroni and mix well.

YIELD: 6 servings

| Total calories: | 3,000 |
|---|---|
| Calories per serving: | 500 |

|  | Grams | % of recipe |
|---|---|---|
| CARB | 64 | 50 |
| PRO | 53 | 45 |
| FAT | 4 | 5 |

## Rigatoni with Roasted Red Pepper Sauce

Red peppers are an expensive but delightfully tasty vegetable. This recipe, submitted by Linda Press Wolfe, capitalizes on their flavor and produces a different pasta meal. The original recipe included no oil; I prefer a little bit to enhance the taste.

3   large red bell peppers, halved and seeded
1   large onion, peeled and cut into 8 chunks
1   to 4 cloves garlic, left whole and unpeeled
8   ounces rigatoni (or macaroni, ziti, twists, etc.)
¼   cup fresh basil, coarsely chopped
1   to 2 tablespoons olive oil
Salt and pepper to taste
**Optional:**
Parmesan cheese

1. Place the pepper halves skin-side-up in an ungreased roasting pan with onion and unpeeled garlic cloves.
2. Roast at 475° for 30 to 40 minutes, until the skin on the pepper turns black. Shake the pan occasionally to prevent the vegetables from sticking. Transfer to a bowl and set aside to cool.
3. Peel and discard the blackened skin from the peppers. Remove the peel from the garlic. Coarsely chop the roasted vegetable mixture. Set it aside and keep it warm.
4. Meanwhile cook the rigatoni according to the directions on the box. Drain and toss with the roasted vegetable mixture, chopped basil, salt, pepper, and oil.
5. Serve with grated Parmesan cheese if desired.

| YIELD: 2 large servings | | |
|---|---|---|
| Total calories: | | 1,100 |
| Calories per serving: | | 550 |

| | Grams | % of recipe |
|---|---|---|
| CARB | 113 | 80 |
| PRO | 20 | 15 |
| FAT | 2 | 5 |

## Tomato Sauce for Pasta

This is a versatile chunky-style sauce with delicate flavor. It makes an excellent pasta, pizza, or lasagna sauce. For a richer taste, add ⅓ cup of red wine before simmering.

1   small onion, finely chopped
2   tablespoons olive oil
1   28-ounce can Italian-style tomatoes, packed in purée (if packed in juice, add 3 tablespoons tomato paste)
1   to 2 cloves garlic, minced
1½  teaspoons dried oregano
1   teaspoon dried basil
2   teaspoons sugar or to taste
1   teaspoon salt or to taste
Freshly ground black pepper

1. In a saucepan heat the oil and lightly sauté the onions over medium heat until translucent.
2. Add the tomatoes and purée to the sautéed onions. Add the garlic and seasonings and bring to a simmer. Stir occasionally to prevent the sauce from sticking to the bottom of the pan. Simmer over low heat for 20 to 30 minutes. Makes about 3 cups.

| YIELD: 3 servings of pasta or 1 big pizza | | |
|---|---|---|
| Total calories: | | 500 |
| Calories per ⅛ recipe: | | 60 |

| | Grams | % of recipe |
|---|---|---|
| CARB | 8 | 50 |
| PRO | 1 | 5 |
| FAT | 3 | 45 |

## Spicy Chinese Noodles

If you were to call this Peanut Butter Pasta, people might groan. Call it Spicy Chinese Noodles and they will come back for seconds. When serving this to guests, be sure no one is allergic to nuts—this dish can fool even the most cautious eaters.

8   ounces dry pasta
⅓   cup peanut butter, preferably chunky
3   tablespoons soy sauce
3   tablespoons vinegar
1   tablespoon sugar or to taste
1   to 2 dashes cayenne pepper or to taste

**Optional:**
Garlic powder
Green bell pepper strips, lightly steamed
Snow peas, lightly steamed
Chopped scallions

1. Cook the pasta according to the package directions. Drain.
2. In a small saucepan combine the peanut butter, soy sauce, vinegar, sugar, cayenne, and garlic powder if desired. Cook over low heat until the mixture is heated, stirring until smooth.
3. In a serving bowl mix together the pasta and peanut butter sauce. Add bell peppers, snow peas, and scallions if desired. If the pasta is dry, add a little water to thin the sauce.

| YIELD: 4 side-dish servings | | |
|---|---|---|
| Total calories: | | 1,500 |
| Calories per serving: | | 375 |

| | Grams | % of recipe |
|---|---|---|
| CARB | 50 | 55 |
| PRO | 15 | 15 |
| FAT | 12 | 30 |

## Pasta with Wine and Olives

I created this delicious recipe one cold winter evening after a hard workout. Since then I have enjoyed it many times. You may omit the olives if you have none, but they really make it special. Whenever I sauté, I use a little bit of real butter in place of some of the oil—a little packs a lot of rich flavor and in such small amounts, doesn't contribute a great deal of cholesterol or saturated fat to the meal.—JLH

2   teaspoons olive oil
1   teaspoon butter
5   Greek olives, pitted and chopped
1   to 2 cloves garlic, minced
¼   cup white wine
2   plum tomatoes, chopped
¼   cup chopped fresh basil
¼   teaspoon oregano
Salt and pepper to taste

¼   pound pasta, cooked
2   tablespoons Parmesan/Romano cheese, grated or feta cheese, crumbled

1. In a skillet heat the oil and butter. Sauté the olives and garlic for about 1 minute.
2. Add the wine, tomatoes, basil, oregano, salt, and pepper. Cook for about 1 minute, until heated through.
3. Add the cooked pasta and toss to combine. Sprinkle with cheese and enjoy.

| YIELD: 1 big serving | | |
|---|---|---|
| Total calories: | | 680 |

| | Grams | % of recipe |
|---|---|---|
| CARB | 105 | 60 |
| PRO | 18 | 10 |
| FAT | 21 | 30 |

> "When you run up First Avenue in New York, if you don't get goose bumps, there's something wrong with you."
>
> —**FRANK SHORTER**, Olympic gold medalist, quoted in Newsday, November 2, 1986

## Low-Fat Noodles Alfredo

Sports nutritionist Barbara Day of Louisville, Kentucky, likes the following recipe because it's easy to make, her family eats it, and it's lower in fat than the real thing.

1 to 1½ tablespoons butter or margarine
½ cup milk
½ to ¾ cup grated Parmesan cheese
Salt and pepper to taste
8 ounces wide egg noodles, cooked
**Optional:**
1 tablespoon fresh or dried parsley flakes
¼ teaspoon oregano

1. In a saucepan melt the butter.
2. Remove the pan from the heat and add the milk, Parmesan, salt, pepper, parsley, and oregano. Stir to blend.
3. Transfer the noodles to a serving dish. Pour the sauce over the hot noodles, stirring gently until well coated.

YIELD: 3 main-dish servings

| Total calories: | 1,200 |
|---|---|
| Calories per serving: | 400 |

| | Grams | % of recipe |
|---|---|---|
| CARB | 53 | 55 |
| PRO | 17 | 20 |
| FAT | 11 | 25 |

## Sesame Pasta with Broccoli I

Sesame paste (tahini) is the secret ingredient in this recipe. If tahini is an unfamiliar ingredient in your household, I recommend that you buy some (at a large supermarket or natural food store) and start introducing this pleasing flavor into your meals. If you can't find it, substitute peanut butter diluted with 1 or 2 tablespoons boiling water.

8 ounces dry pasta
2 cups fresh or frozen broccoli, chopped
¼ cup tahini
**Optional:**
Cayenne pepper
Garlic powder
Vegetables such as celery or scallions, to taste

1. Cook the pasta according to the package directions. Drain.
2. While the pasta is cooking, steam the broccoli until crisp-tender.
3. In a large bowl mix the tahini with the drained pasta. Add the cooked broccoli and the water it was cooked in if the pasta is dry.
4. Add cayenne pepper, garlic powder, and vegetables if desired.

YIELD: 3 main-dish servings

| Total calories: | 1,300 |
|---|---|
| Calories per serving: | 430 |

| | Grams | % of recipe |
|---|---|---|
| CARB | 67 | 60 |
| PRO | 16 | 15 |
| FAT | 11 | 25 |

## Sesame Pasta with Broccoli II

This dish, which is popular with Gloria Averbuch's family, is excellent served warm or cold. Any extra sauce makes a great veggie dip or salad dressing.

8 ounces uncooked pasta
1 head broccoli (or other vegetable)
1 cup plain yogurt
1 tablespoon soy sauce
2 to 3 tablespoons tahini
**Optional:**
1 to 2 cloves garlic, minced
Dash Tabasco
½ teaspoon cumin
Diced red and green bell peppers
Snow peas
Shredded carrots

1. Cook the pasta according to the package directions. Drain.
2. While the pasta is cooking, steam the broccoli until crisp-tender.
3. In a small bowl mix the yogurt, soy sauce, tahini, garlic, Tabasco, and cumin. Add the pasta and toss to coat.
4. Add the bell peppers, snow peas, and carrots.

YIELD: 2 main-dish servings

| Total calories: | 1,100 |
|---|---|
| Calories per serving: | 550 |

| | Grams | % of recipe |
|---|---|---|
| CARB | 96 | 70 |
| PRO | 19 | 15 |
| FAT | 10 | 15 |

# MAJOR PLAYERS

Several athletes have achieved fame in New York and, in turn, have contributed to the reputation and personality of the race by virtue of their achievements. They include Grete Waitz, Bill Rodgers, and Alberto Salazar.

GRETE WAITZ accepted an invitation to the New York City Marathon in 1978 merely to see the sights. Race director Fred Lebow thought Norwegian Waitz—a world record holder in the 3,000 meters—would make a good "rabbit." He assumed she'd set a quick early pace and eventually drop out. It was, after all, her first marathon. Even more remarkable, she had never run farther than 12 miles. In fact, the elementary school teacher was about to retire from competition.

The twenty-five-year old Waitz went on to set a world record that day and returned to New York for a total of nine victories and two more world records, an unprecedented streak. During her reborn career as a road racer, she set scores of records and amassed numerous other victories and honors. She won the 1983 World Championships Marathon, the 1984 Olympic Games marathon silver medal, and was the five-time World Cross Country champion. She remains the "Queen of the Road" in New York and one of the

most beloved sports figures in both the United States and Norway. A statue of Waitz was erected at Oslo's Bislett Stadium.

In 1991, Waitz hung up her racing shoes, but she still runs and is active in a variety of sports. She and her husband Jack divide their time between their native Oslo and Gainesville, Florida. They are involved in sports-related businesses and promotion, including the largest all-women's race in the world, and charitable activities.

ALBERTO SALAZAR, born in Cuba, raised in Massachusetts, and residing in Oregon, symbolizes the cultural diversity of the New York City Marathon. Salazar was a twenty-two-year-old college senior when he decided to test himself over 26.2 miles. The result was an exciting victory over established favorites in the 1980 New York City Marathon, and a then world best for a first-timer at 2:09:41.

The following year both his fame and daring were solidified. Displaying astonishing confidence, Salazar boldly predicted before the race that he would break a twelve-year-old world marathon record. Such a prediction was virtually unheard of for such a difficult event,

*Grete Waitz*

particularly in New York, a course not known for its ease. But Salazar delivered, with a time of 2:08:13.

He notched a third victory the following year with a gutsy sprint at the very end and a 4-second margin over second place, which remains the closest margin of victory in the history of the race. He duplicated this

*continued on page 142*

*Alberto Salazar*

*Bill Rodgers*

American records in the 5,000 and 10,000 meters on the track. He was an Olympic marathoner at the 1984 Games. His career was reignited with a 1994 win in the prestigious Comrades Marathon in South Africa.

Today he lives with his wife and three children in Portland, Oregon. He is a field representative and coach for Nike, Inc.

BILL RODGERS, quite simply, is the greatest American road runner in the history of the sport.

His highly publicized victories in both the New York City and Boston Marathons became a symbol of the running boom of the 1980s. He won the first five-borough New York City Marathon in 1976, and went on to cross the line first the following three years. He also won his hometown Boston Marathon four times (1975, 1978, 1979, and 1980), making him the only runner in history to achieve such a record in major marathon competition.

At one point, Rodgers did not lose a road race, from 10k's to marathons, for nearly three years—an extraordinary feat. He also held American road records for a remarkable range of distances, from 10k's to marathons.

technique in winning the 1982 Boston Marathon. Salazar's remarkable marathons made him famous in New York and around the world.

Salazar was a dominant figure in road racing throughout the early 1980s, setting records at a variety of distances. He also held the

Rodgers still runs as a top masters (over forty) competitor and record-setter. He also does extensive running promotions. He lives with his wife and two daughters in Sherborn, Massachusetts.

## Spaghetti á la Carbonara

I frequently serve this as my standard "company-is-coming" dinner when I have little preparation time. It can be served either as a main dish with a green vegetable or salad or as a side dish for a fish meal.

½ pound spaghetti
1 to 2 tablespoons olive oil
1 large onion, chopped (or ¼ teaspoon onion powder)
1 clove garlic, minced
2 tablespoons parsley
1 teaspoon oregano
½ cup white wine or vermouth
2 eggs (or substitute), beaten
4 to 6 ounces grated low-fat Swiss or Muenster cheese

1. Cook the spaghetti according to the package directions. Drain.
2. Meanwhile, in a large saucepan heat the oil and sauté the onion, garlic, and spices until tender.
3. Add the wine. Add the cooked spaghetti and mix well.
4. Stir in the beaten eggs and grated cheese. Let the spaghetti stand for 1 to 2 minutes to allow the heat of the spaghetti to cook the eggs.

YIELD: 3 main-dish servings

| Total calories: | 1,450 |
|---|---|
| Calories per serving: | 480 |

| | Grams | % of recipe |
|---|---|---|
| CARB | 63 | 55 |
| PRO | 25 | 20 |
| FAT | 14 | 25 |

## Savory Seafood Pasta

Ann Joyal, a nutritionist in Boston, submitted this recipe that works well with rice or pasta.

1 28-ounce can whole tomatoes, drained and chopped
1 cup chopped green and/or red bell peppers
1 cup white wine
2 teaspoons dried basil
Salt to taste

1 to 2 tablespoons cornstarch
2 tablespoons water
1 pound scallops
¾ pound pasta, such as linguine, cooked

### Optional:
1 tablespoon olive oil
1 small onion, chopped
2 cloves garlic, minced
1 bay leaf

1. If garlic and onions are desired, in a large skillet heat the oil and sauté the onions and garlic until tender, about 3 to 5 minutes.
2. In the skillet add (or combine) the tomatoes, bell pepper, wine, basil, bay leaf, and salt to taste. Simmer uncovered for about 10 minutes.
3. In a small bowl dissolve the cornstarch in the water. Add the cornstarch mixture to the skillet. Continue to simmer for 2 minutes.
4. Add the scallops. Cover and simmer for 3 to 5 minutes, or until the scallops are done. Serve over pasta or rice.

YIELD: 4 servings

| Total calories: | 2,100 |
|---|---|
| Calories per serving: | 525 |

| | Grams | % of recipe |
|---|---|---|
| CARB | 82 | 60 |
| PRO | 31 | 25 |
| FAT | 8 | 15 |

## Kathrine Switzer's Smoked Salmon Pasta

By replacing the heavy cream in the original recipe with fat-free or low-fat sour cream, you will be able to enjoy in good health this tasty dish. Some would sprinkle fresh Parmesan on this, but Kathrine says she personally would not as this changes the flavor too much for her. But a fresh grind of pepper is delicious. This is a variable recipe, you can add more or less of things as you like.

1 pound pasta, such as fettuccine
2 cups fresh or frozen peas
4 ounces New Zealand smoked salmon or New York lox
2 to 4 tablespoons fresh pesto sauce (see recipe, page 146)
½ cup fat-free sour cream

1. Cook the pasta according to the package directions.
2. Steam the frozen peas until just thawed and hot.
3. Cut the smoked salmon into ⅓-inch cubes and set it aside.
4. Drain the pasta and return it to the pan. Add the pesto and stir gently until the pasta is well coated. Add the sour cream, peas, and salmon pieces, and toss well. If the pasta is too sticky, add a little very hot water or milk. Serve immediately.

YIELD: 5 main-dish servings

| Total calories: | 2,300 |
|---|---|
| Calories per serving: | 460 |

| | Grams | % of recipe |
|---|---|---|
| CARB | 80 | 70 |
| PRO | 15 | 10 |
| FAT | 9 | 20 |

# PASTA: THE STAPLE OF THE LONG-DISTANCE RUNNER

To endurance athletes, pasta is a tasty vehicle for complex carbohydrates—the best muscle fuel for their activity. But to historians, pasta is a hot topic. According to the Court of Historical Review in San Francisco, the controversy is over the question of who invented spaghetti—the Italians or the Chinese. The popular notion—a myth firmly established by Gary Cooper in the 1938 film *The Adventures of Marco Polo*—is that explorer Polo brought pasta from China to Italy as a result of his travels. Some historians contend the dish was present in Italy even before 1295, when Polo returned from China. However,

one San Francisco restaurateur has given accounts that show the Chinese eating a rice-flour noodle as early as 4,600 years ago.

Pasta was a luxury in Italy in the centuries after Marco Polo, and by 1400 it was sold in shops that retained night watchmen to protect the supply. The huge wave of Italian immigration to America between 1880 and 1921 was responsible for making the dish a staple of the American diet. Eventually, Italians all over the country opened spaghetti houses. Incidentally, "Spago" is "a string;" "spaghetti" are "Many little strings (of dough)."

## Shrimp with Linguine, Olives, and Mushrooms

2    tablespoons olive oil
1    cup sliced mushrooms
½    cup sliced, pitted, brine-cured black olives
¾    cup clam juice
1    tablespoon minced fresh basil
1    tablespoon minced fresh parsley
1    teaspoon dried oregano, crumbled
¾    pound shrimp, shelled and deveined
½    to 1 cup milk
½    to ¾ cup grated fontina or Parmesan cheese
Salt and pepper to taste
1    pound linguine, cooked
**Optional:**
1    to 3 cloves garlic, minced

1. In a large skillet heat the oil and sauté the garlic, mushrooms, and olives over medium heat until almost all of the liquid from the mushrooms has evaporated.
2. Add the clam juice, basil, parsley, and oregano and simmer,

stirring occasionally, until heated through.
3. Add the shrimp and simmer for 1 to 2 minutes, until the shrimp are cooked through. Add the milk, cheese, salt, and pepper and heat until the cheese melts, stirring constantly.
4. In a serving bowl toss the linguine with the shrimp mixture and serve.

YIELD: 5 servings

| Total calories: | | 2,800 |
| Calories per serving: | | 550 |

| | Grams | % of recipe |
| --- | --- | --- |
| CARB | 81 | 60 |
| PRO | 20 | 15 |
| FAT | 16 | 25 |

## Japanese Noodles with Ginger

These noodles are delicious hot or cold, plain, with steamed vegetables, or on top of a salad. If you don't have Japanese noodles, regular pasta noodles such as vermicelli or linguine or Chinese rice noodles

also work nicely. This recipe is a favorite of Patti Catalano Dillon.

1    pound udon noodles (Japanese whole-wheat noodles) or other noodles
2    to 4 cloves garlic
1    2-inch piece fresh ginger (about 1 square inch)
¼    cup tamari sauce or soy sauce
¼    cup honey or ½ cup brown rice syrup
¼    cup oil, preferably sesame

1. Cook the pasta according to the package directions.
2. In a blender or food processor combine the remaining ingredients. Process for 1 to 2 minutes, until smooth.
3. In a serving bowl toss the ginger mixture with the warm noodles. Serve hot or cold.

YIELD: 4 main-dish servings

| Total calories: | | 1,600 |
| Calories per serving: | | 400 |

| | Grams | % of recipe |
| --- | --- | --- |
| CARB | 61 | 60 |
| PRO | 12 | 15 |
| FAT | 12 | 25 |

## Shrimp Fettuccine

This low-fat recipe submitted by Helen Baker of Peyton, Colorado is quick and easy to prepare—the kind of meal runners like.

6   ounces pasta, preferably fettuccine
1   8-ounce package frozen peeled and deveined shrimp
2   cups frozen vegetable mixture of broccoli, carrots, and onions
1   tablespoon margarine or butter
1   tablespoon cornstarch
½   teaspoon instant chicken bouillon granules or 1 cube
¾   to 1 cup low-fat milk
2   tablespoons grated Parmesan cheese
**Optional:**
1   clove garlic, minced
⅛   teaspoon lemon pepper
2   tablespoons white wine
Tomatoes and parsley for garnish

1. In a large saucepan cook the pasta for 8 minutes.
2. Add the shrimp and frozen vegetables and return to a boil. Reduce the heat and simmer for 1 to 3 minutes or until the shrimp turn pink and the pasta is tender. Drain and return to the saucepan.
3. In a small saucepan melt the margarine. Stir in the cornstarch, bouillon, garlic, and lemon pepper. Stir in the milk. Cook, stirring constantly, until thickened and bubbly. Cook for 2 minutes more, stirring constantly. Stir in the cheese and wine as desired.
4. Pour the sauce over the pasta mixture. Toss to combine. Garnish with more Parmesan, tomatoes, and parsley if desired.

YIELD: 2 large servings

| Total calories: | 1,000 |
|---|---|
| Calories per serving: | 500 |

|  | Grams | % of recipe |
|---|---|---|
| CARB | 72 | 60 |
| PRO | 27 | 20 |
| FAT | 11 | 20 |

## Pasta with Clam Sauce

This recipe is from the kitchen of Jeff "Rat" Atkinson of Manhattan Beach, California. Jeff was an Olympic finalist in the 1500m run at Seoul, Korea.

3   tablespoons olive oil
3   cloves garlic, minced
1   medium onion, finely chopped
1   6-ounce can chopped clams
1   8-ounce jar clam juice
Black pepper to taste
Dash crushed red pepper
1   pound pasta, cooked
**Optional:**
¼   cup chopped parsley

1. In a saucepan heat the oil and sauté the garlic and onion until tender.
2. Pour in the clams and clam juice. Season with black and red pepper to taste.
3. In a serving bowl pour the sauce over the pasta. Toss with parsley as desired.

**Variation:** Add 8 ounces of low-fat sour cream instead of the clam juice for a white sauce.

YIELD: 4 servings

| Total calories: | 2,100 |
|---|---|
| Calories per serving: | 525 |

|  | Grams | % of recipe |
|---|---|---|
| CARB | 86 | 65 |
| PRO | 19 | 15 |
| FAT | 12 | 20 |

## Pasta with Chicken and Spinach

Vince Connelly, running chef and a Boston runner, loves to cook, loves to eat, and is happy to share his recipe with us.

1   pound pasta, such as fettuccine
1   pound boneless chicken breasts, thinly sliced
2   tablespoons oil, preferably olive
1   to 4 cloves garlic, finely chopped
1   pound fresh spinach, washed, drained, and roughly chopped
10  ounces mushrooms, sliced
1   10-ounce can chicken broth, regular or low sodium
Salt and pepper to taste
**Optional:**
Parmesan cheese

1. Cook the pasta, according to the package directions.
2. In a large skillet heat the oil and sauté the chicken breasts for 30 seconds.
3. Toss in the garlic and mushrooms and stir well. Cook for 5 minutes.
4. Pour in the chicken broth and bring it to a simmer. Add the spinach, stirring until it wilts.
5. Drain the pasta and return it to the cooking pot. Pour in the chicken/vegetable mixture and toss well. Heat for 2 minutes.
6. Season to taste with salt and pepper, and Parmesan cheese if desired.

YIELD: 5 servings

| Total calories: | 2,700 |
|---|---|
| Calories per serving: | 540 |

|  | Grams | % of recipe |
|---|---|---|
| CARB | 75 | 55 |
| PRO | 38 | 30 |
| FAT | 10 | 15 |

145

## Cajun Shrimp and Scallop Fettuccine

This spicy sauce also works well over rice.

2   tablespoons olive oil
1   onion, chopped
3   cloves garlic, minced
1   tablespoon Cajun seasoning
2   cups (1 14-ounce can) peeled tomatoes with juice
1½ cups tomato juice
½   teaspoon sugar
¼   cup fresh chopped parsley or 1 tablespoon dried
1   cup frozen peas
½   cup chopped roasted red peppers, drained (from a jar)
½   pound jumbo shrimp, peeled and deveined
½   pound scallops
12  ounces fettuccine or other pasta, cooked
½   cup grated Parmesan cheese
**Optional:**
2   cups sliced fresh mushrooms
1   small zucchini, chopped

1. In a large skillet heat the oil over medium-high heat and sauté the onion, garlic, and Cajun seasoning until the onions are slightly softened, about 4 to 6 minutes.
2. Stir in the mushrooms and cook until wilted.
3. Add the tomatoes, tomato juice, sugar, and parsley. Simmer for 15 minutes.
4. Stir in the peas, zucchini, peppers, shrimp, and scallops. Cover and cook for 8 to 10 minutes, or until the shrimp are pink and tender. Season to taste with salt and pepper.
5. Portion the fettuccine into serving bowls. Add sauce to each bowl and sprinkle with Parmesan as desired.

YIELD: 4 servings

| | Total calories: | 2,300 |
| --- | --- | --- |
| | Calories per serving: | 580 |

| | Grams | % of recipe |
| --- | --- | --- |
| CARB | 82 | 55 |
| PRO | 36 | 25 |
| FAT | 12 | 20 |

## Pasta with Ham and Peas

This recipe is adapted from a favorite of Nancy Ditz, who finished 8th in the 1990 New York City Marathon and 17th in the 1988 Olympic Marathon.

The combination of the sweet peas, sweet wine, and salty ham is a change from the standard Italian tomato sauces. The evaporated milk adds a slightly creamy taste.

1   pound uncooked pasta, such as penne, shells, or bowties
1   16-ounce can tomatoes, drained and diced
1   8-ounce can tomato sauce
1   cup sweet wine, vodka, or chicken broth
1   cup evaporated skim milk
¼   to ½ pound ham, diced
1   to 2 cups peas, fresh, or frozen and thawed
**Optional:**
1   to 2 tablespoons oil
1   medium onion, diced
¼   teaspoon crushed red pepper
Parmesan cheese

1. Cook the pasta according to the package directions.
2. If desired, in a large pot heat the oil and sauté the onion in oil until tender, about 5 minutes.
3. Add the tomatoes, tomato sauce, wine, and crushed red pepper if desired, and cook for about 5 minutes.
4. Add the milk, then the ham, peas, and cooked noodles. If

patient, let the mixture cook over low heat for about 5 to 10 minutes, to let the flavors blend. Serve with Parmesan cheese as desired.

YIELD: 4 large servings

| | Total calories: | 2,300 |
| --- | --- | --- |
| | Calories per serving: | 580 |

| | Grams | % of recipe |
| --- | --- | --- |
| CARB | 106 | 75 |
| PRO | 32 | 20 |
| FAT | 3 | 5 |

## Pesto

Pesto has such a wonderful flavor and color, and a little goes a long way. Not only does it make a fantastic pizza sauce, it is good in chicken salad, on sandwiches, and on plain French bread.

1   cup packed fresh basil
2   cloves garlic
¼   cup grated Parmesan cheese
Salt to taste
3   to 4 tablespoons olive oil
¾   pound of pasta, cooked
**Optional:**
2   tablespoons pine nuts

1. In a food processor combine the basil, garlic, Parmesan, salt, and pine nuts. Process until chopped.
2. Slowly add the oil and process until blended. This makes about ½ cup.
3. Add to cooked pasta.

YIELD: 3 main-dish servings

| | Total calories: | 1,400 |
| --- | --- | --- |
| | Calories per serving: | 470 |

| | Grams | % of recipe |
| --- | --- | --- |
| CARB | 75 | 65 |
| PRO | 15 | 10 |
| FAT | 12 | 25 |

# 11 MAIN DISHES WITH CHICKEN AND TURKEY

The white and dark meat of chicken and turkey are excellent examples of muscle physiology. They represent two different types of muscle fibers:

- The white breast meat is primarily fast-twitch fibers that are used for quick bursts of energy, such as sprinting and track events.

- The dark meat in the legs and wings is primarily slow-twitch fibers that function best for endurance exercise.

Elite marathon runners tend to have a high proportion of slow-twitch fibers, but also enough fast-twitch in case they need to sprint to the finish!

Because slow-twitch muscles rely more on fat for fuel, the legs and wings have a higher fat content than does the white breast meat. These darker muscles also have more iron, zinc, and B vitamins—many of the same nutrients found in red meats.

If you do not eat red meat, you might want to include more dark meat from chicken in your sports diet. For the small price of a few grams of fat, you'll get more nutritional value. The fattiest part of the chicken is really the skin, and that's what you should eliminate. To reduce temptation, remove the skin before you cook it!

| Chicken, 4 ounces | Calories | Fat (gm) | Iron (gm) |
|---|---|---|---|
| Breast, white meat: | 200 | 5 | 1.0 |
| Thigh, dark meat: | 235 | 11 | 1.5 |

## Basic Chicken Stir-Fry 101

Stir-frying is nutritious because you cook with only a small amount of liquid, and use that liquid in the sauce. The quick cooking time also minimizes the loss of vitamins. This technique works well not only with chicken but also beef, pork, lamb, and tofu.

If you are unfamiliar with stir-frying, here are a few tips to "wok" you through the process. Actually, you do not need a wok—I prefer to use a cast-iron or nonstick skillet.

½   cup uncooked rice
1   tablespoon cornstarch
2   tablespoons cold water
Seasonings (see note, below)
6   ounces boneless, skinless chicken breast
½   to 1 tablespoon oil, olive, canola, and/or sesame
½   to 1 cup chicken broth
2   to 3 cups chopped mixed vegetables, fresh or frozen

1. Prepare the rice according to the package directions.
2. In a small bowl mix together the cornstarch and cold water. Add seasonings as desired and set the mixture aside.
3. Cut the chicken into thin strips.
4. In a preheated wok or skillet heat the oil. Add the chicken, stirring a bit until done. Remove the chicken to a platter.
5. Add the denser vegetables to the wok first, because they require more cooking time. Add the broth and cover the pan. Add the smaller vegetable pieces after 1 or 2 minutes, and cook until the vegetables are tender-crisp, 2 to 5 minutes.
6. When the vegetables are almost done, add the cornstarch mixture and stir until the broth thickens.
7. Return the chicken to the wok and mix well.

**Note:** Season with your choice of 1 teaspoon of soy sauce and 1 to 2 teaspoons of brown sugar or honey, 2 tablespoons of vinegar or ketchup and a dash of ginger, salt and pepper to taste.

YIELD: 1 large serving

| Total calories: | | 660 |
|---|---|---|

| | Grams | % of recipe |
|---|---|---|
| CARB | 77 | 50 |
| PRO | 41 | 30 |
| FAT | 13 | 20 |

## Steve Jones's Chicken Stir-Fry with Sesame Sauce

Recipe contributor and 1988 NYC Marathon champion Steve Jones suggests you serve this with "vegetable rice." To cooking rice add a handful of fresh or frozen peas, corn, and mushrooms.

1     tablespoon cornstarch
2     tablespoons water
1     tablespoon tahini or peanut butter
¼     cup soy sauce or tamari
½     cup cool chicken broth
½     to 1 tablespoon oil, preferably sesame or olive
1     clove garlic, minced
12    ounces boneless, skinless chicken breasts, cut into strips
4     cups diced vegetables, fresh or frozen (mushrooms, scallions, onions, peas, broccoli, etc.)

1. In a small bowl blend the cornstarch with a small amount of water. Blend in the tahini, soy sauce, and chicken broth.
2. In a large skillet heat the oil. Sauté the garlic briefly. Add the chicken and vegetables and fry over high heat, stirring constantly, for 2 minutes.
3. Pour in the liquid mixture. Stir constantly for 1 minute, until the sauce thickens. Serve immediately.

YIELD: 2 servings

| Total calories: | | 640 |
| Calories per serving: | | 320 |

| | Grams | % of recipe |
| --- | --- | --- |
| CARB | 20 | 25 |
| PRO | 26 | 36 |
| FAT | 15 | 40 |

Calories per serving with 1½ cups rice: 620

| | Grams | % of recipe |
| --- | --- | --- |
| CARB | 86 | 55 |
| PRO | 30 | 20 |
| FAT | 17 | 25 |

## Basic Steamed Chicken

**Per person:**
1   cup water
6   ounces skinless chicken

1. In a saucepan pour ½ inch of water.
2. Add the chicken, cover tightly, and bring just to a boil. Reduce the heat.
3. Simmer over medium-low heat for 15 to 20 minutes or until

---

### SUMMARY OF NEW YORK CITY MARATHON PARTICIPATION

| Year | Starters | Finishers |
| --- | --- | --- |
| 1970 | 127 | 55 |
| 1975 | 534 | 339 |
| 1976 | 2,090 | 1,549 |
| 1979 | 11,533 | 10,477 |
| 1980 | 14,012 | 12,512 |
| 1985 | 16,705 | 15,881 |
| 1987 | 22,523 | 21,244 |
| 1991 | 26,900 | 25,797 |

(25,000 represents the approximate limit of participants allowed, as determined by the marathon organizers and city agencies.)

As of the end of the 1993 race, a total of 302,121 have finished the race out of a field of 321,666 starters.

---

the juices run clear when the chicken is pierced with a fork.

YIELD: 1 serving

| Total calories: | | 165 |

| | Grams | % of recipe |
| --- | --- | --- |
| CARB | 0 | 0 |
| PRO | 25 | 60 |
| FAT | 7 | 40 |

## Orange Chicken with Rice

This one-pot meal is popular among runners who dislike washing many dishes. It goes well with broccoli or a green salad.

6     ounces boneless, skinless chicken
⅓     cup orange juice
⅓     cup water
1     teaspoon soy sauce
½     cup uncooked rice
**Optional:**
½     small onion, sliced or chopped
½     teaspoon curry powder
*Dash garlic powder*
½     green pepper, diced

1. In a pot with a tight cover, combine the chicken, orange juice, water, soy sauce, onion, and seasonings.
2. Cover and bring the mixture to a boil. Add the rice.
3. Reduce the heat and simmer for about 20 minutes, or until the rice is done.
4. Arrange the green peppers on the top if desired. Cover and steam for 2 to 3 minutes.

YIELD: 1 serving

| Total calories: | | 520 |

| | Grams | % of recipe |
| --- | --- | --- |
| CARB | 80 | 60 |
| PRO | 31 | 25 |
| FAT | 8 | 15 |

## FAMOUS FACES WHO'VE RUN THE NYC MARATHON

*Raymond Flynn*, former mayor of Boston and current U.S. ambassador to the Vatican

*Prince Willem-Alexander Claus George Ferdinand*, heir to the throne of Holland

*William Baldwin*, star of the movie *Backdraft*

*Peter Weller*, star of the movie *RoboCop*

*Jacques D'Amboise*, former principal dancer, New York City Ballet.

*Brunson McKinley*, former U.S. ambassador to Haiti.

*Kim Alexis*, supermodel featured on more than four hundred magazine covers

*Lynn Swann*, former Pittsburgh Steelers wide receiver, member of four Super Bowl champion teams

*Bob Nystrom*, former New York Islander and Stanley Cup champion

## BUT THE AVERAGE MARATHONER IS . . .

- in his or her thirties and has been running more than a decade.

- 70 percent of the field has run a marathon before.

- more than twice the number of Marathon men are married than single, while slightly more single women than married women run the race.

- topping the list of professions represented are lawyers and administrators/managers, followed by engineers, then teachers.

## Sesame Chicken

This recipe works equally well with fish. The sesame seeds add a nice flavor, as well as some vitamin E.

6  ounces chicken breast, boned and skinned
1  to 2 tablespoons sesame seeds
1  teaspoon oil, olive, canola, and/or sesame
Salt and pepper to taste

1. Preheat a heavy nonstick skillet.
2. Place the sesame seeds into a flat dish. Dip the chicken breast into them, turning until coated.
3. In the hot skillet heat the oil. Add the chicken and cook about 5 minutes per side.

| YIELD: 1 serving | | |
|---|---|---|
| Total calories: | | 250 |

| | Grams | % of recipe |
|---|---|---|
| CARB | 1 | 0 |
| PRO | 25 | 40 |
| FAT | 16 | 60 |

## Quick One-Pot Chicken Dinner

The one-pot meal is a no-brainer—perfect for when you arrive home hungry and want a quick meal.

**Per person:**
6  ounces boneless, skinless chicken
1  large potato, cut in ¼" slices
1  cup water
Salt and pepper to taste
2  cups vegetables of your choice: peas, green beans, broccoli, etc.

1. In a saucepan with a tight fitting cover combine the chicken, potato, water, and seasonings.
2. Cover, bring to a boil, and simmer for about 10 to 15 minutes.
3. Add the vegetables. Cook for another 5 to 10 minutes or until the vegetables are done.
4. Drain and skim the broth, which you can then drink alongside the dinner.

| YIELD: 1 serving | | |
|---|---|---|
| Total calories: | | 450 |

| | Grams | % of recipe |
|---|---|---|
| CARB | 80 | 65 |
| PRO | 29 | 25 |
| FAT | 7 | 10 |

## Maple Chicken and Rice

The maple syrup adds a slightly different flavor that leaves people wondering what the secret ingredient is.

If you prefer to bake this dish, simply put the ingredients in a covered casserole and bake at 350° for 35 to 45 minutes.

**Per person:**

6  ounces chicken, boned and skinned
1  tablespoon maple syrup
1  teaspoon lemon juice
¾  cup chicken broth, homemade, canned, or from a bouillon cube
Salt and pepper to taste
½  cup rice
**Optional:**
Slivered almonds for garnish

1. In a saucepan with a tight cover, combine the chicken, maple syrup, lemon juice, broth, salt, and pepper. Bring the mixture to a boil.
2. Add the rice. Cover and simmer for 20 minutes or until the rice is done.
3. Garnish with almonds if desired.

YIELD: 1 serving

| Total calories: | | 520 |
| --- | --- | --- |
| | Grams | % of recipe |
| CARB | 81 | 60 |
| PRO | 31 | 25 |
| FAT | 8 | 15 |

## Baked Chicken with Mustard

This simple recipe offers a tasty way to add variety to yet another chicken dinner.

**Per person:**

6  ounces skinless chicken
1  to 2 teaspoons prepared mustard
2  teaspoons grated Parmesan cheese

1. Line a baking pan with aluminum foil for easy cleanup. Place the chicken in the pan.
2. Spread mustard on the chicken. Sprinkle with Parmesan.
3. Bake uncovered at 350° for 20 to 30 minutes.

YIELD: 1 serving

| Total calories: | | 190 |
| --- | --- | --- |
| | Grams | % of recipe |
| CARB | trace | trace |
| PRO | 26 | 55 |
| FAT | 10 | 45 |

## Honey-Baked Chicken

When you're tired of plain baked chicken, this offers a flavor change.

**Per person:**

6  ounces skinless chicken
2  teaspoons honey
¼  teaspoon curry powder

1. Line a baking pan with aluminum foil for easy cleanup. Place the chicken in the pan.
2. Coat the chicken with a thin layer of honey.
3. Sprinkle with curry powder.
4. Bake uncovered at 350° for 20 to 30 minutes.

YIELD: 1 serving

| Total calories: | | 200 |
| --- | --- | --- |
| | Grams | % of recipe |
| CARB | 3 | 5 |
| PRO | 25 | 55 |
| FAT | 9 | 40 |

## Yogurt-Broiled Chicken

This marinade also works well with roasted turkey breast, pork, or beef.

1  cup plain low-fat yogurt
¼  cup firmly packed brown sugar
1  to 4 cloves garlic
3  tablespoons cider vinegar
2  teaspoons Worcestershire sauce
2  dashes hot pepper sauce (Tabasco)
4  boneless, skinless chicken breast halves

1. In a blender or food processor combine all of the ingredients except the chicken. Process until smooth.
2. Arrange the chicken in a shallow baking dish. Pour the marinade evenly over the chicken.
3. Cover and refrigerate for 12 to 48 hours.
4. Broil the chicken for 5 to 7 minutes on each side, basting frequently until done. The chicken may also be grilled.

YIELD: 4 servings

| Total calories: | | 800 |
| --- | --- | --- |
| Calories per serving: | | 200 |
| | Grams | % of recipe |
| CARB | 8 | 15 |
| PRO | 27 | 55 |
| FAT | 7 | 30 |

## Chicken Breasts in Foil I

Baking chicken in foil produces a dinner that's moist and tasty, and also eliminates a dirty baking dish to scrub. You can be creative and package whatever suits your fancy inside the foil. To make good use of the oven, start a potato baking while you prepare the chicken, then place the chicken in the oven about 20 minutes later.

**Per person:**

1    boneless, skinless chicken breast
Diced vegetables of your choice: onion, mushrooms, carrots, potato
Seasonings (garlic, rosemary, thyme, basil)

1. Place the chicken breast in a 12-inch piece of aluminum foil.
2. Add vegetables and seasonings of your choice.
3. Fold the edges of the foil together.
4. Bake at 375° for about 20 minutes. Be careful of steam when opening the foil packet.

YIELD: 1 serving

| Total calories: | | 200 |
|---|---|---|

| | Grams | % of recipe |
|---|---|---|
| CARB | 10 | 20 |
| PRO | 25 | 50 |
| FAT | 7 | 30 |

## Chicken Breasts in Foil II

In this company recipe, chicken breasts are topped with flavorful, sautéed vegetables and then sealed in foil and baked. The result is very succulent, delicious chicken. Thank you, Peter Hermann, for sharing this recipe. It also works well with fish.

In addition to the mushrooms, you may add other vegetables such as zucchini, carrots, or spinach, which can be sautéed with the mushrooms.

4    boneless, skinless chicken breasts (about 6 ounces each), pounded to ¼-inch thick
Salt and pepper to taste
2    teaspoons olive oil
1    to 4 cloves garlic, minced
8    ounces mushrooms, sliced
8    ounces canned crushed tomatoes or 5 to 6 plum tomatoes, peeled and chopped
**Optional:**
1    to 2 shallots, minced or ¼ to ⅓ cup minced onion
½    teaspoon minced fresh rosemary of ¼ teaspoon dried
¼    teaspoon dried thyme
Grated rind of 1 large lemon
2    tablespoons cooking sherry

1. Sprinkle the chicken breasts lightly with salt and pepper.
2. Tear off four 12-inch pieces of aluminum foil. Place one breast on each piece of foil.
3. In a skillet heat the olive oil over medium-low heat and sauté the garlic and shallots until tender.
4. Add the mushrooms, tomatoes, and seasonings as desired and cook for about 8 minutes.
5. Remove the pan from the heat, adjust the seasonings, and pour some of the sauce over each chicken breast.
6. Fold the foil over each breast, sealing the edges. Place the foil packages on a baking sheet. Bake at 375° for 20 minutes. Serve in the foil.

YIELD: 4 servings

| Total calories: | 1,000 |
|---|---|
| Calories per serving: | 250 |

| | Grams | % of recipe |
|---|---|---|
| CARB | 9 | 15 |
| PRO | 25 | 40 |
| FAT | 13 | 45 |

## Orange-Grilled Chicken with Curry

Peter Hermann says this tasty marinade is equally good for seafood.

4    teaspoons Dijon-style mustard
1    cup orange juice
4    teaspoons curry powder
4    teaspoons dried tarragon or 2 tablespoons fresh minced
4    skinless, boneless chicken breast halves (6 ounces each)

1. In a large bowl whisk together the mustard, orange juice, curry powder, and tarragon.
2. Arrange the chicken in a shallow baking dish. Pour the marinade evenly over the chicken.
3. Marinate the chicken for at least 1 hour, or overnight.
4. Grill the chicken breasts for about 5 to 7 minutes on each side or until done. The chicken may also be broiled.

YIELD: 4 servings

| Total calories: | 700 |
|---|---|
| Calories per serving: | 175 |

| | Grams | % of recipe |
|---|---|---|
| CARB | 3 | 5 |
| PRO | 25 | 60 |
| FAT | 7 | 35 |

*More than fifty volunteer bands play at points all along the Marathon course.*

## Chicken with Sweet Potatoes and Prunes

Sweet potatoes are an excellent source of beta-carotene, and they taste great with chicken. The prunes add to the sweetness as well as color contrast.

16  dried prunes
¼  cup vinegar
¼  cup orange juice
1  cup chicken broth
4  tablespoons firmly packed brown sugar
½  teaspoon salt or to taste
4  medium sweet potatoes, peeled and cubed
4  boneless and skinless chicken breast halves
**Optional:**
¾  cup dry vermouth
2  cloves garlic, minced
1  tablespoon oregano
1  tablespoon cornstarch
¼  cup cold water

1. In a large stock pot combine the prunes, vinegar, orange juice, broth, vermouth, garlic, oregano, sugar, and salt. Bring the mixture to a boil.
2. Add the sweet potatoes and cook for about 15 minutes.
3. Place the chicken breasts on top of the potatoes, cover, and cook for about 20 minutes or until the potatoes are done.
4. Skim the fat from the broth. If desired, dissolve the cornstarch in the water and add it to the broth. Cook, stirring constantly, until thick and smooth.

| YIELD: 4 servings | |
| --- | --- |
| Total calories: | 1,900 |
| Calories per serving: | 475 |

| | Grams | % of recipe |
| --- | --- | --- |
| CARB | 75 | 60 |
| PRO | 28 | 25 |
| FAT | 7 | 15 |

## Alberto Salazar's Arroz con Pollo

This dish is of Spanish origin, and it appears with variation in other Spanish-American countries. It is a good example of America's Creole cuisine, which uses rice as a staple in a variety of combinations. This accounts for the name in Spanish being "Rice with Chicken" rather than "Chicken with Rice" as translated into English.—AS

6  boneless, skinless chicken breast halves, cut into large pieces
3  cloves garlic, minced
¼  cup oil, preferably olive
1  large onion, minced
1  large green bell pepper, minced
1  8-ounce can pimiento or roasted red pepper, finely chopped
1  16-ounce can tomato purée or ground tomatoes
3½ cups dry white wine
2  cups chicken broth
Juice of 1 lemon
1  to 2 tablespoons salt, to taste
½  teaspoon pepper
2½ cups rice
½  of a 10-ounce package frozen peas
**Optional:**
¼  teaspoon saffron
1  bay leaf
1 small can asparagus tips for garnish
½  of a 12-ounce can beer

1. Arrange the chicken in a shallow dish. Sprinkle the chicken with the garlic and oil. If time allows refrigerate for 2 hours or overnight.
2. In a large skillet cook the chicken with the marinade until the chicken is lightly browned.

3. Add the onion, green pepper, pimiento, tomato purée, wine, chicken broth, lemon juice, pepper, saffron, and bay leaf, as desired. Simmer for 10 to 15 minutes, until the chicken is about half done.

4. Add small amounts of water or broth as needed to prevent the rice from drying. Add the peas and continue heating for another 2 minutes.

5. Garnish with asparagus. Pour the beer over the dish to enhance the flavor, if desired. Serve immediately from the cooking pot.

YIELD: 6 servings

| Total calories: | 2,400 |
|---|---|
| Calories per serving: | 400 |

| | Grams | % of recipe |
|---|---|---|
| CARB | 44 | 45 |
| PRO | 33 | 35 |
| FAT | 10 | 20 |

The Marathon minyan, a Jewish prayer ceremony, is held at the race start. A Christian service is held nearby.

## Grilled Chicken with Spicy Thai Sauce

Mary Abbott Hess, past-president of the American Dietetic Association and cook par excellence, submitted this recipe. She says the spicy dipping sauce is also good with broiled shrimp or scallops and is good over rice, couscous, or bulgur.

I tried making the sauce with less sugar, but the taste of vinegar was too strong. I then added the full ⅓ cup and found it just right. The few extra carbs are worth the better taste.

4   boneless, skinless chicken breast halves, about 6 ounces each
½   cup chopped red bell pepper
½   cup vinegar
¼   to ⅓ cup sugar
½   teaspoon crushed red hot pepper flakes

**Optional:**
¼   cup lemon juice
2   cloves garlic halves
½   teaspoon salt

1. Optional: Marinate the chicken in the lemon juice for several hours.

2. In a blender or food processor purée the red bell pepper and vinegar. Pour this mixture into a small saucepan. Add the sugar and red pepper flakes, and simmer the sauce for about 10 minutes. Remove the pan from the heat and let the sauce cool.

3. Drain the chicken, rub it with garlic, sprinkle with salt, if desired.

4. Broil the chicken for about 5 to 7 minutes per side or until done.

5. Serve with individual small bowls of dipping sauce.

YIELD: 4 servings

| Total calories: | 900 |
|---|---|
| Calories per serving: | 225 |

| | Grams | % of recipe |
|---|---|---|
| CARB | 16 | 30 |
| PRO | 25 | 45 |
| FAT | 7 | 25 |

153

# WORLD MARATHON RECORDS

| | | | |
|---|---|---|---|
| 2:06:50 | Belayneh Densimo, Ethiopia | Rotterdam | 17 April 1988 |
| 2:21:06 | Ingrid Kristiansen, Norway | London | 21 April 1985 |

# AMERICAN MARATHON RECORDS

| | | | |
|---|---|---|---|
| 2:08:13 | Alberto Salazar, Eugene, OR | New York | 25 October 1981 |
| 2:21:21 | Joan Benoit Samuelson, Freeport, ME | Chicago | 20 October 1985 |

# NEW YORK CITY MARATHON RECORDS

| | | |
|---|---|---|
| 2:08:01 | Juma Ikangaa | 1989 |
| 2:24:40 | Lisa Ondieki | 1992 |

# PAST WINNERS, NEW YORK CITY MARATHON

| Year | Men | Time | Year | Women | Time |
|---|---|---|---|---|---|
| 1970 | Gary Muhrcke | 2:31:39 | 1970 | No Finisher | |
| 1971 | Norman Higgins | 2:22:55 | 1971 | Beth Bonner | 2:55:22 |
| 1972 | Sheldon Karlin | 2:27:53 | 1972 | Nina Kuscsik | 3:08:42 |
| 1973 | Tom Fleming | 2:21:55 | 1973 | Nina Kuscsik | 2:57:08 |
| 1974 | Norbert Sander | 2:26:31 | 1974 | Kathrine Switzer | 3:07:29 |
| 1975 | Tom Fleming | 2:19:27 | 1975 | Kim Merritt | 2:46:15 |
| 1976 | Bill Rodgers | 2:10:10 | 1976 | Miki Gorman | 2:39:11 |
| 1977 | Bill Rodgers | 2:11:28 | 1977 | Miki Gorman | 2:43:10 |
| 1978 | Bill Rodgers | 2:12:12 | 1978 | Grete Waitz | 2:32:30 |
| 1979 | Bill Rodgers | 2:11:42 | 1979 | Grete Waitz | 2:27:33 |
| 1980 | Alberto Salazar | 2:09:41 | 1980 | Grete Waitz | 2:25:41 |
| 1981 | Alberto Salazar | 2:08:13 | 1981 | Allison Roe | 2:25:29 |
| 1982 | Alberto Salazar | 2:09:29 | 1982 | Grete Waitz | 2:27:14 |
| 1983 | Rod Dixon | 2:08:59 | 1983 | Grete Waitz | 2:27:00 |
| 1984 | Orlando Pizzolato | 2:14:53 | 1984 | Grete Waitz | 2:29:30 |
| 1985 | Orlando Pizzolato | 2:11:34 | 1985 | Grete Waitz | 2:28:34 |
| 1986 | Gianni Poli | 2:11:06 | 1986 | Grete Waitz | 2:28:06 |
| 1987 | Ibrahim Hussein | 2:11:01 | 1987 | Priscilla Welch | 2:30:17 |
| 1988 | Steve Jones | 2:08:20 | 1988 | Grete Waitz | 2:28:07 |
| 1989 | Juma Ikangaa | 2:08:01 | 1989 | Ingrid Kristiansen | 2:25:30 |
| 1990 | Douglas Wakiihuri | 2:12:39 | 1990 | Wanda Panfil | 2:30:45 |
| 1991 | Salvador Garcia | 2:09:28 | 1991 | Liz McColgan | 2:27:33 |
| 1992 | Willie Mtolo | 2:09:29 | 1992 | Lisa Ondieki | 2:24:40 |
| 1993 | Andres Espinosa | 2:10:04 | 1993 | Uta Pippig | 2:26:24 |

## Pistachio Chicken with Curry Sauce

This recipe was adapted from one created by Chef Jeffrey Fuelo of Nutley, New Jersey. This dish requires some time to prepare, but the result is well worth the effort and it makes a special company dish. It goes well with rice and a dark green salad.

Note: The Pistachio Chicken may be prepared with any type of chopped nuts. Prechopped peanuts might be the simplest. The original recipe called for dipping the chicken in flour, then in egg, and then the nuts, but this method is simpler. You may prefer the original method. The Curry Sauce tastes great with all of the fruits and vegetables, but you may eliminate one or two of them if they are unavailable or not to your liking.

½ cup chopped celery
½ cup chopped onion
½ cup chopped carrot
½ cup diced banana
½ cup chopped pineapple (fresh or canned)
½ cup chopped apple
¼ cup water

1 teaspoon salt or to taste
1 tablespoon sugar
1 to 2 teaspoons curry powder
½ to 1 cup milk

1 cup finely chopped pistachios
4 boneless, skinless chicken breasts (about 1 pound)
1 to 2 tablespoons vegetable oil
Optional:
1 to 2 teaspoons sugar or to taste

1. In a saucepan combine the celery, onion, carrot, banana, pineapple, apple, and water. Cook over medium-low heat for about 15 minutes.

2. Add 1 teaspoon of salt, 1 tablespoon of sugar, and the curry powder, and simmer until tender, about 10 more minutes.
3. Add the milk. In a blender purée the sauce until smooth. Return the sauce to the pan and adjust the seasonings. Keep the sauce warm.
4. In a shallow dish combine the finely chopped pistachios and 1 teaspoon of sugar.
5. Roll each piece of chicken in the pistachio mixture until coated.
6. In a nonstick skillet heat the oil and sauté the chicken breasts for about 5 minutes on each side.
7. Spoon a portion of the sauce on each of 4 plates. Place a chicken breast on each plate.

YIELD: 4 servings

| Total calories: | 1,460 |
| --- | --- |
| Calories per serving: | 365 |

| | Grams | % of recipe |
| --- | --- | --- |
| CARB | 25 | 25 |
| PRO | 28 | 30 |
| FAT | 17 | 45 |

Calories per serving with 1 cup rice: 565

| | Grams | % of recipe |
| --- | --- | --- |
| CARB | 69 | 50 |
| PRO | 32 | 25 |
| FAT | 18 | 25 |

> "You don't run twenty-six miles at five minutes a mile on good looks and a secret recipe."
>
> —FRANK SHORTER

## Ground Turkey Mix for Spaghetti Sauce or Chili

Sports nutritionist Sue Luke of Charlotte, North Carolina, says this recipe makes a large amount, which is good to keep in the freezer and use as needed. It's a great way to add a little protein to pasta sauce or soups. It also works well for sloppy Joes and tacos.

1½ pounds ground turkey
1 small onion, chopped
1 small green pepper, chopped
8 ounces fresh mushrooms, chopped
1 tablespoon oil, preferably olive

1. In a large nonstick skillet sauté the turkey until cooked. Transfer the turkey to a colander and let any excess fat drip away. Wipe the skillet.
2. In the same skillet heat the oil and sauté the onions and green pepper until tender crisp.
3. Add the mushrooms and continue cooking until the mushrooms are softened.
4. Return the turkey to the pan and mix well. Divide the mixture among 6 small freezer bags.

YIELD: 6 servings

| Total calories: | 1,300 |
| --- | --- |
| Calories per serving: | 215 |

| | Grams | % of recipe |
| --- | --- | --- |
| CARB | 3 | 5 |
| PRO | 34 | 65 |
| FAT | 8 | 30 |

## Turkey Picatta

Deborah Bisson suggests that you serve the turkey picatta with your favorite pasta or roasted red potatoes. It also goes very nicely with rice. This recipe can also be prepared with chicken breasts in place of the turkey.

1   tablespoon butter or margarine
1   pound mushrooms, sliced
1½  pounds turkey breast, flattened to ¼" thickness
1   to 2 tablespoons oil, preferably olive or canola
3   tablespoons dry Madeira wine
1   to 3 tablespoons lemon juice
¼   cup chicken broth
**Optional:**
¼   cup fresh diced Italian parsley
Lemon slices for garnish

1. In a skillet melt the butter and sauté mushrooms over medium-high heat about 5 minutes. Remove the mushrooms from the pan and set them aside.
2. Heat the oil in the pan and add 1 or 2 pieces of turkey breast, sautéing for 2 to 3 minutes per side. Transfer the turkey to a plate and keep it in a warm oven while sautéing the remaining pieces.
3. Drain any excess oil from the pan and stir the wine, lemon juice, and chicken broth, scraping off any browned bits. Boil the sauce for a few minutes, until it is slightly thickened.
4. Pour the sauce over the turkey, top with the mushrooms, and garnish with fresh parsley and lemon slices if desired.

YIELD: 4 servings

| | Total calories: | 1,000 |
| --- | --- | --- |
| | Calories per serving: | 250 |

| | Grams | % of recipe |
| --- | --- | --- |
| CARB | 6 | 10 |
| PRO | 27 | 45 |
| FAT | 13 | 45 |

## Lemon Turkey Breast with Sweet Potatoes and Fruit Stuffing

Sugar-free beverages leave a nice flavor without sweetness, because the aspartame deteriorates with cooking. Andrew Ing and Ingrid Crane of Westhampton Beach, New York, submitted this recipe because it is slightly different, yet tasty and simple. The recipe also works well with chicken.

1   turkey breast half, skinned (about 2 pounds)
4   sweet potatoes, peeled and quartered
2½  cups Crystal Light citrus or lemon drink or chicken broth
Stuffing:
½   cup chopped celery
1   apple, cored and chopped
¼   cup raisins
1   to 1½ cups Crystal Light citrus or lemon drink or chicken broth
1   8-ounce package stuffing mix or seasoned bread cubes
**Optional:**
1   orange, sliced

1. Place the turkey breast in a baking pan. Pour the Crystal Light over the turkey.
2. Arrange the sweet potato quarters and orange slices around the turkey. Cover tightly with foil or a lid.
3. Bake at 350° for 1 hour and 15 minutes or until done.
4. In a large bowl combine the celery, apple, raisins, and Crystal Light. Add the stuffing mix. Transfer the stuffing to a baking dish and cover.
5. Bake at 350° for about 30 minutes.

YIELD: 6 servings

| | Total calories: | 2,400 |
| --- | --- | --- |
| | Calories per serving: | 400 |

| | Grams | % of recipe |
| --- | --- | --- |
| CARB | 56 | 55 |
| PRO | 29 | 30 |
| FAT | 7 | 25 |

YIELD: 6 servings of stuffing

| | Total calories: | 1,100 |
| --- | --- | --- |
| | Calories per serving: | 185 |

| | Grams | % of recipe |
| --- | --- | --- |
| CARB | 44 | 85 |
| PRO | 4 | 10 |
| FAT | 1 | 5 |

# 12 MAIN DISHES WITH SEAFOOD

Cooking with seafood is simple and a pleasure because of it's versatility. You can bake, poach, steam, broil, stir-fry, or grill fish, depending on the type you choose. Nevertheless, many people shy away from seafood. My advice is to learn how to prepare fish because it is not only a great source of low-fat protein, but also of health-protective fish oils.

Here are some fish tips:

- Buy fresh fish that has no "fishy" odor. Ask to smell the fish before purchasing it. Fish odor comes only with age and bacterial contamination.

- To rid your hands of any fishy smell, rub them with lemon juice or vinegar, then wash them.

- Seasonings that go well with fish include lemon, dill, basil, rosemary, and parsley (and paprika for color).

- Use the 10-minute rule for cooking fish: Cook fish 10 minutes per inch of thickness. Fold thin parts under to make the fish as even a thickness as possible. As fish cooks, the flesh turns from translucent to opaque white, similar to egg whites.

- To test for doneness, gently pull the fish apart with a fork. It should flake easily and no longer be translucent. Do not overcook fish. Perfectly cooked fish is moist and has a delicate flavor, unlike overcooked fish that is dry and tasteless.

| Fish (4 ounces cooked, or 6 ounces raw) | Calories | Gm Pro | Gm Fat |
|---|---|---|---|
| Bluefish | 210 | 34 | 7 |
| Catfish | 200 | 31 | 7 |
| Clams (8 large or 18 small) | 130 | 22 | 2 |
| Cod | 140 | 30 | 1 |
| Grouper | 160 | 33 | 2 |
| Haddock | 150 | 32 | 1 |
| Salmon, Atlantic | 240 | 34 | 11 |
| Salmon, sockeye | 190 | 36 | 15 |
| Shrimp (24 large) | 180 | 35 | 3 |
| Snapper | 170 | 35 | 2 |
| Swordfish | 210 | 36 | 7 |
| Tuna, fresh | 240 | 40 | 8 |

- If possible, cook fish in its serving dish; fish is fragile and more attractive the less it is handled.

Fish that are low in fat are also low in calories. But the fish that are high in fat offer better protection against heart disease.

## Gary Muhrcke's Shrimp with Feta Cheese

Serve this dish over rice. Very quick and easy!

2   to 4 cloves garlic, chopped
1   pound cleaned and deveined uncooked shrimp
1   28-ounce can crushed tomatoes
½   pound feta cheese
**Optional:**
½   cup chopped fresh parsley

1. Spray a large skillet with cooking spray. Sauté the garlic and shrimp until the shrimp turns pink, about 1 minute. Add a little water or broth if the shrimp stick to the pan.
2. Add the tomatoes and simmer for 2 to 5 minutes.
3. Add the crumbled feta. Add the parsley just before serving.

YIELD: 4 servings

| Total calories: | 1,200 |
|---|---|
| Calories per serving: | 300 |

| | Grams | % of recipe |
|---|---|---|
| CARB | 13 | 20 |
| PRO | 33 | 40 |
| FAT | 13 | 40 |

Calories with 1 cup rice per serving: 500

| | Grams | % of recipe |
|---|---|---|
| CARB | 57 | 45 |
| PRO | 35 | 25 |
| FAT | 15 | 30 |

# MARATHON MELTING POT

Through all five boroughs of the city and over five bridges, the twenty-five-thousand marathoners experience the sights, sounds, and ambience that is quintessentially New York. To welcome them, the New York City Fire Department hangs signs in the various neighborhoods. Here's a tour of where they run:

The race begins on the Staten Island side of the Verrazano-Narrows Bridge, America's longest single suspension bridge, built in 1964. (Staten Island became a part of New York City as a prize in a sailing contest sponsored by the Duke of York in 1687.)

After running 2 miles over the bridge, the Marathoners enter Brooklyn for an 11-mile stretch, making it the most heavily traversed borough. Brooklyn, which is 78.8 square miles, was once spelled Breukelen, and means "broken lands" in Dutch. For the first half of the race, Manhattan is always in view, with glimpses of such landmarks as the World Trade Center, the Empire State Building, and the Chrysler Building.

The first Brooklyn neighborhood is Bay Ridge, originally settled by the Dutch, later becoming a refuge for Norwegians seeking religious freedom. The area is now sprinkled with Italians and Irish.

The runners next pass Sunset Park, once Finnish, now largely Latin American and Chinese.

The race proceeds through the Gowanus section of Brooklyn, named for the Mohawk Indian chief Gowane. Gowanus was the scene of the battle of Long Island, George Washington's first engagement of the Revolution.

In Fort Greene, the three Marathon starts merge at the 8-mile mark, site of the Williamsburg Savings Bank Tower. Built in 1929, it is Brooklyn's tallest building at 512 feet. Also situated here is the Brooklyn Academy of Music, where the great Enrico Caruso once sang, and the offices of the old Brooklyn *Daily Eagle,* which in 1810 published the poetry of Walt Whitman, a local resident.

After 9 miles the runners approach Bedford-Stuyvesant, the largest African-American community in New York. Runners next enter the world of Williamsburg, the site of the world's large Hasidic Jew population. This area also provided the setting for Betty Smith's acclaimed novel, *A Tree Grows in Brooklyn.*

Winding through Greenpoint, the runners can hear cheers from the sizeable Polish population and the German, Ukrainian, and Russian communities.

In 1969, a little-known archbishop from Poland visited this area. Years later, the neighborhood named a segment of a local street Pope John Paul II Square in honor of their guest.

The Pulaski Bridge at the halfway point (13.1 miles) separates Queens from Manhattan. The first male and female runners to reach this point receive an award, appropriately from the Polish Embassy.

Runners next pass the Long Island City section of Queens. Once farmland, it is now the site of Silvercup Studios, a three-block long complex some consider Hollywood East. At the 15-mile mark, the runners face the one-mile run across the Queensboro Bridge. (After it opened in 1909, the Queensboro Bridge precipitated the quadrupling of the Queens population.)

Manhattan is what many think of as "New York." The course's largest and loudest crowds are here along First Avenue, part of the Upper East Side. Although now an affluent section, this area was once farmland spotted with foraging pigs.

The Lower Seventies were once known as Little Bohemia, and the local public library maintained a collection of fifteen thousand books—in Czech. The Eighties form the heart of Yorkville, New York's German community.

After Yorkville, the marathoners enter the lively section of Spanish Harlem and El Barrio ("The Neighborhood"). Crossing the Harlem River on the Willis Avenue Bridge and entering the South Bronx, runners now hit the 20-mile point in the race. After traversing the short, flat, Madison Avenue Bridge, they are back in Manhattan, the last borough.

Harlem is next, home to America's most famous Jazz Age nightspots and the center of African-American

*continued on next page*

## Shrimp Creole

This recipe was submitted by nutritionist Georgia Kostas and originally appeared in *What's Cooking at the Cooper Clinic.*

| 1   | to 2 tablespoons butter or margarine |
|-----|---|
| ½   | cup diced onion |
| ½   | cup diced celery |
| ½   | cup diced green bell pepper |
| ½   | teaspoon minced garlic |
| 2   | 8-ounce cans tomato sauce |
| ⅛   | teaspoon pepper |
| ¼   | teaspoon chili powder |
| 1   | pound small shrimp, cooked, peeled, and cut in pieces |
| 4   | cups cooked rice (1⅓ cups raw) |

1. In a large skillet melt the butter and sauté the onion, celery, bell pepper, and garlic until tender.
2. Add the tomato sauce, pepper, and chili powder, and simmer for 15 minutes.
3. Add the cooked shrimp and heat through.
4. Serve over rice.

YIELD: 3 servings

| Total calories: | 1,200 |
|---|---|
| Calories per serving: | 400 |

|       | Grams | % of recipe |
|-------|-------|-------------|
| CARB  | 48    | 50          |
| PRO   | 36    | 35          |
| FAT   | 7     | 15          |

## Paella

Paella is a popular dish among people of Spanish descent. To make paella, simply use Alberto Salazar's recipe for Arroz con Pollo (page 152), with the following addition. Serve with bread, to boost the carbohydrates in the meal.

| ½ | pound raw shrimp |
|---|---|
| ½ | pound raw clams |

1. Ten minutes before the rice is done, arrange the shrimp and clams on top of the casserole.
2. Cover and continue cooking for the last 10 minutes.

YIELD: 6 servings

| Total calories: | 2,700 |
|---|---|
| Calories per serving: | 450 |

|       | Grams | % of recipe |
|-------|-------|-------------|
| CARB  | 46    | 40          |
| PRO   | 44    | 40          |
| FAT   | 10    | 20          |

## Dijon Fish

This recipe was submitted by sports nutritionist Barbara Day of Louisville, Kentucky. She notes that it is easy and tastes good, too.

| 3 | tablespoons Dijon mustard |
|---|---|
| ⅓ | cup plain nonfat yogurt |
| 1 | pound halibut or other fish |
|   | Pepper to taste |
| ⅓ | cup vermouth or dry white wine |

1. In a small bowl combine the mustard and yogurt.
2. Arrange the fish in a baking dish. Season with pepper. Spread the mustard-yogurt mixture over the fish.
3. Pour vermouth or wine around the fish.
4. Bake uncovered at 400° for 15 to 20 minutes or until the fish flakes easily.

YIELD: 3 servings

| Total calories: | 660 |
|---|---|
| Calories per serving: | 220 |

|       | Grams | % of recipe |
|-------|-------|-------------|
| CARB  | 4     | 5           |
| PRO   | 37    | 70          |
| FAT   | 6     | 20          |

culture for nearly a century. Runners make their way down Fifth Avenue and around Marcus Garvey Park, named for the African-American leader who preached self-reliance when he arrived in Harlem in 1916. The route now enters the runners' mecca, Central Park, at the 23-mile mark.

The final three miles feature a brief departure from the park onto Fifty-ninth Street near the elegant Plaza Hotel. Runners re-enter the park at Columbus Circle for the final quarter-mile dash adjacent to the restaurant, The Tavern on the Green.

Central Park is a national monument and scenic landmark. At 840 acres, it is larger than the country of Monaco. The finish line is part of a park that took twenty years to build and involved moving ten million horse cartloads of stone, earth, and topsoil. Sheep Meadow, located near the finish, was populated with sheep until they were banned in 1934.

## Clam Pilaf

This dish makes a complete meal that goes well with a spinach salad.

1  cup uncooked rice
2  cups chicken broth (homemade or from bouillon) or clam juice
3  6½-ounce cans chopped or minced clams, drained
1  10-ounce package frozen peas, thawed

**Optional:**
1  tablespoon oil
2  tablespoons minced onion
2  cups sliced celery
1  to 2 cloves garlic, minced
½  teaspoon tarragon leaves
½  teaspoon dried basil leaves
1  tablespoon fresh minced parsley
Salt and pepper to taste
1  cup sliced mushrooms

1. If desired, in a saucepan heat the oil and sauté the onions, celery, garlic, and seasonings until softened, about 3 to 5 minutes.
2. Add the broth or clam juice and bring the mixture to a boil. Cover and simmer gently for 15 minutes.
3. Add the clams, peas, and mushrooms. Cover and cook for 10 minutes, or until the rice is tender and the liquid is absorbed.

YIELD: 4 servings

| Total calories: | | 1,200 |
| Calories per serving: | | 300 |

| | Grams | % of recipe |
| --- | --- | --- |
| CARB | 47 | 65 |
| PRO | 23 | 30 |
| FAT | 2 | 5 |

## Kathrine Switzer's Mussels from the Sea

You must be in New Zealand or in another pollution-free sea environment to do this. Wearing your old running shoes, wade out in the surf with a plastic bucket and knife and cut or pull the mussel shells off the rocks. Put them in the bucket, fill the bucket with clean sea water, and place it in a cool shady place overnight to let the mussels clean themselves of sand.
—KS

Fresh mussels
**Optional:**
Melted butter
Soy sauce
Crushed garlic

1. Scrub the mussel shells and cut off the "beards" with scissors and put the mussels in a steamer on the stove, or spread out on a cookie sheet in a hot oven.
2. When they are open (about 3 to 8 minutes), serve in the shell. Any that are not open, throw away; they are not good.
3. Dip the warm mussels in melted butter or a mixture of soy sauce and chopped garlic. White wine is a good accompaniment to this!

| Total calories 3 ounces of mussels without shell: | | 70 |

| | Grams | % of recipe |
| --- | --- | --- |
| CARB | 3 | 20 |
| PRO | 10 | 55 |
| FAT | 2 | 25 |

## Creamy Fish Bake

This recipe from Barbara Day was submitted because it's easy to prepare, nutritious, and the kids like it, too.

1½  pounds halibut fillets or steaks
½  cup plain low-fat or nonfat yogurt
1  tablespoon reduced fat or fat-free mayonnaise
2  tablespoons minced onion
1  teaspoon dried basil

1. Place the halibut in a baking pan.
2. In a small bowl combine the remaining ingredients.
3. Spread the yogurt mixture over the halibut.
4. Bake uncovered at 400° for 10 to 15 minutes, until the fish flakes easily.

YIELD: 3 servings

| Total calories: | | 960 |
| Calories per serving: | | 320 |

| | Grams | % of recipe |
| --- | --- | --- |
| CARB | 5 | 5 |
| PRO | 57 | 70 |
| FAT | 8 | 25 |

According to American Sports Data, Inc. of Hartsdale, New York, there are 8.8 million runners who frequently pound the pavement at least 100 times during the year. According to USA Track & Field in Santa Barbara, California, 301,500 ran U.S. marathons in 1993, an increase of 5 percent over the previous year.

## Baked Fish with Dill

Simple yet elegant.

2  pounds fish steaks such as halibut, cut ¾-inch thick
1  to 2 tablespoons butter or margarine
¼  teaspoon dried dill
2  tablespoons vermouth
Salt and pepper to taste

1. Pat the fish dry and cut it into serving pieces.
2. In a glass dish place the butter and dill. Microwave or heat in the oven until the butter is melted. Stir in the vermouth.
3. Arrange the fish in a single layer on the bottom of the baking dish. Spoon some of the sauce over the fish.
4. *Oven directions:* Cover the dish. Bake at 350° for about 15 to 20 minutes. Turn fish over halfway during the baking, for best flavor.
   *Microwave directions:* Cover the dish with waxed paper. Microwave on high for 5 to 7 minutes. Turn fish over halfway through the cooking.
5. Transfer the fish to a platter. Season the pan juices with salt and pepper to taste. Spoon the juices over the fish.

YIELD: 4 servings

| Total calories: | | 1,000 |
| --- | --- | --- |
| Calories per serving: | | 250 |

| | Grams | % of recipe |
| --- | --- | --- |
| CARB | 0 | 0 |
| PRO | 45 | 70 |
| FAT | 8 | 30 |

Orlando Pizzolato (on right) won the race twice, in 1984 and 1985, and became a hero in his native Italy.

## Baked Fish with Wine

Vermouth or dry white wine adds a nice flavor to fish—and is a nice way to use leftover wine. Instead of baking this in the oven, it may be prepared in a skillet on top of the stove. (For best results, put the fish on top of the vegetables.)

1½  pounds white fish (scrod, sole, or haddock)
½  cup vermouth or dry white wine
1  large onion, sliced
1  tablespoon flour
½  cup milk
Salt and pepper to taste
**Optional:**
Sliced mushrooms

1. Place the fish in a casserole dish. Add the vermouth, onions, and mushrooms. Cover.
2. Bake at 350° for 30 minutes.
3. Transfer the fish to a serving platter.
4. In a small bowl blend the flour into the cold milk. Add the mixture to the sauce.
5. Bring the sauce to a boil and cook until thickened, stirring constantly. Season with salt and pepper.
6. Pour the sauce over the fish.

YIELD: 3 servings

| Total calories: | | 810 |
| --- | --- | --- |
| Calories per serving: | | 270 |

| | Grams | % of recipe |
| --- | --- | --- |
| CARB | 9 | 15 |
| PRO | 48 | 70 |
| FAT | 5 | 15 |

### Kathrine Switzer's Fish in Foil

This method of cooking fish works well with most varieties, including Kathrine's favorite, orange roughy. Orange roughy is a native New Zealand fish, found in very deep water, and thus is good for you because it has cold water fish oils. Kathrine likes it because it is a beautiful white fish with a lovely delicate flavor. The scales on the outside are bright orange, but you almost never see this as the fish shop already has the fish cut into boneless fillets. Orange roughy has become "fashionable" in the United States and is available in supermarkets. Cook this fish plainly, otherwise you can't taste it. This is a very fast and easy way.

**Per Person:**

1   *fillet, about ½ pound, rinsed and dried*
⅓   *teaspoon olive oil*
*Fresh herbs*

1. Tear off 1 piece of aluminum foil, about twice the size of the fish fillet.
2. Spread the oil over the surface of the foil.
3. Place a fillet on the foil and sprinkle with fresh herbs. Bring up the sides of the foil and fold over at the top, making a closed "tent."
4. Place the foil tent on a baking sheet.
5. Bake at 375° for about 8 minutes.
6. Open tent to check for doneness. The fish will be very opaque white.
7. Slide the fillet onto your serving plate. Lightly garnish with sprigs of fresh herbs.

Yield: 1 serving

| Total calories: | | 180 |
| --- | --- | --- |

| | Grams | % of recipe |
| --- | --- | --- |
| CARB | 0 | 0 |
| PRO | 34 | 75 |
| FAT | 5 | 25 |

### Joan Benoit Samuelson's Mustard-Dill Salmon

1   *pound fresh salmon fillets or steaks*
¼   *cup of your favorite mustard*
*Juice of ½ lemon*
*Fresh dill*
**Optional:**
*Slivered almonds*

1. Cut the salmon into 3 serving pieces. Place the salmon in a glass dish. Spread each piece with mustard.
2. Squeeze lemon juice over the salmon and top with fresh dill.
3. Bake at 325° for 20 to 25 minutes, or grill for 3 to 7 minutes on each side, depending upon thickness. Top with slivered almonds, if desired.

Yield: 3 servings

| Total calories: | | 660 |
| --- | --- | --- |
| Calories per serving: | | 220 |

| | Grams | % of recipe |
| --- | --- | --- |
| CARB | 2 | 5 |
| PRO | 30 | 55 |
| FAT | 10 | 40 |

*The annual pasta party features a variety of unique recipes.*

## Fish in Lime

This recipe was submitted by Lori Fujihawa from Hawaii, where fish is a popular entrée. This is an easy, tasty, and low-fat way to prepare it.

1    *pound fresh or frozen white fish fillets*
⅓    *cup water*
⅓    *cup lime juice*
2    *tablespoons honey*
1    *teaspoon oil, preferably olive*
1    *teaspoon dried dill*

1. Cut the fish into 4 portions and place it in a shallow pan.
2. In a small bowl combine the remaining ingredients. Pour the marinade over the fish.
3. Cover the fish and refrigerate for 3 hours or overnight. Turn the fish occasionally.
4. Spray a broiler pan with nonstick cooking spray. Place the fish on the prepared pan. Tuck under any thin edges so the fish will cook evenly. Broil the fish 4 inches from the heat until the fish flakes easily. Allow 5 minutes for each half-inch of thickness. If the pieces are more than one-inch thick, turn halfway through the cooking time.
5. Baste the fish often with marinade during broiling. Brush with marinade just before serving.

YIELD: 3 servings

| Total calories: | | 660 |
| --- | --- | --- |
| Calories per serving: | | 220 |

| | Grams | % of recipe |
| --- | --- | --- |
| CARB | 10 | 20 |
| PRO | 38 | 70 |
| FAT | 3 | 10 |

*Running a marathon takes enormous concentration.*

## Fish Kabobs with Citrus Marinade

This tangy marinade also works well with chicken.

¼    *cup orange juice*
1    *tablespoon vegetable oil*
*Juice of ½ lime*
2    *cloves garlic, minced*
*Salt and pepper to taste*
1½ *pounds firm-fleshed seafood such as swordfish, shark, or tuna, cut into 1½-inch pieces or 1½ pounds whole scallops or shrimp*
1    *red bell pepper, chopped into 1½-inch square pieces*
1    *green bell pepper, chopped into 1½-inch square pieces*
1    *onion, quartered and separated into pieces*
1    *zucchini, cut in half lengthwise and cut into ½-inch pieces*
*Vegetable oil*
**Optional:**
2    *teaspoons minced fresh ginger root*
1    *teaspoon grated orange peel*

1. In a large bowl or dish combine the orange juice, 1 tablespoon of oil, lime juice, garlic, ginger root, orange peel, salt, and pepper.
2. Add the seafood and toss to coat. Cover and refrigerate for 1 hour or overnight.
3. Drain the seafood. Alternately skewer pieces of seafood, red and green pepper, zucchini slices, and onion pieces. Brush the vegetables with a small amount of oil.
4. Broil the kabobs for 2 to 3 minutes on each side or until cooked. Serve over rice if desired.

YIELD: 4 servings

| Total calories: | | 960 |
| --- | --- | --- |
| Calories per serving: | | 240 |

| | Grams | % of recipe |
| --- | --- | --- |
| CARB | 8 | 15 |
| PRO | 34 | 60 |
| FAT | 7 | 25 |

## Poached Salmon with Ginger and Soy Sauce

Poaching makes salmon so juicy and tender, and the liquid then makes a great sauce. There are endless possibilities for poaching ingredients. The following recipe combines a few favorites.

1   1-inch piece ginger root, thinly sliced
1   large clove garlic, crushed (not minced)
2   tablespoons soy sauce
1   cup water, fish stock, or vegetable stock
2   salmon steaks (about ¾ pound)
**Optional:**
2   slices lemon
⅓   cup white wine
1   tablespoon minced parsley

1. In a medium sauté pan combine the ginger, garlic, lemon slices, soy sauce, water, and wine. Heat to simmering.
2. Add the salmon steaks to the liquid, cover and simmer over medium heat until the fish is consistently light pink and just barely flakes, about 10 minutes or less. If the steaks are thick, you may need to turn them over or add more liquid to the pan. Be careful not to overcook the salmon or it will fall apart in the pan.
3. Remove the salmon to serving plates.
4. Whisk together ¼ cup of the poaching liquid and the parsley, and pour the sauce over the salmon.

*New York City Marathon race director Fred Lebow celebrated his remission from brain cancer by running the 1992 Marathon with "coach" Grete Waitz. (See page 194.)*

## TRANSLATORS

More than 450 linguists volunteer to help with every aspect of the Marathon, from working the international booth at the Expo to being part of 400 race-day linguists from start to finish. The linguists are stationed throughout the entire finish area because organizers have found that this is where tired international runners are most prone to forget their English. The linguists, who represent more than eight languages (the most widely used are Italian, German, Spanish, French, Japanese, and Swedish) are recruited from the Marathon Volunteer Corps, United Nations volunteers, and Metro International, a group of exchange students.

| YIELD: 2 servings | |
|---|---|
| Total calories: | 450 |
| Calories per serving: | 225 |

| | Grams | % of recipe |
|---|---|---|
| CARB | 2 | 5 |
| PRO | 34 | 60 |
| FAT | 9 | 35 |

## Salmon Casserole

Prepare this early in the day for the evening's dinner. If you want a slightly richer sauce, use part evaporated milk. Serve with a tossed green salad.

8 ounces noodles
2 to 4 tablespoons margarine
¼ cup flour
2 cups milk
Salt and pepper to taste
1 8-ounce can salmon
1 10-ounce package frozen peas
1 6-ounce can mushrooms

1. In a saucepan cook noodles according to the package directions.
2. In a separate saucepan melt the margarine. Stir in the flour. When the mixture is thickened, gradually add the milk. Season with salt and pepper to taste.
3. Remove the pan from the heat. Add salmon, peas, mushrooms, and then the noodles.
4. Pour the mixture into a casserole dish. Bake at 350° for 30 minutes to blend the flavors.

| YIELD: 4 servings | |
|---|---|
| Total calories: | 1,800 |
| Calories per serving: | 450 |

| | Grams | % of recipe |
|---|---|---|
| CARB | 63 | 55 |
| PRO | 25 | 25 |
| FAT | 11 | 20 |

## VOLUNTEERS

Recruiting the nearly 10,000 Marathon volunteers is a year-long process accomplished by the New York Road Runners Club (NYRRC) Volunteer Office, which spends the summer planning and enlisting recruits. According to Volunteer Coordinator Marilyn Shaw, a mailing of 8,000 volunteer applications is directed to the previous year's volunteers. Then volunteers are recruited at fall street fairs and even among the playgoers at Shakespeare in the Park.

There are two dozen possible assignments. In addition to standard tasks such as handing out medals and roses, there are jobs such as working with the "Late Crew"—a 3:00–10:00 P.M. clean-up group in Central Park.

Leading up to the race is the Packet Stuffing Party and the Food Packing Carnival. Packet stuffing involves 500 volunteers in an all-day assembling of more than 30 items in 33,000 bags. Food packing involves loading 30,000 lunch bags to be distributed to the runners after the race. Volunteers also help with the Pasta Party and the International Breakfast Run. Rubbing shoulders with international runners makes this one of the most popular Marathon jobs.

The Expo is the hub of the action during race week, and volunteers include everyone from high school students to doctors and teachers. They roll Marathon posters, iron and sew for the store set-up, direct traffic, and interpret.

By race day there are thousands of additional volunteers recruited by the mayor's office from Community Boards to work the water stations along the course. There are 1,000 volunteers in Central Park. To obtain one of the coveted finish-line jobs, a person is required to work at other races such as the Marathon Computer Run, a five-mile rehearsal race conducted the week before the big day.

A unique volunteer job is that of bandit catcher. Although runners are individually screened at the start by computer and video cameras, some runners without numbers jump in along the course and try to cross the finish line. Seventy bandit catchers—all runners and fit to give chase—are placed along the final mile of the course. They wear Marathon T-shirts that are imprinted on the back: EXIT GUIDE FOR UNNUMBERED RUNNERS.

Volunteering often leads to unexpected opportunities. Lucille Singleton, one of the stalwart Marathon "grunt" crew who has been working at NYRRC races for well over a decade, has a lot of experience lifting heavy wooden barricades. It was this experience, claims Volunteer Coordinator Marilyn Shaw, that may have aided the seventy-year-old Singleton in acquiring her 1994 job: in construction.

## Tuna-Noodle Casserole I

This classic casserole is even better the second day, when the flavors have had time to blend.

1  8-ounce package noodles
1  7-ounce can tuna, drained
1  10½-ounce can cream of mushroom soup
½  soup can milk
Salt and pepper to taste

1. Cook the noodles according to the package directions.
2. In a saucepan combine the tuna, soup, and milk. Season with salt and pepper to taste.
3. Add the noodles.
4. Serve as is, or bake at 350° for 20 minutes to allow the flavors to blend.

YIELD: 3 servings

| | | |
|---|---|---|
| Total calories: | | 1,400 |
| Calories per serving: | | 470 |

| | Grams | % of recipe |
|---|---|---|
| CARB | 66 | 55 |
| PRO | 26 | 25 |
| FAT | 11 | 20 |

## Tuna-Noodle Casserole II

This is almost as easy as Tuna Noodle Casserole I, but has much more flavor and makes a delicious supper. Vary it by adding pimientos, brine-cured olives, sherry, or chopped cooked spinach.

1  to 2 tablespoons butter, margarine, or oil
1  cup sliced fresh mushrooms
⅓  cup chopped onion
1  6-ounce can water-packed tuna, drained and flaked
¼  cup milk
½  pound pasta noodles (rotelli, shells, etc.), cooked al dente
1  10½-ounce can cream of mushroom soup (reduced fat variety)
Salt and pepper to taste
**Optional:**
¼  teaspoon garlic powder or 1 clove fresh minced
¼  teaspoon celery seed
¼  teaspoon dried dill
1  to 2 tablespoons sherry
1  tablespoon chopped pimiento
8  to 10 brine-cured black olives, chopped
½  cup chopped, cooked spinach
Parmesan cheese

1. In a small skillet heat the oil and sauté the mushrooms and onion until the onion is translucent.
2. In a large bowl combine the remaining ingredients. Add the mushroom and onion mixture and blend well.
3. Transfer the mixture to a 1½-quart glass baking dish. Sprinkle with Parmesan cheese if desired.
4. Bake uncovered at 350° for 30 minutes.

YIELD: 3 servings

| | | |
|---|---|---|
| Total calories: | | 1,400 |
| Calories per serving: | | 470 |

| | Grams | % of recipe |
|---|---|---|
| CARB | 67 | 55 |
| PRO | 28 | 25 |
| FAT | 10 | 20 |

# 13 MAIN DISHES WITH BEEF, PORK, AND LAMB

Red meats such as beef, pork, and lamb are an excellent addition to a sports diet because they are not only a good source of protein but also iron, zinc, and B vitamins. (See chapter 2 for more details.) The trick is to choose the cuts of meat that look the leanest. Then, trim any visible fat before cooking, and eat the meat only in small portions as the accompaniment to the meal, so that one pound of meat stretches to feed four people.

The leanest cuts of meat include:

Lean beef: Round steak, top and bottom round roast, eye of the round, boneless rump roast, tip steak, lean stew beef, strip steak, flank steak, more than 85 percent lean hamburger

Pork: sirloin roast or chops, loin chops, top loin roast, tenderloin, cutlets

Ham: lean and extra-lean cured ham (labeled 93 to 97 percent fat-free), center-cut ham, Canadian bacon

Veal: Loin roast and chop, leg steak, rump roast, cutlets, arm roast, and steak

Lamb: sirloin roast, loin chops, leg roast

To further reduce the fat content, cook the meat appropriately:

- Broil, grill, bake, or roast the meat, trying not to overcook.
- When roasting, use a rack so the fat will drain away from the meat.
- Use nonstick skillets for browning, adding little or no extra fat.
- Because lean meats may be tougher than fattier cuts, they cook best when thinly sliced (for stir-fry dishes) or made into soups and stews (for moistness).
- After making a soup or stew, either cool it and skim the fat from the top, or if time allows, refrigerate it until the fat solidifies on the top, then scrape off the fat before reheating.
- When making gravy, drain the fat from the pan, then add water to liquify the drippings, and pour it into a smaller saucepan. Skim the fat off this drippings water, heat to a boil, and thicken with a mixture of 1 to 1½ tablespoons flour mixed into cold water per cup of broth.

> "The most surprising part is that an event that ties up this much traffic doesn't have the name Trump in the title."
>
> —PHIL MUSHNICK, New York Post, on the 1989 Marathon

## Sweet 'n' Spicy Orange Beef

This is a welcome treat after a hard workout, when you're hungry for something sweet but healthful.

1   cup uncooked rice
1   pound extra-lean ground beef
¼   cup orange marmalade
¼   teaspoon red pepper flakes
**Optional:**
*Cayenne pepper to taste*
*Cooked peas*
*Diced celery*
*Green bell pepper*
*Pineapple chunks*

1. Cook the rice according to the package directions.
2. In a skillet sauté the beef until browned. Drain the fat.
3. Add the marmalade, hot pepper, and cooked rice. Mix well. Add any of the optional ingredients as desired.

YIELD: 4 servings

| Total calories: | | 1,500 |
|---|---|---|
| Calories per serving: | | 375 |

|  | Grams | % of recipe |
|---|---|---|
| CARB | 52 | 55 |
| PRO | 33 | 35 |
| FAT | 4 | 10 |

*Finishing a marathon is an unforgettable experience because each finisher is a winner.*

its unusual yellowish-brown color, but he quickly came to appreciate its sweet and spicy flavor and the change it offers from his more traditional pizza dinners.

2   *pounds extra-lean ground beef*
1   *medium onion, chopped*
2   *tablespoons lemon juice*
2   *teaspoons curry powder*
1   *teaspoon turmeric*
1   *tablespoon apricot jam or orange marmalade*
1   *tablespoon fruit chutney*
*Salt and pepper to taste*
½   *cup raisins*
3   *eggs (or substitute)*
1   *cup milk*
**Optional:**
½   *cup slivered almonds*
2   *bay leaves*

1. Mix together the ground beef, chopped onion, lemon juice, curry powder, turmeric, jam, chutney, salt, pepper, raisins, and almonds, if desired.
2. Brown this meat mixture in a nonstick skillet then put it in to a 2-quart casserole.
3. Beat together the eggs and the milk. Pour the mixture over the meat, then top with the whole bay leaves, if desired. Bake at 350° for about 30 to 40 minutes or until set. Remove the bay leaves before serving.

Yield: 8 servings

| | Total calories: | 2,600 |
|---|---|---|
| | Calories per serving: | 325 |

| | Grams | % of recipe |
|---|---|---|
| CARB | 14 | 15 |
| PRO | 27 | 35 |
| FAT | 18 | 50 |

Calories with 1 cup rice per serving:   535

| | Grams | % of recipe |
|---|---|---|
| CARB | 58 | 45 |
| PRO | 29 | 25 |
| FAT | 19 | 40 |

## Goulash

The original recipe calls for stew beef but I generally make this with hamburger since it takes less cooking time. Serve with noodles, peas, and bread to boost the carbohydrates.

1   *pound lean hamburger*
1   *large onion, chopped*
1   *clove garlic, crushed*
1   *8-ounce can tomato sauce*
*Salt and pepper to taste*
*Dash cloves*
*Pinch basil*
1   *tablespoon molasses*

1. In a large skillet brown the hamburger, onion, and garlic. Drain the grease.
2. Add the tomato sauce and seasonings. Cover and simmer for 20 minutes to 2 hours. The longer the goulash cooks, the better the flavor.

YIELD: 4 servings

| Total calories: | 1,200 |
|---|---|
| Calories per serving: | 300 |

| | Grams | % of recipe |
|---|---|---|
| CARB | 11 | 15 |
| PRO | 28 | 40 |
| FAT | 16 | 45 |

Calories with 1 cup noodles per serving:   510

| | Grams | % of recipe |
|---|---|---|
| CARB | 53 | 40 |
| PRO | 35 | 30 |
| FAT | 16 | 30 |

## South African Bobotie

Pronounced bob-bootie, this South African meal is a favorite with two-time New York City Marathon winner Tom Fleming and his wife Barbara who is from South Africa. When Tom first looked at this dish he was somewhat skeptical due to

## Meatballs and Variations

This recipe calls for beef, but ground turkey or chicken can be substituted. Sue Luke, sports nutritionist in Charlotte, North Carolina, says they are an excellent, low-fat way to get some protein with your pasta.

2   pounds extra-lean ground beef
4   eggs (or substitute)
1½  cups seasoned bread crumbs
3   cloves garlic, minced
2   teaspoons Italian seasoning
Salt and pepper to taste
¼   to ½ cup milk, beer, or tomato juice to moisten

**Optional:**
1   chopped onion
¼   cup Parmesan cheese, or ½ cup low-fat Cheddar cheese

1. In a mixing bowl combine all of the ingredients. Shape the mixture into balls.
2. Place the meatballs on a baking sheet. Bake at 350° for 15 to 20 minutes.
3. When the meatballs have cooled, place them in a freezer bag and use them as needed. They may be dropped into spaghetti sauce 15 or 20 minutes before serving.

YIELD: about 24 golf-ball size meatballs

| Total calories: | | 2,900 |
| Calories per meatball: | | 120 |

|  | Grams | % of recipe |
| --- | --- | --- |
| CARB | 5 | 15 |
| PRO | 11 | 40 |
| FAT | 6 | 45 |

## Taco Salad

Stacy Flickner says this is a quick and easy Mexican dish that is popular after a busy day at work. Don't forget the salsa for that spicy touch! You can also use leftover chili in place of the taco beef mixture. To boost the carbohydrate value, simply add an extra can of beans and/or eliminate or reduce the meat.

½   to 1 pound lean ground beef or turkey
1   packet taco seasoning
1   16-ounce can kidney beans, drained
6   ounces fat-free tortilla chips
4   ounces (1 cup) shredded low-fat Cheddar cheese
4   cups shredded lettuce
1   cup sliced fresh tomatoes

**Optional:**
Salsa
Low-fat sour cream
Guacamole

1. In a skillet brown the beef. Drain the fat.
2. Add the taco seasoning.
3. Add the beans and heat through.
4. In a 2-quart casserole dish layer in order the tortilla chips, hot meat mixture, cheese, lettuce, and tomatoes.
5. Top with a dollop of salsa, low-fat sour cream, or guacamole if desired. Serve immediately.

YIELD: 4 servings

| Total calories: | | 1,700 |
| Calories per serving: | | 425 |

|  | Grams | % of recipe |
| --- | --- | --- |
| CARB | 48 | 45 |
| PRO | 30 | 30 |
| FAT | 13 | 25 |

## THE RED CROSS

More than two hundred volunteers from the American Red Cross are on duty on race day. They assist the City's Emergency Medical Services teams by providing nonemergency first-aid treatment at two locations along the Marathon route. Red Cross volunteers also support the acute care medical tent in Central Park, acting as stretcher bearers. Early in the day, the Red Cross serves a light breakfast at the Staten Island Naval Base. In Central Park, food stations provide coffee, donuts, and snacks at the Family Reunion Area.

Typically, the Red Cross will serve:
32,000 cups of coffee
12,000 cups of hot chocolate
6,000 cups of tea
5,600 sandwiches
15,600 donuts
8,400 rolls

The Red Cross will have on hand:
40,000 packets of sugar and sugar substitute
50,000 paper cups
40,000 plastic stirrers
24,000 paper napkins
2,200 garbage bags
1,000 cots and blankets

## Beef and Bean Burritos

The meat in this recipe may be omitted, as well as the cheese, for a lower fat meatless version. Note how easily the combination of just a little extra-lean meat and low-fat cheese add up the grams of fat.

½  pound extra-lean ground beef or turkey
½  packet taco seasoning mix (see note, below)
1  16-ounce can black or pinto beans
4  large flour tortillas
4  ounces (1 cup) grated low-fat Cheddar or Monterey Jack cheese
2  cups shredded lettuce
2  medium tomatoes, diced
**Optional:**
1  small green onion, diced
Sliced jalapeño peppers
Salsa
Low-fat sour cream
Guacamole

1. In a large skillet brown the beef or turkey. Drain the fat.
2. Add the taco seasoning and drained beans, and heat through.
3. Onto each tortilla spoon a portion of the meat and bean mixture. Top with cheese. Roll the tortillas up into burritos.
4. Arrange the burritos in a glass baking dish. Microwave on high for 30 to 45 seconds. Or place the burritos on a baking sheet and broil in the oven until lightly browned on top.

5. Place the burritos on serving plates. Top with the remaining ingredients, as desired.

**Note:** The taco seasoning may be replaced with the following seasoning mixture. Combine ⅛ teaspoon cumin, ⅛ teaspoon oregano, ⅛ teaspoon garlic powder, ¼ teaspoon chili powder, a dash of cayenne pepper or 3 dashes of Tabasco, salt, and pepper to taste.

YIELD: 4 burritos

| Total calories: | | 1,300 |
| Calories per serving: | | 325 |

| | Grams | % of recipe |
| --- | --- | --- |
| CARB | 29 | 35 |
| PRO | 27 | 35 |
| FAT | 12 | 30 |

---

## TIMING IS EVERYTHING

At peak Marathon time, which is about 2:45 P.M., more than three hundred runners a minute cross the finish line. In order to accommodate so many, three separate finish lines are used, breaking the number down to ninety-five to one hundred runners per minute. This matches the race start, which features three separate, but simultaneous, starting lines.

---

## Easy Enchilada Stack

This recipe is from the kitchen of Arturo Barrios and Joy Rochester of Boulder, Colorado. You may boost the carbohydrates by adding canned beans.

½  to 1 pound extra-lean ground beef, or turkey or chicken cubes
1  cup chopped onion
1  8-ounce jar salsa
1  8-ounce can diced green chilies
1  8-ounce carton plain nonfat yogurt
2  ounces (½ cup) low-fat Cheddar cheese, shredded
4  flour tortillas

1. In a large skillet cook the ground beef and onion until browned. Reserve a small amount of salsa and chilies for garnish, and add the remaining salsa and chilies. Mix well. Cover and simmer for 5 to 10 minutes. Drain slightly if there is any excess liquid.
2. In a casserole dish alternately layer a tortilla, ⅓ of the meat mixture, ⅓ of the yogurt, and ⅓ of the cheese. Repeat the layers 3 times, ending with a tortilla.
3. Sprinkle the reserved salsa and cheese over the layers. Bake at 350° for 5 to 10 minutes.

YIELD: 3 servings

| Total calories: | | 1,300 |
| Calories per serving: | | 430 |

| | Grams | % of recipe |
| --- | --- | --- |
| CARB | 46 | 45 |
| PRO | 29 | 25 |
| FAT | 14 | 30 |

## Sloppy Joes

These make a favorite for a Saturday lunch—spicy and a change from a cold sandwich. By cooking this in a cast-iron skillet, you will get more nutritional value from additional iron in the sauce. You can also make this with tofu instead of beef for a vegetarian meal.

1   pound extra-lean hamburger
1   12-ounce bottle chili sauce
8   hamburger buns or English muffins
**Optional:**
Grated cheese

1. In a skillet brown the hamburger. Drain well.
2. Add the chili sauce and heat through.
3. Serve over hamburger buns or English muffins. Sprinkle with grated cheese, if desired.

YIELD: 4 servings

| Total calories: | | 2,100 |
| --- | --- | --- |
| Calories per serving (2 buns): | | 525 |

| | Grams | % of recipe |
| --- | --- | --- |
| CARB | 68 | 50 |
| PRO | 30 | 15 |
| FAT | 15 | 25 |

## Kathrine Switzer's Rack of Lamb with Rosemary

Kathrine is a great believer in a diet that has some red meat in it; she's particularly fond of lamb. It is a real treat in America, but ordinary fare in New Zealand. It's funny to see the most expensive item on an American menu being so common in New Zealand.

1   lamb rack; enough for 2 people
1   teaspoon dried rosemary

1. Have the butcher trim down most of the fat from the outside of the lamb rack and between the bones about ½ inch from the loin. This makes it healthier (less fat) and prettier to serve.
2. Dampen the lamb rack and press crushed rosemary on it. (It won't stick unless the lamb is damp). Put lamb on a metal or wire rack in a broiler or roaster pan; this way it cooks with the fat dripping off of the meat.
3. Put it in a 450° oven for 10 minutes, then turn the heat down to about 350° to 375°. (This seals the outside of the meat and keeps juices in.) Cook for about 25 minutes more, then take a look at the meat, maybe even cutting into it to test for doneness. If you like lamb medium-rare, watch this timing pretty carefully. In any case, it will be completely done within 40 or more minutes, or a total cooking time of 50 minutes.
4. A lovely presentation is to serve the whole rack on a platter with watercress, grilled tomato halves and roasted potatoes. Put those frilly paper hats on the end of the bones for a great look.

YIELD: 2 servings

| Calories per 4-ounce serving: | | 230 |
| --- | --- | --- |
| | Grams | % of recipe |
| CARB | 0 | 0 |
| PRO | 33 | 55 |
| FAT | 11 | 45 |

## Sweet and Sour Pork Chops

Excellent with rice and peas.

4   lean pork chops, well trimmed
1   13½-ounce can pineapple
    chunks with juice reserved
¼   cup molasses
½   cup vinegar
1   tablespoon soy sauce
2   teaspoons cornstarch
1   tablespoon water

**Optional:**
½   teaspoon ginger
1   11-ounce can mandarin oranges

1. In a large skillet brown the pork
   chops. Drain the fat.
2. Add the pineapple juice,
   molasses, vinegar, soy sauce,
   and ginger. Cover and simmer
   for 30 minutes.
3. Skim the fat.
5. In a small bowl dissolve the
   cornstarch in the water. Blend
   the mixture into the sauce.
   Cook, stirring constantly, until
   thickened.
6. Add the pineapple chunks and
   mandarin oranges, and heat
   through.

YIELD: 4 servings

| Total calories: | 1,500 |
|---|---|
| Calories per serving: | 375 |

|  | Grams | % of recipe |
|---|---|---|
| CARB | 32 | 35 |
| PRO | 28 | 30 |
| FAT | 15 | 35 |

*One of the two hundred to three hundred
runners in the Marathon representing the
New York Police Department*

# 14 VEGETARIAN MAIN DISHES, BEANS, AND GRAINS

Whereas vegetarian runners used to be considered somewhat "nutty," vegetarian cookery is popular among most of today's runners. They enjoy not only the fine flavor of meatless meals but also the carbohydrate-rich beans and grains that are the foundation of a vegetarian diet.

Most of the meatless meals have been included with the Pasta, Soups, Stews, and Chilis, and Breakfasts and Brunches chapters. Hence, this chapter contains only a few additional recipes.

### BEANS

Without a doubt, cooking with canned beans is far quicker than cooking you own. But if you prefer home cooked, here are some tips:

- Beans (except for lentils) should be soaked overnight or for 6 to 8 hours in room-temperature water. This shortens the cooking time and improves the flavor, tex-

| Bean | Cooking time | Yield from one cup dry |
|------|--------------|------------------------|
| Garbanzo | 3 hours | 4 cups |
| Kidney | 1½ | 2 |
| Lentils | 1 | 2+ |
| Pinto | 2½ | 2 |

ture, and appearance of the beans. Soaking also reduces the gas-causing qualities.

If you want to speed the soaking process, add beans to a large pot of boiling water and boil for 2 minutes. Cover, then remove the pot from the heat and let it stand for an hour. Drain and rinse, and then they'll be ready to cook.

- Beans cook nicely in a Crock-Pot (5 to 10 hours, moderate heat) or pressure cooker (10 to 35 minutes), depending upon how well-done you like them.

- Be sure to use a large enough kettle. Beans expand!!!

- Cook enough beans for more than one meal. They refrigerate and freeze well. For convenience, freeze them in individual portions.

- Because beans lack the amino acid methionine, simply serve them with methionine-rich foods such as rice or corn or milk products to enhance their protein value.

- Beans are not only a good source of protein, but also carbohydrates, B vitamins such as folic acid, and fiber. When added to an overall low-fat diet, they can help lower elevated blood cholesterol levels.

- If beans cause you intestinal problems, eat small amounts, and be sure to soak them long enough before cooking. You can also try Beano, a product that when added to beans helps reduce gas formation.

### BEAN IDEAS

- In a blender, mix black beans, salsa, and cheese. Heat in the microwave and use as a dip or on top of tortillas or potato.

- Sauté garlic and onions in a little oil; add canned beans (whole or mashed) and heat together.

> "The starting line of the New York City Marathon is kind of like a giant time bomb behind you about to go off . . . it is the most spectacular start in the sport."
>
> **—BILL RODGERS,**
> *1987 television coverage*

> "You go across the whole city and not one person gives you the finger."
>
> —Marathoner **CURTIS TRIPP,**
> *New York Times,*
> *November 5, 1990*

- *Add to salads, spaghetti sauce, soups, and stews for a protein booster.*

## GRAINS

*The most commonly eaten grains include rice, wheat, corn, and oats. Grains less familiar to U.S. runners include buckwheat, bulgur, millet, wild rice, and rye. Many runners in other countries, however, thrive on these foods. The Kenyan runners, for example, have done very well without pasta! Perhaps we have something to learn?*

*If you want to experiment with eating more grains, go to the health food store and ask someone to help you select a mixture, such as Kashi. Cook grains in quantity, and then add them to your meals:*

- *For breakfast, most grains can be eaten as a hot cereal with banana, raisins, and yogurt.*

- *Add cooked grains to soups, for more substance.*

- *In dinners, replace pasta and rice with grains.*

## CORN

*Although corn is eaten in the United States primarily as a vegetable side dish (corn on the cob) or as a snack (popcorn), this grain is a staple in the diet of many runners—particularly those from Africa and South America, as well as Italy and many other countries. Cornmeal is popularly made into polenta (Italian), ugali (Kenyan), or cornmeal mush (southern United States).*

## COUSCOUS

*Couscous is a tiny, pellet-like grain made from wheat in United States, or from cracked millet in North Africa (much like bulgur of the Middle Eastern countries).*

*Couscous is best know to many runners as the main ingredient in Tabouli.*

## Tabouli

Light, refreshing, and a nice change from pasta salads.

1   cup bulgur or couscous
2   cups boiling water
2   tomatoes, diced
½   cucumber, diced
1   cup fresh parsley, chopped
1   to 2 tablespoons olive oil
2   tablespoons lemon juice
1   clove garlic, finely chopped
½   teaspoon salt, as desired
**Optional:**
3   scallions, diced
3   tablespoons chopped fresh mint

1. Place the bulgur in a medium bowl and cover with the boiling water. Let the bulgur soak for an hour refrigerated or overnight.
2. Drain the bulgur well in a strainer. In a serving dish combine the bulgur, diced tomatoes, cucumber, scallions, and parsley. Mix well.
3. Mix the oil, lemon juice, garlic, mint, and salt. Add the mixture to the tabouli within 1 hour of serving.

YIELD: 3 servings

| Total calories: | 600 |
|---|---|
| Calories per serving: | 200 |

|  | Grams | % of recipe |
|---|---|---|
| CARB | 38 | 75 |
| PRO | 3 | 5 |
| FAT | 4 | 20 |

## ONLY IN NEW YORK . . .

### MULTI-LINGUAL MARATHON

The Marathon entry form is printed in five languages. The 13,700 No Parking signs along the course for race day are in three languages: Spanish, Yiddish, and English.

### MARATHON ANGST

Calming runners is an important job. Marathoners are concerned about everything from finishing the race to fears of crowds and bridges. The long wait at the race start and the extreme fatigue at the end can exacerbate these anxieties. Enter the psyching team—a group of about one hundred psychiatrists, psychologists, and social workers. An estimated fifteen hundred runners at the start and finish take advantage of the group's expertise.

### KEEPING WARM

When the engine stops running, the body gets cold. That's why runners wrap themselves in metalized thermal blankets given out at the Marathon finish. This keeps them warm until they can retrieve their gear. If laid end to end, the blankets would extend 7.89 miles longer than the Marathon's 26.2 miles. It takes more than forty volunteers to distribute the blankets.

*continued on page 176*

## Beans and Rice

Black beans with brown rice. Red beans with white rice. Beans and rice in any combination together provide complete protein without fat. Beans are also a good source of fiber. Although delicious as is, this dish makes a great taco filling, using corn tortillas, hot sauce, lettuce, and cheese.

2   tablespoons oil
½   cup chopped onion
½   cup chopped celery
2   cups cooked white or brown rice
1   16-ounce can or 2 cups cooked pinto, kidney, or other beans of your choice

**Optional:**
1   tablespoon chopped parsley
½   teaspoon garlic powder or 2 cloves fresh garlic, minced
Several dashes Tabasco sauce
Salt and pepper to taste

1. In a large skillet heat the oil and sauté the onion and celery until tender.
2. Add the remaining ingredients and simmer for 5 minutes to blend the flavors.

YIELD: 3 servings

| Total calories: | | 1,200 |
| --- | --- | --- |
| Calories per serving: | | 400 |

| | Grams | % of recipe |
| --- | --- | --- |
| CARB | 63 | 65 |
| PRO | 15 | 15 |
| FAT | 10 | 20 |

*"I don't know if you'd call it a zoo, a circus, or a party, maybe a little bit of each."*
—Corey McPherrin, reporting on the start of the 1987 NYC Marathon for WABC-TV New York.

## Ugali

This Kenyan dish is a staple that is eaten both at lunch and dinner—as well as pre-marathon. The Kenyans generally eat generous amounts of it along with their typical meals of chicken, cabbage, and rice. Because the flavor and texture differs depending upon the use of white or yellow cornmeal, you might want to try both, then make your choice. Ugali made with white cornmeal tends to be more popular among Americans.

4   cups water
1   cup cornmeal, white or yellow
Salt to taste

1. In a saucepan bring the water to a rapid boil.
2. Slowly sprinkle the cornmeal into the rapidly boiling water, stirring continuously for about 5 minutes.
3. When the ugali has become thick (about 3 to 5 minutes), remove the pan from the heat.
4. Serve with chicken and cabbage for a traditional Kenyan meal.

YIELD: 2 servings

| Total calories: | | 500 |
| --- | --- | --- |
| Calories per serving: | | 250 |

| | Grams | % of recipe |
| --- | --- | --- |
| CARB | 55 | 85 |
| PRO | 6 | 10 |
| FAT | 1 | 5 |

## Mexican Bean Bake

This recipe is reprinted with permission from *The Balancing Act Nutrition and Weight Guide*, by Georgia Kostas, R.D., nutritionist at the Cooper Clinic in Dallas, Texas.

2   cups cooked (1 16-ounce can) kidney beans (or other beans of your choice)
1   tablespoon dried basil
1   tablespoon dried oregano
1   bouillon cube
1   15-ounce can tomato sauce
1   8-ounce can tomato paste
½   cup low-fat Ricotta cheese
6   tortillas, corn or flour
1   cup (4 ounces) grated part-skim mozzarella cheese

**Optional:**
1   onion, chopped
1   clove garlic, minced
⅛   teaspoon pepper
1   teaspoon dried parsley

1. In a saucepan stir together and heat the beans, onion, garlic, seasonings, and bouillon cube.
2. Add the tomato sauce and paste and cook for 20 minutes, stirring occasionally.
3. Add the Ricotta cheese, stir, and continue cooking.
4. Line the bottom of an 11x7-inch shallow glass baking dish with 6 tortillas. Spread with the bean mixture and then the Mozzarella cheese. Bake uncovered at 400° for 30 minutes.

YIELD: 4 servings

| Total calories: | | 1,800 |
|---|---|---|
| Calories per serving: | | 450 |

| | Grams | % of recipe |
|---|---|---|
| CARB | 59 | 55 |
| PRO | 25 | 20 |
| FAT | 13 | 25 |

## Polenta

This recipe from Sharon Barbano's Italian grandmother is similar to the Kenyan Ugali. Sharon recommends serving it with tomato sauce and grated cheese for dinner (as she enjoyed every Christmas Eve after midnight mass), or else with maple syrup, honey, molasses, and/or milk for a hearty breakfast after winter running.

4   cups boiling water or hot milk or combination
1   cup white or yellow cornmeal
½   cup cold water
1   teaspoon salt

1. Place boiling water or hot milk or combination in the top of a double boiler over simmering water.
2. In a small bowl combine the cornmeal, cold water, and salt.
3. Gradually stir the cornmeal mixture into the hot liquid. Cook and stir the mixture for 2 to 3 minutes over high heat.
4. Cover and steam over medium heat for 25 to 30 minutes, stirring frequently.

YIELD: 2 servings

| Total calories: | | 500 |
|---|---|---|
| Calories per serving: | | 250 |

| | Grams | % of recipe |
|---|---|---|
| CARB | 55 | 85 |
| PRO | 6 | 10 |
| FAT | 1 | 5 |

### FRUIT OF THE VINE

In one Italian area along the course, red-and-white checkered tablecloths have been topped with glasses of wine for the Marathoners—the residents' version of an aid station.

### MUSIC, MUSIC EVERYWHERE

Runners get psyched with the music of more than fifty volunteer bands along the course. The bands make every kind of music, from funk to salsa and ragtime. One group dresses in tuxedos and plays classical music.

The increase in the number of bands began in the mid-1980s, after race director Fred Lebow heard music during the London Marathon. However, New York's tunes date back to 1979, when the proud and hearty Bishop Loughlin High School band started blasting out the theme from the movie *Rocky*. Stationed at the site of their school, they're still at it. Every year, they play variations of the *Rocky* theme from the first runner to the last.

### MARATHON MOTIVATION

During the 1984 NYC Marathon, when eventual winter Orlando Pizzolato of Italy frequently stopped while cramping in the heat, motorcycle police officer Ralph Viscio was there to encourage him. *"Cinquanta mille dollari,"* Viscio would tell him in Italian ("fifty thousand dollars," the total value of the prize money for winning that year), and Pizzolato would start running again.

## Refried Beans

This recipe for refried beans is a low-fat version of what you generally get from a can or in a restaurant. If you don't have a food processor, simply mash the beans with the back of a fork. This recipe, submitted by Karen Angevine, R.D., is reprinted with permission from *What's Cooking at the Cooper Clinic*.

3  cups cooked pinto beans
¼  cup chicken broth or liquid from beans
1  tablespoon vegetable oil
½  cup chopped onion
1  teaspoon minced garlic
¼  teaspoon garlic powder
¼  teaspoon cayenne pepper
Salt and pepper to taste

1. In a food processor combine the beans and chicken broth. Process until puréed.
2. In a large skillet heat the oil over medium-high heat and sauté the onions and garlic until tender.
3. Pour the bean purée into the skillet. Stir constantly until thickened.
4. Season with garlic powder, cayenne, salt, and pepper. Serve hot.

YIELD: 4 servings

| Total calories: | 1,000 |
|---|---|
| Calories per serving: | 250 |

|  | Grams | % of recipe |
|---|---|---|
| CARB | 42 | 65 |
| PRO | 12 | 20 |
| FAT | 4 | 15 |

## Hummus

Traditional hummus, made with olive oil and tahini, can be a surprisingly high-fat meal. This recipe reduces the fat by half.

Besides eating hummus on a pita or bagel, you might try it on hot pasta. What a flavorful meatless meal.

1  16-ounce can chickpeas
1  to 3 cloves garlic
2  to 4 tablespoons sesame tahini (or peanut butter)
1  to 2 tablespoons lemon juice
¼  cup water or liquid from the canned chickpeas
Salt and pepper to taste
**Optional:**
*Dash cayenne*
1  tablespoon parsley
½  teaspoon cumin

1. In a food processor combine the chickpeas and garlic and process until coarsely chopped.
2. Add the remaining ingredients and process until smooth. Add additional water as needed for consistency.

YIELD: 3 servings

| Total calories: | 600 |
|---|---|
| Calories per serving: | 200 |

|  | Grams | % of recipe |
|---|---|---|
| CARB | 27 | 55 |
| PRO | 9 | 15 |
| FAT | 6 | 30 |

### ELITE WHEELS

Members of the elite Highway Unit Motorcycle Patrol escort the lead runners in the Marathon, including the lead women. These riders are the same ones who precede presidential motorcades. Both the president and the Marathon require more than thirty-five motorcycles.

### IT TAKES ALL KINDS

One year an English runner played "When the Saints Come Marching In" on the clarinet for the entire race, while another ran wearing a halo and angel's wings. Another year a Dutchman ran in traditional wooden shoes. In 1993, fifteen young men in full rhino costumes, weighing thirty pounds each, ran the race in an effort to raise money for Save the Rhino International.

### WEDDING BELLS

Taking time out from their 26.2 mile run, Pam Kezios and Tom Young, both of Chicago, were married at the 8-mile mark of the 1993 Marathon. Their four-person wedding party ran the race with them.

### MASS MEDIA

New York proudly lives up to its reputation as the media capital of the world. In addition to three television broadcasts in the U.S. alone, the 1993 Marathon was covered by six local radio stations. Press credentials are issued to approximately two thousand worldwide media.

## Enchilada Casserole

Joan Benoit Samuelson adapted this recipe from a pregnant runner who, during her second pregnancy, pushed the first child in the baby jogger at altitude. This must be a high-energy meal!!!

You can make this recipe with ground beef, ground turkey, tofu, and/or canned beans. This version with beans is highest in carbohydrates. If you want to prepare it ahead, simply refrigerate it, then bake it for an extra 10 to 15 minutes.

1   onion chopped
1   16-ounce can pinto or kidney beans and/or ground turkey, lean beef, or tofu
2   8-ounce cans tomato sauce
1   12-ounce can mild enchilada sauce
1   11-ounce can corn with peppers
½   teaspoon chili powder
¼   teaspoon dried oregano
12  corn tortillas
4   to 6 ounces low-fat Cheddar cheese, grated

**Optional:**
Chopped lettuce, tomatoes, and low-fat ranch salad dressing or fat-free sour cream

1. In a large saucepan combine the onion, beans, tomato sauce, enchilada sauce, chili powder, and oregano. Or, in a large skillet, brown the onion with beef or ground turkey, drain, then add the sauces and seasonings.
2. Bring to a boil, then simmer for 5 minutes.
3. Place 4 tortillas in the bottom of a 9x13-inch baking dish. Pour half of the bean mixture over the tortillas. Sprinkle with half the cheese. Repeat layers, ending with 4 tortillas.
4. Cover with foil. Bake at 350° for 20 minutes. Uncover and bake 5 more minutes.
5. Garnish with chopped lettuce, tomatoes, and low-fat ranch salad dressing as desired.

YIELD: 5 servings

| | | |
|---|---|---|
| Total calories: | | 2,200 |
| Calories per serving: | | 440 |

| | Grams | % of recipe |
|---|---|---|
| CARB | 66 | 60 |
| PRO | 21 | 20 |
| FAT | 10 | 2 |

Because so many of the recipes in other chapters include meatless meals, we have chosen to cross-reference them, rather than to include them in this chapter with vegetarian cookery. Your best bet for a wider variety of meatless meals is to look at the following recipes:

*Bob Kempainen of the United States (#25) and Andres Espinosa of Mexico (#2) battled over the final miles in the 1993 race. Espinosa finished first and Kempainen second.*

TOP: *The leaders set the pace.*

RIGHT: *The New York City Fire Department fields one of the largest groups in the Marathon.*

BELOW: *Grete Waitz leads the charge up the Queensboro Bridge.*

*There's no other race like the New York City Marathon. Even Pope John Paul II called it "a fantastic event."*

RIGHT: *The effort of the Achilles Track Club for the disabled isone of the inspiring aspects of the race.*

BELOW: *More than twenty-six thousand balloons decorate the Marathon course.*

LEFT:  *The women's race in the New York City Marathon is credited with encouraging the inclusion of the event in the 1984 Olympic Games.*

BELOW:  *The runners become human traffic on New York City's bridges.*

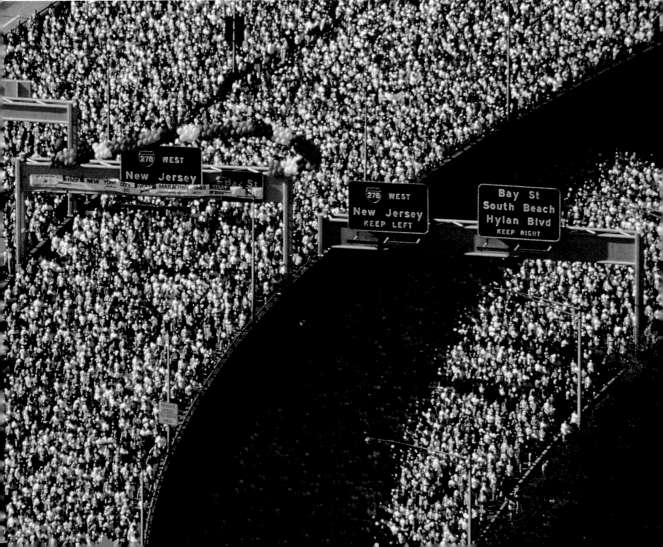

RIGHT: *A runner puts in a final effort at the finish line.*

BELOW: *Almost at the finish line, the marathoners enter Central Park.*

LEFT: *Australia's Lisa Ondieki and South Africa's Willie Mtolo were crowned victorious with the traditional laurel wreaths after the 1992 Marathon.*

BELOW: *More than two thousand journalists from around the world cover the Marathon. A coveted position is at the finish line.*

FINISH NEW YORK CITY FINISH MARATHON 1988

NEW YORK RUNNERS CLUB  MANUFACTURERS HANOVER  asics  John Hancock  MERCEDES-BENZ  Rudin family  RUNNE

*Nine-time New York City Marathon
Champion Grete Waitz wins her eighth
victory in 1986.*

*An ecstatic Alberto Salazar breaks a
twelve-year-old Marathon world record
in 1981.*

# 15 POTATOES AND RICE

Although pasta wins the race for the most popular runner's carbohydrate, rice and potato are close seconds. The following recipes and ideas can enhance their presence in your meals.

## POTATOES

Norwegian, German, and Irish runners are among the many who thrive on potatoes. This carbohydrate-rich food is a vegetable that actually offers more vitamins and minerals than does plain rice or pasta (see chapter 1). To help you include more potatoes in your sports diet, here are some tips:

- Potatoes come in different varieties, with some varieties best suited for baking (russets),

> "Running was an extension of my life. . . . As a kid I ran on the farm, I ran two miles to school. In New York, I used to run to work, 20 or 30 miles every morning, depending on how I felt."
>
> —OLYMPIAN **TED CORBITT**, veteran of 198 marathons and ultramarathons, and one of the inspirations behind the New York City Marathon

others for boiling (red or white rounds). Ask the produce manager at your grocery store for guidance.

- Potatoes are best stored in a cool, humid (but not wet) place that is well ventilated, such as your cellar. Do not refrigerate potatoes because they will become sweet and off-colored.

- Rather than peel the skin (under which is stored most of the vitamin C), scrub the skin well and cook it, skin and all. Yes, even mashed potatoes can be made unpeeled!

- One pound of potatoes = three medium = two large. The large "restaurant size" potato generally has about 200 calories.

- To bake a potato in the oven, allow about 40 minutes at 400° for a medium potato, closer to an hour for a large potato. Because potatoes can be baked at any temperature, you can simply adjust the cooking time to whatever else is in the oven.

- You can tell if the potato is done if you can easily pierce it with a fork.

- To cook a potato in the microwave oven, prick the skin in several places with a fork, place it on some paper towels in the bottom of the microwave, and cook it for about 4 minutes if it is medium-sized, 6 to 10 minutes if large. Cooking time will vary

according to the size of the potato, the power of your oven, and the number of potatoes being cooked. Turn the potato over halfway through cooking. Remove the potato from the oven, wrap it in a towel, and allow it to finish cooking for about 3 to 5 minutes.

## QUICK AND EASY BAKED POTATO TOPPINGS

To spice-up your potato, try the following toppings:

- Plain yogurt
- Imitation butter granules (such as Molly McButter) and milk
- Mustard
- Mustard and Worcestershire sauce
- Vinegar and flavored vinegars
- Soy sauce
- Pesto
- Chopped chives and green onion
- Herbs such as dill, parsley, chopped chives
- Steamed broccoli or other cooked vegetables
- Chopped jalapeño peppers
- Low- or nonfat salad dressing
- Nonfat sour cream, chopped onion, and grated low-fat Cheddar cheese
- Cottage cheese and garlic powder
- Cottage cheese and salsa

- Soup broth
- Milk mashed into the potato
- Lentils or lentil soup
- Applesauce

## RICE

For the runners in China, Japan, and other Asian countries, rice is the staple of their sports diet. A meal isn't a meal unless it contains rice. After wheat and corn, rice is the world's third leading grain.

Brown rice is made into white rice when the fiber-rich bran is removed during the refining process. This also removes some of the nutrients, but you can compensate for this loss (if you prefer white over brown rice) by eating other whole grains (such as bran cereals and whole-wheat breads) at your other meals.

Cooking tips:

- Because of its tough bran coat and germ, brown rice needs

about 45 to 50 minutes to cook; white rice only about 20 to 30 minutes.

- Consider cooking rice in the morning while you are getting ready for work, so that it will be waiting to be simply reheated when you get home.

- When cooking rice make double amounts to have leftovers that you can either freeze or refrigerate.

- Portions: 1 cup raw white rice = 3 cups cooked = about 600 calories 1 cup raw brown rice = 3–4 cups cooked = about 600 calories

- Rice is popularly cooked by two methods:

1. Bring a saucepan of water to a full boil, stir in ⅓ to ½ cup rice per person plus 1 to 2 teaspoons salt, as desired. Simmer about 20 minutes, or until a grain of rice is tender when you bite into it. Drain into a colander, rinse it under hot tap water to remove the sticky starch, and put it back into the saucepan. Keep the rice warm over low heat, fluffing it with a fork.

2. For each cup of rice, put 2 cups of water into a saucepan, and a teaspoon salt, as desired. Bring to a boil, then cover and turn the heat down low. Let the rice cook undisturbed until it is tender and all the water has been absorbed. Then stir gently with a fork. (Stirring too much may result in a gluey mess.) This method retains more of the vitamins that otherwise get lost into the cooking water.

## QUICK AND EASY RICE IDEAS

Here are a few rice suggestions for hungry marathoners.

Bill Rodgers, four-time NYC Marathon and four-time Boston Marathon winner, helped to spur the running boom in America.

Cook rice in:

- *Chicken or beef broth*
- *Mixture of orange or apple juice and water*
- *Water with seasonings: cinnamon, soy sauce, oregano, curry, chili powder, or whatever might nicely blend with the menu.*

Top rice with:

- *Leftover chili*
- *Low- or nonfat Italian dressing and mustard*

- *Toasted sesame seeds*
- *Steamed vegetables*
- *Chopped mushrooms and green peppers, either raw or sautéed*
- *Nonfat sour cream, raisins, tuna, and curry powder*
- *Raisins, cinnamon, and applesauce.*

## Potato Pancakes

Although Fred Lebow is not known for his cooking, his sister, Sarah Katz, is an excellent cook. She shares this traditional food they ate during Passovers in Romania. (Most families served Latkes at Chanukah.) These are commonly made with flour and onion, but the basic recipe tasted best to me. Onion lovers, however, might prefer to add the optional ingredients. Latkes are popularly served with applesauce or low-fat sour cream.

2   *eggs (or substitute)*
2   *large potatoes, grated*
*Salt and pepper to taste*
1   *to 2 tablespoons oil, preferably olive or canola*
**Optional:**
½   *to 1 onion, grated*
3   *tablespoons flour*

1. In a medium bowl beat the eggs until fluffy. Add the grated potato and onion if desired. Season to taste with salt and pepper. Add the flour if desired.
2. In a large skillet heat the oil. Drop the potato mixture by the tablespoonful into the hot oil. Flatten with the back of the spoon.
3. Cook until the pancakes are golden brown and cooked through, 5 to 7 minutes per side. Be sure to cook them enough or you will have somewhat crunchy pancakes. Test the first pancake and proceed from there.
4. Line a dish with paper towels. Place the cooked pancakes in the dish and keep them warm in the oven while you cook the remaining pancakes.

YIELD: 3 servings

| Total calories: | | 800 |
|---|---|---|
| Calories per serving: | | 270 |

| | Grams | % of recipe |
|---|---|---|
| CARB | 42 | 65 |
| PRO | 7 | 10 |
| FAT | 8 | 25 |

## Grete Waitz's Baked Potato

Grete Waitz has mastered the art of preparing potatoes effortlessly. Here is her standard fare.

1   *large (7 ounce) baking potato*
*Salad seasonings sprinkled on top*
½   *cup low-fat cottage cheese*

1. Cook the potato in the microwave oven (or conventional oven, as time allows) until it feels soft when pierced with a fork.
2. Remove the potato from the oven. Cut an X on the top and puff up the potato meat.
3. Sprinkle generously with salad seasonings and top with a spoonful of cottage cheese.

YIELD: 1 serving

| Total calories: | | 300 |
|---|---|---|

| | Grams | % of recipe |
|---|---|---|
| CARB | 55 | 70 |
| PRO | 18 | 25 |
| FAT | 1 | 5 |

## Red Potato Salad

This recipe, adapted from *What's Cooking at the Cooper Clinic*, was submitted by nutritionist Veronica Coronado. It is a tasty low-fat potato salad. The nonfat sour cream adds flavor, but you may eliminate this if desired.

Although this salad can be made with any type of potato, you'll get the best results using small red potatoes because they hold their shape well and don't crumble into mush.

2    pounds small red potatoes
1    to 2 small onions, chopped
½    cup white wine vinegar
2    tablespoons Dijon mustard
2    tablespoons oil, preferably olive
Salt and pepper to taste
**Optional:**
½    cup nonfat sour cream
¼    cup fresh dill

1. Wash the potatoes. In a large pot of boiling water cook the potatoes whole just until tender.
2. In a small bowl combine the onions, vinegar, mustard, oil, dill, salt, or pepper to taste.
3. Drain the potatoes and rinse them with cold water to cool them off. Cut the potatoes into quarters or cubes when cool enough to handle. Place the potatoes in a large bowl.
4. Pour the dressing over the potatoes, tossing gently.
5. Fold in the sour cream.
6. For best flavor, allow the salad to stand at least 30 minutes before serving.

YIELD: 4 servings

| Total calories: | 1,000 |
|---|---|
| Calories per serving: | 250 |

|  | Grams | % of recipe |
|---|---|---|
| CARB | 45 | 70 |
| PRO | 6 | 10 |
| FAT | 5 | 20 |

## Sweet Potato and Bell Pepper Salad

Peter Herman loves this sweet potato salad not only because it is pretty to look at but it also tastes good. Plus, it's filled with healthful vegetables. You can't go wrong.

4    medium sweet potatoes, peeled and cut into uniform pieces
½    green bell pepper, seeded and diced
½    sweet red bell pepper, diced
½    large red onion, diced
**Dressing:**
3    tablespoons Dijon mustard
3    tablespoons ketchup
1    clove garlic, minced
3    to 6 tablespoons olive oil
¼    cup vinegar
1    tablespoon Worcestershire sauce
2    tablespoons lime juice (lemon will do, but it's not as good)
Salt and pepper to taste
¼    cup finely chopped fresh parsley

1. In a large pot cover the sweet potato pieces with water and cook until just done, about 10 minutes. Do not overcook, or they will fall apart in the salad.
2. Drain the potatoes immediately and rinse them with cold water. After they have cooled, about 1 minute, drain them again and place them in a large bowl.
3. Add the bell peppers and onion, and toss lightly.
4. In a separate bowl combine the remaining ingredients. Adjust the seasonings as needed.
5. Pour the dressing over the potato mixture and toss care-

fully. Serve immediately or refrigerate overnight to allow the flavors to blend.

YIELD: 4 servings

| Total calories: | 1,000 |
|---|---|
| Calories per serving: | 250 |

|  | Grams | % of recipe |
|---|---|---|
| CARB | 40 | 65 |
| PRO | 3 | 5 |
| FAT | 9 | 30 |

## Egg and Potato Dinner

This meal is designed for those who hate to wash dishes.

1    large baking potato
1    egg
1    ounce low-fat cheese
Salt and pepper to taste
**Optional:**
1    teaspoon margarine

1. Pierce the potato in several places with a fork. Bake at 400° for 1 hour or until done.
2. Cut a cross in the top. Fluff the insides with a fork, making a well.
3. Add margarine, if desired. Break the egg into the potato, top with salt, pepper, and cheese.
4. Return the potato to the oven and bake for about 15 minutes, until the egg is cooked.

YIELD: 1 serving

| Total calories: | 400 |
|---|---|

|  | Grams | % of recipe |
|---|---|---|
| CARB | 61 | 60 |
| PRO | 18 | 20 |
| FAT | 9 | 20 |

## Rice with Celery and Caraway

This is a nice change-of-pace from plain rice, and the subtly different flavor blends well with chicken or fish.

1    tablespoon olive oil, butter, or
     combination
2    stalks celery, thinly sliced
½    cup uncooked long-grain rice
¼    teaspoon caraway seeds
1    cup water or broth
Salt and pepper to taste
**Optional:**
1    onion, finely chopped

1. In a small heavy saucepan heat the oil and/or butter and cook the celery and onion until soft over medium-high heat.
2. Add the rice and caraway seeds and sauté the mixture, stirring constantly, for about 1 minute.
3. Add the broth, salt, and pepper to taste. Bring to a boil and cover. Simmer for 15 to 20 minutes, or until the rice is tender and the liquid is absorbed.
4. Remove the pan from the heat. Let the pot sit, covered, for about 5 minutes. Fluff with a fork and serve.

**Variation:** In a saucepan bring the water to a boil. Add all of the ingredients, without first sautéing the celery or onion. Cover and simmer for 20 to 25 minutes, as in step 3.

YIELD: 2 servings

| Total calories: | 420 |
| --- | --- |
| Calories per serving: | 210 |

|  | Grams | % of recipe |
| --- | --- | --- |
| CARB | 40 | 75 |
| PRO | 3 | 5 |
| FAT | 4 | 20 |

# IT'S ALL IN THE NUMBERS

30,000 finisher's medals
25,041 rejected entries
36,340 runners & officials T-shirts
25,000 computer-printed numbers
1,850 woolen blankets
33,000 heat-retaining blankets
1,260 stretchers
30 medical units
1 major field hospital
13,700 No Parking signs
13,315 (estimated) volunteers including 7,875 race day volunteers, among them 450 linguists and 1,625 course marshals, 1,940 medical volunteers, and 400 volunteer ham radio operators
2,700 police
262 City of New York Parks and Recreation staff
10,000 credentials for staff, volunteers, and press
87 domestic race directors, observing race procedures
100 international race officials observing race procedures
37 computer terminals
18,000 yards of barricade tape
120,000 safety pins
22,050 feet of rope
550 portable toilets
500 six-foot tables
10,000 feet of snowfencing
1.5 miles of wire for public address system at the start
300 gallons of "Marathon Blue" paint

32,000 cups of coffee
1,600,000 paper cups
4.5 tons of ice
3 tons of bagels
1,600 banners along the course
8,000 roses
69,000 square feet for seven tents at the race start
32,000 runners' packets with nearly 30 items
5,000 pounds of pasta
2,500 gallons of sauce
185 custom crystal awards
135 buses making 297 trips to transport runners
10,500 clothing items returned to runners at finish
26,000 balloons
3,800 gallons of sports drink
150,000 bottles of spring water
300 signs at race start
342 signs in Central Park, the race finish
75,000 items sold in Marathon store at the Expo (including 35,000 T-shirts)
75 cellular phones
60,000 people who attend the Marathon Expo
60,000 New York City Marathon posters distributed
30,000 sponges
80 "kiddie" swimming pools
500 rakes to clean paper cups at water stations
76,000 photos (2,000 rolls of film) taken of 25,000 runners

## German Potato Salad

This salad not only tastes delicious but also has a wonderful aroma. Mary Schran of Media, Pennsylvania, says it is best served while still piping hot.

For best results, use new potatoes such as Red Bliss potatoes. Otherwise you could end up with potato mush rather than cubes that hold their shape.

8   new potatoes, washed
2   to 3 tablespoons oil, preferably olive
1   small onion, chopped
2   tablespoons flour
⅓   cup cider vinegar
¾   cup water
1   to 1½ tablespoons sugar or to taste
¾   teaspoon dry mustard
Salt and pepper to taste
**Optional:**
1   tablespoon dried parsley

1. Slice the potatoes into ½-inch thick wedges, preferably leaving the skin on. Place the potatoes in a saucepan.
2. Add enough water to steam the potatoes. Cover and cook until tender. Drain.
3. In a small skillet heat the oil and sauté the onions until tender. Add the flour and cook for 2 minutes.
4. Add the remaining ingredients and cook until bubbly and thick, about 2 minutes.
5. Pour the dressing over the cooked potatoes and stir gently until well combined. Serve immediately or chill and serve cold.

YIELD: 4 servings

| Total calories: | 1,100 |
|---|---|
| Calories per seving: | 275 |

|  | Grams | % of recipe |
|---|---|---|
| CARB | 51 | 75 |
| PRO | 4 | 5 |
| FAT | 6 | 20 |

## Oven French Fries I

Runner and nutritionist Ann LeBarron of Waldorf, Maryland, selected this low-fat French fry recipe because it is an American favorite food, healthy, and potassium-rich. No one will know these are low-fat!

**Per Person:**
1   large baking potato per person, cleaned, unpeeled
1   teaspoon canola oil
Cooking spray
Salt and pepper to taste

1. Cut the potato lengthwise into 10 or 12 pieces. Place in a large bowl.
2. Rub with oil and sprinkle with the salt and pepper, as desired.
3. Spray a baking sheet thoroughly with cooking spray and place the potatoes evenly on it.
4. Bake at 400° for 20 minutes. Turn the potatoes over and continue baking for another 10 to 15 minutes. Serve immediately. Be careful, the potatoes will be very hot!

YIELD: 1 serving

| Total calories: | 260 |
|---|---|

|  | Grams | % of recipe |
|---|---|---|
| CARB | 52 | 80 |
| PRO | 4 | 5 |
| FAT | 4 | 15 |

## Oven French Fries II

These tasty spears have more spices and taste than the prior recipe. They go nicely with any dish—or even for munching on for snacks.

**Per Person:**
1   large russet potato, cut into tenths lengthwise
1   teaspoon olive oil
1   tablespoon Parmesan cheese
**Your choice of:**
Dried crushed red pepper
Dried crushed basil
Garlic cloves, pressed
Dried oregano
Salt and pepper

1. In a bowl combine the potatoes, oil, and any of the seasonings desired. Toss to coat.
2. Transfer the potatoes to a baking sheet treated with cooking spray. Bake at 400° for about 20 minutes.
3. Top with cheese and continue baking for 10 to 15 minutes, or until tender with golden brown crisp edges.

YIELD: 1 serving

| Total calories: | 320 |
|---|---|

|  | Grams | % of recipe |
|---|---|---|
| CARB | 51 | 65 |
| PRO | 12 | 15 |
| FAT | 7 | 20 |

## Rice and Eggplant "Lasagna"

Who says lasagna has to be made with noodles? Here's a variety of lasagna that uses rice instead.

1½ cups uncooked rice
1  large eggplant
1  28-ounce jar spaghetti sauce
**Optional:**
1  to 2 cups cottage cheese
3  to 6 ounces low-fat mozzarella cheese
¼  cup Parmesan cheese
2  cups additional vegetables (sautéed or steamed onions, mushrooms, zucchini)

1. Cook rice according to directions on the package.
2. While the rice is cooking, slice eggplant lengthwise into "lasagna noodles." Arrange the eggplant on a baking sheet sprayed with cooking spray. Bake at 350° for 20 minutes.
3. In a casserole pan layer the cooked rice, spaghetti sauce, eggplant, and optional ingredients. Heat in the oven for about 20 to 30 minutes.

YIELD: 4 servings

| Total calories: | | 1,600 |
| --- | --- | --- |
| Calories per serving: | | 400 |

| | Grams | % of recipe |
| --- | --- | --- |
| CARB | 75 | 75 |
| PRO | 9 | 10 |
| FAT | 7 | 15 |

## Sopa de Arroz (Mexican Rice)

This recipe, submitted by Cecilia Chapman, was adapted from the Spanish rice paella that came with the Spaniards in the early 1800s to

Olympic marathon gold medalist Gelindo Bordin (#4) is flanked by two of his Italian countrymen. The New York City Marathon is so prestigious in Italy, it is broadcast on national television.

the northern region of Mexico, southern Texas, and New Mexico. These areas were far away from the ocean fronts, so the Spanish were unable to include the fish, shrimp, and shellfish used in their traditional paella. Meat and chicken were not plentiful either, so paella became a very simple rice dish with few ingredients. This dish is still enjoyed today and is an important staple food, almost always served as a side order with beans.

1  tablespoon vegetable oil
1  cup rice
¼  cup chopped onion
1  clove garlic, left whole
2  cups chicken stock
½  cup tomato sauce
½  cup frozen peas
Salt and pepper to taste

1. In a deep saucepan heat the oil and sauté the rice, onion, and garlic until the rice turns white or lightly brown. Remove the pan from the heat and set aside to cool for a few minutes.
2. Add the remaining ingredients and bring the mixture to a boil. Reduce the heat to the lowest setting. Cover and simmer for 20 minutes.
3. Serve. The person who receives the whole garlic in his/her serving will receive good fortune.

YIELD: 4 servings

| Total calories: | | 840 |
| --- | --- | --- |
| Calories per serving: | | 210 |

| | Grams | % of recipe |
| --- | --- | --- |
| CARB | 40 | 75 |
| PRO | 4 | 10 |
| FAT | 4 | 15 |

185

## Hawaiian Curried Rice

This recipe was submitted by Lori Fujikawa. This is a quick and easy dish to prepare. It combines both rice and the curry flavor so popular in Hawaii.

2    cups vegetable broth
¼    teaspoon curry powder
1    cup white rice, uncooked
3    tablespoons golden raisins
**Optional:**
3    tablespoons sliced almonds

1. In a saucepan combine the broth and curry powder. Bring the mixture to a boil.
2. Gradually add the rice, maintaining a boil.
3. Add the raisins and stir once. Reduce the heat, cover, and simmer for 25 minutes without lifting the lid.
4. Stir the rice and add the almonds if desired.

YIELD: 3 servings

| Total calories: | 700 |
|---|---|
| Calories per serving: | 230 |

|  | Grams | % of recipe |
|---|---|---|
| CARB | 52 | 90 |
| PRO | 3 | 5 |
| FAT | 1 | 5 |

## Orange Rice

This rice goes well with chicken or fish.

2    cups water
½    cup orange juice
2    to 3 chicken bouillon cubes
1    cup rice
**Optional:**
1    to 2 tablespoons butter or margarine

1. In a saucepan bring the water, juice, bouillon, and butter or margarine to a boil.
2. Add the rice and stir. Cover and cook over low heat without stirring for 20 minutes or until tender.

YIELD: 3 servings

| Total calories: | 700 |
|---|---|
| Calories per serving: | 235 |

|  | Grams | % of recipe |
|---|---|---|
| CARB | 50 | 90 |
| PRO | 3 | 5 |
| FAT | 1 | 5 |

## Chicken Fried Rice

The chances are this is lower in fat than what you'll get from a restaurant, and just as tasty. Don't hesitate to be creative and add lots of extras, depending on what you have on hand.

2    to 3 tablespoons oil
2    cups diced cooked chicken
4    cups cooked rice
½    cup frozen peas
¾    teaspoon sugar or to taste
¼    cup soy sauce
**Optional:**
2    cups sliced green onions
¼    pound mushrooms, sliced
¼    teaspoon ginger
1    to 2 scrambled eggs

1. In a large skillet or wok heat the oil. If onions and mushrooms are desired, sauté them in the hot oil, stirring constantly until the mushrooms are golden, about 5 minutes.
2. Add the chicken, rice, and remaining ingredients. Cook for about 5 minutes more, stirring constantly until heated.

YIELD: 4 servings

| Total calories: | 1,800 |
|---|---|
| Calories per serving: | 450 |

|  | Grams | % of recipe |
|---|---|---|
| CARB | 60 | 55 |
| PRO | 32 | 25 |
| FAT | 9 | 20 |

# 16 VEGETABLES

Vegetables are the edible parts of plants: the flower (broccoli), berry (pepper), root, bulb or tuber (carrots, potatoes), stems or shoots (celery, asparagus), or leaves (spinach, lettuce). Vegetables are also excellent sources of "all natural" vitamins that are generally packaged as low-fat, carbohydrate-rich sports foods.

Little compares with the nice taste of plain, fresh vegetables cooked until just tender-crisp. If you wish to add some seasonings, here are some good combinations:*

| | |
|---|---|
| Basil | Green beans, tomatoes, zucchini |
| Oregano | Zucchini, mushrooms, tomatoes, onions |
| Dill | Green beans, carrots, peas, potatoes |
| Cinnamon | Spinach, winter squash, sweet potatoes |
| Marjoram | Celery, greens |
| Nutmeg | Corn, cauliflower, beans |
| Thyme | Artichokes, mushrooms, peas, carrots |
| Parsley | Sprinkled on any vegetable |

* Adapted from The American Heart Association Cookbook, (New York: Ballantine Books, 1975).

## SAVING THE NUTRIENTS

To get the most nutrients out of your vegetables, handle them properly so they have minimal exposure to the four elements that reduce their nutritional value: air, heat, water, and light.

| Problem | Solution |
|---|---|
| Air | Store fresh vegetables in plastic containers. Cook covered. |
| Heat | Store fresh vegetables in the refrigerator. Cook only slightly until crisp-tender, not mushy. Minimize cooking time to enhance the flavor and nutritional value. |
| Water | Do not soak vegetables in water. Cook in minimal water, stir-fry, or microwave. |
| Light | Store in a dark place (inside the fridge!) Cook in a covered pan. |

The following tips for cooking vegetables are taken from my Sports Nutrition Guidebook (Leisure Press, 1990).

## BASIC STEAMED VEGETABLES

1. Wash vegetables thoroughly; prepare and cut into pieces keeping the skin or peel, if appropriate.

2. Put ½ inch of water in the bottom of a pan that has a tight cover.

3. Bring the water to a boil. Add the vegetables. Or, put the vegetables in a steamer basket and put this in the saucepan with 1 inch of water.

4. Cover the pan tightly and cook over medium heat until the vegetables are tender crisp—about 3 minutes for spinach, 10 minutes for broccoli, 15 minutes for sliced carrots.

5. Drain the vegetables, reserving the cooking water for soup or sauces, or simply drink it as a broth.

## BASIC MICROWAVED VEGETABLES

Microwave cookery is perfect for vegetables because it cooks them quickly and without water, thereby retaining a greater percentage of the nutrients than with conventional methods.

1. Wash the vegetables and cut them into bite-sized pieces. Put them in a microwavable container with a cover, or on a plate and then cover with a plastic bag or plastic wrap. If the pieces vary in thickness arrange them in a ring, with the thicker portions toward the outside of the dish.
   Optional: Sprinkle with herbs (basil, oregano, parsley, garlic

powder), soy sauce, or whatever suits your taste.

2. Microwave until tender crisp. The amount of time will vary according to your particular microwave oven and the amount of vegetable you are cooking. Start off with 3 minutes for a single serving; larger servings take longer. The vegetables will continue cooking after you remove them from the oven, so plan that into your cooking time.

### BASIC STIR-FRIED VEGETABLES

Vegetables stir-fried until tender-crisp are very flavorful, colorful, and nutritious—but they do have more fat than if steamed. Be sure to add only a minimal amount of oil (olive, canola, sesame) to the cooking pan. I prefer to use a heavy skillet for stir-frying, rather than a wok—it does a fine job!

Some popular stir-fry combinations include:

- Carrots, broccoli, and mushrooms
- Onions, green peppers, zucchini, and tomatoes
- Chinese cabbage, bok choy, and water chestnuts

1. Wash, drain well (to prevent the water from spattering when the vegetables are added) and cut the vegetables of your choice into bite-sized pieces or ⅛-inch slices. Whenever possible, slice the vegetables diagonally to increase the surface area; this allows for faster cooking. Try to make the pieces uniform so they will cook evenly.

2. Heat the skillet or wok over high heat. Add 1 to 3 teaspoons of oil—just enough to coat the bottom of the pan.

---

## MARATHON CARPET

When race officials saw the bloodied feet of top runner Chris Stewart after the 1976 Marathon, they came up with the idea of carpeting the grating on the bridges, which had affected the feet of Stewart and many others. Since then, one mile of carpet is installed on four bridges. The Queensboro Bridge carpet is laid out twenty-four hours before the race. Another race takes place when the other three bridges are each carpeted a mere one hour before the runners arrive. The carpet is removed after the last runner has crossed each bridge.

The carpet is 115 times larger than the average living room and in a few hours will endure more traffic than a front hallway does in a year.

---

Optional: add a slice of ginger root or some minced garlic, stir-frying for one minute to add flavor.

3. Begin with the vegetables that take longest to cook (carrots, cauliflower, broccoli). A few minutes later add the remaining ones (mushrooms, bean sprouts, cabbage, spinach). Constantly lift and turn the vegetables to coat them with oil.

4. Add a little bit of water (¼ to ½ cup), then cover and steam the vegetables for 2 to 5 minutes. Adjust the heat to prevent scorching.

5. Don't overcrowd the pan. Cook small batches at a time.

6. Optional add-ins: soy sauce, stir-fried beef, chicken, tofu, rice, or noodles.

7. To thicken the juices, stir in a mixture of 2 teaspoons of cornstarch dissolved into 1 tablespoon of water. Add more water or broth if this makes the sauce too thick.
Optional: Garnish with toasted sesame seeds, mandarin orange sections, or pineapple chunks.

### BASIC BAKED VEGETABLES

If you are baking chicken, potatoes, or a casserole, you might as well make good use of the oven and bake the vegetables too. Some popular suggestions include:

- eggplant halves sprinkled with garlic powder
- zucchini with onions and oregano
- carrots with ginger
- sliced sweet potato with apple

1. In a covered baking dish season the vegetables and add a small amount of water, or wrap them in foil.

2. Bake at 350° for 20 to 30 minutes (depending on the size of the chunks) until crisp-tender. Caution—with foil-wrapped vegetables, be careful when opening the foil. The escaping steam might burn you.

## Baked Vegetable Medley

New York Road Runners Club member and nutrition consultant Christine Schlott recommends this combination of vegetables to bake.

4   medium potatoes, cut in eighths
3   bell peppers, green, red, and/or yellow, cut into 1-inch squares
3   tomatoes, cut into wedges
4   medium onions, peeled and cut in quarters
2   to 4 tablespoons olive oil
Salt and pepper to taste

1. Place the vegetables in a 9x13-inch baking dish.
2. Pour the oil into the palm of your hands and then rub it over the vegetables. Sprinkle with salt and pepper to taste.
3. Bake at 400° for about 45 minutes, stirring every 15 minutes. The vegetables may char a bit, but don't worry. This only enhances their flavor.
4. If the vegetables have an excess of liquid near the end of the baking period, raise the oven temperature to 450° until most of the liquid evaporates.
5. Transfer to a warm serving dish.

YIELD: 4 servings

| Total calories: | | 1,100 |
| Calories per serving: | | 275 |

|  | Grams | % of recipe |
| --- | --- | --- |
| CARB | 53 | 75 |
| PRO | 3 | 5 |
| FAT | 6 | 20 |

## Nina Kuscsik's "Eat Your Spinach" Creamed Spinach

1   10-ounce package frozen chopped spinach or 1 pound fresh spinach
2   teaspoons butter or margarine
1½  tablespoons all-purpose flour
¾   cup low-fat milk
¼   teaspoon sugar to taste
Salt and pepper to taste

1. Cook and drain the frozen spinach. Or prepare the fresh spinach by washing and then cooking in 1 tablespoon of water in a covered pot over medium heat until the leaves are wilted, 2 to 3 minutes. Drain and chop.
2. In a saucepan melt the butter or margarine and add the flour gradually. Stir constantly with a wire wisk until smooth.
3. Add the milk gradually, stirring constantly. Cook until thickened.
4. Add the salt, pepper, and cooked spinach.

> In the greatest ever NYC Marathon duel, second place finisher Geoff Smith of Great Britian fell to the ground after crossing the finish line. Was he emotionally overwhelmed by the defeat? "Just tired," he said. "I wanted to sit down. They didn't have a chair, so I had to lie down."
>
> —Adapted from New York Newsday, November 8, 1993

YIELD: 3 servings

| Total calories: | | 300 |
| Calories per serving: | | 100 |

|  | Grams | % of recipe |
| --- | --- | --- |
| CARB | 13 | 45 |
| PRO | 5 | 25 |
| FAT | 3 | 30 |

## Spinach with Garlic

Spinach, like all dark green vegetables, is rich in vitamin A. One-third cup provides 100 percent of your daily need. Spinach is also a good source of folic acid, vitamin C, riboflavin, and many other nutrients. By cooking it in oil rather than water it will retain more nutritional value—but also add more calories.

1   pound fresh spinach
1   tablespoon oil
1   clove garlic, crushed, or ¼ teaspoon garlic powder

1. Wash the spinach and remove the tough stems. Drain well.
2. In a skillet heat the oil. Add the garlic and sauté for 1 to 2 minutes. Add the spinach and stir to coat. Cover and cook for 1 minute over medium-high heat.
3. Uncover and stir gently. Cook for 1 to 2 more minutes.

YIELD: 3 servings

| Total calories: | | 210 |
| Calories per serving: | | 70 |

|  | Grams | % of recipe |
| --- | --- | --- |
| CARB | 5 | 30 |
| PRO | 4 | 25 |
| FAT | 4 | 45 |

# THE NEW YORK CITY MARATHON IS . . .

- The largest marathon in the world with 26,597 finishers in 1993.
- The largest women's marathon field in the world with more than 6,000 participants.
- The largest live single-day spectator sporting event in the world.
- According to the New York City Police Department, nearly two million people line the streets during the race.
- The site of three women's world records, one men's world record, and twelve sub-2:10 times for men.
- The largest field of international runners of any marathon (8,000 from 91 countries in 1993). The international contingent alone would rank as one of the largest marathons in the country.
- Other "world records" include the world's longest carpet (one mile by three feet wide on the Queensboro Bridge), the world's longest urinal, 328 feet, and the greatest number of volunteers for any mass sporting event, an estimated 13,315.

## Spinach and Cheese Casserole

This recipe is from *What's Cooking at the Cooper Clinic* and was submitted by their sports nutritionist, Georgia Kostas.

2   10-ounce packages frozen chopped spinach, thawed
1   cup low-fat cottage cheese
½   package dry onion soup mix
¼   cup grated part-skim mozzarella cheese
**Optional:**
2   teaspoons dill
½   cup sliced water chestnuts

1. Cook the spinach according to the package directions. Drain and squeeze out the excess water. Return it to the cooking pot.
2. In a blender combine the cottage cheese, soup mix, and dill. Process until blended.
3. To the cooled spinach add the mozzarella and water chestnuts, if desired, and the cottage cheese mixture, stirring well.
4. Pour into a casserole dish and bake covered at 350° for 30 minutes.

YIELD: 4 servings

| Total calories: | | 480 |
| --- | --- | --- |
| Calories per serving: | | 120 |

| | Grams | % of recipe |
| --- | --- | --- |
| CARB | 12 | 40 |
| PRO | 13 | 40 |
| FAT | 2 | 20 |

## Corn and Broccoli Bake

This recipe makes a favorite dish that is simple, tasty, and unique. The creamed corn combines nicely with broccoli. The type of cracker will slightly influence the flavor. Saltines and stoned wheat work well, as do Ritz.

1   16-ounce can creamed corn
1   10-ounce box frozen chopped broccoli, cooked and drained
1   to 2 eggs (or substitute), slightly beaten
2   teaspoons dehydrated onion
Salt and pepper, as desired
¾   cup cracker crumbs (for example, about 15 saltines)

1. In a large bowl combine the corn, broccoli, egg, onion, salt, and pepper.
2. Mix in half of the cracker crumbs.
3. Spread the mixture in a 1-quart casserole dish. Top with the remaining cracker crumbs.
4. Bake at 350° for 35 minutes.

YIELD: 6 servings

| Total calories: | | 660 |
| --- | --- | --- |
| Calories per serving: | | 110 |

| | Grams | % of recipe |
| --- | --- | --- |
| CARB | 18 | 70 |
| PRO | 5 | 15 |
| FAT | 2 | 15 |

## Potato and Carrot Casserole

Patty Evanitsky of East Brunswick, New Jersey, says this is one of her favorite recipes. It's simple, yet high in carbohydrate and vitamins A and C.

3   medium potatoes, diced
3   medium carrots, diced
1   cup warm milk
Salt and pepper to taste
**Optional:**
1   to 2 tablespoons butter or margarine
1   to 2 ounces Cheddar cheese, grated

1. In a vegetable steamer or microwave, steam the potatoes and carrots in a small amount of water until tender.
2. Drain the excess water and mash the potatoes and carrots together.
3. Add the milk and butter, and continue to mash or beat the mixture until fluffy.
4. Season with salt and pepper to taste. Grease a casserole dish. Spread the mixture into the prepared dish.
5. Garnish with sliced, cooked carrots or grated Cheddar cheese. Bake at 350° for 20 minutes to allow the flavors to blend.

Yield: 6 servings

| | Total calories: | 900 |
|---|---|---|
| | Calories per serving: | 150 |

| | Grams | % of recipe |
|---|---|---|
| CARB | 30 | 80 |
| PRO | 4 | 10 |
| FAT | 2 | 10 |

## Sweet and Dilly Carrots

Veronica Coronado, nutritionist at the Cooper Clinic, submitted this recipe from the book, *What's Cooking at the Cooper Clinic.*

2   cups carrots, peeled and sliced
2   tablespoons honey
⅛   teaspoon dill weed
Salt to taste
**Optional:**
1   to 2 teaspoons margarine
¼   teaspoon lemon pepper

1. In a steamer or microwave, steam the carrots until tender.
2. Drain the cooked carrots well and put them in a serving dish.
3. Add the remaining ingredients. Mix well. Serve hot.

Yield: 4 servings

| | Total calories: | 200 |
|---|---|---|
| | Calories per serving: | 50 |

| | Grams | % of recipe |
|---|---|---|
| CARB | 11 | 90 |
| PRO | 1 | 10 |
| FAT | 0 | 0 |

The 1992 Marathon was held shortly after sanctions were lifted banning South Africa from international athletic competition. Willie Mtolo (#1) became a national hero in South Africa after he won the race.

## Curried Carrots

The combination of flavors in this simple dish nicely complements the sweet carrots. If you have any leftovers, refrigerate them and add them to a green salad.

4   large carrots, peeled and sliced
½   teaspoon curry powder
2   tablespoons orange juice
1   teaspoon sugar to taste
Salt and pepper to taste
**Optional:**
2   teaspoons butter or margarine

1. In a vegetable steamer or microwave cook the carrots until tender. Drain.
2. In a saucepan melt the butter if desired. Add the curry powder, orange juice, and sugar, and cook until bubbly.
3. Add the carrots and stir to coat. Season with salt and pepper to taste.

YIELD: 2 servings

| Total calories: | 150 |
|---|---|
| Calories per serving: | 75 |

|  | Grams | % of recipe |
|---|---|---|
| CARB | 17 | 95 |
| PRO | 2 | 5 |
| FAT | 0 | 0 |

> **"Long distance runners have to be very strange people. . . . Yes, yes, me, too."**
>
> —*TED CORBITT*, as quoted in *The New York Times*, November 12, 1993

*Olympic gold medalist Frank Shorter (#4) ran the first five-borough NYC Marathon in 1976.*

## Eggplant Italiano I

This is a favorite pre-race meal of Cindy Millar of Mesa, Arizona. It is similar to eggplant Parmesan, but there is no frying. It is all cooked in the microwave. Cindy serves it with pasta for dinner, and uses the leftovers for eggplant subs.

16  ounces (2 cups) spaghetti sauce
1   medium eggplant, sliced into ⅛-inch rounds
½   cup grated Parmesan or Romano (or any cheese)
4   to 6 ounces (1 to 1½ cups) sliced low-fat mozzarella
**Optional:**
2   teaspoons leaf oregano
½   teaspoon garlic powder

1. Season the spaghetti sauce with oregano and garlic powder if desired. Spread ¼ cup of sauce in the bottom of a 2-quart casserole dish.
2. Layer half of the eggplant over the sauce. Spread half of the remaining sauce over the eggplant. Sprinkle with half of the Parmesan.
3. Repeat the layers, using all of the eggplant, sauce, and Parmesan.
4. Microwave on high for 13 minutes.
5. Top the casserole with the mozzarella slices. Microwave on high for 1 minute or until the cheese melts.

YIELD: 4 servings

| Total calories: | 1,000 |
|---|---|
| Calories per serving: | 250 |

|  | Grams | % of recipe |
|---|---|---|
| CARB | 18 | 50 |
| PRO | 13 | 20 |
| FAT | 14 | 30 |

## Eggplant Italiano II

Eggplant is a high-fiber, low-calorie vegetable. It is mostly water, with insignificant amounts of nutrients until you boost the vitamin A with the tomato sauce, and the protein and calcium when the cheese is added.

To simplify the recipe, use a jar of spaghetti sauce. For a high-carbohydrate sports dinner, serve this with rice or pasta.

1   large eggplant
1   28-ounce can tomato purée
1   tablespoon oregano
1   clove garlic, crushed or ¼ teaspoon garlic powder
1   tablespoon molasses
1   pound low-fat cottage cheese
1   teaspoon oregano
¼   teaspoon garlic powder
2   tablespoons flour
4   ounces (1 cup) grated mozzarella
2   tablespoons Parmesan cheese

1. Slice the eggplant into ½-inch wheels. Steam for 10 minutes. Drain.
2. In a saucepan combine the tomato purée with 1 tablespoon of oregano, garlic, and molasses. Heat through.
3. In a medium bowl combine the cottage cheese, 1 teaspoon of oregano, garlic powder, and flour. Blend well.
4. In a casserole dish layer half of the eggplant, cottage cheese, and tomato sauce. Repeat the layers.
5. Top with grated mozzarella and Parmesan.
6. Bake at 350° for 20 minutes.

YIELD: 4 servings

| Total calories: | | 1,300 |
|---|---|---|
| Calories per serving: | | 325 |

| | Grams | % of recipe |
|---|---|---|
| CARB | 26 | 35 |
| PRO | 25 | 30 |
| FAT | 13 | 35 |

Calories per serving with 1½ cups rice: 620

| | Grams | % of recipe |
|---|---|---|
| CARB | 92 | 60 |
| PRO | 31 | 20 |
| FAT | 14 | 20 |

## Sautéed Zucchini

Zucchini and summer squash are watery vegetables with insignificant nutritional value other than some fiber. They are low in calories until you add oil and cheese.

4   medium zucchini
2   tablespoons olive oil
1   to 2 tablespoons Parmesan cheese, as desired

1. Slice the zucchini very thinly.
2. In a skillet heat the oil and sauté the zucchini gently until tender, about 1 to 2 minutes.
3. Top with Parmesan cheese.

YIELD: 4 servings

| Total calories: | | 400 |
|---|---|---|
| Calories per serving: | | 100 |

| | Grams | % of recipe |
|---|---|---|
| CARB | 9 | 30 |
| PRO | 2 | 10 |
| FAT | 6 | 60 |

## Zucchini Stuffing Casserole

This side dish provides a nice change of pace served with chicken or fish. For extra color cook grated carrot along with the zucchini.

3   medium zucchini, sliced
1   onion, sliced
½   cup water
1   10½-ounce can cream of chicken (or mushroom) soup
1   soup can milk
3   cups stuffing mix
**Optional:**
⅓   cup grated cheese

1. In a saucepan combine the zucchini, onions, and water. Cover and bring to a boil. Simmer for 5 minutes.
2. Add the soup and milk, and heat through.
3. In the bottom of a shallow casserole spread the stuffing. Pour the zucchini mixture over the stuffing. Top with cheese, if desired.
4. Cover and bake at 350° for 20 minutes.

YIELD: 5 servings

| Total calories: | | 1,400 |
|---|---|---|
| Calories per serving: | | 280 |

| | Grams | % of recipe |
|---|---|---|
| CARB | 45 | 65 |
| PRO | 7 | 10 |
| FAT | 7 | 25 |

# THE RACE OF A LIFETIME

In 1990,. Fred Lebow, then president of the NYRRC found he had brain cancer. He recalls the experience, in 1992, when Grete Waitz ran the Marathon with him.

The vow I made to finish the Marathon goes back to the day when I found out I had cancer. I couldn't sleep that night. The tears rolled down my face as I thought about dying, and a stinging regret hit me: I had never run the five-borough marathon. I realize this must seem insane to people who aren't runners. This guy's lucky to be alive, and he's worried about running a marathon? Yet every runner who takes on the challenge of a marathon, for whatever reason, doesn't have to ask why. When you are forced to face your own mortality so dramatically day after day, something has to sustain you. In addition to my family, my friends, a sense of my religious roots, and the best medical care—my running kept me alive.

*For the first eight miles, I obsess over the organization of the race. I manage only to walk most of the first mile on the bridge. Then we increase to about a 12-minute pace, as planned. Word comes that the lead men are engaged in a dramatic duel. I am told Lisa Ondieki is on course-record pace. The race is okay. I begin to run for myself.*

In the weeks that followed my brain biopsy, I ran or walked every day, circling the hospital roof or running the hallways. Did I do all this for my body? Of course not. It was for my mind. "Why are you running around like that?" the other patients would ask. "The question is not why I'm doing it," I replied. "The question is why aren't you doing it too."

*At the 10-mile mark, I notice a mixture of spectators— Hasidic Jews, Hispanics, and African-Americans—united as spectators. As the Hasidic girls, wearing their finest dresses, hand me candy and water, I reflect on this unity with some price. The New York City Marathon is more than just a footrace.*

Day by day, month by month, I returned to my former life. As my cancer went into remission, I did more running and then made a firm resolution. I wanted to run my marathon in 1992.

*For a mile and a half on the Queensboro Bridge, we run essentially in silence. Grete periodically asks how I feel. Coming off the Queensboro Bridge and onto First Avenue in Manhattan, everything changes. The power of this race— which for so many years I have experienced from the pace car—hits me as one of the runners. The cheering is incredi-ble. I can't believe the throngs of people have waited this long for runners at my pace! The Crown Prince of Holland is running the race, but now I feel like I am the royal prince.*

Initially I told no one of my resolution. Then I confided in a few close friends. In Norway, Jack Waitz asked me if his wife, with nine wins in the race, could run the marathon with me.

*At 18 miles, my knee starts to hurt and my legs are tightening. Our pace slows. But time really doesn't matter. At 19 miles, I ask for a piece of sports bar. At 20 miles, Grete and I each hit our own wall. At mile 21, I ask Grete to stop and help me put on my knee brace.*

By late summer, I announced that I was planning to run the marathon. Why did I tell all the world I was doing this? One reason was to get the moral support and to solidify my commitment to run; the second was to answer all those who have contacted me since I got cancer—the other victims of this disease who looked for a bit of inspiration or advice.

*"You're where it's happening, Fred," shouts a smiling woman in Harlem. Then we realize that we are close to Central Park. When I pass 90th Street and Fifth Avenue, 80-year-old Joe Kleinerman, the anchor of the NYRRC, moves toward me—for the first time in ages without his cane. There are tears in his eyes. He hugs me and plants a kiss on my cheek. This is all it takes. I begin to cry. Then Grete begins to cry.*

I had one reason for running the marathon that far out-weighed all others: It meant that I had conquered cancer.

*We're approaching the finish. Grete and I and everyone around us are crying uncontrollably. After I cross the blue finish line, I bend down to kiss it—reminiscent of the custom of those Jews who, on first arriving to the Holy Land, bend down to kiss the ground. But I have to laugh amid the tears. After I bend down, I can't get up! Grete helps me up. My first words draw a laugh: "I never realized a marathon could be so long."*

The most important feeling that remains is that I have taken my life back. As I wrote in *The New York Road Runners Club Complete Book of Running*, "The real change is inside me, a change I understand best through my running. I'm glad to be alive, and I live with that feeling every day. It's like being a beginner again, in love with the idea of my body moving along, content with the weather, the season, and the sound of each footfall."

## Baked Tomato

These tomatoes are so simple to make and are a delicious accompaniment to most meals, particularly salmon. For efficient use of the oven, JoAnn Walters suggests you make them when you bake entrées.

*1   fresh tomato per person*
*Salt and pepper to taste*
*Pinch sugar*
*Parmesan cheese*

1. Slice a dime-sized sliver off the bottom of the tomato so that it will sit evenly. Slice about ⅛ inch off the top of the tomato. Core the tomato, removing the green and white portion and leaving a 1-inch hole in the center.
2. Place the tomato in a baking dish. Sprinkle with salt, pepper, and sugar. Fill the hole with Parmesan and sprinkle Parmesan around the top. Bake at 350° for 20 to 30 minutes.

YIELD: 1 serving

| Total calories: | | 65 |
|---|---|---|

|  | Grams | % of recipe |
|---|---|---|
| CARB | 11 | 65 |
| PRO | 1 | 10 |
| FAT | 2 | 25 |

*Thomas Young and Pamela Kezios were married at the 8-mile mark of the 1993 NYC Marathon. After their brief vows, they took off and finished the race.*

## Summer Squash and Onion Casserole

What do you do with all those squash exploding in the garden? Here's one solution from Veronica Coronado and *What's Cooking at the Cooper Clinic.*

*1   pound yellow summer squash*
*⅓   cup chopped onion*
*¼   cup water*
*¼   cup bread crumbs*
*1   teaspoon margarine*
*2   teaspoons sugar*
*Salt and pepper to taste*

1. Slice the squash and onions into a casserole dish. Add the water.
2. In a small bowl combine the remaining ingredients. Sprinkle the mixture over the squash.
3. Cover and bake at 350° for 30 minutes.

YIELD: 2 servings

| Total calories: | | 160 |
|---|---|---|
| Calories per serving: | | 80 |

|  | Grams | % of recipe |
|---|---|---|
| CARB | 14 | 65 |
| PRO | 3 | 15 |
| FAT | 2 | 20 |

195

## Acorn Squash with Walnuts and Applesauce

Winter squash, like most colorful vegetables, is rich in vitamin A. One ¾-cup serving supplies 100 percent of your daily need. Squash is also a good source of potassium, fiber, and carbohydrates. I recommend it as a part of your regular sports diet. That's why the recipe is for two squash—cook enough for leftovers while you are cooking!

2   *acorn squash*
1   *cup applesauce*
2   *tablespoons firmly packed brown sugar*
2   *tablespoons raisins*
2   *tablespoons walnuts*
¼   *teaspoon cinnamon*

1. Cut the squash in half and scoop out all of the seeds. If needed, cut a slice from the bottom so the squash will sit flat.
2. In a small bowl combine the remaining ingredients. Portion the mixture into the squash halves.
3. Place ½ inch of water in a baking pan. Place the squash in the pan.
4. Cover and bake at 350° for 30 minutes.
5. Uncover and bake an additional 30 minutes or until the squash are tender when pierced with a fork.

YIELD: 4 servings

| Total calories: | | 1,000 |
|---|---|---|
| Calories per serving: | | 250 |

| | Grams | % of recipe |
|---|---|---|
| CARB | 48 | 75 |
| PRO | 5 | 10 |
| FAT | 4 | 15 |

## Winter Squash with Orange and Pineapple

This recipe from Chicago-area sports nutritionist Jacqueline Marcus is tasty and different—but so easy.

1   *package frozen mashed squash, thawed*
2   *tablespoons low-fat sour cream*
½   *cup pineapple chunks, packed in juice or water*
½   *cup orange segments, cut into chunks*

**Optional:**
*Fresh mint, chopped*
8   *walnut halves*

1. In a medium bowl beat together the mashed squash and sour cream. Add the pineapple and orange chunks.
2. Transfer the mixture to a small casserole dish.
3. Bake at 350° for 15 to 20 minutes or until hot.
4. Sprinkle with mint and walnut halves, if desired.

YIELD: 3 servings

| Total calories: | | 330 |
|---|---|---|
| Calories per serving: | | 110 |

| | Grams | % of recipe |
|---|---|---|
| CARB | 25 | 90 |
| PRO | 2 | 10 |
| FAT | 0 | 0 |

# 17 MUNCHIES AND PIZZA

*The following recipes may be used for snacks, lunches, or suppers, depending upon your mood.*

## Bean Dip

This is good not only as a dip for fat-free tortilla chips, but also for filling a tortilla, then rolling it up with diced tomatoes and lettuce, if desired, to add crunch.

| 1 | 16-ounce can vegetarian refried beans |
| 1 | 16-ounce can vegetarian chili |
| 6 | ounces (1½ cups) grated low-fat Cheddar cheese |

1. In the bottom of a pie plate or shallow casserole dish spread the refried beans, then the vegetarian chili.
2. Sprinkle the cheese on top.
3. Heat in the microwave until bubbling.

YIELD: 10 servings

| Total calories: | 1,300 |
| Calories per serving: | 130 |

|  | Grams | % of recipe |
|---|---|---|
| CARB | 18 | 55 |
| PRO | 10 | 30 |
| FAT | 2 | 15 |

## Focaccia

Bill Fischer discovered the wonders of focaccia when marathon training. He says it sure tastes good and can be either a spicy snack by itself, a nice accompaniment to soup, or used to make a carbo-loaded sandwich.

He credits the recipes as being adapted from the *Fields of Green Cookbook* (1993).

| 2 | packages active dry yeast |
| 2 | cups lukewarm water (110°) |
| 1 | tablespoon honey or sugar |
| ¼ | to ½ cup oil, preferably olive or canola |
| 2 | tablespoons fresh rosemary, finely chopped (or 1 to 2 teaspoons dried) |
| 3 | tablespoons fresh sage, finely chopped (or 1 to 2 teaspoons dried) |
| ½ | cup sun-dried tomatoes, chopped |
| 2 | teaspoons salt |
| 5 | cups flour, preferably half white, half whole-wheat |
| 1 | tablespoon oil, preferably roasted garlic oil, to brush the bread |

1. In a large bowl combine the yeast, ½ cup of water, and honey or sugar. Set aside until foamy.
2. Add the oil, remaining water, rosemary, sage, sun-dried tomatoes, and salt.
3. Add 4 cups of flour. Turn the dough on to a floured board and knead in the last cup. Knead well for 10 minutes, adding more flour as needed.
4. Put the dough in an oiled bowl, turning it over so the top has oil coating the surface. Cover and let the dough rise in a warm place for about 1 hour and 30 minutes.
5. Punch down the dough, and turn it onto a lightly oiled 11x16-inch baking sheet. Flatten the dough so that it covers as much of the surface as possible. (The thicker the dough in the pan, the thicker the finished product. If you want to make thinner breads, use 2 pans.)
6. Cover and let the dough rise for 30 minutes. Dimple the dough with your fingertips, then brush with roasted garlic oil (or any good-tasting oil).
7. Place in a 450° oven. Reduce the temperature to 375° and bake for 25 minutes, until golden brown. Cool on a rack.

YIELD: 1 large focaccia or 2 mediums

| Total calories: | 2,900 |
| Calories per serving (1⁄16 recipe): | 180 |

|  | Grams | % of recipe |
|---|---|---|
| CARB | 32 | 70 |
| PRO | 4 | 10 |
| FAT | 4 | 20 |

*To save precious time, serious runners must perfect the art of drinking on the run.*

## Pizza Fondue

This recipe, which is taken from *Nancy Clark's Sports Nutrition Guidebook* (Leisure Press, 1990), is fun for children and grown-ups alike. The trick is to eat enough bread with the fondue so that you carbo-load instead of fill up on the cheese.

1   16-ounce jar spaghetti or pizza sauce
8   ounces (2 cups) grated  low-fat mozzarella cheese
2   tablespoons flour
1   loaf French or Italian bread, broken into chunks
**Optional:**
*Celery chunks, green bell pepper cubes, mushroom caps for dipping*

1. In a fondue pot or medium-sized saucepan heat the spaghetti sauce.
2. Shake together the grated cheese and flour.
3. Gradually melt the cheese into the spaghetti sauce, stirring constantly.
4. Keep the fondue warm by placing the pot on a fondue-pot stand, heating tray, or camp stove.
5. Using forks, dip chunks of bread or raw vegetables into the pizza fondue.

YIELD: 4 servings

| Total calories: | | 2,200 |
|---|---|---|
| Calories per serving: | | 550 |

|  | Grams | % of recipe |
|---|---|---|
| CARB | 77 | 55 |
| PRO | 27 | 20 |
| FAT | 15 | 25 |

## Herbed Cheese Spread

This has great flavor and is low in fat. Serve it as an appetizer with crackers, toasted pita bread, or bread sticks.

1   cup yogurt "cream cheese" (see following recipe) or 1 8-ounce package low-fat cream cheese (fat free makes this recipe too watery)
1   teaspoon honey
½   cup unsweetened crushed pineapple, drained
⅓   cup chopped red and/or green bell pepper
*Salt and pepper to taste*
**Optional:**
⅓   cup chopped green onions
1   teaspoon dried dill
¼   teaspoon garlic or onion powder
2   tablespoons hulled salted or unsalted sunflower seeds

1. In a medium bowl blend together the "cream" cheese and honey. Blend in the pineapple, bell pepper, salt, pepper, onions, dill, and garlic powder.
2. Transfer the spread to the serving bowl.
3. Sprinkle sunflower seeds over the spread if desired.

YIELD: 1½ cups

| Total calories: | | 540 |
|---|---|---|
| Calories per serving (about 2 tablespoons): | | 45 |

|  | Grams | % of recipe |
|---|---|---|
| CARB | 7 | 70 |
| PRO | 4 | 30 |
| FAT | 0 | 0 |

## Yogurt "Cream" Cheese

This is surprisingly good and a healthy alternative to the traditional bagel spread. For a special touch, blend the yogurt cheese with chopped scallions and garlic powder, fresh chopped fruit, or honey, dates, and walnuts.

1  paper coffee filter, drip type
1  16-ounce carton plain low-fat yogurt that contains no gelatin

1. Place the filter in a strainer or colander and set it over a mixing bowl. Spoon the yogurt into the filter. Cover, refrigerate, and let drip at least 3 hours or overnight.
2. When the yogurt is the consistency of softened cream cheese, spoon it into an airtight container and discard the whey. Store in refrigerator.

YIELD: 4–6 tablespoons

| Total calories: | | 100 |
| Calories per serving: | | 25 |

| | Grams | % of recipe |
| --- | --- | --- |
| CARB | 4 | 55 |
| PRO | 3 | 45 |
| FAT | 0 | 0 |

*Hasidic Jewish girls in Williamsburg, Brooklyn, greet the runners. The first few years of the race, few of these conservative religious residents came out along the streets.*

## Spicy Spinach Dip

This recipe was submitted by Marilyn Burnett of Scottsdale, Arizona. Leftovers reheat well in the microwave, and make a great topping for baked potatoes or pasta. However, Marilyn says there are rarely any leftovers! Serve with tortilla chips, pita, or crackers.

1   10-ounce package frozen chopped spinach
4   jalapeño peppers, seeded and chopped
½   red bell pepper, chopped
1   small onion, chopped
8   ounces (2 cups) shredded fat-free Monterey Jack cheese
12  ounces fat-free cream cheese or yogurt cream cheese
¾   cup skim milk
1   teaspoon cider vinegar
**Optional:**
*Dash Tabasco sauce*

1. Thaw the spinach and squeeze out as much liquid as possible.
2. In a baking dish combine the spinach and the remaining ingredients. Mix well.
3. Bake at 400° for 15 to 20 minutes, or until bubbly around the edges.
4. Let the dip cool for 10 minutes before serving, if possible. Just before serving, dash Tabasco sauce over the top, if desired.

YIELD: 10 servings

| Total calories: | | 650 |
| Calories per serving (about ¼ cup): | | 65 |

| | Grams | % of recipe |
| --- | --- | --- |
| CARB | 5 | 30 |
| PRO | 11 | 70 |
| FAT | 0 | 0 |

## Tortilla Crisps

Gloria Averbuch submitted this idea for a snack that is tasty and so much more nutritious than the high-fat variety. For a special touch, before toasting, sprinkle each tortilla with spices such as garlic powder and chili powder, cumin and onion powder, or just simply salt and pepper. Top with your favorite beans, plain yogurt, reduced-fat sour cream, low-fat grated cheese, and salsa.

*Oil or cooking spray*
*Corn tortilla*

1. Either brush a very small amount of oil on a corn tortilla or spray lightly with cooking spray.
2. Toast in an oven or toaster oven until crisp.

| Calories per tortilla: | | 85 |
| --- | --- | --- |
| | Grams | % of recipe |
| CARB | 12 | 60 |
| PRO | 2 | 10 |
| FAT | 3 | 30 |

## Pita Chips

*1   medium pita bread*
**Optional:**
*Cooking spray*
*Garlic salt*
*Chili powder*
*Taco seasoning mix*
*Oregano*

1. Split the pita bread lengthwise and then cut into chip-sized wedges. Place the wedges on a baking sheet.
2. Spray the pita wedges with cooking spray if desired. Sprinkle with seasonings as desired.
3. Bake at 250° for 20 minutes or until golden. Serve with your favorite dip or salsa.

| Calories per pita: | | 220 |
| --- | --- | --- |
| | Grams | % of recipe |
| CARB | 40 | 75 |
| PRO | 8 | 15 |
| FAT | 3 | 10 |

## Crunchy Gorp

Sports nutritionist Barbara Day of Louisville, Kentucky, submitted this recipe that is easy to prepare, crunchy, and energy-packed. Eat it on the run!

¼  *cup Wheat Chex*
¼  *cup Corn Chex*
¼  *cup pretzels*
¼  *cup raisins*
2   *tablespoons peanuts*

1. In a lunch bag combine all of the ingredients.
2. Shake, shake, shake, then munch, munch, munch.

YIELD: 1 serving

| Total calories (about 1 cup): | | 340 |
| --- | --- | --- |
| | Grams | % of recipe |
| CARB | 60 | 70 |
| PRO | 7 | 10 |
| FAT | 8 | 20 |

# THE WORLD'S LARGEST DINNER PARTY

It's the Marathon Pasta Party, of course! According to Fred Lebow, the New York City Marathon has held some sort of pre-race "feed" since 1976. The current pasta party holds the unofficial title of "the world's largest dinner party."

Between 4:00 and 9:00 P.M., approximately 14,000 runners consume 5,000 pounds of pasta and 2,500 gallons of sauce. The leftover pasta from the pasta party is donated to an organization to help feed New York's hungry.

How much is 5,000 pounds of pasta? If laid out, end to end, the spaghetti would stretch 54 miles. That's 285,174 feet, or:

- Enough pasta for one person to eat a pasta dinner every day for 38 years
- .06 times the length of the NYC Marathon route
- 4⅛ times the length of Manhattan
- 47,608 times the height of Fred Lebow
- 44 times the length of the Queens Midtown Tunnel
- 585 times the height of the United Nations Building
- 24 times the average depth of the Atlantic Ocean
- 935 times the height of the Statue of Liberty

## Seasoned Popcorn

Popcorn makes a fun, low-calorie snack as long as it's prepared without lots of butter or oil. If you don't have an air popper or a no-fat microwave popper, try this low-fat method for stove-top popcorn.

| 1 | tablespoon oil, preferably safflower or canola |
| 2 | tablespoons popcorn kernels |

1. Heat the oil in the bottom of a saucepan. Add the corn kernels.
2. When the popcorn is just about to start popping, carefully drain off half the oil.
3. Resume cooking, allowing the corn to pop without the oil.
4. Season with: garlic or onion powder or salt; curry powder; basil, oregano, and/or other Italian seasonings, powdered salad dressing mixes; combination of paprika and red pepper; soy sauce; grated Parmesan or mozzarella; taco seasoning mix; cinnamon. To get the seasonings to "stick" without butter, spray the popcorn with cooking spray, then sprinkle the seasonings, buy seasoned popcorn sprays, or mix salt and water (or soy sauce) in a spray bottle and mist the popcorn with the salt solution (note: people with high blood pressure should limit their intake of salted popcorn).

Yield: 1 serving (4 cups)

| Calories per serving with half the oil drained: | | 150 |
| --- | --- | --- |
|  | Grams | % of recipe |
| CARB | 20 | 55 |
| PRO | 3 | 5 |
| FAT | 7 | 40 |

## Chunky Salsa

Stacy Flickner submitted this family favorite that can be added to meats, simmered with vegetables, or eaten with various Mexican dishes. It is an old Mexican salsa recipe given to her aunt by a migrant Mexican worker who worked in the produce fields of the Snake River Valley near Wilder, Idaho—a major producer of fresh vegetables sold all across the United States.

| 3 | cups chopped and peeled fresh, ripe tomatoes |
| 2 | cups chopped onions |
| ½ | cup (or more depending on your taste) chopped red or green jalapeño peppers |
| ¼ | cup white vinegar |
| ½ | teaspoon salt or to taste |

**Optional:**

| ¼ | cup chopped fresh cilantro |
| 2 | cloves garlic, crushed |
| ½ | teaspoon sugar |

1. In a large bowl combine the tomatoes, onions, peppers, vinegar, and salt.
2. Add the cilantro, garlic, and sugar if desired. Adjust the peppers, salt, garlic, etc. to taste.

YIELD: 20 servings

| Total calories: | | 200 |
| --- | --- | --- |
| Calories per serving (about ¼ cup): | | 10 |
|  | Grams | % of recipe |
| CARB | 3 | 100 |
| PRO | 0 | 0 |
| FAT | 0 | 0 |

## Frozen Fruit Nuggets

Popping a few of these frozen fruit chunks in your mouth is a refreshing treat after a hot summer workout. Frozen bananas are particularly good—similar to banana ice cream! Frozen chunks also whip up into

Kathrine Switzer, who won the Marathon in 1974, went on to become a broadcaster and champion of women's running.

delightful shakes when blenderized with either milk or juice.

*Grapes, bananas, strawberries, watermelon, cantaloupe, or other fruits of your choice*

1. Cut the fruit into bite-sized pieces.
2. Spread the fruit pieces on a flat pan and place in the freezer for 1 hour. When frozen, place the pieces into baggies, so they'll be ready when the munchies strike!

| Calories per cup of nuggets: | | 50 |
| --- | --- | --- |
|  | Grams | % or recipe |
| CARB | 12 | 90 |
| PRO | - | 5 |
| FAT | - | - |

# PIZZA IDEAS

If you don't want to make your own pizza dough using the following recipes, use:

- dough bought from your local pizza shop or grocery store
- Boboli
- English muffins
- Syrian (pita) bread

Top the pizza crust with sauce. A 12-inch pizza should use about ¾ to 1 cup of sauce, more or less as desired. Choose your toppings. The possibilities are endless. The goal is to have fun and eat well! Here is where you and your family can be creative.

- Try different cheeses like Ricotta, feta, and Cheddar (a 12-inch pizza will need about 4 ounces of cheese or more).
- Vegetables such as sun-dried tomatoes, steamed broccoli, fresh mushrooms, and onions make a wonderful combination.
- Pesto makes a fantastic sauce.
- Or try a white Roman pizza—a pizza without sauce, just cheese and/or toppings.

Bake a large pizza (12- or 14-inch) at 475° for 12 to 15 minutes or until the cheese is bubbly and turning golden-brown. Smaller pizzas such as English muffin or pita pizzas may be baked in the toaster oven.

## Whole-Wheat Pizza Dough

Here is a crust for those who prefer whole wheat. I recommend using only part whole wheat, otherwise the flavor becomes overwhelming and the crust tends to be dry.—JLH

1   cup lukewarm water (110°)
1   package active dry yeast
1   to 3 teaspoons salt, as desired
3   tablespoons olive oil, or less as desired
2   tablespoons sugar
1   cup whole-wheat flour
1½ to 2 cups white flour

1. Place the warm water in a large mixing bowl, and sprinkle the yeast over the top. Mix gently until fully dissolved.

2. Stir in the salt, oil, and sugar, and half the flour. Combine well. Keep adding small amounts of the flour and continue to mix until the dough begins to stick together in a ball and begins to pull away from the sides of the bowl.

3. Turn the dough out on to a floured surface and begin to knead. Continue kneading, adding small amounts of flour, until the dough is no longer sticky.

4. Place the ball of dough in a large oiled bowl. Turn the dough over to cover it with oil and cover the top of the bowl with plastic wrap or a damp, warm towel. Let the bowl stand in a warm place for about 1½ to 2 hours or until the dough has doubled in size.

5. Uncover the bowl and punch down the risen dough.

6. Place the dough on a lightly floured work surface. Unless you are an adept pizzamaker, use a rolling pin to roll the dough into either a circle or a rectangle (about 10x13 inches). Allow the dough to relax for a minute or two before transferring it to a pizza pan or cookie sheet, treated with cooking spray. You are now ready to assemble your pizza.

YIELD: dough for one big pizza (8 slices)

| Total calories: | 1,500 |
|---|---|
| Calories per slice: | 190 |

|  | Grams | % of recipe |
|---|---|---|
| CARB | 32 | 65 |
| PRO | 4 | 10 |
| FAT | 5 | 25 |

## Spinach Dough

This is an easy pizza crust because it requires no yeast or rising time. It's delicious with just cheese topping—mix together favorites such as feta, low-fat Monterey Jack, and mozzarella. If you prefer a chewier crust, roll it thicker using only part of the pan. Rolling it out thinly makes a crispy crust. Your kids will love it!

| | |
|---|---|
| 1 | 10-ounce package frozen chopped spinach, thawed |
| 3 | tablespoons olive oil |
| ½ | cup milk |
| 1 | egg (or substitute), slightly beaten |
| 2 | cups flour, half white, half whole-wheat, as desired |
| 1 | tablespoon baking powder |
| ½ | teaspoon salt |

1. Drain the thawed spinach in a colander and press out most of the moisture.
2. In a small saucepan heat the oil and add the spinach. Cook over low heat for 5 minutes.
3. Remove the pan from the heat, cool slightly, and then stir in the milk and egg.
4. In a separate bowl combine the flour, baking powder, and salt. Mix well and add the spinach mixture. The dough will be very sticky and wet.
5. Turn the dough onto a greased 12-inch pizza pan or a 10x14-inch cookie sheet and cover with waxed paper. Using your hands or a rolling pin, spread the dough out to an even layer, pushing up around the edges to form a border. Remove the waxed paper.
6. Bake the crust at 450° for 15 to 20 minutes.
7. Add the toppings and bake until done.

YIELD: dough for 1 pizza, 8 slices

| | | |
|---|---|---|
| Total calories: | | 1,350 |
| Calories per serving: | | 170 |

| | Grams | % of recipe |
|---|---|---|
| CARB | 26 | 60 |
| PRO | 5 | 15 |
| FAT | 5 | 25 |

## Pizza Sauce

If you're ever in Boston for the BAA Marathon, stop by Newbury Pizza on Newbury Street and try a slice of one of the best pizzas in town. This recipe was adapted from their basic pizza sauce. You won't believe how delicious and easy it is.

| | |
|---|---|
| 1 | 16-ounce can crushed peeled tomatoes |
| 1 | 6-ounce can tomato paste |
| ½ | cup water |
| 1 | tablespoon sugar |
| 1 | tablespoon oregano |
| 1½ | teaspoons pepper |
| 1 | teaspoon salt |

1. In a large bowl combine all of the ingredients.
2. Spread on pizza dough as desired.

YIELD: enough for 1 big pizza

| | | |
|---|---|---|
| Total calories: | | 240 |
| Calories per ⅛ recipe: | | 30 |

| | Grams | % of recipe |
|---|---|---|
| CARB | 6 | 85 |
| PRO | 1 | 15 |
| FAT | 0 | 0 |

I have been asked everywhere I go: Why do people run the Marathon? Sure, there is a sense of status we gain among our peers. But I think the real reasons are more personal. I think it is because we need to test our physical, emotional, or creative abilities. After all, in practical life we cannot all "give it our all." We can't grow wings and fly. We can't sing without a great voice, or dance when we aren't dancers. Most of us won't perform on a stage. But whether a person is a world-class athlete or a four-hour runner, the Marathon gives us a stage. In this case, it's the road, where we can perform and be proud, while millions of people applaud. It's like being on Broadway and getting a standing ovation!

For another thing, in an unequal world, in this one endeavor people of vastly differing abilities share something in common: the act of going the distance. Whether it's two hours or four or five, the effort and achievement are similar.

—FRED LEBOW

203

## Sun-Dried Tomato Sauce

This sauce is so flavorful that there is no need to add salt, pepper, or spices. It is good with pasta, and goes especially well with red peppers and goat cheese.

1  *cup sun-dried tomatoes packed in oil, drained*
1  *clove garlic, minced*
1  *cup water*
1  *cup tomato sauce*

1. In a saucepan cook the sun-dried tomatoes and garlic in the water, uncovered for about 20 minutes, or until the tomatoes are plump and tender.
2. Reduce the heat, add the tomato sauce, and simmer for another 10 minutes.
3. In a blender or food processor purée the mixture until smooth.

YIELD: 8 servings

| Total calories: | 320 |
| --- | --- |
| Calories per serving: | 40 |

| | Grams | % of recipe |
| --- | --- | --- |
| CARB | 5 | 50 |
| PRO | 1 | 10 |
| FAT | 2 | 40 |

## Veggie Calzones

Ann Joyal of Boston submitted this recipe because it is easy and fun—with a yummy surprise inside!

1  *10-ounce tube refrigerated pizza dough or homemade recipe*
1  *cup pizza sauce, homemade or canned*

**Your choice of:**
½  *cup sliced mushrooms*
½  *cup chopped bell peppers*
½  *cup grated low-fat cheese (Cheddar or mozzarella)*
½  *cup grated carrot*
½  *cup olives*
½  *cup chopped onion*
½  *cup chopped broccoli or spinach*

**Optional:**
½  *teaspoon dried basil*
¼  *teaspoon garlic powder or 1 clove fresh, minced*
*Salt and pepper as desired*

1. Unroll and stretch the dough to approximately 6 to 8 inches wide. Spread the dough with pizza sauce. Set aside.
2. Microwave or steam the vegetables lightly until tender crisp.

Place the vegetables in the center of the dough. Top with cheese.
3. Sprinkle with basil, garlic, salt, and pepper as desired. Fold half the circle of dough over and seal the edges. Place on a lightly oiled baking sheet.
4. Bake at 425° for 10 to 15 minutes.

YIELD: 2 generous servings

| Total calories: | 1,000 |
| --- | --- |
| Calories per ½ calzone: | 500 |

| | Grams | % of recipe |
| --- | --- | --- |
| CARB | 77 | 60 |
| PRO | 21 | 15 |
| FAT | 14 | 25 |

# 18 *DESSERTS*

Whether you are recovering from a training run or the marathon itself, a scrumptious dessert can be a fun reward. You need not feel guilty about enjoying a sweet treat, assuming that you balance it into your day's food allowance. Simply get out your calculator:

6 miles x 100 calories/mile = 600 calories
= two pieces of Fred Lebow's favorite Big Apple Cake or
= 5 of Joan Benoit Samuelson's chocolate chip cookies . . .

The following collection of dessert recipes includes healthful, semi-healthful, and decadent sweets and treats.

## *Warm Peach Dessert*

When you want something sweet but healthful for dessert, try this simple standby. Like most warm fruit desserts, this goes nicely when topped with frozen yogurt or ice cream!

Although this recipe uses the microwave oven, you can also bake the peaches in a regular oven (or toaster oven) at 350° for 10 to 15 minutes or even sauté them in a nonstick pan on the stovetop.

4   *halves canned peaches*
2   *teaspoons brown sugar*
**Optional:**
1   *teaspoon margarine or butter*
*Sprinkling of cinnamon or nutmeg*

1. Place the peaches pit-side-up in a microwavable dish.
2. Put ½ teaspoon of brown sugar and ¼ teaspoon of butter if desired in the center of each peach.
3. Sprinkle with cinnamon. Microwave for about 2 to 4 minutes or until hot.

YIELD: 1 serving

| Total calories: | | 110 |
|---|---|---|
| Calories per serving: | | 110 |

| | Grams | % of recipe |
|---|---|---|
| CARB | 28 | 100 |
| PRO | 0 | 0 |
| FAT | 0 | 0 |

## *Bananas with Maple Syrup or Honey*

When confronted with an abundance of bananas that are quickly ripening, this dessert can solve the "how to use the bananas" problem.

1   *tablespoon maple syrup or honey*
1   *big banana, sliced*
**Optional:**
1   *teaspoon butter or margarine*
1   *teaspoon lemon juice*
*Sprinkling of cinnamon*

1. Melt the butter in a microwaveable bowl if desired.
2. Add the maple syrup and banana slices. Coat the banana slices with the syrup and butter mixture.
3. Microwave for 1 to 3 minutes, or until warm.
4. If desired, sprinkle with lemon juice and/or cinnamon.

YIELD: 1 serving

| Total calories: | | 220 |
|---|---|---|

| | Grams | % of recipe |
|---|---|---|
| CARB | 53 | 95 |
| PRO | 2 | 5 |
| FAT | 0 | 0 |

## Fruit Pizza I

This fruit pizza has been a favorite celebration dessert in Amy Pohlman's family. She says it is almost as fun to make as it is to eat. She recommends that you be creative and make designs with the fruit, such as a flag or a huge heart or a Big Apple.

This dessert has extra special meaning for Amy because she was eating this when her boyfriend proposed to her. She hopes it will have equally nice memories for you!

1   20-ounce roll prepared sugar cookie dough
1   8-ounce package softened low-fat cream cheese
2   tablespoons milk (or ¼ cup low-fat sour cream)
2   tablespoons sugar
½   teaspoon almond or vanilla extract
3   to 4 cups assorted fruits for the topping (berries, sliced peaches, kiwi, etc.)
2   tablespoons apricot jam

1. Cut the cookie dough into ⅛-inch slices.
2. Line the sides and bottom of a greased 14-inch pizza pan or baking sheet with the cookie dough slices.
3. Bake at 350° for 12 to 14 minutes, or until golden brown. Let the crust cool.
4. Beat together the cream cheese, milk (or sour cream), sugar, and almond (or vanilla) extract. Spread over the cooled crust.
5. Slice favorite fruits and arrange on top of the cream cheese.

"That was Fred Lebow's contribution. I think he had a vision—that running could or should be adapted to participation by masses of people. . . . Primarily with his New York City Marathon . . . It was such a magnet to people's imaginations, a wonderful, thrilling affair."

—**JIM FIXX**, author of the influential bestseller, The Complete Book of Running

6. Melt the apricot jam and brush a little over the fruit to help the fruit stay fresh-looking, if desired.
7. Refrigerate until ready to serve.

YIELD: 16 servings

| Total calories: | | 3,200 |
|---|---|---|
| Calories per serving: | | 190 |

| | Grams | % of recipe |
|---|---|---|
| CARB | 26 | 55 |
| PRO | 2 | 5 |
| FAT | 9 | 40 |

## Fruit Pizza II (Low-Fat)

2   cups Light Cool Whip
1   large sponge cake shell (from the supermarket)
3   to 4 cups assorted fruits: banana, grapes, strawberries, peaches, blueberries, kiwi, etc.

1. Spread the Cool Whip on the spongecake.
2. Arrange your favorite fruits on top.

YIELD: 12 servings

| Total calories: | | 1,800 |
|---|---|---|
| Calories per serving: | | 150 |

| | Grams | % of recipe |
|---|---|---|
| CARB | 25 | 65 |
| PRO | 3 | 10 |
| FAT | 4 | 25 |

## Strawberry-Lemon Yogurt

This colorful and visually appealing dessert is a great source of calcium, vitamin C, and carbohydrates—to say nothing of being quick and easy.

1   cup lemon yogurt, nonfat or low-fat
1   cup strawberries, sliced
**Optional:**
¼   cup toasted, slivered almonds

1. In a glass bowl layer or mix the yogurt and strawberries.
2. Garnish with toasted almonds if desired.

YIELD: 1 serving

| Total calories: | | 220 |
|---|---|---|

| | Grams | % of recipe |
|---|---|---|
| CARB | 40 | 75 |
| PRO | 14 | 25 |
| FAT | 0 | 0 |

## Chocolate Chip Cookies (Low-Fat)

Rachel Berger submitted this recipe because the cookies are not only easy to prepare (less than 5 minutes) but also very low in fat. The applesauce is an excellent nonfat replacement for butter (and may be used in other recipes—½ cup of applesauce can replace ½ cup [1 stick] butter). When Rachel first read about this applesauce replacement, she was skeptical. But now she says she is converted! Perhaps you will be, too.

2   eggs or 1 egg plus 1 egg white
½   cup sugar
½   cup firmly packed brown sugar
1   cup unsweetened applesauce
1   to 2 teaspoons vanilla extract
1   teaspoon baking soda
1   teaspoon salt
2¼  cups flour, preferable half white, half whole-wheat
1   cup (1 6-ounce package) chocolate chips

1.  Spray a cookie sheet with cooking spray. Preheat oven to 350°.
2.  In a large bowl mix together the eggs, sugar, brown sugar, applesauce, and vanilla.
3.  Add the baking soda, salt, and flour, mixing until combined. Fold in the chocolate chips.
4.  Drop by teaspoon onto the prepared cookie sheet.
5.  Bake at 350° for 15 to 20 minutes.

YIELD: 24 cookies

| Total calories: | | 3,000 |
| --- | --- | --- |
| Calories per cookie: | | 125 |

|  | Grams | % of recipe |
| --- | --- | --- |
| CARB | 24 | 75 |
| PRO | 2 | 5 |
| FAT | 2 | 20 |

More than two million spectators line New York's streets on Marathon Sunday, making it the world's largest single-day spectator sporting event.

## Joan Benoit Samuelson's Chocolate Chip Oatmeal Cookies

Joan says she generally keeps her cookie jar well stocked with these tasty treats that are enjoyed by family and friends alike. The cookies are cakey and have a nice taste of oatmeal. She claims they help her run through the Maine winters without missing a step.

1   cup margarine or butter
2   eggs (or substitute)
¾   cup sugar
¾   cup firmly packed brown sugar
2   cups oatmeal, instant or old-fashioned
1   teaspoon baking soda
½   to 1 teaspoon salt, as desired
2½  cups flour, half white, half whole-wheat, as desired
1   to 2 tablespoons vanilla
1   cup (6 ounces) chocolate chips

**Optional:**

1   cup raisins or sliced almonds
½   teaspoon cinnamon

1.  In a large bowl mix the ingredients the Samuelson way, "all together—it doesn't matter in what order."
2.  Drop by rounded spoonfuls onto an ungreased cookie sheet. Bake at 350° for about 15 minutes.

YIELD: 36 cookies

| Total calories: | | 5,600 |
| --- | --- | --- |
| Calories per cookie: | | 155 |

|  | Grams | % of recipe |
| --- | --- | --- |
| CARB | 21 | 55 |
| PRO | 2 | 5 |
| FAT | 7 | 40 |

## Ricotta Cheesecake

This Ricotta cheesecake, unlike ones made with cream cheese, has a light texture. It is a favorite of the Lebow family. Fred's sister, Sarah Katz, claims that this will put a smile on the face of any hungry runner who wants to deviate from his or her standard low-fat sports diet. The crumble topping adds a nice appearance and texture.

To save on fat and calories, you can omit the crust and crumble topping. You'll still have a low-carbohydrate dessert—so pile on the strawberries!

**Crust:**

½   cup sugar
¼   to ½ cup butter or margarine
1   cup flour
1   teaspoon baking powder
1   egg (or substitute)
1   teaspoon salt
2   teaspoons cinnamon

**Filling:**

4   eggs, separated
½   cup sugar
2   cups (1 pound) part-skim Ricotta or farmer cheese
1   cup sour cream, reduced-fat
2   tablespoons flour
½   tablespoon salt
2   teaspoons vanilla extract
2   tablespoons orange juice

**Topping:**

½   cup reserved crust mixture
¼   cup oatmeal, uncooked
1   teaspoon cinnamon

1. Make the crust by combining the ½ cup sugar, ¼ cup butter, 1 cup flour, baking powder, eggs, salt, and 2 teaspoons cinnamon. Form it into a soft dough. Reserve about ½ cup for the topping, then chill the rest in the refrigerator to make it easier to handle.
2. In a medium bowl beat the egg whites until stiff.
3. In a large bowl combine the ½ cup sugar, Ricotta cheese, sour cream, 2 tablespoons flour, salt, vanilla, and orange juice. Fold in the egg whites.
4. Press the chilled dough into a 10-inch springform pan that has been treated with cooking spray. Pour in the filling.
5. To the reserved crust mixture add ¼ cup oatmeal and another teaspoon of cinnamon. Mix well, then crumble it on top of the cheesecake.
6. Bake at 350° for 45 to 60 minutes, or until a knife inserted near the center comes out clean.

YIELD: 16 servings

| | |
|---|---|
| Total calories with crust: | 3,500 |
| Calories per serving: | 220 |

| | Grams | % of recipe |
|---|---|---|
| CARB | 24 | 45 |
| PRO | 6 | 10 |
| FAT | 11 | 45 |
| Total calories without crust: | | 2,000 |
| Calories per serving: | | 125 |

| | Grams | % of recipe |
|---|---|---|
| CARB | 9 | 30 |
| PRO | 4 | 15 |
| FAT | 8 | 55 |

## Yogurt Topping for Fresh Fruit

This adds a festive flavor to cut-up fruit salads.

1   cup plain yogurt, nonfat or low-fat
1   to 2 tablespoons firmly packed brown sugar or honey
⅛   teaspoon nutmeg

**Optional:**

¼   teaspoon vanilla extract or a drop of almond extract
¼   teaspoon cinnamon

1. In a small bowl mix together the yogurt, brown sugar, and nutmeg.
2. Serve over cut-up fruits of your choice.

YIELD: 2 servings

| | |
|---|---|
| Total calories (without fruit): | 180 |
| Calories per serving: | 90 |

| | Grams | % of recipe |
|---|---|---|
| CARB | 15 | 70 |
| PRO | 6 | 30 |
| FAT | 0 | 0 |

## CALORIES AND MORE CALORIES

Runners typically burn between 100 and 150 calories per mile, or 2,600 to 3,500 calories per marathon. To replace those calories, basic nutritional needs aside, a runner would need to eat one of the following:

- 2 to 3 dozen bagels
- 35 to 47 peaches
- 11 to 15 servings of regular yogurt with fruit
- about 2 pounds of plain cooked pasta.

(Source: Gatorade Exercise Physiology Lab)

## WATER, WATER EVERYWHERE

The runners' life's blood is water. Some one hundred thousand bottles of water are served at the start of the marathon. Aid stations are also stocked with water and sports drinks and are set up at every mile along the route and at the finish. The prevailing wisdom is that endurance athletes should consume 12 to 16 ounces of fluid prior to a race. Along the course, they need between 4 and 8 ounces every 15 to 20 minutes.

### Creamy Cheesecake (Low-Fat)

If you keep the secret, no one will guess this is (relatively) low in fat. It's a fine alternative to the standard cheesecake recipes! Give it a try. As with most cheesecakes, this tastes great with a fruit topping.

| | |
|---|---|
| 1 | cup graham cracker crumbs (about 8 squares; 4 sheets) |
| 1 | tablespoon margarine |
| 1 | teaspoon cinnamon |
| 1 | tablespoon water |
| 12 | ounces low-fat cream cheese |
| 1 | cup sugar |
| ¼ | cup cornstarch |
| 2 | eggs (or substitute) |
| 2 | cups nonfat vanilla yogurt |

1. Treat a 9-inch springform pan with nonstick cooking spray or lightly coat with oil.
2. In a medium bowl combine the graham cracker crumbs, margarine, cinnamon, and water. Press evenly into a thin layer on the bottom of the pan.
3. In a large mixing bowl beat the cream cheese, sugar, cornstarch and eggs until smooth and creamy. Slowly beat in the yogurt.
4. Pour the batter into the crust. Bake at 350° for about 1 hour and 10 minutes or until a knife inserted near the center comes out clean.
5. Turn off the oven and leave the cake inside with the door closed for about 30 minutes. Remove from the oven, cool it, then chill it in the refrigerator.
6. Serve with fresh fruit topping, such as peaches or strawberries, if desired.

YIELD: 12 servings

| Total calories: | | 2,400 |
|---|---|---|
| Calories per serving: | | 200 |

| | Grams | % of recipe |
|---|---|---|
| CARB | 27 | 55 |
| PRO | 5 | 10 |
| FAT | 8 | 35 |

### Creamy Cheesecake (Decadent)

This cheesecake is popular among the members of the Greater Boston Track Club who participate in the Sunday long runs when they are hosted by Jean Smith. Many members run a few extra miles, knowing their appetites will be more than satisfied afterward with this delicious treat. As Jean says "This is a party food," not a standard part of a sports diet, but rather a special treat.

Because this has such a high-fat content, be sure to serve it with lots of fruit on top, plus include plenty of carbs in the rest of your low-fat diet. Otherwise, you'll easily fat-load, not carbo-load.

| | |
|---|---|
| 4 | 8-ounce ounce packages cream cheese, whipped |
| ½ | cup butter |
| 1 | 16-ounce carton sour cream |
| 2 | tablespoons cornstarch |
| 1½ | cups sugar |
| 1 | teaspoon vanilla extract |
| 1 | teaspoon lemon juice |
| 5 | eggs (or substitute) |
| 1 | teaspoon grated lemon rind |

1. Let the cream cheese, butter, and sour cream come to room temperature.
2. In a large bowl whip the cream cheese, then all of the ingredients except the eggs.
3. Beat in the eggs one at a time, mixing well after each addition.
4. Pour the mixture into a 10" springform pan that has been treated with cooking spray.
5. Cover the outside of the pan with aluminum foil (to prevent leaks), then rest it in a large roasting pan half-filled with water.
6. Bake at 375° for about 1 hour. Allow to cool in the pan, and be sure to plan a long run to burn off the calories if you want to eat more than one portion!

YIELD: 20 servings

| Total calories: | | 6,000 |
|---|---|---|
| Calories per serving: | | 300 |

| | Grams | % of recipe |
|---|---|---|
| CARB | 16 | 20 |
| PRO | 6 | 10 |
| FAT | 23 | 70 |

## The Big Apple Cake

Fred Lebow's sister, Sarah Katz, provided this recipe for a big and rich Big Apple Cake. It can double either as a dessert or a coffeecake, depending on if you are recovering from a morning long run or participating in an evening celebration. Although this cake's high-fat content will dip into your day's fat budget, the pleasurable taste sure is worthwhile. To lower the fat content, you could replace ½ cup of the oil with ½ cup of applesauce.

4  to 5 large cooking apples (such as MacIntosh or Cortland)
¼  cup sugar
2  tablespoons cinnamon
¼  cup orange juice
4  eggs (or substitute)
1½ to 2 cups sugar
1  cup oil, preferably canola
½  cup milk
2  teaspoons vanilla extract
1½ teaspoons salt
1  tablespoon baking powder
3  cups flour

1. Core the apples and slice them thinly into a large bowl. Sprinkle with ¼ cup sugar, cinnamon, and orange juice. Set the bowl aside.
2. In a separate bowl beat together the eggs, 1½ cups of sugar, and oil. Add the milk, vanilla, and salt. Mix in the baking powder and flour. Beat well with an electric mixer.
3. Spray a tube, bundt, or large springform pan with cooking spray or oil. Pour in ⅓ of the cake batter, then half the apples, another layer of cake batter, the rest of the apples, and finish with the last third of the cake batter.

4. Pour the remaining juice from the apples on top of the batter.
5. Bake at 350° for 45 to 50 minutes, or until a toothpick inserted in the center comes out clean.

Yield: 1 big cake; 16 slices

| Total calories: | | 5,000 |
| Calories per serving: | | 310 |

| | Grams | % of recipe |
| --- | --- | --- |
| CARB | 41 | 55 |
| PRO | 4 | 5 |
| FAT | 14 | 40 |

If made with ½ cup oil and ½ cup applesauce:

| Total calories: | | 4,100 |
| Calories per serving: | | 255 |

| | Grams | % of recipe |
| --- | --- | --- |
| CARB | 42 | 65 |
| PRO | 4 | 5 |
| FAT | 8 | 30 |

## The Big Apple Pie

This cookbook would be incomplete with out the all-American favorite! Enjoy this in the spirit of the Big Apple. Relatively high in fat (15 grams) but also carbohydrates and calories, this clearly needs to be balanced into your overall low-fat diet. If desired, you can eliminate half the fat by using only a top crust. No one will care!

Sweet-tart apples such as MacIntosh, Granny Smith, or Jonathan cook the best.

**Crust:**
2  cups flour
½  teaspoon salt
⅔  cup cold butter or margarine
6  to 7 tablespoons iced water
**Optional:**
2  teaspoons sugar
**Filling:**
5  to 6 cups apples, sliced (about ⅛-inch thick)
⅔  cup sugar
1½ tablespoons cornstarch
1  teaspoon cinnamon
**Optional:**
Juice of ¼ lemon
⅛  teaspoon cloves
⅛  teaspoon nutmeg

1. In a bowl or food processor combine the flour, salt, butter, and 2 teaspoons of sugar until the mixture resembles coarse meal.
2. Sprinkle 1 tablespoon of water over the mixture and toss with a fork. Continue until all is moistened.
3. Divide the dough in half, and flatten onto plates, being careful not to over-handle. Chill the dough in the freezer or refrigerator to make it easier to handle.
4. Prepare the apples and place them in a large bowl. Sprinkle the lemon juice over them if desired, and toss to coat.
5. In a separate bowl combine the sugar, cornstarch, and spices until well blended. Pour the sugar mixture over the apples and stir to evenly coat.
6. Place the dough on a lightly floured pastry board and quickly roll each ball into a 12- to 14-inch circle. Wrap the half of the pastry around the rolling pin (or beer bottle or soda can, if that's what you have) and transfer it to a 9-inch pie plate. Refrigerate the remaining pastry until needed.

7. Fit the pastry into the pie plate, being careful not to stretch the dough. Trim the edges even with the rim of the pie plate. Refrigerate until needed.
8. Pour the apple mixture into the pie shell. Top with the remaining crust. With a paring knife, cut small decorative slivers on top of the top crust to let the steam escape when cooking.
9. Bake at 450° for 10 minutes. Reduce the temperature to 350° and continue to bake for 35 minutes.

YIELD: 8 servings

| Total calories: | 2,800 |
| Calories per serving: | 350 |

| | Grams | % of recipe |
| --- | --- | --- |
| CARB | 52 | 60 |
| PRO | 2 | 5 |
| FAT | 15 | 35 |

Mavis Lindgren began marathoning at age 70. At age 86, the retired nurse from California completed the 1993 NYC Marathon, bringing her marathon total to 65. She was the first woman over age 80 to finish the NYC Marathon.

## Big Apple Crumble

British runner David R. Clark shares this dessert than can help maintain muscle glycogen stores. Perhaps if you eat this before the New York City Marathon, you won't crumble! The recipe also works well with blueberries, peaches, or 1½–2 pounds of any fruit of your choice.

2   to 4 tablespoons butter or margarine
½   cup flour, preferably whole-wheat
½   to ¾ cup sugar, brown or white
1   cup muesli with dried fruits and nuts (or plain rolled oats)
4   to 6 apples, sliced

**Optional:**
2   to 4 teaspoons cinnamon
½   cup chopped nuts
½   cup raisins

1. Using your hands, rub the butter or margarine into the flour and sugar until it forms a crumb mixture. Add the muesli.
2. Place the fruit in an 8-inch square baking dish. Add 2 tablespoons of water. Sprinkle the crumb mixture over the fruit. Base at 350° for about 45 to 50 minutes, until brown.

YIELD: 6 servings

| Total calories: | 1,800 |
| Calories per serving: | 300 |

| | Grams | % of recipe |
| --- | --- | --- |
| CARB | 60 | 80 |
| PRO | 3 | 5 |
| FAT | 5 | 15 |

## The Big Apple Bread Pudding

This dessert is not only nutritious, but also doubles as an excellent breakfast. Enjoy the leftovers the next morning for a special treat! Different types of breads vary the flavor. Cracked wheat is a favorite. Serve plain, with yogurt topping, or with light ice cream.

6   slices bread, cubed
4   medium apples, diced
3   cups milk, preferably low-fat
3   eggs (or substitute)
½   cup sugar
½   teaspoon salt
2   teaspoons cinnamon
2   tablespoons sugar
1   teaspoon cinnamon

1. Treat an 8-inch baking dish with cooking spray
2. In a mixing bowl toss together the bread cubes and apples. Transfer the mixture to the prepared dish.
3. In a separate bowl combine the milk, eggs, ½ cup of sugar, salt, and 2 teaspoons of cinnamon.
4. Pour the liquid mixture over the apples and bread.
5. Mix together 2 tablespoons of sugar and 1 teaspoon of cinnamon. Sprinkle the mixture over the pudding.
6. Cover. Bake at 325° for 45 minutes or until set. The pudding is done when a knife inserted near the center comes out clean.

YIELD: 6 servings

| Total calories: | 1,600 |
| Calories per serving: | 270 |

| | Grams | % of recipe |
| --- | --- | --- |
| CARB | 51 | 75 |
| PRO | 10 | 15 |
| FAT | 3 | 10 |

*Top masters (over 40) runner Ryszard Marczak of Poland*

## Blueberry Slump

This dessert (or even breakfast!) is wonderful for carbohydrate-loading because it is low in fat and high in taste.

1   quart blueberries, fresh or
    frozen
½   cup water
½   cup sugar
**Dumplings:**
1   cup flour
½   teaspoon salt
2   tablespoons sugar
2   teaspoons baking powder
⅓   cup milk
2   tablespoons oil

1. In a 2-quart saucepan combine the blueberries, water, and

sugar, and bring the water to a boil.
2. In a medium bowl combine the remaining ingredients and lightly mix them together.
3. Drop the dumpling dough by spoonfuls into the boiling blueberries.
4. Cover and cook for 20 minutes over moderate heat.

YIELD: 5 servings

| | |
|---|---|
| Total calories: | 1,500 |
| Calories per serving: | 300 |

| | Grams | % of recipe |
|---|---|---|
| CARB | 60 | 80 |
| PRO | 4 | 5 |
| FAT | 5 | 15 |

## Raspberry Freeze

Denise Coyle submitted this recipe for a refreshing summer cooler. The lemonade cuts the sweetness of the gelatin, making this a tart and tangy treat. The recipe can be made without the frozen yogurt and simply chilled in the refrigerator, then eaten as a gelatin-type dessert.

3   ounces red raspberry gelatin
    (small box)
2   cups boiling water
1   cup red raspberries, fresh or
    frozen
3   ounces (half of a 6-ounce can)
    frozen pink lemonade
    concentrate
1   pint vanilla frozen yogurt

1. Dissolve the gelatin in the boiling water.
2. Add the raspberries and lemonade with the juice. Add the frozen yogurt. Mix well and freeze.

YIELD: 6 servings

| | |
|---|---|
| Total calories: | 680 |
| Calories per serving: | 110 |

| | Grams | % of recipe |
|---|---|---|
| CARB | 25 | 90 |
| PRO | 3 | 10 |
| FAT | 0 | 0 |

## Frozen Fruit and Yogurt Bars

On a hot summer evening these fat-free bars are a refreshing, high-carb treat. They are yummy with blueberries, and strawberries also work well. Your kids will love them, too!

1   cup plain yogurt
2   to 3 tablespoons honey
1   cup fresh fruit, diced
⅓   cup nonfat dry milk
¾   cup Grape-Nuts cereal
⅓   cup dry oatmeal

1. In a blender or food processor blend the yogurt, honey, and fruit.
2. In a medium bowl combine the dry milk, Grape Nuts, and oatmeal. Pour the yogurt mixture over the dry ingredients and mix well.
3. Pour the mixture into an 8-inch square pan and freeze. Cut into 9 bars before they are completely frozen. Continue freezing until hard.
4. Wrap each bar separately in plastic wrap and store in the freezer.

YIELD: 9 bars

| | |
|---|---|
| Total calories: | 810 |
| Calories per bar: | 90 |

| | Grams | % of recipe |
|---|---|---|
| CARB | 18 | 80 |
| PRO | 4 | 20 |
| FAT | 0 | 0 |

## Carrot Cake

This carrot cake is a favorite among the Hegmann family. They devour it within two days. Hungry runners can probably do the same! In case that happens, I've reduced the fat content somewhat, to assist with carbo-loading as compared to fat-loading. (If you need to justify this, remember that the ingredients include a wholesome blend of fruit, vegetables, protein, and grains!)

1½ cups sugar
¾ cup oil, preferably canola
3 eggs (or substitute)
2 cups grated carrot
1 cup crushed, canned pineapple with juice
2 teaspoons vanilla extract
1 teaspoon salt
1 teaspoon baking powder
½ teaspoon baking soda
2½ cups flour
**Optional:**
1 teaspoon cinnamon
1 cup chopped walnuts
**Frosting:**
4 ounces low-fat cream cheese, at room temperature
½ pound (about 2¼ cups) confectioners' sugar, sifted
1 teaspoon vanilla extract
1 to 2 tablespoons milk or orange juice
**Optional:**
2 teaspoons grated orange peel

1. Treat a 9x13-inch pan with cooking spray.
2. In a mixing bowl beat together the sugar and oil, then the eggs.
3. Add the carrot, pineapple and its juice, and 2 teaspoons of vanilla. Mix well.
4. Add the salt, cinnamon, and nuts if desired, baking powder, and soda. Gently blend in the flour, being careful not to over-beat.
5. Pour the batter into the prepared pan. Bake at 350° for 35 to 40 minutes. Cool completely before frosting.
6. In a mixing bowl beat the cream cheese and confectioners' sugar.
7. Add 1 teaspoon of vanilla and the milk, and beat until smooth, creamy, and the desired consistency.
8. Spread the frosting on the cake.

YIELD: 24 pieces

| Total calories plain cake: | | 4,200 |
|---|---|---|
| Calories per serving: | | 175 |

| | Grams | % of recipe |
|---|---|---|
| CARB | 26 | 60 |
| PRO | 2 | 5 |
| FAT | 7 | 35 |

| Total calories cake with frosting: | | 5,500 |
|---|---|---|
| Calories per serving: | | 230 |

| | Grams | % of recipe |
|---|---|---|
| CARB | 37 | 65 |
| PRO | 3 | 5 |
| FAT | 8 | 30 |

## Brownies from a Mix (Low-Fat)

This recipe produces rich, moist brownies without all of the fat. It was adapted from Duncan Hines and Dannon Yogurt recipes and is given to us by Georgia Kostas, sports nutritionist of the Cooper Clinic in Dallas and author of *The Balancing Act*.

1 box brownie mix
½ to 1 cup nonfat plain yogurt
1 to 2 egg whites
Water

1. Treat a 9x12-inch square baking pan with cooking spray.
2. Omit the oil and eggs from the brownie recipe. Instead, add an equivalent amount of yogurt for the oil and one egg white for each egg. Add water according to the brownie recipe. Mix well. The mixture will probably be very thick.
3. Pour the batter into the prepared pan. Bake at 350° for about 30 minutes, or as directed on the package.

YIELD: 24 brownies

| Total calories: | | 2,900 |
|---|---|---|
| Calories per serving: | | 120 |

| | Grams | % of recipe |
|---|---|---|
| CARB | 22 | 75 |
| PRO | 1 | 5 |
| FAT | 3 | 20 |

*Metalized space blankets keep the runners warm after they cross the finish line.*

## Chocolate Lush (Low-Fat)

This brownie pudding is a tasty treat for those who want a high-carbohydrate dessert after a wholesome meal. It forms its own sauce during baking.

1    cup flour
¾    cup sugar
2    tablespoons unsweetened cocoa powder
2    teaspoons baking powder
1    teaspoon salt
½    cup milk
2    tablespoons oil, preferably canola

**Topping:**
2    teaspoons vanilla extract
¾    cup firmly packed brown sugar
¼    cup unsweetened cocoa powder
1¾   cups hot water

**Optional:**
½    cup chopped nuts

1. Treat an 8-inch square baking pan with cooking spray.
2. In a medium bowl stir together the flour, ¾ cup of sugar, 2 tablespoons of cocoa, baking powder, and salt. Add the milk, oil, and vanilla. Mix until smooth. Add nuts, if desired.
3. Pour the batter into the prepared pan.
4. In a separate bowl combine the brown sugar, cocoa, and hot water. Pour this mixture on top of the batter in the pan.
5. Bake at 350° for 40 minutes, or until lightly browned and bubbly.

YIELD: 9 servings

| Total calories: | | 2,100 |
|---|---|---|
| Calories per serving: | | 230 |

| | Grams | % of recipe |
|---|---|---|
| CARB | 46 | 80 |
| PRO | 3 | 5 |
| FAT | 4 | 15 |

The 1991 NYC Marathon women's field was dubbed "the race of the mothers." Although not from 1991, this photo shows Australia's Lisa Ondieki celebrating with her family.

## Decadent Brownies

These are dense and chewy and worth every calorie, a special treat to be balanced into your sports diet if you want a chocolate fix!

4    1-ounce squares unsweetened baking chocolate
½    cup butter or margarine
1    cup sugar
½    cup firmly packed brown sugar
2    eggs (or substitute)
2    teaspoons vanilla extract
½    teaspoon salt
1    cup flour

**Optional:**
Light rum

1. Treat a 9x13-inch baking pan with cooking spray.
2. In a glass mixing bowl or saucepan melt the chocolate and butter together in the microwave or over low heat. Melt just until the butter is liquid, then stir until the chocolate finishes melting.
3. In a large mixing bowl combine the melted chocolate, butter, sugar, and brown sugar.
4. Stir in the eggs, vanilla, and salt until completely mixed.
5. Add the flour and mix well.
6. Spread the batter in the prepared baking pan. Bake at 350° for 25 to 35 minutes or until a toothpick inserted in the center comes out slightly sticky. If desired, while the brownies are

still warm prick holes with a toothpick 1 inch apart. Drizzle light rum over the brownies, more or less as desired. It will sink into the holes and add a wonderful flavor.

7. Once slightly cooled, cut into 24 squares.

Yield: 24 brownies

| Total calories: | | 3,500 |
|---|---|---|
| Calories per brownie: | | 145 |

| | Grams | % of recipe |
|---|---|---|
| CARB | 20 | 50 |
| PRO | 2 | 5 |
| FAT | 7 | 45 |

## Brownies (Low-Fat)

Nutritionist and runner Natalie Updegrove Partridge selected this recipe because many people think something that contains chocolate can't be low-fat. Not the case.

The original recipe called for 1 cup ripe, mashed bananas, but I prefer using 1 cup of applesauce instead—the flavor of the applesauce is milder and you won't even know it's one of the ingredients. But if you are a banana fan, you might enjoy the banana flavor that sneaks through the chocolate.

1   cup applesauce or mashed, old bananas (about 2 bananas)
1   egg (or substitute)
¼   cup oil, preferably canola
¾   cup sugar, white or brown sugar or combination
2   teaspoons vanilla extract
½   cup plain yogurt
½   cup unsweetened cocoa powder
1   teaspoon salt
½   teaspoon baking soda
1½  cups flour

**Optional:**
⅓   cup chocolate chips
⅓   cup chopped walnuts

## FOOD AT THE FINISH

What's a marathon without a post-run lunch? Every finisher of the race receives a bag lunch. Although some of the items vary, what has remained constant for nearly two decades is the bagel and the apple. According to Marathon volunteer (and former chef) Jon Kranz, both are symbols of New York City.

1. Treat a 9-inch square baking pan with cooking spray.
2. In a large bowl combine the applesauce and egg. Mix well.
3. Add the oil, sugar, vanilla, and yogurt. Blend in the cocoa, salt, and baking soda.
4. Gently stir in the flour. Mix until just blended.
5. Pour the batter in to the prepared pan. Top with chocolate chips and/or walnuts if desired.
6. Bake at 350° for 25 to 30 minutes. Cool in the pan.

Yield: 16 brownies

| Total calories: | | 2,250 |
|---|---|---|
| Calories per brownie: | | 140 |

| | Grams | % of recipe |
|---|---|---|
| CARB | 23 | 65 |
| PRO | 3 | 10 |
| FAT | 4 | 25 |

## Pumpkin Oat Cookies (Low-Fat)

These cookies are tasty, moist, and nourishing, and an easy way to sneak some vegetables into your diet if you need to rationalize baking these cookies! You wouldn't know they have only 3 grams of fat per cookie.

⅓   cup oil
¾   cup firmly packed brown sugar
1   egg (or substitute)
1½  cups canned pumpkin
1   teaspoon cinnamon
½   teaspoon nutmeg
½   teaspoon salt
1   cup rolled oats
2   teaspoons baking powder
½   teaspoon baking soda
1½  cups flour, half white, half whole-wheat, as desired

**Optional:**
⅛   teaspoon ginger
⅛   teaspoon cloves
½   cup chopped walnuts
½   cup raisins

1. In a large mixing bowl beat together the oil, sugar, egg, and pumpkin. Mix well.
2. Add the cinnamon, nutmeg, ginger, cloves, and salt. Fold in the oats, baking powder, and soda. Gently blend in the flour.
3. Drop the batter by tablespoons onto a nonstick cookie sheet.
4. Bake at 350° for 10 to 12 minutes.

Yield: about 30 cookies

| Total calories: | | 2,700 |
|---|---|---|
| Calories per cookie: | | 90 |

| | Grams | % of recipe |
|---|---|---|
| CARB | 13 | 60 |
| PRO | 2 | 5 |
| FAT | 3 | 35 |

*The view of the famous Manhattan skyline is one of the notable landmarks along the course.*

## Crisp and Chewies

As the name suggests these cookies are crisp, yet chewy—and delightfully different. As with most cookies that are crisp, the fat content is relatively high. Be sure to balance them into your overall low-fat diet.

¾   cup butter or margarine
1   egg (or substitute)
¼   cup molasses
1   cup sugar
½   teaspoon ginger
½   teaspoon cloves
½   teaspoon salt
1   teaspoon baking soda
1½  cups flour
¾   cup rolled oats

1. In a medium bowl cream together the margarine, egg, and molasses.
2. Add the remaining ingredients, stirring the oats in last.

3. Place dough by tablespoonfuls 2 inches apart on an ungreased cookie sheet.
4. Bake at 375° for 8 to 10 minutes. The cookie will puff up while baking, and "fall" when it is done. Remove the cookies from the oven just after they "fall." If you overbake these cookies they will be crisp but not chewy.
5. Allow the cookies to cool on the cookie sheet for 1 to 2 minutes before removing.
6. Store in a tightly covered container.

YIELD: about 36 cookies

| Total calories: | | 3,200 |
| Calories per cookie: | | 90 |

| | Grams | % of recipe |
| --- | --- | --- |
| CARB | 12 | 55 |
| PRO | 1 | 5 |
| FAT | 4 | 40 |

## Oatmeal Cookies

These cakey, simple cookies digest easily and are good for a pre-exercise snack or recovery food. Sports nutritionist and runner Natalie Updegrove Partridge of Rockville, Maryland, reports that the members of her track club love them.

This recipe makes about 5 dozen cookies—enough to feed the whole team! If you are cooking for yourself, you might want to cut the recipe in half.

1¼  cups milk
1   cup oil, preferably canola
2   eggs (or substitute)
2   teaspoons vanilla extract
¾   cup sugar
1   cup firmly packed brown sugar
4   cups oatmeal
2   teaspoons baking soda
2   teaspoons salt
2   teaspoons cinnamon
1   cup raisins
3   cups flour, half white, half whole-wheat, as desired

1. In a large bowl beat together the milk, oil, eggs, and vanilla. Mix in the sugar and brown sugar. Add the oatmeal.
2. Blend in the baking soda, salt, cinnamon, and raisins. Fold in the flour.
3. Drop by tablespoons onto an ungreased cookie sheet. Bake at 350° for 15 to 18 minutes.

YIELD: about 60 cookies

| Total calories: | | 6,500 |
| Calories per cookie: | | 110 |

| | Grams | % of recipe |
| --- | --- | --- |
| CARB | 16 | 60 |
| PRO | 2 | 10 |
| FAT | 4 | 30 |

## Almond Biscotti

These Italian cookies are definitely for dunking in a cup of tea . . . they are hard and crunchy! But they are very low in fat (mostly what is in the almonds), high in carbs, and slow-to-eat, so that you feel satisfied with one or two.

1    cup sugar
2    cups flour
⅛    teaspoon baking soda
½    teaspoon salt
2    eggs (or substitute)
1    teaspoon butter or margarine,
      preferably at room temperature
1    teaspoon vanilla extract
¼    teaspoon almond extract
½    cup whole almonds
      (lightly toasted at 300° for
      about 10 minutes)

1. Treat a large cookie sheet with cooking spray.
2. In a large bowl combine the sugar, flour, baking soda, and salt. Add the eggs, butter, and vanilla and almond extracts, and mix just until combined. Stir in the almonds.
3. Transfer the dough to a well-floured surface. Using well-floured hands, form the dough into 3 1x6-inch logs. Space the logs 2½ inches apart on the prepared sheet.
4. Bake at 300° for about 1 hour, until light golden brown. The logs will spread and flatten. Cool slightly.
5. Transfer the logs to a cutting board and using a serrated knife, slice logs diagonally into ½-inch wide biscotti. Place the biscotti on the cookie sheet, cut surface down.
6. Bake until golden brown, about 30 minutes. Cool completely on a rack.

*Patented "Marathon Blue" is used to paint a line along the entire Marathon course. The New York Road Runners Club apple logo (in white) adorns the finish line.*

YIELD: about 18 slices

| | |
|---|---|
| Total calories: | 2,100 |
| Calories per piece: | 115 |

| | Grams | % of recipe |
|---|---|---|
| CARB | 22 | 75 |
| PRO | 3 | 10 |
| FAT | 2 | 15 |

## Date Bars

Sweet and rich in wholesome carbohydrates, these bars are good for snacks and recovery foods.

¼    cup butter or margarine
8    ounces (1 cup) chopped dates
2    eggs (or substitute)
½    to 1 cup sugar
½    teaspoon salt
¼    teaspoon baking powder
½    cup flour
**Optional:**
1    cup walnuts, chopped
½    teaspoon cinnamon

1. Treat a 9-inch square pan with cooking spray.
2. In a saucepan melt the butter or margarine (or microwave it until melted).
3. Remove the pan from the heat and add the dates, eggs, sugar, and salt. Beat well.
4. Mix in the baking powder, and then gently stir in the flour.
5. Pour the batter into the prepared pan. Bake at 350° for 45 minutes, or until a toothpick inserted near the center comes out clean.

YIELD: 12 servings

| | |
|---|---|
| Total calories: | 1,900 |
| Calories per serving: | 160 |

| | Grams | % of recipe |
|---|---|---|
| CARB | 26 | 70 |
| PRO | 2 | 5 |
| FAT | 5 | 25 |

## Peanut Brittle

Amy Roeder was introduced to this easy treat on a cold winter's day in Vermont. It's a relatively high-carb candy, but you can justify eating it because of the (little bit of) nutrition added by the peanuts. Better for refueling than just sugary jelly beans . . . !

1  cup sugar
½  cup light corn syrup
1  cup roasted peanuts, unsalted
1  teaspoon butter or margarine
1  teaspoon vanilla extract
1  teaspoon baking soda

1. In a 1½ quart casserole dish mix the sugar and corn syrup. Cook on high in the microwave for 4 minutes, or on the stove top just until the mixture comes to a boil.
2. Add the peanuts and microwave on high for 3 to 5 minutes until the mixture is light brown. Or boil gently on the stove top without stirring.
3. Blend in the butter and vanilla.
4. Cook for 2 to 3 minutes more.
5. Add the baking soda and mix until foamy.
6. Pour into oiled sheet pan and allow to cool.

YIELD: about 10 large chunks

| Total calories: | 2,100 |
| Calories per serving: | 210 |

|  | Grams | % of recipe |
| --- | --- | --- |
| CARB | 34 | 65 |
| PRO | 3 | 5 |
| FAT | 7 | 30 |

## Raspberry Sauce

Deborah Bisson says this recipe is a favorite in her family and is usually served with angel food cake for birthdays and holidays. What a festive low-fat treat!

2  cups fresh or frozen raspberries
½  cup confectioners' sugar
1  tablespoon raspberry liqueur
1  tablespoon lemon juice

1. In a blender or food processor purée the raspberries.
2. Add the remaining ingredients. Process until smooth.
3. Strain sauce to remove the seeds.

YIELD: about 1¾ cups

| Total calories: | 550 |
| Calories per ¼ cup: | 80 |

|  | Grams | % of recipe |
| --- | --- | --- |
| CARB | 20 | 100 |
| PRO | 0 | 0 |
| FAT | 0 | 0 |

## Brandied Apricot Sauce

This sauce is superb over frozen yogurt or vanilla ice cream. If you mix it with a little milk, it also goes well over hot bread pudding.

1  cup dried apricots
⅔  cup water
⅓  cup sugar
2  tablespoons brandy
1½  tablespoons orange juice

1. In a small saucepan combine the apricots, water, and sugar. Bring the mixture to a boil.
2. Reduce the heat and simmer, uncovered, for 12 minutes.
3. In a blender or food processor purée the apricot mixture.
4. Stir in the brandy and orange juice.

YIELD: about 1¼ cups, 5 servings

| Total calories: | 650 |
| Calories per serving: | 130 |

|  | Grams | % of recipe |
| --- | --- | --- |
| CARB | 32 | 100 |
| PRO | 0 | 0 |
| FAT | 0 | 0 |

# 19 BEVERAGES AND FLUIDS

One key to staying well hydrated is to have readily available good tasting beverages, because you will tend to drink more of a fluid that you like. The following recipes include an assortment of beverages that you can make to rehydrate, refresh, and refuel yourself after a sweaty workout. They will replace not only lost fluids but also depleted carbohydrates. The fruit-based beverages offer potassium, as well. The heartier shakes and smoothies can be used as meal replacers or even weight-gain drinks if you consume them in addition to hearty meals.

Drink to your health!

## Strawberry Shake

This recipe from the New England Dairy and Food Council is a calcium and protein booster, and a fun way to get the nutrients needed for strong bones and muscles.

1    cup sliced strawberries
1    cup strawberry low-fat yogurt
1    cup ice cubes
1    cup milk, preferably low-fat
¼    cup nonfat dry milk
2    tablespoons sugar

1. In a blender combine all of the ingredients.
2. Blend until smooth, 1 to 2 minutes. Serve immediately.

YIELD: 2 servings

| | | |
|---|---|---|
| Total calories: | | 550 |
| Calories per serving: | | 225 |

| | Grams | % of recipe |
|---|---|---|
| CARB | 47 | 80 |
| PRO | 7 | 15 |
| FAT | 1 | 5 |

## White Grape Spritzer

Melissa Kalman of Boston claims this is a very refreshing drink after a long workout, especially on a hot summer day.

1    12-ounce can frozen white grape juice concentrate, thawed
1    1-quart bottle sparkling white grape juice, chilled
1    1-quart bottle club soda
**Optional:**
Lemon and lime slices as desired for garnish

1. In a pitcher or punch bowl combine the grape juice concentrate, grape juice, and club soda.
2. Pour over ice and garnish each serving with lemon or lime slices.

YIELD: about 2½ quarts

| | | |
|---|---|---|
| Total calories: | | 1,300 |
| Calories per 8 ounces: | | 130 |

| | Grams | % of recipe |
|---|---|---|
| CARB | 32 | 100 |
| PRO | 1 | 5 |
| FAT | 0 | 0 |

## Homemade Sports Drink

The main ingredients in the commercial fluid replacers include:
- a 5 to 7 percent sugar solution (about 50 calories per 8 ounces, equal to 12 grams carbohydrates or about 3 teaspoons sugar),
- about 50 to 110 milligrams sodium (the amount in ¹⁄₁₆ teaspoon salt or 1 pinch), and
- 24 to 45 milligrams potassium (the amount is 1 tablespoon orange juice or 2 tablespoons lemon juice) to enhance the rate the fluid gets absorbed from your stomach into your system. This recipe comes close enough. Give a try if you want a low-cost fluid replacer.

1    tablespoon sugar
1    pinch (¹⁄₁₆ teaspoon) salt
1    tablespoon orange juice or 2 tablespoons lemon juice
7½ ounces ice water

1. In a glass dissolve the sugar and salt in a little bit of hot water.
2. Add the juice and remaining ice water.
3. Quench that thirst!

YIELD: 1 serving

| | |
|---|---|
| Total calories: | 50 |
| mg sodium | 110 |
| mg potassium | 30 |

*Twenty-two-year-old Tom Fleming of Bloomfield, N.J. (#10) eventually wins the 1973 race.*

## Watermelon Sparkling Punch

Buff Hastry submitted this recipe as a fun and refreshing drink to serve at a "recovery party" after the marathon. The watermelon shell makes a festive punch bowl.

1     large watermelon
2     cups fresh strawberries
1½  cups sugar
1     cup orange juice
5     cups lemon-flavored sparkling
       mineral water, chilled

1. Cut a thin slice from the bottom of the melon, if necessary, to prevent rolling. Cut off one-third of the top. Scoop the pulp from the melon and remove the seeds. Use a U-shaped knife or paring knife to cut a decorative edge around the melon shell. Set the shell aside.
2. In a blender combine the melon pulp and strawberries in batches. Process until puréed.
3. In a saucepan combine the sugar and orange juice. Bring the mixture to a boil, reduce the heat, and simmer for 5 minutes.
4. Add the orange juice mixture to the watermelon mixture. Cover and refrigerate until chilled.
5. Just before serving, stir in the mineral water. Serve in the watermelon shell.

YIELD: 5 quarts (20 servings)

| Total calories: | | 2,000 |
|---|---|---|
| Calories per 8-ounce serving: | | 200 |

| | Grams | % of recipe |
|---|---|---|
| CARB | 24 | 95 |
| PRO | 1 | 5 |
| FAT | 0 | 0 |

## Old-Fashioned Lemonade

Somehow a heat wave can become a useful excuse to sit on the porch and drink homemade lemonade. Because sugar dissolves poorly in cold water, you'll get the best results by first dissolving the sugar in hot water. Adjust the sugar according to your tastes—this will make you pucker!

¾  to 1 cup sugar or honey, to taste
     or equivalent in alternative
     sweetener
1   cup boiling water
3   to 4 lemons, juiced
2   quarts cold water

1. Dissolve the sugar in the boiling water.
2. Pour the lemon juice into a 2-quart container.
3. Add the sugar solution plus enough water to make about 2 quarts, or to taste.
4. Relax and enjoy the heat wave!

YIELD: 2 quarts

| Total calories: | | 600 to 800 |
|---|---|---|
| Calories per 8 ounces: | | 75 to 100 |

| | Grams | % of recipe |
|---|---|---|
| CARB | 19 | 100 |
| PRO | 0 | 0 |
| FAT | 0 | 0 |

## Banana-Pine-Orange Smoothie

This "slushy" drink is loaded with potassium, vitamin C, and carbohydrates, a delicious and appropriate post-run refresher. When you're confronted with too many bananas that are ripening, peel some of them and store them in a plastic bag in the freezer. They'll be ready and waiting to be made into this frostie drink.

1   small banana, frozen
½   cup crushed pineapple, chilled
¾   cup orange juice, chilled
**Optional:**
¼   cup nonfat dry milk for extra calcium and protein

1. In a blender combine all of the ingredients.
2. Process until smooth. Serve immediately.

YIELD: 1 smoothie

| Total calories: | | 220 |
| --- | --- | --- |
| | Grams | % of recipe |
| CARB | 53 | 95 |
| PRO | 1 | 5 |
| FAT | 0 | 0 |

## Pudding Shake

Molly Shipp submitted this recipe because it's a great milkshake alternative. The instant pudding adds a nice thick texture, and the ice cubes make it a frosty and refreshing drink. By varying the flavor of the pudding (vanilla, lemon, and chocolate), yogurt (plain, lemon, blueberry) and the fruits, you can create numerous variations.

2   cups skim milk
1   3½-ounce package instant pudding
8   ounces low-fat yogurt
1   cup crushed ice
1   cup strawberries or any fruit, fresh, frozen, or canned

1. In a blender combine all of the ingredients.
2. Process until smooth. Serve immediately.

YIELD: 3 servings

| Total calories: | | 750 |
| --- | --- | --- |
| Calories per serving: | | 250 |
| | Grams | % of recipe |
| CARB | 53 | 85 |
| PRO | 10 | 15 |
| FAT | 0 | 0 |

## Banana Blast

Elizabeth "Buff" Hastry, dietetic intern at Beth Israel Hospital in Boston, submitted this recipe because it is a quick and easy booster before or after a run. The ice cubes make it thick but thirst-quenching.

1   medium ripe banana
½   cup skim milk
½   teaspoon vanilla extract
5   ice cubes

1. In a blender combine all of the ingredients.
2. Process until smooth. Serve immediately.

YIELD: 1 serving

| Total calories: | | 150 |
| --- | --- | --- |
| | Grams | % of recipe |
| CARB | 33 | 85 |
| PRO | 5 | 15 |
| FAT | 0 | 0 |

## Citrus Refresher

Chicago-area sports nutritionist Jacqueline Marcus says this punch is a welcome refresher for thirsty runners. In the winter, serve it warm; in the summer add sparkling water and serve it cold.

4   cups apple cider
12  whole cloves
2   cinnamon sticks
¼   teaspoon nutmeg
3   cups orange juice
3   cups grapefruit juice
Juice of 1 lemon
**Optional:**
1   grapefruit, sliced
1   orange, sliced
1   lemon, sliced

1. In a large pot combine the cider, cloves, cinnamon, and nutmeg. Bring the mixture to a boil, reduce the heat, and simmer for 10 to 15 minutes.
2. Remove the spices. Add the orange juice, grapefruit juice, and lemon juice. Heat through.
3. Garnish with the sliced fruit.

YIELD: 10 servings

| Total calories: | | 1,100 |
| --- | --- | --- |
| Calories per 8 ounces: | | 110 |
| | Grams | % of recipe |
| CARB | 27 | 95 |
| PRO | 1 | 5 |
| FAT | 0 | 0 |

221

## Calcium-Rich Super Shake

This shake is a super-smart choice for women who need extra calcium. By making this large amount, you can stock it in the refrigerator, ready and waiting for a quick meal or snack.

2½ cups milk
½ cup plain yogurt
½ small can frozen orange juice concentrate (about ⅓ cup)
¼ cup nonfat dry milk
3 tablespoons honey or sugar
1 teaspoon vanilla extract

**Optional:**
2 tablespoons unsweetened cocoa powder

1. In a blender or container with a lid combine all of the ingredients.
2. Cover and shake vigorously until completely blended.

YIELD: 3 servings

| Total calories: | | 700 |
|---|---|---|
| Calories per serving: | | 235 |

| | Grams | % of recipe |
|---|---|---|
| CARB | 45 | 75 |
| PRO | 13 | 25 |
| FAT | 0 | 0 |

## Hot Fruit Punch

Here's a potful of punch to refuel a team of cold runners.

2 pounds dried mixed fruit
3 quarts water
20 whole cloves
1 whole orange
1 cup honey, or to taste
8 cinnamon sticks
6 oranges, sliced
6 lemons, sliced
½ gallon cider

**Optional:**
Rum
Brandy

1. In a large pot cook the dried fruit with water for 15 minutes.
2. Stick the cloves into a whole orange. Add the orange to the fruit.
3. Add the remaining ingredients. Heat the punch for 15 minutes. If you add alcohol, do not bring it to a boil, or most of the alcohol will evaporate.

YIELD: 24 servings

| Total calories: | | 4,600 |
|---|---|---|
| Calories per 8-ounce serving: | | 190 |

| | Grams | % of recipe |
|---|---|---|
| CARB | 47 | 95 |
| PRO | 2 | 5 |
| FAT | 0 | 0 |

## Mulled Cranberry Cider

This is delicious hot or cold. The spices give it wonderful aroma, especially appealing on a wintry day.

4 cups cranberry juice
4 cups apple cider
1 orange, washed and sliced
2 cinnamon sticks
8 whole cloves

**Optional:**
¼ cup firmly packed brown sugar
¼ teaspoon allspice
⅛ teaspoon nutmeg

1. In a saucepan combine all of the ingredients.
2. Bring the mixture to a boil, reduce the heat, and simmer for 30 minutes or longer.

YIELD: 8 servings

| Total calories: | | 1,200 |
|---|---|---|
| Calories per 8 ounces: | | 150 |

| | Grams | % of recipe |
|---|---|---|
| CARB | 38 | 100 |
| PRO | 0 | 0 |
| FAT | 0 | 0 |

# SELECTED REFERENCES

## Chapters 1, 2, and 3

Brouns, Fred. *Nutritional Needs of Athletes.* West Sussex, England: John Wiley and Sons, 1993.
———, W. Saris, and N. Rehrer. "Abdominal Complaints and Gastro-intestinal Function during Long-lasting Exercise." *International Journal of Sports Medicine* 8 (1987): 175–89.

Bucci, Luke. *Nutrients as Ergogenic Aids for Sports and Exercise.* Boca Raton, Fla.: CRC Press, 1993.

Costill, D. L. "Carbohydrates for Exercise: Dietary Demands for Optimal Performance." *International Journal of Sports Medicine* 9 (1988): 1–18.

Coyle, E. F., and E. Coyle. "Carbohydrates That Speed Recovery from Training." *Physician and Sportsmedicine* 21, no. 2 (1993): 111–23.

Jenkins, D. J., et al. "Glycemic Index of Foods: A Physiological Basis for Carbohydrate Exchange." *American Journal of Clinical Nutrition* 34 (1981): 362–66.

McArdle, W. F. Karch, and V. Katch. *Exercise Physiology: Energy, Nutrition and Human Performance.* Philadelphia: Lea & Febiger, 1994.

National Research Council. *Recommended Dietary Allowances.* 10th edition. Washington D.C.: National Academy Press, 1989.

Nishimune, T., et al. "Glycemic Index and Fiber Content of Some Foods." *American Journal of Clinical Nutrition* 54 (1991): 414–19.

Rehrer, N., et al. "Effects of Dehydration on Gastric Emptying and Gastrointestinal Distress while Running." *Medicine and Science in Sports and Exercise* 22, no. 6 (1990): 790–95.

Sherman, W. "Muscle Glycogen Supercompensation during the Week before Athletic Competition." *Sports Science Exchange* (The Gatorade Institute) 2, no. 16 (June 1989).

Wilmore, J., and D. Costill. *Physiology of Sport and Exercise.* Champaign, Ill.: Human Kinetics Publisher, 1994.

## Chapters 4 and 5

Andon, M., et al. "Spinal Bone Density and Calcium Intake in Healthy Postmenopausal Women." *American Journal of Clinical Nutrition* 54 (1991): 927–29.

Bouchard, C., et al. "The Response to Long Term Overfeeding in Identical Twins. *New England Journal of Medicine* 322 (1990): 1477–82.

Brownell, K., S. Steen, and J. Wilmore. "Weight Regulation Practices in Athletes: Analysis of Metabolic and Health Effects." *Medicine and Science in Sports and Exercise* 19, no. 6 (1987): 546–56.

Caldwell, F. "Menstrual Irregularity in Athletes: The Unanswered Question." *Physician and Sports Medicine* 10, no. 5 (1982): 142.

Clark, N., M. Nelson, and W. Evans. "Nutrition Education for Elite Women Runners." *Physician and Sports Medicine* 16, no. 2 (1988): 124–34.

DeSouza, M. J., and D. Metzger. "Reproductive Dysfunction in Amenorrheic Athletes and Anorexic Patients: A Review." *Medicine and Science in Sports and Exercise* 23, no. 9 (1991): 995–1007.

Deuster, P. A., et al. "Nutritional Intake and Status of Highly Trained Amenorrheic and Eumenorrheic Women Runners." *American Journal of Clinical Nutrition* 46 (1986): 636–43.

*continued on page 226*

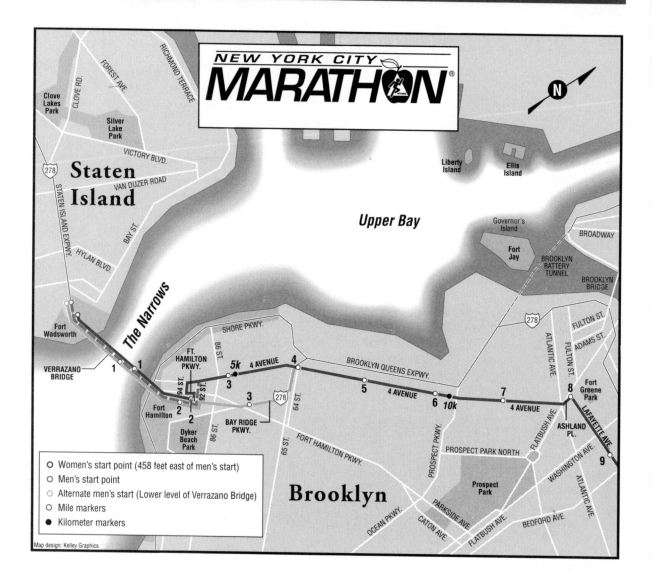

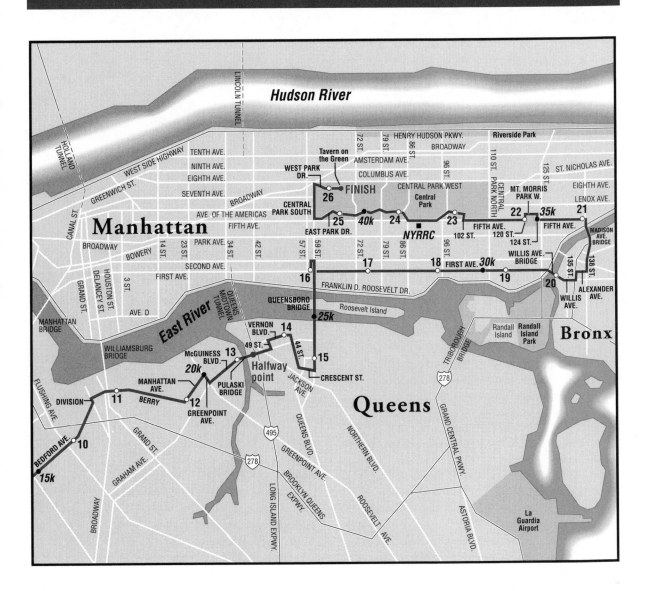

Hudson River

LINCOLN TUNNEL

HOLLAND TUNNEL

WEST SIDE HIGHWAY

GREENWICH ST.

CANAL ST.

**Manhattan**

TENTH AVE.
NINTH AVE.
EIGHTH AVE.
SEVENTH AVE.
BROADWAY
AVE. OF THE AMERICAS
FIFTH AVE.

WEST PARK DR.

Tavern on the Green

CENTRAL PARK SOUTH

HENRY HUDSON PKWY.
BROADWAY
AMSTERDAM AVE.
COLUMBUS AVE.

72 ST.
79 ST.
86 ST.

Riverside Park

Central Park West

**FINISH**
26

25
EAST PARK DR.
40k
24

Central Park

NYRRC

23
102 ST.

96 ST.
110 ST.
CENTRAL PARK NORTH

CENTRAL PARK
22
FIFTH AVE.
120 ST.
124 ST.

MT. MORRIS PARK W.
35k

125 ST.
ST. NICHOLAS AVE.
EIGHTH AVE.
LENOX AVE.

21
FIFTH AVE.
MADISON AVE. BRIDGE

BROADWAY
14 ST.
23 ST.
34 ST.
42 ST.
PARK AVE.
SECOND AVE.
FIRST AVE.

BOWERY
3 ST.
AVE. D

57 ST.
59 ST.
72 ST.
79 ST.
86 ST.
96 ST.

16
17
18
FIRST AVE.
30k
19
20

135 ST.
138 ST.
WILLIS
AVE.
ALEXANDER AVE.

WILLIS AVE. BRIDGE

FRANKLIN D. ROOSEVELT DR.

HOUSTON ST.
DELANCEY ST.
GRAND ST.

MANHATTAN BRIDGE

WILLIAMSBURG BRIDGE

**East River**

QUEENS MIDTOWN TUNNEL

QUEENSBORO BRIDGE

Roosevelt Island

25k

VERNON BLVD.
14
49 ST.

McGUINESS BLVD.
13
PULASKI BRIDGE

Halfway point

44 ST.
JACKSON AVE.
15
CRESCENT ST.

**Queens**

Randall Island
Randall Island Park

**Bronx**

TRIBOROUGH BRIDGE

278

FLUSHING AVE.
DIVISION
11
BERRY
MANHATTAN AVE.
20k
12
GREENPOINT AVE.

BEDFORD AVE.
10
15k

GRAHAM AVE.
GRAND ST.

BROADWAY

495

278

GREENPOINT AVE.

QUEENS BLVD.

NORTHERN BLVD.

ROOSEVELT AVE.

LONG ISLAND EXPWY.

BROOKLYN QUEENS EXPWY.

GRAND CENTRAL PKWY.

ASTORIA BLVD.

La Guardia Airport

Kaiserauer, S., et al. "Nutritional, Physiological, and Menstrual Status in Distance Runners." *Medicine and Science in Sports and Exercise* 21 (1989): 120–25.

Lloyd, T., et al. "Interrelationships of Diet, Athletic Activity, Menstrual Status and Bone Density in Collegiate Women." *American Journal of Clinical Nutrition* 46 (1987): 681–84.

———, et al. "Women Athletes with Menstrual Irregularity Have Increased Musculoskeletal Injuries." *Medicine and Science in Sports and Exercise* 18, no. 4 (1986): 374–79.

Manos T., et al. "Physiological Parameters Related to 10K Performance in Elite Women Race Walkers." *Medicine and Science in Sports and Exercise* 22, no. 2, sup. S124 (1990).

Mulligan, K., and G. Butterfield. "Discrepancies Between Energy Intake and Expenditure in Physically Active Women." *British Journal of Nutrition* 64 (1990): 23–26.

Myerson, M., et al. "Resting Metabolic Rate and Energy Balance in Amenorrheic and Eumenorrheic Runners." *Medicine and Science in Sports and Exercise* 23 (1991): 15–22.

Nelson, M., et al. "Diet and Bone Status in Amenorrheic Runners." *American Journal of Clinical Nutrition* 43 (1986): 910–16.

Pedersen, A., et al. "Menstrual Differences due to Vegetarian and Non-vegetarian Diets." *American Journal of Clinical Nutrition* 53 (1991): 879–85.

Rosen L., et al. "Pathogenic Weight Control Behaviors in Female Athletes." *Physician and Sports Medicine* 14, no. 1 (1986): 79–86.

Sanborn, C., B. Albrecht, and W. Wagner. "Athletic Amenorrhea: Lack of Association with Body Fat. *Medicine and Science in Sports and Exercise* 19, no. 3 (1987): 207–12.

Schulz, L. O., et al. "Energy Expenditure of Elite Female Runners Measured by Respiratory Chamber and Doubly Labeled Water." *Journal of Applied Physiology* 72, no. 1 (1992): 23–28.

Thompson, R., and R. Sherman. *Helping Athletes with Eating Disorders.* Champaign, Ill.: Human Kinetics Publishers, 1993.

Wilmore, J., et al. "Is There Energy Conservation in Amenorrheic Compared with Eumenorrheic Distance Runners?" *Journal of Applied Physiology* 72, no. 1 (1992): 15–22.

## Recommended Reading

Brouns, Fred. *Nutritional Needs of Athletes.* Sussex, England: John Wiley and Sons, 1993.

Bucci, L. *Nutrients and Ergogenic Aids for Sports and Exercise.* Boca Raton, Fla.: CRC Press, 1994.

Clark, N. *Nancy Clark's Sports Nutrition Guidebook.* Champaign, Ill.: Leisure Press, 1990.

McArdle, W., F. Katch, and V. Katch. *Essentials of Exercise Physiology.* Philadelphia: Lea & Febiger, 1994.

Thompson, R., and R. Sherman. *Helping Athletes with Eating Disorders.* Champaign, Ill.: Human Kinetics Publishers, 1993.

Noakes, Tim. *Lore of Running.* Champaign, Ill.: Leisure Press, 1991.

Wilmore, Jack, and D. Costill. *Physiology of Sport and Exercise.* Champaign, Ill.: Human Kinetics Publishers, 1994.

## High-Carbohydrate Cookbooks

Baird, P. *Quick Harvest: A Vegetarian's Guide to Microwave Cooking.* Englewood Cliffs, N.J.: Prentice Hall, 1991.

Brody, J. *Jane Brody's Good Food Book: Living the High Carbohydrate Way.* New York: W. W. Norton & Co., 1985.

Clark, N. *Nancy Clark's Sports Nutrition Guidebook.* Champaign, Ill.: Leisure Press, 1990.

Hinman, B. *Lean and Luscious and Meatless.* Rocklin, Calif.: Prima Publishing, 1991.

Robertson, L., C. Flinders, and B. Ruppenthal. *The New Laurel's Kitchen.* Berkeley, Calif.: Ten Speed Press, 1986.

# RECIPE CONTRIBUTORS

The recipes in this book are compiled from a variety of sources—all of whom love to eat and enjoy great food. Special thanks goes to:

## SPORTS NUTRITIONISTS AND DIETITIANS

Karen Angevine, Dallas, TX—Refried Beans

Merle Best, Euclid, NJ—Central Park Salad with Chicken

Veronica Coronado, Dallas, TX—Sweet and Dilly Carrots, Red Potato Salad, Summer Squash with Onion Casserole

Barbara Day, Louisville, KY—Low-Fat Noodles Alfredo, Dijon Fish, Creamy Fish Bake, Chicken Salad, Crunchy Gorp

Lisa Dorfman, Miami, FL—Spiced Turkey Salad, Tropical Pasta Salad with Chickpeas

Roseann Ferrini, Brookline, MA—Peanut Butter Granola

Mary Abbott Hess, Chicago, IL—Italian Bread Salad, Grilled Chicken with Spicy Thai Sauce

Ann Joyal, Boston, MA—Savory Seafood Pasta, Strawberry Shake, Veggie Calzones

Georgia Kostas, Dallas, TX—Spinach and Cheese Casserole, Shrimp Creole, Mexican Bean Bake, Brownies from a Mix (Low-Fat)

Ann LeBarron, Waldorf, MD—Oven French Fries I

Marci Leeds, Pittsburgh, PA—Basic Fruit Muffins

Sue Luke, Charlotte, NC—Almond Biscotti, Ground Turkey Mix for Spaghetti Sauce or Chili, Meatballs and Variations

Jacqueline Marcus, Chicago, IL—Cabbage and Carrot Salad, Tunisian Pita Salad, Winter Squash with Orange and Pineapple, Citrus Refresher

Mary-Giselle Rathgeber, New York, NY—Tabouli, Gazpacho

Terri Lee Smith, Boston, MA—Pasta and White Bean Soup with Sun-Dried Tomatoes

Natalie Updegrove Partridge, Rockville, ME—Chili (∨egetarian, Turkey, or Beef), Brownies (Low-Fat), ∣ Cookies

## ∣TERNS

∨egetable Soup with Beef or

Deborah Bisson, Boston, MA—Turkey Picatta, Raspberry Sauce

Cecelia Chapman, Cambridge, MA—Mexican Rice

Denise Coyle, Allston, MA—Raspberry Freeze

Stacy Flickner, Kingman, KS—Taco Salad, Chunky Salsa

Lori Fujikawa, Boston, MA—Hawaiian Curried Rice, Fish in Lime

Elizabeth Hastry, Boston, MA—Banana Blast, Watermelon Sparkling Punch

Melissa Kalman, Brookline, MA—White Grape Spritzer, Fresh Fruit Salad with Yogurt Dressing

Amy Pohlman, Omaha, NE—Breadsticks, Fruit Pizza

Amy Roeder, Brighton, MA—Peanut Brittle

Molly Schipp, Wellesly Hills, MA—Pudding Shake

## ELITE RUNNERS

(*indicates the recipes are courtesy of Christine Schlott's New York Running News column, "Eating Elite")

*Gabrielle Andersen, Switzerland/SunValley, ID—Swiss Bircher Muesli

*Jeff Atkinson, Manhattan Beach, CA—Pasta with Clam Sauce

*Ann Audain, New Zealand—Honey Nut Granola

Sharon Barbano, Boston, MA—Polenta

*Arturo Barrios, Colorado—Easy Enchilada Stack

*David Clark, England—Big Apple Crumble

*Patti Catalano Dillon, Atlanta, GA—Japanese Noodles with Ginger

*Nancy Ditz, Woodside, CA—Pasta with Ham and Peas

Tom Fleming, Glen Ridge, NJ—South African Bobotie, South African Fruit Platter with Yogurt and Honey Dressing

Jeff Galloway, Atlanta, GA—Oat Bran Muffins

*Margaret Groos, Tennessee—Whole-Wheat Yogurt Biscuits

*Angella Hearn, New York, NY—Oriental Spinach Salad with Soy Sauce and Sesame Dressing

*Steve Jones, Wales, Colorado—Chicken Stir-Fry with Sesame Sauce

Nina Kuscsik, New York, NY—"Eat Your Spinach" Creamed Spinach, Holiday Pulla Bread

Gary Muhrcke, New York, NY—Shrimp with Feta Cheese

Uta Pippig, Germany/Colorado—Pasta Dinner

*Orlando Pizzolato, Ferrara, Italy—Pasta e Fagioli

Bill Rodgers, Sherborn, MA—Spinach Salad with Sweet and Sour Dressing

Alberto Salazar, Beaverton, OR—Arroz con Pollo

Joan Benoit Samuelson, Freeport, ME—Blueberry Muffins, Spinach Lasagna, Minestrone Soup, Enchilada Casserole, Vegetable Cheese Chowder, Oatmeal Yeast Bread, Mustard-Dill Salmon, Chocolate Chip Oatmeal Cookies

Norb Sander, New York, NY—French Toast

Kathrine Switzer, New Zealand—Toast with Manuka Honey, Smoked Salmon Pasta, Fish in Foil, Mussels from the Sea, Rack of Lamb with Rosemary

*John Treacy, Ireland—Irish Stew

Grete Waitz, Norway/Florida—High-Fiber Breakfast, Baked Potato

Priscilla Welch, England/Colorado—Banana Bread

## RUNNING COOKS

Barbara Anderson, New York, NY—Macrobiotic Soup

Gloria Averbuch, Upper Montclair, NJ—Sesame Pasta with Broccoli II, Tortilla Crisps

Helen Baker, Peyton, CO—Shrimp Fettuccine

Barbara Barran, Brooklyn, NY—Mango-Chicken-Rice Salad, Sea Legs Salad with Sun-Dried Tomatoes, Avocado-Black Bean Pasta Salad

Rachael Berger, New York, NY—Chocolate Chip Cookies (Low-Fat)

Marilyn Burnett, Scottsdale, AZ—Spicy Spinach Dip

Vince Connelly, Brookline, MA—Pasta with Chicken and Spinach

Ingrid Crane, Westhampton Beach, NY—Lemon Turkey Breast with Sweet Potatoes and Fruit Stuffing

Joy Cunningham, Chicago, IL—Colorful Vegetable Pasta Salad with Honey-Mustard Dressing

Patty Evanitsky, East Brunswick, NJ—Potato and Carrot Casserole

Bill Fischer, New York, NY—Focaccia

Paul Friedman, Upper Montclair, NJ—Blue-Ribbon Breakfast Cereal

Loretta Gascoigne, Redmond, WA—Breakfast Bars

Michael Keohane, New York, NY—Runner's Basic One-Pot Pasta

Susan and Terry Martell, Richland, WA—Bagels

Cindy Millar, Mesa, AZ—Eggplant Italiano

Dennis Monahan, Mililani, HI—Simple Chili

Judy Morrill, New York, NY—Runner's Basic Pasta with Vegetables

Linda Press Wolfe, Cross River, NY—Gourmet Vegetarian Lasagna, Rigatoni with Roasted Red Pepper Sauce

Christine Schlott, Whitestone, NY—Baked Vegetable Medley, Wild Rice Chicken Salad

Jean Smith, Newton, MA—Creamy Cheesecake, Single-Rise Yeast Bread

## FAMILY AND FRIENDS

Mary Bernazani, Roslindale, MA—Breakfast Cookie

Barbara Boen, Boston, MA—Soufflé à la Stale Bagels

Janice Clark, Little Compton, RI—Crisp and Chewies

Molly Curran, Lynnfield, MA—Honey-Baked Chicken

Annie Hale, Holliston, MA—Egg and Potato Dinner

Janet Hegmann, Boise, ID—Sunset French Dressing, Cauliflower Soup, Big Apple Pie

Madeline Hegmann, Wellsboro, PA—Baked "Big Apple" French Toast

Mary Hegmann, Boise, ID—Decadent Brownies

Ellen Herbert, Newton, MA—Pizza Fondue

Peter Herman, Cambridge, MA—Sweet Potato and Pepper Salad, Pumpkin Soup, Snow Pea-Cucumber Salad, Chicken in Foil, Orange-Grilled Chicken with Curry

Sarah Katz, Monsey, NY—Orzo, Cheese Danish, Ricotta Cheesecake, Potato Pancakes, Big Apple Cake

Tim Maggs, Scotia, NY—Ugali

Kay McGrath, Buffalo, NY—Whole-Wheat Raisin Quick Bread

Fran Richman, Brighton, MA—Pasta Omelette

Jackie Schneider, Gardiner, MT—Chocolate Lush

Mary Schran, Media, PA—German Potato Salad

Peter Schran, Media, PA—Pumpkin Oat Cookies (Low-Fat)

Diane Sinski, Belmont, MA—Egg Drop Soup

Joann Walters, Mechanicsburg, PA—Baked Tomato

Sue Westin, Brockton, MA—French-Toasted Cheese Sandwiches

# INDEX